10th Workshop on Representation Learning for NLP (RepL4NLP-2025)

Albuquerque, New Mexico, USA
4 May 2025

ISBN: 979-8-3313-1928-1

Printed from e-media with permission by:

Curran Associates, Inc.
57 Morehouse Lane
Red Hook, NY 12571

Some format issues inherent in the e-media version may also appear in this print version.

Association for Computational Linguistics
209 N. Eighth Street
Stroudsburg, Pennsylvania 18360

Phone: 1-570-476-8006
Fax: 1-570-476-0860

acl@aclweb.org

Additional copies of this publication are available from:

Curran Associates, Inc.
57 Morehouse Lane
Red Hook, NY 12571 USA
Phone: 845-758-0400
Fax: 845-758-2633
Email: curran@proceedings.com
Web: www.proceedings.com

RepL4NLP 2025

10th Workshop on Representation Learning for NLP

Proceedings of the Workshop

May 4, 2025

The RepL4NLP organizers gratefully acknowledge the support from the following sponsors.

Gold

Order copies of this and other ACL proceedings from:

Association for Computational Linguistics (ACL)
317 Sidney Baker St. S
Suite 400 - 134
Kerrville, TX 78028
USA
Tel: +1-855-225-1962
acl@aclweb.org

Introduction

Welcome to RepL4NLP 2025, The 10th Workshop on Representation Learning for NLP. Co-located with NAACL 2025, this workshop is scheduled for May 4, 2025 to be held in Albuquerque, New Mexico.

The 10th Workshop on Representation Learning for NLP (RepL4NLP) at NAACL 2025 is dedicated to exploring linguistic information representation within computational models, a critical aspect of modern Natural Language Processing. A core focus of the workshop will be on the efficient learning of representations, examining methods to create effective linguistic representations while minimizing computational resources and optimizing training processes. Another key area of exploration is the dynamic evolution of representations during training, seeking to understand how vector spaces change over time and what factors influence these transformations. The workshop will also address the critical challenge of evaluating existing representations, aiming to establish robust benchmarks and methodologies for assessing their quality. A deeper understanding of the relationship between representations and model behaviors is another central theme, investigating how representation choices impact model performance and outcomes. Recognizing the importance of multilingual NLP, the workshop extends its scope beyond English, encouraging the development and evaluation of representations for diverse languages and modalities, including those with limited resources and multimodal datasets. By fostering collaboration among researchers from various disciplines, the workshop aims to drive innovation and progress in the field of linguistic representation learning.
This year, there were a total of 19 archival and non-archival submissions to the RepL4NLP workshop, of which a total of 13 were accepted. All these works have been included in our proceedings.

In addition to poster sessions where accepted works will be presented, the Workshop also will also host talks and a panel discussion with four invited speakers: Akari Asai, Najoung Kim, Ana Marasovic, and Yoav Artzi.

Finally, we would like to express our gratitude to all the authors, committee members, invited speakers, and participants for helping make this workshop possible. We would also like to gratefully acknowledge our sponsor, Google DeepMind, for their support.

Organizing Committee

Program Chairs

Alexandra Chronopoulou, Google DeepMind, USA
Xiang Lorraine Li, University of Pittsburgh, USA
Bodhisattwa Prasad Majumder, Allen Institute for Artificial Intelligence, USA
Freda Shi, University of Waterloo and Vector Institute, Canada
Giorgos Vernikos, Google DeepMind, Switzerland
Vaibhav Adlakha, McGill University, Canada

Program Committee

Program Chairs

Alexandra Chronopoulou, Google DeepMind
Xiang Lorraine Li, University of Pittsburgh
Bodhisattwa Prasad Majumder, Allen Institute for Artificial Intelligence
Freda Shi, University of Waterloo and Vector Institute
Giorgos Vernikos, Google DeepMind
Vaibhav Adlakha, McGill University

Reviewers

Taichi Aida
Nicholas Andrews
Andreas Athanasopoulos
Bhiman Kumar Baghel
Yuntao Bai
Steven Bedrick
Gábor Berend
Bernd Bohnet
Necva Bölücü
Danlu Chen
Anni Chen
Yue Chen
Lin Chen
Srinivasarao Daruna
Christopher Davis
Zifeng Ding
Andrew Drozdov
Vladimir Eidelman
Alina Fastowski
Félix Gaschi
Valentin Hofmann
Zhaoyi Joey Hou
Jiaji Huang
Katharina Hämmerl
Etsuko Ishii
Amit Jaspal
Fran Jelenić
Ashvini Kumar Jindal
Jatin Khilnani
Hyunjong Kim
Shankar Kumar
Matthieu Labeau
Seungil Chad Lee
Zhu Liu
Chen Cecilia Liu
Yiwei Lyu
Kimberly Mai

Sheikh Mannan
Kelly Marchisio
Antonio Valerio Miceli Barone
Tsvetomila Mihaylova
Ashutosh Modi
Truc-Vien T. Nguyen
Stephen Obadinma
Tsuyoshi Okita
Ankur Padia
Ankur Padia
Yuval Pinter
Meghana Puvvadi
Rahul Raja
Tharindu Ranasinghe
Simon Razniewski
Angelika Romanou
Frank Rudzicz
Kaushik Ram Sadagopan
Sai Ashish Somayajula
Karolina Stanczak
Bilal Taha
Sowmya Vajjala
Eva Maria Vecchi
Qingyun Wang
Bin Wang
Takateru Yamakoshi
Hong Yu
Menno Van Zaanen
Kai Zhang
Xinran Zhao
Wenbo Zhao
Dong Zhou
Imed Zitouni

Table of Contents

DEPTH: Discourse Education through Pre-Training Hierarchically

Zachary Elisha Bamberger
Technion
zachary@campus.technion.ac.il

Ofek Glick
Technion
ofek.glick@campus.technion.ac.il

Chaim Baskin
Ben-Gurion University of the Negev
chaimbaskin@bgu.ac.il

Yonatan Belinkov
Technion
belinkov@technion.ac.il

Abstract

Language Models (LMs) struggle with linguistic understanding at the discourse level, even though discourse patterns such as coherence, cohesion, and narrative flow are prevalent in their pre-training data. To improve the discourse capabilities of LMs already at the pre-training stage, we introduce DEPTH, an encoder-decoder model that learns latent representations for sentences using a discourse-oriented pre-training objective. DEPTH combines hierarchical sentence representations with two objectives: (1) *Sentence Un-Shuffling*, and (2) *Span-Corruption*. Our approach trains the model to represent both sub-word-level and sentence-level dependencies over a pre-training corpora. When trained either from scratch or continuing from a pre-trained T5 checkpoint, DEPTH learns semantic and discourse-level representations faster than T5, outperforming it in span-corruption loss despite the additional sentence-un-shuffling objective. Evaluations on the GLUE, DiscoEval, and NI benchmarks demonstrate DEPTH's ability to quickly learn diverse downstream tasks, which require syntactic, semantic, and discourse capabilities. Our approach extends the discourse capabilities of T5, while minimally impacting other natural language understanding (NLU) capabilities in the resulting LM. We share ur codebse for reproducibility: https://github.com/zbambergerNLP/depth.git

1 Introduction

Discourse understanding—the ability to understand how sentences and broader textual units form cohesive narratives (Miltsakaki et al., 2004; Prasad et al., 2008; Jernite et al., 2017; Prasad et al., 2018)—is fundamental to effective communication. However, LMs often struggle with this, especially when dealing with long and complex inputs, hindering their performance on tasks like persuasive argumentation (Durmus et al., 2019; Hidey et al., 2017; Chakrabarty et al., 2019), summarization (Zhao et al., 2022), essay scoring (Mim et al., 2021), dialogue systems (Hua et al., 2023), and following instructions (Wei et al., 2022a). Recent evidence from Yu et al. (2024) reinforces this view, demonstrating that human language comprehension occurs at multiple levels and that incorporating discourse-level objectives like next sentence prediction (NSP) can lead to more human-like language representations and improved contextual understanding.

Early attempts to incorporate discourse awareness into pre-training, such as Next Sentence Prediction (NSP) in BERT (Devlin et al., 2019) and Sentence Order Prediction (SOP) in ALBERT (Lan et al., 2020), proved overly simplistic and hindered learning effective discourse representations (Liu et al., 2019; Lan et al., 2020; Raffel et al., 2020). Subsequent encoder models like Sentence-level Language Model (SLM) (Lee et al., 2020), CONPONO (Iter et al., 2020), and Hi-Transformer (Wu et al., 2021) improved discourse capabilities in LMs but lacked generative capabilities.

Unlike the pre-training tasks for encoder LMs, next-token prediction provides decoder LMs like GPT (Radford et al., 2018, 2019; Brown et al., 2020; OpenAI et al., 2023) with powerful generative capabilities. However, without a dedicated and costly alignment phase (Ouyang et al., 2022; Wei et al., 2022a; Bai et al., 2022), these LMs tend to falter in understanding and executing human queries.

Even with a dedicated alignment phase, large decoder-only models generally perform poorly on discourse-oriented benchmarks that measure coherence and cohesion (Chen et al., 2019; Maimon and Tsarfaty, 2023a,b; Wang et al., 2023). Encoder-decoder models such as T5 (Raffel et al., 2020) and BART (Lewis et al., 2020a) consistently outperform much larger ($\approx 400\times$) decoder-only models like GPT-3 (Brown et al., 2020) and GPT-4 (OpenAI et al., 2023) on these tasks. Recent work

Proceedings of the 10th Workshop on Representation Learning for NLP (RepL4NLP-2025), pages 1–25
May 4, 2025 ©2025 Association for Computational Linguistics

by Katz et al. (2024) indicates that incorporating encoder-decoder attention mechanisms into modern decoder-only models like Llama-3 (Grattafiori et al., 2024), Qwen-2.5 (Qwen et al., 2025), and Mistral (Jiang et al., 2023) also boosts performance, suggesting potential additional benefits from pre-training models with such attention schemes.

To improve the discourse-capabilities of encoder-decoders already at the pre-training stage, we propose DEPTH (**D**iscourse-**E**ducation through **P**re-**T**raining **H**ierarchically), a hierarchical language model that learns representations for both sub-word and sentence-level tokens. DEPTH extends the pre-training objective of SLM from encoder-only models like BERT, to encoder-decoder models like T5. Notably, DEPTH introduces latent, heirarchical representations for sentences (as in Lee et al. (2020); Yang et al. (2021); Yu et al. (2024)) directly into the objective of a *generative* pre-training task. By employing a hierarchical attention mechanism across sub-word and sentence level tokens, DEPTH captures both fine-grained semantic dependencies and broader inter-sentence relationships. When pre-trained from scratch, our DEPTH model obtains meaningful representations for downstream tasks much faster than our baseline T5. Continuously pre-training T5 models with the DEPTH objective improves the discourse capabilities of the resulting models, without sacrificing performance in downstream NLU tasks.

2 Method

Pre-training DEPTH involves simultaneously performing span corruption (Raffel et al., 2020), while also un-shuffling sentences as in Lee et al. (2020). In Section 2.1 we introduce a new tokenizer for DEPTH, which combines T5's tokenizer with the sentence segmentation operation required for sentence un-shuffling. In Section 2.2, we detail how we combined the pre-training objectives of both models into the sequence-to-sequence framework of T5. Next, in Section 2.3, we discuss how we introduce hierarchical representations during pre-training, and how this hierarchy encourages the model to learn discourse representations. Finally, in Section 2.4, we demonstrate how to combine the losses of T5 and SLM into a unified objective that is conducive to traditional teacher-forcing.

2.1 Tokenization

We introduce a tokenization function, t, which transforms an input string, s, into a sequence of tokens, $X = (x_{1,1}, x_{1,2}, \ldots, x_{m,\text{len}(m)})$, in our vocabulary, V. Each token $x_{i,j}$ denotes the j'th token of the i'th sentence, where m is the number of sentences and len(i) is the length of the i'th sentence. V includes special tokens <EOS>, <BOS>, <PAD>, and sentinel tokens V_{sentinel} of the form <special_token_z> as in the original T5 paper.

To facilitate DEPTH's hierarchical structure, we segment sentences using NLTK (Bird and Loper, 2004) and create $k + 1$ new tokens[1]:

$$S = \{\texttt{<SENT\_1>}, \ldots, \texttt{<SENT\_k>}, \texttt{<EOSEN>}\}$$
$$V' = V \cup S$$

We augment our tokenizer function t to form t', which maps sequence s to tokens in V'. In each sentence, we prepend a <SENT_i> token and append a <EOSEN> token:

$$X = \{\texttt{<SENT\_a>}, x_{1,1}, x_{1,2}, \ldots, x_{1,\text{len}(1)}, \texttt{<EOSEN>}, \ldots, x_{m,\text{len}(m)}, \texttt{<EOSEN>}, \texttt{<EOS>}\}$$

The integer i in <SENT_i> represents a sentence's index, sampled uniformly at random from $\{1, \ldots, k\}$ without replacement. We truncate sentences beyond the k'th to limit vocabulary size.

Unlike SLM (an encoder-only LM with an auxiliary pointer-decoder), DEPTH is an encoder-decoder that predicts <SENT_i> and <EOSEN> token IDs directly. The <EOSEN> token signals the next token is either <SENT_i> or <EOS>, allowing for dynamic attention masking in the decoder.

Formally, we define a pre-tokenization function $f : s \rightarrow s'$, where s' includes <SENT_i> and <EOSEN> tokens. The tokenized input for DEPTH is produced with $T(s) = t(f(s)) = X$. We use the SentencePiece (Kudo and Richardson, 2018) tokenizer as t, adjusted to support DEPTH's sentence-level pre-training objective.

2.2 Corruption

Span-Masking: We apply a corruption process to each batch of tokenized sequences. We sample masked spans using a geometric distribution (as in Joshi et al. (2020) and Raffel et al. (2020)), parameterized with an average span length of λ and a masking probability of p. Spans overlapping with sentence tokens (<EOSEN> or <SENT_i>) are ignored. Masked token spans are replaced with a single sentinel token <special_token_z>, where

[1] We follow Lee et al. (2020), using $k = 20$ sentence tokens.

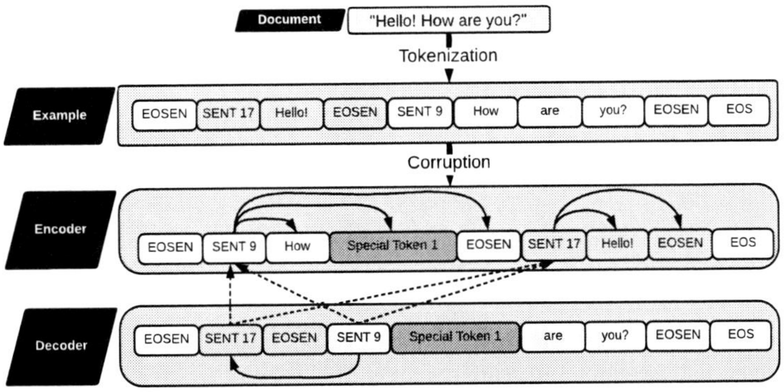

Figure 1: DEPTH tokenization and corruption process. Given an input document, DEPTH introduces sentence tokens (<SENT_i> and <EOSEN>), applies span masking, and shuffles sentences with probability 0.5. Attention patterns are shown with arrows (dotted for cross-attention, solid for self-attention).

(z) is a uniformly sampled integer from $0, \ldots, 99$. The missing token sequences appear after the corresponding sentinel token in the labels. Note that in the original T5 implementation, sentinel tokens appear in the same incrementally decreasing order in each example (<special_token_99> followed by <special_token_98>, etc...). We randomly sample sentinel token ID's for DEPTH to eliminate hints about sentence positions from the sentinel tokens. For example, with the T5 scheme for span-masking, the presence of <special_token_99> indicates that the sentence in which it appears comes first, making sentence un-shuffling too easy.

Sentence Un-Shuffling: Given an input sequence of up to k sentences, we randomly shuffle the order of sentences in the model input[2]. We then task the model with reconstructing the original order of the sentence tokens in the target. We shuffle all examples in a batch with probability $p = 0.5$ (as in SLM). By disrupting the original sentence order, DEPTH encourages learning of (1) the complete meaning of individual sentences, independent of their surrounding context, and (2) representations that encode how sentences relate to each other[3]. We show DEPTH's corruption process in Figure 1.

2.3 Attention masks

Our baseline model (T5) utilizes bidirectional attention in the encoder, auto-regressive attention in the decoder, and full cross attention from the decoder to the encoder. However, T5's formulation does not account for the hierarchical treatment of sentences used by SLM and DEPTH.

We define *non-sentence* tokens, x_{reg}, as tokens $x \in X$ where $x \notin S$. We compose attention masks to impose hierarchy. As part of encoder self-attention, non-sentence tokens can attend to all other tokens in the corrupted input sequence, while <SENT_i> tokens can only attend to tokens within their own sentence (including sentinel tokens). As part of decoder self-attention, all tokens have an auto-regressive attention mask, but <SENT_i> tokens can only attend to past sentence tokens. Finally, as part of cross attention, non-sentence tokens in the decoder can attend to the entire input in the encoder, while sentence tokens in the decoder can only attend to sentence tokens in the encoder. This scheme is depicted in Figure 1.

This scheme encourages the model to use sentence token representations in the encoder to predict the next sentence token in the decoder via cross-attention. It also ensures that non-sentence tokens in the encoder provide relevant discourse information to their corresponding sentence tokens.

2.4 Loss Formulation

Let $Y = \{y_{1,1}, y_{1,2}, \ldots, y_{m,\text{len}(m)}\}$ be the target sequence, where each token $y_{i,j}$ belongs either to the span-masking task (non-sentence tokens) or to the sentence un-shuffling task (sentence tokens). We denote by $\hat{S}$ the set of all sentence tokens in Y. The model prediction is given by $\hat{Y} = \{\hat{y}_{1,1}, \hat{y}_{1,2}, \ldots, \hat{y}_{m,\text{len}(m)}\}$, where $\hat{y}_{i,j}$ represents the predicted probability distribution over the vocabulary for token $y_{i,j}$. Let the total number of tokens be $N = |Y|$.

The loss for DEPTH, which jointly optimizes the reconstruction (span-masking) and sentence un-shuffling tasks, is defined as the token-averaged

[2] We do not shuffle the order of tokens within a sentence

[3] E.g., discourse markers, co-reference, and entailment

cross-entropy:

$$L_{\text{DEPTH}} = -\frac{1}{N}\sum_{i=1}^{m}\sum_{j=1}^{\text{len}(i)} y_{i,j} \cdot \log \hat{y}_{i,j}$$

$$= \underbrace{-\frac{1}{N}\sum_{y_{i,j}\in Y\cap\hat{S}} y_{i,j} \cdot \log \hat{y}_{i,j}}_{\text{Sentence Loss}} \underbrace{-\frac{1}{N}\sum_{y_{i,j}\in Y\setminus\hat{S}} y_{i,j} \cdot \log \hat{y}_{i,j}}_{\text{Reconstruction Loss}}$$

In this formulation, the summation runs over all sentences in the input (i.e., up to m sentences, where $1 \leq m \leq k$), and within each sentence over its tokens. This allows us to decompose the model's performance into the contributions from the sentence un-shuffling and the span-masking tasks. We explore additional loss formulations and weighting schemes in Appendix B.1.

3 Experimental setup

The aim of our experiments is to measure the effectiveness of DEPTH against a standard encoder-decoder model. Accordingly, our experiments explore the learning dynamics of DEPTH model relative to a T5-Base (220M parameter) baseline. We pre-train both models on the C4 dataset (Raffel et al., 2020; Dodge et al., 2021) to resemble the manner in which the original T5 was trained (see additional reasoning in Appendix D.2). We chose to use Base-sized models given limited computational resources, and ease of reproducibility (following the example of Lee et al. (2020); Levine et al. (2020); Zhang et al. (2020); Raffel et al. (2020)). We did not use SLM as our baseline since its codebase and checkpoints are not released, and it cannot perform free-form text generation.

We chose to run our experiments without example packing since this is how the SLM model, which inspired DEPTH, was trained. Furthermore, example-packing in T5 enables unrelated examples to impact the model's decisions, thereby harming performance (Krell et al., 2021; Shi et al., 2024). While example-packing is critical for more computationally-efficient training (Ding et al., 2024), we were interested in measuring which model was able to use training examples more effectively. We examine the impacts of avoiding example packing in Appendix A.2.

Consistent with Nawrot (2023), we found that the Adafactor optimizer (Shazeer and Stern, 2018), while more computationally efficient, slightly harmed model performance. We therefore use AdamW (Loshchilov and Hutter, 2019) instead. We use a linearly increasing learning rate during the first $10,000$ steps, and then reduce the learning rate linearly for DEPTH (as in SLM), and with an inverse square learning rate ratio for T5 (as in the original T5 paper). We chose to use a masking probability of $p = 0.3$,[4] and an average span length of $\lambda = 3$. Our mask probability is higher than the advised 0.15 from T5 to accommodate for the fact that sentence-tokens within DEPTH cannot be masked.

We conduct two types of pre-training experiments:

1. **From Scratch (FS)**: Both T5 and DEPTH models are randomly initialized, and pre-trained on C4 with their respective objectives.

2. **Continuous Pre-Training (CPT)**: Both T5 and DEPTH models are initialized from the T5-Base checkpoint on HuggingFace (Wolf et al., 2019), and continue to pre-train on C4 with their respective objectives.

We note that our CPT experiments build on top of T5 models that have been trained for over 1T tokens, whereas the amount of tokens they see during continuous pre-training is relatively minuscule ($\approx 67\times$ fewer tokens for T5, and $\approx 80\times$ fewer tokens for DEPTH). We compare configurations of similar-sized models in Appendix D.1.

3.1 Fine-tuning experiments

We follow up our pre-training experiments with a collection of downstream tasks. We evaluate our models on natural language inference (MNLI, Williams et al. (2018)), sentiment analysis (SST2, Socher et al. (2013)), and grammar (CoLA, Warstadt et al. (2019)) within the GLUE benchmark (Wang et al., 2018). We also use the DiscoEval suite (Chen et al., 2019) to evaluate models on their understanding of discourse. We use two tasks from DiscoEval: Sentence Permutation (SP) and Discourse Coherence (DC). SP involves identifying the correct position of a removed, while DC involves predicting whether or not a paragraph was coherent. Finally, we measure our model's generative abilities on the Natural Instructions (NI) dataset (Mishra et al., 2022), which measures the ability of LMs to follow instructions, and served as a benchmark for NanoT5 (Nawrot, 2023).

[4] Raffel et al. (2020) reports that this span corruption ratio does not adversely impact downstream performance, although recently Ankner et al. (2024) suggested a dynamic masking rate tends to perform best.

Our experimental framework is inspired by Pythia (Biderman et al., 2023), which evaluates the performance of LMs on downstream tasks from intermediate checkpoints. We run evaluation with checkpoints from both T5 and DEPTH models, gathered at steps $\{2K, 4K, \ldots, 512K, 1M\}$ in order to examine these models' emergent capabilities. The exponential distance between these checkpoints allows us to scale intermediate checkpoint evaluation to much longer training runs.[5]

4 Results

4.1 C4 pre-training

During pre-training, we find that DEPTH consistently achieves a lower validation loss than a comparably trained T5 model. This is true for both FS and CPT. Furthermore, when we isolate the reconstruction loss (the objective used by T5, without sentence tokens), we find that DEPTH outperforms T5 despite balancing an additional pre-training objective (Figure 2 for FS and Figure 3 for CPT). These results are consistent with the findings in SLM, where their model converged faster, and on fewer tokens than models such as BERT and T5.

While we were not able to match the performance of the baseline model of Raffel et al. (2020) (see Appendix A for speculations on why), we have obtained the lowest loss scores among PyTorch implementations of T5 models. Specifically, in our FS setting, we find that our randomly initialized T5 model outperforms the validation loss of NanoT5, achieving 1.65 vs. 1.95 at step 64,000.

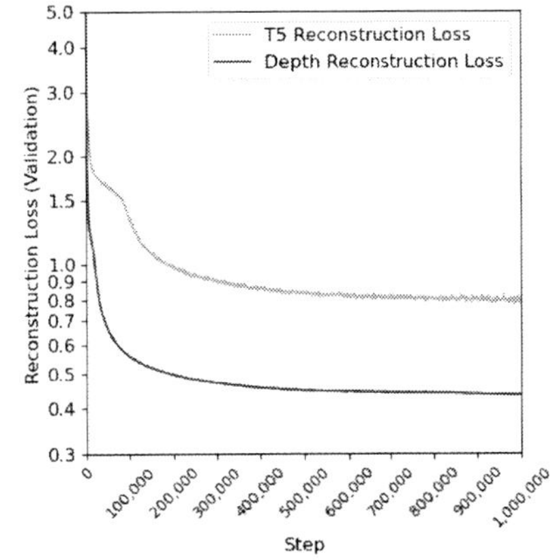

Figure 2: From Scratch Pre-Training loss (validation) for both T5 and DEPTH

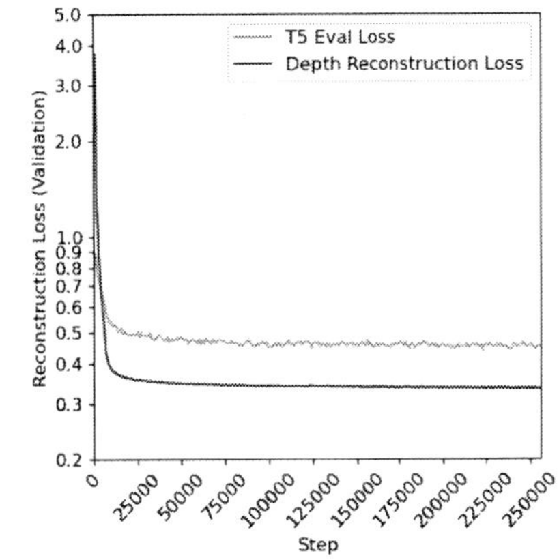

Figure 3: Continuous Pre-Training loss (validation) for both T5 and DEPTH.

4.2 GLUE fine-tuning

We found that over the course of FS pre-training, both models improved on GLUE tasks. However, T5's improvement pattern was slower than DEPTH's (top row of Figure 4). We found it difficult to replicate the results of the original T5 (both on GLUE tasks and the pre-training loss) as discussed in Appendix A. We project that with more substantial training (i.e., 1–3M pre-training steps, and $\geq$ 2048 examples per batch, as in T5), DEPTH could match or exceed the performance of T5 and SLM on downstream tasks.

In the CPT setting (Figure 4, bottom row), we found that DEPTH and T5 perform similarly, both improving only slightly beyond the baseline. Fine-tuning DEPTH on early CPT checkpoints performs worse than fine-tuning comparable T5-CPT checkpoints. We speculate that this dip in performance is related to the change in objective from span-masking to span-masking *and* sentence unshuffling. We share our full results on GLUE in Appendix F.

4.3 DiscoEval fine-tuning

We find that in the FS setting DEPTH consistently outperforms T5 across DC tasks, indicating its robustness in understanding discourse [6] (Figure 5, top row). This suggests DEPTH's pre-training objective is particularly beneficial for tasks that require a deep understanding of narrative structures (both in conversations as in DC-Chat, and more formal and informative texts as in DC-Wiki). We note that between steps 32k and 64k, DEPTH ex-

[5] Evaluating intermediate checkpoint performance every 10,000 steps (as was done in Pythia) on datasets as large as MNLI is unfeasible with our limited computational resources.

[6] In particular, sentence-level discourse relations, as discussed in Jernite et al. (2017)

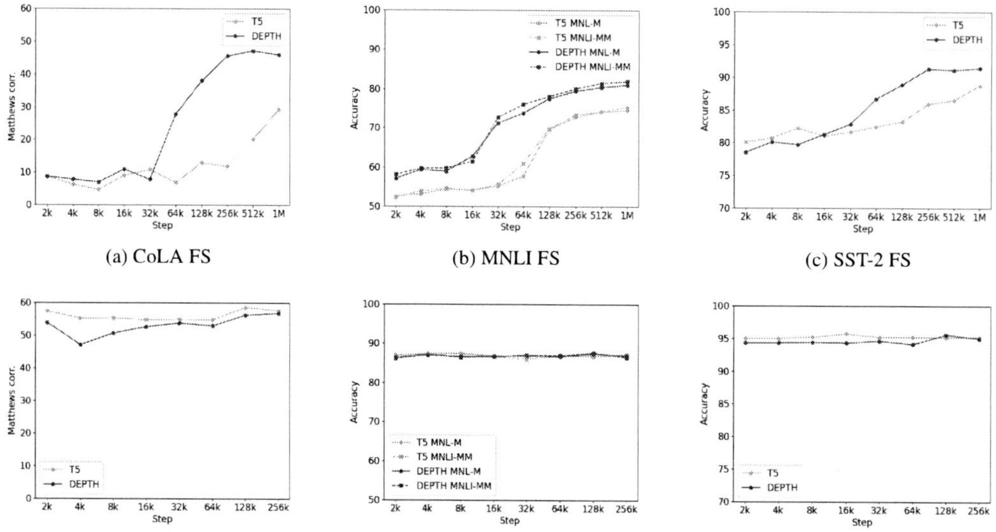

(a) CoLA FS (b) MNLI FS (c) SST-2 FS

(d) CoLA CPT (e) MNLI CPT (f) SST-2 CPT

Figure 4: GLUE results for FS and CPT models. Top row: From Scratch (FS), Bottom row: From Pretrained (CPT).

perienced a large positive boost in performance on DC-Wiki, perhaps indicative of an emergence (Wei et al., 2022b) of discourse understanding during this phase of pre-training. For T5, we found that the model struggled to learn the SP-Arxiv task, achieving random-guess accuracy late in pre-training. However, in SP-Wiki and SP-Rocstory, T5 improves in performances between steps 64k and 128k, perhaps indicating an emergent ability occurring within this timeframe. We report our full results on DiscoEval in Appendix G.

While DEPTH outperformed other models in DC tasks, it failed to reach a high performance level on SP tasks (under-performing relative to SLM, as seen in Table 1). This problem stems already from the pre-training stage, where DEPTH's sentence un-shuffling accuracy is relatively low ($\leq 5\%$ accuracy on shuffled sentence tokens; see Appendix B for additional details). This highlights the complexity of sentence un-shuffling relative to older discourse objectives like NSP and SOP. Surprisingly, while this task was challenging for DEPTH, SLM reported strong performance on sentence un-shuffling. SLM used a dedicated pointer-generator network that consists of a shallow DNN. This module "points" to one of at most k sentences as it iterates over a target sequence consisting of **only** sentence tokens. Also, SLM's non-sentence tokens cannot observe sentence-level tokens as part of the reconstruction loss, avoiding a potential "distraction" in their task.

Model	SP	DC
RoBERTa-Base	38.7	58.4
BERT-Base	53.1	58.9
BERT-Large	53.8	59.6
CONPONO	60.7	72.9
SLM (1M)	72.4	75.4
SLM (3M)	**73.4**	76.1
T5-Base	58.1	80.5
T5-FS	40.91	63.31
T5-CPT	59.48	<u>82.27</u>
DEPTH-FS	55.45	76.22
DEPTH-CPT	<u>65.59</u>	**82.49**

Table 1: Comparison of various models on the SP and DC tasks within DiscoEval. All models aside from T5 and DEPTH and encoder-only models trained with discourse-oriented objectives.

4.4 NI fine-tuning

In the FS setting (Figure 6a), we observe that DEPTH outperforms T5 in the NI benchmark, with a notable leap in performance between steps 16k and 32k. T5, by comparison, only improves significantly after step 64k, and obtains worse performance than DEPTH by the end of training. However, in the CPT setting (Figure 6b), DEPTH's pre-training appears to hinder downstream perfor-

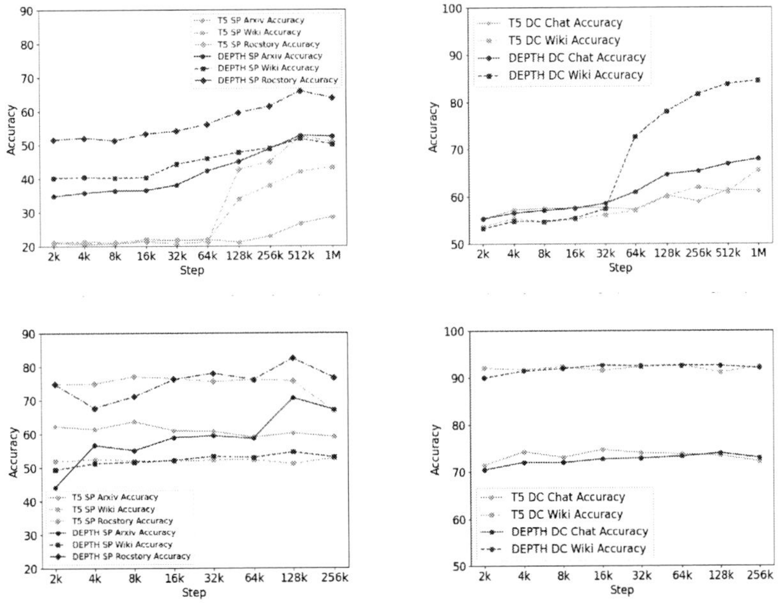

(c) Sentence Permutation (SP) CPT

(d) Discourse Coherence (DC) CPT

Figure 5: DiscoEval results for DEPTH and T5 models. Top row: From Scratch (FS), Bottom row: From Pretrained (CPT).

mance compared to T5, possibly due to the domain shift from T5's pre-training task to DEPTH's pre-training task, which involves learning from shuffled inputs. We present a more complete analysis of these results in Appendix H.

4.5 Error Analysis

We performed error analysis on the DiscoEval benchmark to better understand the nature of discourse errors that DEPTH and T5 made. For the SP task, we show in Table 3 that DEPTH made more reasonable mistakes than T5. For example, in SP-Arxiv FS, 23% of DEPTH's mistakes were reasonable, relative to 7% by T5). We define "reasonable" mistakes as incorrect predictions that would have still resulted in a coherent sentence ordering. Both models struggled with pronoun resolution, which frequently led to incorrect predictions (accounting for 10-30% of all predictions we observed). T5-FS, in particular, often failed to recognize when a removed sentence should come first, a mistake largely resolved in T5-CPT. We note that some examples correctly predicted by FS models were incorrectly predicted by CPT models, and vice versa.

In the DC task, we noted a significant number of incorrectly formatted predictions (e.g., "cooherent" rather than "coherent"), especially in the DC-Chat subset. Each of these incorrectly formatted predictions, when adjusted to a correctly formatted prediction, were incorrect (e.g., an example that the model predicted "cooherent" is labeled "incoherent"). We show in Table 4, that DEPTH-FS was incorrect in DC-Chat examples that humans might find ambiguous (i.e., replacing a random sentence leaves the resulting passage coherent), reinforcing its strength in handling more complex discourse structures. We discuss this further in Appendix E.

5 Related work

The potential of encoder-decoder architectures in today's NLP landscape cannot be overstated. These architectures dominate context-heavy tasks ranging from translation (Üstün et al., 2024; Xue et al., 2021; Tay et al., 2022) to summarization (Zhang et al., 2020; Guo et al., 2022; Tay et al., 2022), and even following instructions across diverse domains (Aribandi et al., 2022; Wei et al., 2022a; Chung et al., 2024). Like their decoder-only counterparts, encoder-decoders are able to accommodate long inputs (Guo et al., 2022), and scale effectively effectively as a function of model size and training data (Sutawika et al., 2024). Ormazabal et al. (2024) released a series of encoder-decoder models, where their dense 21B parameter model outperformed all models of its size in the lmsys

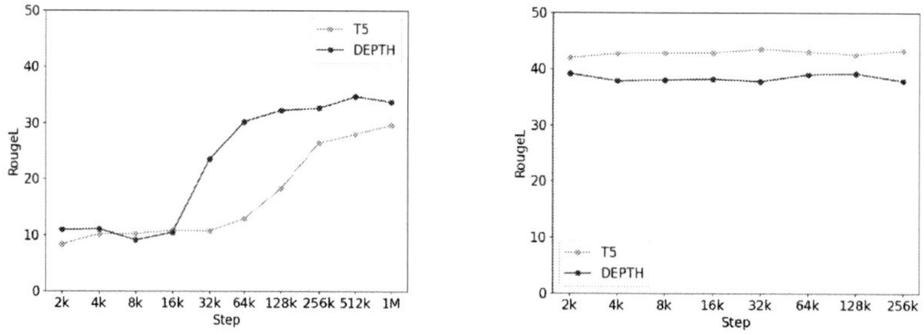

(a) Natural Instructions (NI) FS

(b) Natural Instructions (NI) CPT

Figure 6: NI results for DEPTH and T5 models.

benchmark (Zheng et al., 2023).[7] Encoder-deocder models are also strong multi-modal learners (Ormazabal et al., 2024; Wu et al., 2023; Dosovitskiy et al., 2021; Zhai et al., 2022). When scaled sufficiently, encoder-decoders like Reca-Core may be competitive with state of the art models like GPT-4 (OpenAI et al., 2023), Gemini (Team et al., 2023), and Claude-3.

While specialized encoder-decoder models such as PEGASUS (Zhang et al., 2020), DialogVED (Chen et al., 2022), and a multi-party dialogue pre-training model (Li et al., 2023) demonstrate the value of discourse-oriented tasks for encoder-decoder models, they have limited utility for broader tasks. Long-T5 (Guo et al., 2022) and UL2 (Tay et al., 2022) improved the ability of encoder-decoders to handle long contexts, but did not explicitly tackle discourse understanding. Flan-T5 (Wei et al., 2022a) and Ex-T5 (Aribandi et al., 2022) demonstrated the applicability of encoder-decoders across a variety of tasks, including ones that are heavily discourse dependent. However, these models depend on a vast yet costly annotated dataset to learn human preferences. Finally, BART (Lewis et al., 2020a) is an encoder-decoder which leverages sentence shuffling during pre-training, but does not train dedicated hierarchical representations for sentences (essentially behaving like a DEPTH model without sentence-tokens, and without attention-mask induced hierarchy).

6 Limitations

Given our lack of computational resources (Appendix C), we were not able to pre-train our models with a batch size that would allow an aggressive learning rate like that used in Raffel et al. (2020)'s T5 (see Appendix A for additional details). We also pre-trained on substantially fewer tokens than T5. As a result, our model converges to a worse loss during pre-training, and performs worse on downstream tasks. We also lacked computational resources to compute confidence intervals or statistical significance for our downstream experiments.[8]

Encoder-decoder LMs have fewer tools available for computationally efficient pre-training. For example, FlashAttention (Dao et al., 2022; Dao, 2023), which provides a massive training speedup, is not available for encoder-decoder models. It is therefore difficult to create scalable pre-training experiments with new encoder-decoder architectures and objectives.

7 Conclusions and future work

DEPTH's new pre-training objective and hierarchical representations complement efforts to scale model size, parallelize architectures, and acquire high quality data for pre-training. Despite training over fewer tokens, DEPTH significantly outperformed T5 both during pre-training and during fine-tuning. DEPTH's remarkably efficient learning and downstream performance on discourse oriented tasks underscore the importance of discourse-oriented pre-training.

Looking forward, the application of DEPTH to RAG (Lewis et al., 2020b), especially over sentence "chunks", presents an exciting avenue for future research. Additionally, extending DEPTH's pre-training objectives to encompass higher-level discourse units—such as paragraphs, chapters, and

[7] This Reka model is competitve with mixtral 8x22b (Jiang et al., 2024) (which was trained with significantly more parameters using a mixture-of-experts architecture).

[8] Running a single downstream experiment on MNLI takes 5-7.5 hours. We run $\approx$ 120 experiments for each of 10 benchmarks, and do not have the capacity to repeat experiments $\geq 5\times$ to obtain statistical significance.

whole documents—offers further flexibility emerging hierarchical RAG systems (Chen et al., 2024). Moreover, conducting further experiments with larger DEPTH models is helpful for understanding the scalability of discourse-focused training objectives. Such investigations could reveal whether the promising capabilities observed in DEPTH are amplified with increased model capacity. Finally, sentence-level pre-training tasks such as next-sentence prediction (as in Krishna et al. (2022) and Zhang et al. (2020)) may prove powerful alternatives to sentence un-shuffling.

Acknowledgments

This research was supported by the Israel Science Foundation (grant No. 448/20), an Azrieli Foundation Early Career Faculty Fellowship, and an AI Alignment grant from Open Philanthropy.

References

Zachary Ankner, Naomi Saphra, Davis Blalock, Jonathan Frankle, and Matthew Leavitt. 2024. Dynamic masking rate schedules for MLM pretraining. In *Proceedings of the 18th Conference of the European Chapter of the Association for Computational Linguistics (Volume 2: Short Papers)*, pages 477–487, St. Julian's, Malta. Association for Computational Linguistics.

Vamsi Aribandi, Yi Tay, Tal Schuster, Jinfeng Rao, Huaixiu Steven Zheng, Sanket Vaibhav Mehta, Honglei Zhuang, Vinh Q. Tran, Dara Bahri, Jianmo Ni, Jai Gupta, Kai Hui, Sebastian Ruder, and Donald Metzler. 2022. Ext5: Towards extreme multi-task scaling for transfer learning. In *International Conference on Learning Representations*.

Yuntao Bai, Saurav Kadavath, Sandipan Kundu, Amanda Askell, Jackson Kernion, Andy Jones, Anna Chen, Anna Goldie, Azalia Mirhoseini, Cameron McKinnon, Carol Chen, Catherine Olsson, Christopher Olah, Danny Hernandez, Dawn Drain, Deep Ganguli, Dustin Li, Eli Tran-Johnson, Ethan Perez, Jamie Kerr, Jared Mueller, Jeffrey Ladish, Joshua Landau, Kamal Ndousse, Kamile Lukosuite, Liane Lovitt, Michael Sellitto, Nelson Elhage, Nicholas Schiefer, Noemi Mercado, Nova DasSarma, Robert Lasenby, Robin Larson, Sam Ringer, Scott Johnston, Shauna Kravec, Sheer El Showk, Stanislav Fort, Tamera Lanham, Timothy Telleen-Lawton, Tom Conerly, Tom Henighan, Tristan Hume, Samuel R. Bowman, Zac Hatfield-Dodds, Ben Mann, Dario Amodei, Nicholas Joseph, Sam McCandlish, Tom Brown, and Jared Kaplan. 2022. Constitutional ai: Harmlessness from ai feedback. *Preprint*, arXiv:2212.08073.

Stella Biderman, USVSN Sai Prashanth, Lintang Sutawika, Hailey Schoelkopf, Quentin Anthony, Shivanshu Purohit, and Edward Raff. 2023. Emergent and predictable memorization in large language models.

Steven Bird and Edward Loper. 2004. NLTK: The natural language toolkit. In *Proceedings of the ACL Interactive Poster and Demonstration Sessions*, pages 214–217, Barcelona, Spain. Association for Computational Linguistics.

Tom Brown, Benjamin Mann, Nick Ryder, Melanie Subbiah, Jared D Kaplan, Prafulla Dhariwal, Arvind Neelakantan, Pranav Shyam, Girish Sastry, Amanda Askell, Sandhini Agarwal, Ariel Herbert-Voss, Gretchen Krueger, Tom Henighan, Rewon Child, Aditya Ramesh, Daniel Ziegler, Jeffrey Wu, Clemens Winter, Chris Hesse, Mark Chen, Eric Sigler, Mateusz Litwin, Scott Gray, Benjamin Chess, Jack Clark, Christopher Berner, Sam McCandlish, Alec Radford, Ilya Sutskever, and Dario Amodei. 2020. Language models are few-shot learners. In *Advances in Neural Information Processing Systems*, volume 33, pages 1877–1901. Curran Associates, Inc.

Tuhin Chakrabarty, Christopher Hidey, Smaranda Muresan, Kathy McKeown, and Alyssa Hwang. 2019. AMPERSAND: Argument mining for PERSuAsive oNline discussions. In *Proceedings of the 2019 Conference on Empirical Methods in Natural Language Processing and the 9th International Joint Conference on Natural Language Processing (EMNLP-IJCNLP)*, pages 2933–2943, Hong Kong, China. Association for Computational Linguistics.

Mingda Chen, Zewei Chu, and Kevin Gimpel. 2019. Evaluation benchmarks and learning criteria for discourse-aware sentence representations. In *Proceedings of the 2019 Conference on Empirical Methods in Natural Language Processing and the 9th International Joint Conference on Natural Language Processing (EMNLP-IJCNLP)*, pages 649–662, Hong Kong, China. Association for Computational Linguistics.

Wei Chen, Yeyun Gong, Song Wang, Bolun Yao, Weizhen Qi, Zhongyu Wei, Xiaowu Hu, Bartuer Zhou, Yi Mao, Weizhu Chen, Biao Cheng, and Nan Duan. 2022. DialogVED: A pre-trained latent variable encoder-decoder model for dialog response generation. In *Proceedings of the 60th Annual Meeting of the Association for Computational Linguistics (Volume 1: Long Papers)*, pages 4852–4864, Dublin, Ireland. Association for Computational Linguistics.

Xinyue Chen, Pengyu Gao, Jiangjiang Song, and Xiaoyang Tan. 2024. Hiqa: A hierarchical contextual augmentation rag for massive documents qa. *Preprint*, arXiv:2402.01767.

Hyung Won Chung, Le Hou, Shayne Longpre, Barret Zoph, Yi Tay, William Fedus, Yunxuan Li, Xuezhi Wang, Mostafa Dehghani, Siddhartha Brahma, et al. 2024. Scaling instruction-finetuned language models. *Journal of Machine Learning Research*, 25(70):1–53.

Together Computer. 2023. Redpajama: an open dataset for training large language models.

Tri Dao. 2023. FlashAttention-2: Faster attention with better parallelism and work partitioning.

Tri Dao, Daniel Y. Fu, Stefano Ermon, Atri Rudra, and Christopher Ré. 2022. FlashAttention: Fast and memory-efficient exact attention with IO-awareness. In *Advances in Neural Information Processing Systems*.

Jacob Devlin, Ming-Wei Chang, Kenton Lee, and Kristina Toutanova. 2019. BERT: Pre-training of deep bidirectional transformers for language understanding. In *Proceedings of the 2019 Conference of the North American Chapter of the Association for Computational Linguistics: Human Language Technologies, Volume 1 (Long and Short Papers)*, pages 4171–4186, Minneapolis, Minnesota. Association for Computational Linguistics.

Hantian Ding, Zijian Wang, Giovanni Paolini, Varun Kumar, Anoop Deoras, Dan Roth, and Stefano Soatto. 2024. Fewer truncations improve language modeling. *arXiv preprint arXiv:2404.10830*.

Jesse Dodge, Maarten Sap, Ana Marasović, William Agnew, Gabriel Ilharco, Dirk Groeneveld, Margaret Mitchell, and Matt Gardner. 2021. Documenting large webtext corpora: A case study on the colossal clean crawled corpus. In *Proceedings of the 2021 Conference on Empirical Methods in Natural Language Processing*, pages 1286–1305, Online and Punta Cana, Dominican Republic. Association for Computational Linguistics.

Alexey Dosovitskiy, Lucas Beyer, Alexander Kolesnikov, Dirk Weissenborn, Xiaohua Zhai, Thomas Unterthiner, Mostafa Dehghani, Matthias Minderer, Georg Heigold, Sylvain Gelly, Jakob Uszkoreit, and Neil Houlsby. 2021. An image is worth 16x16 words: Transformers for image recognition at scale. In *International Conference on Learning Representations*.

Esin Durmus, Faisal Ladhak, and Claire Cardie. 2019. The role of pragmatic and discourse context in determining argument impact. In *Conference on Empirical Methods in Natural Language Processing*.

Aaron Grattafiori, Abhimanyu Dubey, Abhinav Jauhri, Abhinav Pandey, Abhishek Kadian, Ahmad Al-Dahle, Aiesha Letman, Akhil Mathur, Alan Schelten, Alex Vaughan, et al. 2024. The llama 3 herd of models. *arXiv preprint arXiv:2407.21783*.

Dirk Groeneveld, Iz Beltagy, Pete Walsh, Akshita Bhagia, Rodney Kinney, Oyvind Tafjord, Ananya Harsh Jha, Hamish Ivison, Ian Magnusson, Yizhong Wang, Shane Arora, David Atkinson, Russell Authur, Khyathi Chandu, Arman Cohan, Jennifer Dumas, Yanai Elazar, Yuling Gu, Jack Hessel, Tushar Khot, William Merrill, Jacob Morrison, Niklas Muennighoff, Aakanksha Naik, Crystal Nam, Matthew E. Peters, Valentina Pyatkin, Abhilasha Ravichander, Dustin Schwenk, Saurabh Shah, Will Smith, Nishant Subramani, Mitchell Wortsman, Pradeep Dasigi, Nathan Lambert, Kyle Richardson, Jesse Dodge, Kyle Lo, Luca Soldaini, Noah A. Smith, and Hannaneh Hajishirzi. 2024. Olmo: Accelerating the science of language models. *Preprint*.

Mandy Guo, Joshua Ainslie, David Uthus, Santiago Ontanon, Jianmo Ni, Yun-Hsuan Sung, and Yinfei Yang. 2022. LongT5: Efficient text-to-text transformer for long sequences. In *Findings of the Association for Computational Linguistics: NAACL 2022*, pages 724–736, Seattle, United States. Association for Computational Linguistics.

Christopher Hidey, Elena Musi, Alyssa Hwang, Smaranda Muresan, and Kathy McKeown. 2017. Analyzing the semantic types of claims and premises in an online persuasive forum. In *Proceedings of the 4th Workshop on Argument Mining*, pages 11–21, Copenhagen, Denmark. Association for Computational Linguistics.

Yilun Hua, Zhaoyuan Deng, and Kathleen McKeown. 2023. Improving long dialogue summarization with semantic graph representation. In *Findings of the Association for Computational Linguistics: ACL 2023*, pages 13851–13883, Toronto, Canada. Association for Computational Linguistics.

Dan Iter, Kelvin Guu, Larry Lansing, and Dan Jurafsky. 2020. Pretraining with contrastive sentence objectives improves discourse performance of language models. In *Proceedings of the 58th Annual Meeting of the Association for Computational Linguistics*, pages 4859–4870, Online. Association for Computational Linguistics.

Yacine Jernite, Samuel R. Bowman, and David Sontag. 2017. Discourse-based objectives for fast unsupervised sentence representation learning. *Preprint*, arXiv:1705.00557.

Albert Q. Jiang, Alexandre Sablayrolles, Arthur Mensch, Chris Bamford, Devendra Singh Chaplot, Diego de las Casas, Florian Bressand, Gianna Lengyel, Guillaume Lample, Lucile Saulnier, Lélio Renard Lavaud, Marie-Anne Lachaux, Pierre Stock, Teven Le Scao, Thibaut Lavril, Thomas Wang, Timothée Lacroix, and William El Sayed. 2023. Mistral 7b. *Preprint*, arXiv:2310.06825.

Albert Q Jiang, Alexandre Sablayrolles, Antoine Roux, Arthur Mensch, Blanche Savary, Chris Bamford, Devendra Singh Chaplot, Diego de las Casas, Emma Bou Hanna, Florian Bressand, et al. 2024. Mixtral of experts. *arXiv preprint arXiv:2401.04088*.

Mandar Joshi, Danqi Chen, Yinhan Liu, Daniel S. Weld, Luke Zettlemoyer, and Omer Levy. 2020. SpanBERT: Improving pre-training by representing and predicting spans. *Transactions of the Association for Computational Linguistics*, 8:64–77.

Shahar Katz, Liran Ringel, Yaniv Romano, and Lior Wolf. 2024. Segment-based attention masking for gpts. *Preprint*, arXiv:2412.18487.

Mario Michael Krell, Matej Kosec, Sergio P Perez, and Andrew Fitzgibbon. 2021. Efficient sequence packing without cross-contamination: Accelerating large language models without impacting performance. *arXiv preprint arXiv:2107.02027*.

Kalpesh Krishna, Yapei Chang, John Wieting, and Mohit Iyyer. 2022. RankGen: Improving text generation with large ranking models. In *Proceedings of the 2022 Conference on Empirical Methods in Natural Language Processing*, pages 199–232, Abu Dhabi, United Arab Emirates. Association for Computational Linguistics.

Taku Kudo and John Richardson. 2018. SentencePiece: A simple and language independent subword tokenizer and detokenizer for neural text processing. In *Proceedings of the 2018 Conference on Empirical Methods in Natural Language Processing: System Demonstrations*, pages 66–71, Brussels, Belgium. Association for Computational Linguistics.

Zhenzhong Lan, Mingda Chen, Sebastian Goodman, Kevin Gimpel, Piyush Sharma, and Radu Soricut. 2020. Albert: A lite bert for self-supervised learning of language representations. In *International Conference on Learning Representations*.

Haejun Lee, Drew A. Hudson, Kangwook Lee, and Christopher D. Manning. 2020. SLM: Learning a discourse language representation with sentence unshuffling. In *Proceedings of the 2020 Conference on Empirical Methods in Natural Language Processing (EMNLP)*, pages 1551–1562, Online. Association for Computational Linguistics.

Yoav Levine, Barak Lenz, Opher Lieber, Omri Abend, Kevin Leyton-Brown, Moshe Tennenholtz, and Yoav Shoham. 2020. Pmi-masking: Principled masking of correlated spans. In *International Conference on Learning Representations*.

Mike Lewis, Yinhan Liu, Naman Goyal, Marjan Ghazvininejad, Abdelrahman Mohamed, Omer Levy, Veselin Stoyanov, and Luke Zettlemoyer. 2020a. BART: Denoising sequence-to-sequence pre-training for natural language generation, translation, and comprehension. In *Proceedings of the 58th Annual Meeting of the Association for Computational Linguistics*, pages 7871–7880, Online. Association for Computational Linguistics.

Patrick Lewis, Ethan Perez, Aleksandara Piktus, Fabio Petroni, Vladimir Karpukhin, Naman Goyal, Heinrich Kuttler, Mike Lewis, Wen tau Yih, Tim Rocktäschel, Sebastian Riedel, and Douwe Kiela. 2020b. Retrieval-augmented generation for knowledge-intensive nlp tasks. *ArXiv*, abs/2005.11401.

Yiyang Li, Xinting Huang, Wei Bi, and Hai Zhao. 2023. Pre-training multi-party dialogue models with latent discourse inference. In *Proceedings of the 61st Annual Meeting of the Association for Computational Linguistics (Volume 1: Long Papers)*, pages 9584–9599, Toronto, Canada. Association for Computational Linguistics.

Yinhan Liu, Myle Ott, Naman Goyal, Jingfei Du, Mandar Joshi, Danqi Chen, Omer Levy, Mike Lewis, Luke Zettlemoyer, and Veselin Stoyanov. 2019. Roberta: A robustly optimized bert pretraining approach. *Preprint*, arXiv:1907.11692.

Ilya Loshchilov and Frank Hutter. 2019. Decoupled weight decay regularization. In *International Conference on Learning Representations*.

Aviya Maimon and Reut Tsarfaty. 2023a. COHESENTIA: A novel benchmark of incremental versus holistic assessment of coherence in generated texts. In *Proceedings of the 2023 Conference on Empirical Methods in Natural Language Processing*, pages 5328–5343, Singapore. Association for Computational Linguistics.

Aviya Maimon and Reut Tsarfaty. 2023b. A novel computational and modeling foundation for automatic coherence assessment. *Preprint*, arXiv:2310.00598.

Eleni Miltsakaki, Rashmi Prasad, Aravind Joshi, and Bonnie Webber. 2004. The Penn Discourse Treebank. In *Proceedings of the Fourth International Conference on Language Resources and Evaluation (LREC'04)*, Lisbon, Portugal. European Language Resources Association (ELRA).

Farjana Sultana Mim, Naoya Inoue, Paul Reisert, Hiroki Ouchi, and Kentaro Inui. 2021. Corruption is not all bad: Incorporating discourse structure into pre-training via corruption for essay scoring. *IEEE/ACM Transactions on Audio, Speech, and Language Processing*, 29:2202–2215.

Swaroop Mishra, Daniel Khashabi, Chitta Baral, and Hannaneh Hajishirzi. 2022. Cross-task generalization via natural language crowdsourcing instructions. In *Proceedings of the 60th Annual Meeting of the Association for Computational Linguistics (Volume 1: Long Papers)*, pages 3470–3487, Dublin, Ireland. Association for Computational Linguistics.

Niklas Muennighoff, Alexander M Rush, Boaz Barak, Teven Le Scao, Nouamane Tazi, Aleksandra Piktus, Sampo Pyysalo, Thomas Wolf, and Colin Raffel. 2023. Scaling data-constrained language models. In *Thirty-seventh Conference on Neural Information Processing Systems*.

Piotr Nawrot. 2023. nanoT5: Fast & simple pre-training and fine-tuning of t5 models with limited resources. In *Proceedings of the 3rd Workshop for Natural Language Processing Open Source Software (NLP-OSS 2023)*, pages 95–101, Singapore. Association for Computational Linguistics.

OpenAI, :, Josh Achiam, Steven Adler, Sandhini Agarwal, Lama Ahmad, Ilge Akkaya, Florencia Leoni Aleman, Diogo Almeida, Janko Altenschmidt, Sam Altman, Shyamal Anadkat, Red Avila, Igor Babuschkin, Suchir Balaji, Valerie Balcom, Paul Baltescu, Haiming Bao, Mo Bavarian, Jeff Belgum, Irwan Bello,

Jake Berdine, Gabriel Bernadett-Shapiro, Christopher Berner, Lenny Bogdonoff, Oleg Boiko, Madelaine Boyd, Anna-Luisa Brakman, Greg Brockman, Tim Brooks, Miles Brundage, Kevin Button, Trevor Cai, Rosie Campbell, Andrew Cann, Brittany Carey, Chelsea Carlson, Rory Carmichael, Brooke Chan, Che Chang, Fotis Chantzis, Derek Chen, Sully Chen, Ruby Chen, Jason Chen, Mark Chen, Ben Chess, Chester Cho, Casey Chu, Hyung Won Chung, Dave Cummings, Jeremiah Currier, Yunxing Dai, Cory Decareaux, Thomas Degry, Noah Deutsch, Damien Deville, Arka Dhar, David Dohan, Steve Dowling, Sheila Dunning, Adrien Ecoffet, Atty Eleti, Tyna Eloundou, David Farhi, Liam Fedus, Niko Felix, Simón Posada Fishman, Juston Forte, Isabella Fulford, Leo Gao, Elie Georges, Christian Gibson, Vik Goel, Tarun Gogineni, Gabriel Goh, Rapha Gontijo-Lopes, Jonathan Gordon, Morgan Grafstein, Scott Gray, Ryan Greene, Joshua Gross, Shixiang Shane Gu, Yufei Guo, Chris Hallacy, Jesse Han, Jeff Harris, Yuchen He, Mike Heaton, Johannes Heidecke, Chris Hesse, Alan Hickey, Wade Hickey, Peter Hoeschele, Brandon Houghton, Kenny Hsu, Shengli Hu, Xin Hu, Joost Huizinga, Shantanu Jain, Shawn Jain, Joanne Jang, Angela Jiang, Roger Jiang, Haozhun Jin, Denny Jin, Shino Jomoto, Billie Jonn, Heewoo Jun, Tomer Kaftan, Łukasz Kaiser, Ali Kamali, Ingmar Kanitscheider, Nitish Shirish Keskar, Tabarak Khan, Logan Kilpatrick, Jong Wook Kim, Christina Kim, Yongjik Kim, Hendrik Kirchner, Jamie Kiros, Matt Knight, Daniel Kokotajlo, Łukasz Kondraciuk, Andrew Kondrich, Aris Konstantinidis, Kyle Kosic, Gretchen Krueger, Vishal Kuo, Michael Lampe, Ikai Lan, Teddy Lee, Jan Leike, Jade Leung, Daniel Levy, Chak Ming Li, Rachel Lim, Molly Lin, Stephanie Lin, Mateusz Litwin, Theresa Lopez, Ryan Lowe, Patricia Lue, Anna Makanju, Kim Malfacini, Sam Manning, Todor Markov, Yaniv Markovski, Bianca Martin, Katie Mayer, Andrew Mayne, Bob McGrew, Scott Mayer McKinney, Christine McLeavey, Paul McMillan, Jake McNeil, David Medina, Aalok Mehta, Jacob Menick, Luke Metz, Andrey Mishchenko, Pamela Mishkin, Vinnie Monaco, Evan Morikawa, Daniel Mossing, Tong Mu, Mira Murati, Oleg Murk, David Mély, Ashvin Nair, Reiichiro Nakano, Rajeev Nayak, Arvind Neelakantan, Richard Ngo, Hyeonwoo Noh, Long Ouyang, Cullen O'Keefe, Jakub Pachocki, Alex Paino, Joe Palermo, Ashley Pantuliano, Giambattista Parascandolo, Joel Parish, Emy Parparita, Alex Passos, Mikhail Pavlov, Andrew Peng, Adam Perelman, Filipe de Avila Belbute Peres, Michael Petrov, Henrique Ponde de Oliveira Pinto, Michael, Pokorny, Michelle Pokrass, Vitchyr Pong, Tolly Powell, Alethea Power, Boris Power, Elizabeth Proehl, Raul Puri, Alec Radford, Jack Rae, Aditya Ramesh, Cameron Raymond, Francis Real, Kendra Rimbach, Carl Ross, Bob Rotsted, Henri Roussez, Nick Ryder, Mario Saltarelli, Ted Sanders, Shibani Santurkar, Girish Sastry, Heather Schmidt, David Schnurr, John Schulman, Daniel Selsam, Kyla Sheppard, Toki Sherbakov, Jessica Shieh, Sarah Shoker, Pranav Shyam, Szymon Sidor, Eric Sigler, Maddie Simens, Jordan Sitkin, Katarina Slama, Ian Sohl, Benjamin Sokolowsky, Yang Song, Natalie Staudacher, Felipe Petroski Such, Natalie Summers, Ilya Sutskever, Jie Tang, Nikolas Tezak, Madeleine Thompson, Phil Tillet, Amin Tootoonchian, Elizabeth Tseng, Preston Tuggle, Nick Turley, Jerry Tworek, Juan Felipe Cerón Uribe, Andrea Vallone, Arun Vijayvergiya, Chelsea Voss, Carroll Wainwright, Justin Jay Wang, Alvin Wang, Ben Wang, Jonathan Ward, Jason Wei, CJ Weinmann, Akila Welihinda, Peter Welinder, Jiayi Weng, Lilian Weng, Matt Wiethoff, Dave Willner, Clemens Winter, Samuel Wolrich, Hannah Wong, Lauren Workman, Sherwin Wu, Jeff Wu, Michael Wu, Kai Xiao, Tao Xu, Sarah Yoo, Kevin Yu, Qiming Yuan, Wojciech Zaremba, Rowan Zellers, Chong Zhang, Marvin Zhang, Shengjia Zhao, Tianhao Zheng, Juntang Zhuang, William Zhuk, and Barret Zoph. 2023. Gpt-4 technical report. *Preprint*, arXiv:2303.08774.

Aitor Ormazabal, Che Zheng, Cyprien de Masson d'Autume, Dani Yogatama, Deyu Fu, Donovan Ong, Eric Chen, Eugenie Lamprecht, Hai Pham, Isaac Ong, Kaloyan Aleksiev, Lei Li, Matthew Henderson, Max Bain, Mikel Artetxe, Nishant Relan, Piotr Padlewski, Qi Liu, Ren Chen, Samuel Phua, Yazheng Yang, Yi Tay, Yuqi Wang, Zhongkai Zhu, and Zhihui Xie. 2024. Reka core, flash, and edge: A series of powerful multimodal language models. *Preprint*, arXiv:2404.12387.

Long Ouyang, Jeffrey Wu, Xu Jiang, Diogo Almeida, Carroll Wainwright, Pamela Mishkin, Chong Zhang, Sandhini Agarwal, Katarina Slama, Alex Ray, John Schulman, Jacob Hilton, Fraser Kelton, Luke Miller, Maddie Simens, Amanda Askell, Peter Welinder, Paul F Christiano, Jan Leike, and Ryan Lowe. 2022. Training language models to follow instructions with human feedback. In *Advances in Neural Information Processing Systems*, volume 35, pages 27730–27744. Curran Associates, Inc.

Rashmi Prasad, Nikhil Dinesh, Alan Lee, Eleni Miltsakaki, Livio Robaldo, Aravind Joshi, and Bonnie Webber. 2008. The Penn Discourse TreeBank 2.0. In *Proceedings of the Sixth International Conference on Language Resources and Evaluation (LREC'08)*, Marrakech, Morocco. European Language Resources Association (ELRA).

Rashmi Prasad, Bonnie Webber, and Alan Lee. 2018. Discourse annotation in the PDTB: The next generation. In *Proceedings of the 14th Joint ACL-ISO Workshop on Interoperable Semantic Annotation*, pages 87–97, Santa Fe, New Mexico, USA. Association for Computational Linguistics.

Qwen, :, An Yang, Baosong Yang, Beichen Zhang, Binyuan Hui, Bo Zheng, Bowen Yu, Chengyuan Li, Dayiheng Liu, Fei Huang, Haoran Wei, Huan Lin, Jian Yang, Jianhong Tu, Jianwei Zhang, Jianxin Yang, Jiaxi Yang, Jingren Zhou, Junyang Lin, Kai Dang, Keming Lu, Keqin Bao, Kexin Yang, Le Yu, Mei Li, Mingfeng Xue, Pei Zhang, Qin Zhu, Rui Men, Runji Lin, Tianhao Li, Tianyi Tang, Tingyu Xia, Xingzhang Ren, Xuancheng Ren, Yang Fan, Yang Su, Yichang

Zhang, Yu Wan, Yuqiong Liu, Zeyu Cui, Zhenru Zhang, and Zihan Qiu. 2025. Qwen2.5 technical report. *Preprint*, arXiv:2412.15115.

Alec Radford, Karthik Narasimhan, Tim Salimans, and Ilya Sutskever. 2018. Improving language understanding by generative pre-training.

Alec Radford, Jeff Wu, Rewon Child, David Luan, Dario Amodei, and Ilya Sutskever. 2019. Language models are unsupervised multitask learners.

Colin Raffel, Noam Shazeer, Adam Roberts, Katherine Lee, Sharan Narang, Michael Matena, Yanqi Zhou, Wei Li, and Peter J Liu. 2020. Exploring the limits of transfer learning with a unified text-to-text transformer. *The Journal of Machine Learning Research*, 21(1):5485–5551.

Samyam Rajbhandari, Jeff Rasley, Olatunji Ruwase, and Yuxiong He. 2020. Zero: memory optimizations toward training trillion parameter models. In *Proceedings of the International Conference for High Performance Computing, Networking, Storage and Analysis*, SC '20. IEEE Press.

Noam Shazeer and Mitchell Stern. 2018. Adafactor: Adaptive learning rates with sublinear memory cost. In *Proceedings of the 35th International Conference on Machine Learning*, volume 80 of *Proceedings of Machine Learning Research*, pages 4596–4604. PMLR.

Weijia Shi, Sewon Min, Maria Lomeli, Chunting Zhou, Margaret Li, Xi Victoria Lin, Noah A. Smith, Luke Zettlemoyer, Wen tau Yih, and Mike Lewis. 2024. In-context pretraining: Language modeling beyond document boundaries. In *The Twelfth International Conference on Learning Representations*.

Richard Socher, Alex Perelygin, Jean Wu, Jason Chuang, Christopher D. Manning, Andrew Ng, and Christopher Potts. 2013. Recursive deep models for semantic compositionality over a sentiment treebank. In *Proceedings of the 2013 Conference on Empirical Methods in Natural Language Processing*, pages 1631–1642, Seattle, Washington, USA. Association for Computational Linguistics.

Luca Soldaini, Rodney Kinney, Akshita Bhagia, Dustin Schwenk, David Atkinson, Russell Authur, Ben Bogin, Khyathi Chandu, Jennifer Dumas, Yanai Elazar, Valentin Hofmann, Ananya Harsh Jha, Sachin Kumar, Li Lucy, Xinxi Lyu, Nathan Lambert, Ian Magnusson, Jacob Morrison, Niklas Muennighoff, Aakanksha Naik, Crystal Nam, Matthew E. Peters, Abhilasha Ravichander, Kyle Richardson, Zejiang Shen, Emma Strubell, Nishant Subramani, Oyvind Tafjord, Pete Walsh, Luke Zettlemoyer, Noah A. Smith, Hannaneh Hajishirzi, Iz Beltagy, Dirk Groeneveld, Jesse Dodge, and Kyle Lo. 2024. Dolma: An Open Corpus of Three Trillion Tokens for Language Model Pretraining Research. *arXiv preprint*.

Lintang Sutawika, Aran Komatsuzaki, and Colin Raffel. 2024. Pile-t5. Blog post.

Yi Tay, Mostafa Dehghani, Vinh Q. Tran, Xavier García, Jason Wei, Xuezhi Wang, Hyung Won Chung, Dara Bahri, Tal Schuster, Huaixiu Steven Zheng, Denny Zhou, Neil Houlsby, and Donald Metzler. 2022. Ul2: Unifying language learning paradigms. In *International Conference on Learning Representations*.

Gemini Team, Rohan Anil, Sebastian Borgeaud, Yonghui Wu, Jean-Baptiste Alayrac, Jiahui Yu, Radu Soricut, Johan Schalkwyk, Andrew M. Dai, Anja Hauth, Katie Millican, David Silver, Slav Petrov, Melvin Johnson, Ioannis Antonoglou, Julian Schrittwieser, Amelia Glaese, Jilin Chen, Emily Pitler, Timothy Lillicrap, Angeliki Lazaridou, Orhan Firat, James Molloy, Michael Isard, Paul R. Barham, Tom Hennigan, Benjamin Lee, Fabio Viola, Malcolm Reynolds, Yuanzhong Xu, Ryan Doherty, Eli Collins, Clemens Meyer, Eliza Rutherford, Erica Moreira, Kareem Ayoub, Megha Goel, George Tucker, Enrique Piqueras, Maxim Krikun, Iain Barr, Nikolay Savinov, Ivo Danihelka, Becca Roelofs, Anaïs White, Anders Andreassen, Tamara von Glehn, Lakshman Yagati, Mehran Kazemi, Lucas Gonzalez, Misha Khalman, Jakub Sygnowski, Alexandre Frechette, Charlotte Smith, Laura Culp, Lev Proleev, Yi Luan, Xi Chen, James Lottes, Nathan Schucher, Federico Lebron, Alban Rrustemi, Natalie Clay, Phil Crone, Tomas Kocisky, Jeffrey Zhao, Bartek Perz, Dian Yu, Heidi Howard, Adam Bloniarz, Jack W. Rae, Han Lu, Laurent Sifre, Marcello Maggioni, Fred Alcober, Dan Garrette, Megan Barnes, Shantanu Thakoor, Jacob Austin, Gabriel Barth-Maron, William Wong, Rishabh Joshi, Rahma Chaabouni, Deeni Fatiha, Arun Ahuja, Ruibo Liu, Yunxuan Li, Sarah Cogan, Jeremy Chen, Chao Jia, Chenjie Gu, Qiao Zhang, Jordan Grimstad, Ale Jakse Hartman, Martin Chadwick, Gaurav Singh Tomar, Xavier Garcia, Evan Senter, Emanuel Taropa, Thanumalayan Sankaranarayana Pillai, Jacob Devlin, Michael Laskin, Diego de Las Casas, Dasha Valter, Connie Tao, Lorenzo Blanco, Adrià Puigdomènech Badia, David Reitter, Mianna Chen, Jenny Brennan, Clara Rivera, Sergey Brin, Shariq Iqbal, Gabriela Surita, Jane Labanowski, Abhi Rao, Stephanie Winkler, Emilio Parisotto, Yiming Gu, Kate Olszewska, Yujing Zhang, Ravi Addanki, Antoine Miech, Annie Louis, Laurent El Shafey, Denis Teplyashin, Geoff Brown, Elliot Catt, Nithya Attaluri, Jan Balaguer, Jackie Xiang, Pidong Wang, Zoe Ashwood, Anton Briukhov, Albert Webson, Sanjay Ganapathy, Smit Sanghavi, Ajay Kannan, Ming-Wei Chang, Axel Stjerngren, Josip Djolonga, Yuting Sun, Ankur Bapna, Matthew Aitchison, Pedram Pejman, Henryk Michalewski, Tianhe Yu, Cindy Wang, Juliette Love, Junwhan Ahn, Dawn Bloxwich, Kehang Han, Peter Humphreys, Thibault Sellam, James Bradbury, Varun Godbole, Sina Samangooei, Bogdan Damoc, Alex Kaskasoli, Sébastien M. R. Arnold, Vijay Vasudevan, Shubham Agrawal, Jason Riesa, Dmitry Lepikhin, Richard Tanburn, Srivatsan Srinivasan, Hyeontaek Lim, Sarah Hodkinson, Pranav Shyam, Johan Ferret, Steven Hand, Ankush Garg, Tom Le Paine, Jian Li, Yujia Li, Minh Giang, Alexander Neitz, Zaheer Abbas, Sarah York, Machel Reid, Elizabeth Cole, Aakanksha

Chowdhery, Dipanjan Das, Dominika Rogozińska, Vitaly Nikolaev, Pablo Sprechmann, Zachary Nado, Lukas Zilka, Flavien Prost, Luheng He, Marianne Monteiro, Gaurav Mishra, Chris Welty, Josh Newlan, Dawei Jia, Miltiadis Allamanis, Clara Huiyi Hu, Raoul de Liedekerke, Justin Gilmer, Carl Saroufim, Shruti Rijhwani, Shaobo Hou, Disha Shrivastava, Anirudh Baddepudi, Alex Goldin, Adnan Ozturel, Albin Cassirer, Yunhan Xu, Daniel Sohn, Devendra Sachan, Reinald Kim Amplayo, Craig Swanson, Dessie Petrova, Shashi Narayan, Arthur Guez, Siddhartha Brahma, Jessica Landon, Miteyan Patel, Ruizhe Zhao, Kevin Villela, Luyu Wang, Wenhao Jia, Matthew Rahtz, Mai Giménez, Legg Yeung, Hanzhao Lin, James Keeling, Petko Georgiev, Diana Mincu, Boxi Wu, Salem Haykal, Rachel Saputro, Kiran Vodrahalli, James Qin, Zeynep Cankara, Abhanshu Sharma, Nick Fernando, Will Hawkins, Behnam Neyshabur, Solomon Kim, Adrian Hutter, Priyanka Agrawal, Alex Castro-Ros, George van den Driessche, Tao Wang, Fan Yang, Shuo yiin Chang, Paul Komarek, Ross McIlroy, Mario Lučić, Guodong Zhang, Wael Farhan, Michael Sharman, Paul Natsev, Paul Michel, Yong Cheng, Yamini Bansal, Siyuan Qiao, Kris Cao, Siamak Shakeri, Christina Butterfield, Justin Chung, Paul Kishan Rubenstein, Shivani Agrawal, Arthur Mensch, Kedar Soparkar, Karel Lenc, Timothy Chung, Aedan Pope, Loren Maggiore, Jackie Kay, Priya Jhakra, Shibo Wang, Joshua Maynez, Mary Phuong, Taylor Tobin, Andrea Tacchetti, Maja Trebacz, Kevin Robinson, Yash Katariya, Sebastian Riedel, Paige Bailey, Kefan Xiao, Nimesh Ghelani, Lora Aroyo, Ambrose Slone, Neil Houlsby, Xuehan Xiong, Zhen Yang, Elena Gribovskaya, Jonas Adler, Mateo Wirth, Lisa Lee, Music Li, Thais Kagohara, Jay Pavagadhi, Sophie Bridgers, Anna Bortsova, Sanjay Ghemawat, Zafarali Ahmed, Tianqi Liu, Richard Powell, Vijay Bolina, Mariko Iinuma, Polina Zablotskaia, James Besley, Da-Woon Chung, Timothy Dozat, Ramona Comanescu, Xiance Si, Jeremy Greer, Guolong Su, Martin Polacek, Raphaël Lopez Kaufman, Simon Tokumine, Hexiang Hu, Elena Buchatskaya, Yingjie Miao, Mohamed Elhawaty, Aditya Siddhant, Nenad Tomasev, Jinwei Xing, Christina Greer, Helen Miller, Shereen Ashraf, Aurko Roy, Zizhao Zhang, Ada Ma, Angelos Filos, Milos Besta, Rory Blevins, Ted Klimenko, Chih-Kuan Yeh, Soravit Changpinyo, Jiaqi Mu, Oscar Chang, Mantas Pajarskas, Carrie Muir, Vered Cohen, Charline Le Lan, Krishna Haridasan, Amit Marathe, Steven Hansen, Sholto Douglas, Rajkumar Samuel, Mingqiu Wang, Sophia Austin, Chang Lan, Jiepu Jiang, Justin Chiu, Jaime Alonso Lorenzo, Lars Lowe Sjösund, Sébastien Cevey, Zach Gleicher, Thi Avrahami, Anudhyan Boral, Hansa Srinivasan, Vittorio Selo, Rhys May, Konstantinos Aisopos, Léonard Hussenot, Livio Baldini Soares, Kate Baumli, Michael B. Chang, Adrià Recasens, Ben Caine, Alexander Pritzel, Filip Pavetic, Fabio Pardo, Anita Gergely, Justin Frye, Vinay Ramasesh, Dan Horgan, Kartikeya Badola, Nora Kassner, Subhrajit Roy, Ethan Dyer, Víctor Campos, Alex Tomala, Yunhao Tang, Dalia El Badawy, Elspeth White, Basil Mustafa, Oran Lang, Abhishek Jindal, Sharad Vikram, Zhitao Gong, Sergi Caelles, Ross Hemsley, Gregory Thornton, Fangxiaoyu Feng, Wojciech Stokowiec, Ce Zheng, Phoebe Thacker, Çağlar Ünlü, Zhishuai Zhang, Mohammad Saleh, James Svensson, Max Bileschi, Piyush Patil, Ankesh Anand, Roman Ring, Katerina Tsihlas, Arpi Vezer, Marco Selvi, Toby Shevlane, Mikel Rodriguez, Tom Kwiatkowski, Samira Daruki, Keran Rong, Allan Dafoe, Nicholas FitzGerald, Keren Gu-Lemberg, Mina Khan, Lisa Anne Hendricks, Marie Pellat, Vladimir Feinberg, James Cobon-Kerr, Tara Sainath, Maribeth Rauh, Sayed Hadi Hashemi, Richard Ives, Yana Hasson, YaGuang Li, Eric Noland, Yuan Cao, Nathan Byrd, Le Hou, Qingze Wang, Thibault Sottiaux, Michela Paganini, Jean-Baptiste Lespiau, Alexandre Moufarek, Samer Hassan, Kaushik Shivakumar, Joost van Amersfoort, Amol Mandhane, Pratik Joshi, Anirudh Goyal, Matthew Tung, Andrew Brock, Hannah Sheahan, Vedant Misra, Cheng Li, Nemanja Rakićević, Mostafa Dehghani, Fangyu Liu, Sid Mittal, Junhyuk Oh, Seb Noury, Eren Sezener, Fantine Huot, Matthew Lamm, Nicola De Cao, Charlie Chen, Gamaleldin Elsayed, Ed Chi, Mahdis Mahdieh, Ian Tenney, Nan Hua, Ivan Petrychenko, Patrick Kane, Dylan Scandinaro, Rishub Jain, Jonathan Uesato, Romina Datta, Adam Sadovsky, Oskar Bunyan, Dominik Rabiej, Shimu Wu, John Zhang, Gautam Vasudevan, Edouard Leurent, Mahmoud Alnahlawi, Ionut Georgescu, Nan Wei, Ivy Zheng, Betty Chan, Pam G Rabinovitch, Piotr Stanczyk, Ye Zhang, David Steiner, Subhajit Naskar, Michael Azzam, Matthew Johnson, Adam Paszke, Chung-Cheng Chiu, Jaume Sanchez Elias, Afroz Mohiuddin, Faizan Muhammad, Jin Miao, Andrew Lee, Nino Vieillard, Sahitya Potluri, Jane Park, Elnaz Davoodi, Jiageng Zhang, Jeff Stanway, Drew Garmon, Abhijit Karmarkar, Zhe Dong, Jong Lee, Aviral Kumar, Luowei Zhou, Jonathan Evens, William Isaac, Zhe Chen, Johnson Jia, Anselm Levskaya, Zhenkai Zhu, Chris Gorgolewski, Peter Grabowski, Yu Mao, Alberto Magni, Kaisheng Yao, Javier Snaider, Norman Casagrande, Paul Suganthan, Evan Palmer, Geoffrey Irving, Edward Loper, Manaal Faruqui, Isha Arkatkar, Nanxin Chen, Izhak Shafran, Michael Fink, Alfonso Castaño, Irene Giannoumis, Wooyeol Kim, Mikołaj Rybiński, Ashwin Sreevatsa, Jennifer Prendki, David Soergel, Adrian Goedeckemeyer, Willi Gierke, Mohsen Jafari, Meenu Gaba, Jeremy Wiesner, Diana Gage Wright, Yawen Wei, Harsha Vashisht, Yana Kulizhskaya, Jay Hoover, Maigo Le, Lu Li, Chimezie Iwuanyanwu, Lu Liu, Kevin Ramirez, Andrey Khorlin, Albert Cui, Tian LIN, Marin Georgiev, Marcus Wu, Ricardo Aguilar, Keith Pallo, Abhishek Chakladar, Alena Repina, Xihui Wu, Tom van der Weide, Priya Ponnapalli, Caroline Kaplan, Jiri Simsa, Shuangfeng Li, Olivier Dousse, Fan Yang, Jeff Piper, Nathan Ie, Minnie Lui, Rama Pasumarthi, Nathan Lintz, Anitha Vijayakumar, Lam Nguyen Thiet, Daniel Andor, Pedro Valenzuela, Cosmin Paduraru, Daiyi Peng, Katherine Lee, Shuyuan Zhang, Somer Greene, Duc Dung Nguyen, Paula Kurylowicz, Sarmishta Velury, Sebastian Krause, Cassidy Hardin, Lucas Dixon, Lili Janzer, Kiam Choo, Ziqiang Feng, Biao Zhang,

Achintya Singhal, Tejasi Latkar, Mingyang Zhang, Quoc Le, Elena Allica Abellan, Dayou Du, Dan McKinnon, Natasha Antropova, Tolga Bolukbasi, Orgad Keller, David Reid, Daniel Finchelstein, Maria Abi Raad, Remi Crocker, Peter Hawkins, Robert Dadashi, Colin Gaffney, Sid Lall, Ken Franko, Egor Filonov, Anna Bulanova, Rémi Leblond, Vikas Yadav, Shirley Chung, Harry Askham, Luis C. Cobo, Kelvin Xu, Felix Fischer, Jun Xu, Christina Sorokin, Chris Alberti, Chu-Cheng Lin, Colin Evans, Hao Zhou, Alek Dimitriev, Hannah Forbes, Dylan Banarse, Zora Tung, Jeremiah Liu, Mark Omernick, Colton Bishop, Chintu Kumar, Rachel Sterneck, Ryan Foley, Rohan Jain, Swaroop Mishra, Jiawei Xia, Taylor Bos, Geoffrey Cideron, Ehsan Amid, Francesco Piccinno, Xingyu Wang, Praseem Banzal, Petru Gurita, Hila Noga, Premal Shah, Daniel J. Mankowitz, Alex Polozov, Nate Kushman, Victoria Krakovna, Sasha Brown, MohammadHossein Bateni, Dennis Duan, Vlad Firoiu, Meghana Thotakuri, Tom Natan, Anhad Mohananey, Matthieu Geist, Sidharth Mudgal, Sertan Girgin, Hui Li, Jiayu Ye, Ofir Roval, Reiko Tojo, Michael Kwong, James Lee-Thorp, Christopher Yew, Quan Yuan, Sumit Bagri, Danila Sinopalnikov, Sabela Ramos, John Mellor, Abhishek Sharma, Aliaksei Severyn, Jonathan Lai, Kathy Wu, Heng-Tze Cheng, David Miller, Nicolas Sonnerat, Denis Vnukov, Rory Greig, Jennifer Beattie, Emily Caveness, Libin Bai, Julian Eisenschlos, Alex Korchemniy, Tomy Tsai, Mimi Jasarevic, Weize Kong, Phuong Dao, Zeyu Zheng, Frederick Liu, Fan Yang, Rui Zhu, Mark Geller, Tian Huey Teh, Jason Sanmiya, Evgeny Gladchenko, Nejc Trdin, Andrei Sozanschi, Daniel Toyama, Evan Rosen, Sasan Tavakkol, Linting Xue, Chen Elkind, Oliver Woodman, John Carpenter, George Papamakarios, Rupert Kemp, Sushant Kafle, Tanya Grunina, Rishika Sinha, Alice Talbert, Abhimanyu Goyal, Diane Wu, Denese Owusu-Afriyie, Cosmo Du, Chloe Thornton, Jordi Pont-Tuset, Pradyumna Narayana, Jing Li, Sabaer Fatehi, John Wieting, Omar Ajmeri, Benigno Uria, Tao Zhu, Yeongil Ko, Laura Knight, Amélie Héliou, Ning Niu, Shane Gu, Chenxi Pang, Dustin Tran, Yeqing Li, Nir Levine, Ariel Stolovich, Norbert Kalb, Rebeca Santamaria-Fernandez, Sonam Goenka, Wenny Yustalim, Robin Strudel, Ali Elqursh, Balaji Lakshminarayanan, Charlie Deck, Shyam Upadhyay, Hyo Lee, Mike Dusenberry, Zonglin Li, Xuezhi Wang, Kyle Levin, Raphael Hoffmann, Dan Holtmann-Rice, Olivier Bachem, Summer Yue, Sho Arora, Eric Malmi, Daniil Mirylenka, Qijun Tan, Christy Koh, Soheil Hassas Yeganeh, Siim Põder, Steven Zheng, Francesco Pongetti, Mukarram Tariq, Yanhua Sun, Lucian Ionita, Mojtaba Seyedhosseini, Pouya Tafti, Ragha Kotikalapudi, Zhiyu Liu, Anmol Gulati, Jasmine Liu, Xinyu Ye, Bart Chrzaszcz, Lily Wang, Nikhil Sethi, Tianrun Li, Ben Brown, Shreya Singh, Wei Fan, Aaron Parisi, Joe Stanton, Chenkai Kuang, Vinod Koverkathu, Christopher A. Choquette-Choo, Yunjie Li, TJ Lu, Abe Ittycheriah, Prakash Shroff, Pei Sun, Mani Varadarajan, Sanaz Bahargam, Rob Willoughby, David Gaddy, Ishita Dasgupta, Guillaume Desjardins, Marco Cornero, Brona Robenek, Bhavishya Mittal, Ben Albrecht, Ashish Shenoy, Fedor Moiseev, Henrik Jacobsson, Alireza Ghaffarkhah, Morgane Rivière, Alanna Walton, Clément Crepy, Alicia Parrish, Yuan Liu, Zongwei Zhou, Clement Farabet, Carey Radebaugh, Praveen Srinivasan, Claudia van der Salm, Andreas Fidjeland, Salvatore Scellato, Eri Latorre-Chimoto, Hanna Klimczak-Plucińska, David Bridson, Dario de Cesare, Tom Hudson, Piermaria Mendolicchio, Lexi Walker, Alex Morris, Ivo Penchev, Matthew Mauger, Alexey Guseynov, Alison Reid, Seth Odoom, Lucia Loher, Victor Cotruta, Madhavi Yenugula, Dominik Grewe, Anastasia Petrushkina, Tom Duerig, Antonio Sanchez, Steve Yadlowsky, Amy Shen, Amir Globerson, Adam Kurzrok, Lynette Webb, Sahil Dua, Dong Li, Preethi Lahoti, Surya Bhupatiraju, Dan Hurt, Haroon Qureshi, Ananth Agarwal, Tomer Shani, Matan Eyal, Anuj Khare, Shreyas Rammohan Belle, Lei Wang, Chetan Tekur, Mihir Sanjay Kale, Jinliang Wei, Ruoxin Sang, Brennan Saeta, Tyler Liechty, Yi Sun, Yao Zhao, Stephan Lee, Pandu Nayak, Doug Fritz, Manish Reddy Vuyyuru, John Aslanides, Nidhi Vyas, Martin Wicke, Xiao Ma, Taylan Bilal, Evgenii Eltyshev, Daniel Balle, Nina Martin, Hardie Cate, James Manyika, Keyvan Amiri, Yelin Kim, Xi Xiong, Kai Kang, Florian Luisier, Nilesh Tripuraneni, David Madras, Mandy Guo, Austin Waters, Oliver Wang, Joshua Ainslie, Jason Baldridge, Han Zhang, Garima Pruthi, Jakob Bauer, Feng Yang, Riham Mansour, Jason Gelman, Yang Xu, George Polovets, Ji Liu, Honglong Cai, Warren Chen, XiangHai Sheng, Emily Xue, Sherjil Ozair, Adams Yu, Christof Angermueller, Xiaowei Li, Weiren Wang, Julia Wiesinger, Emmanouil Koukoumidis, Yuan Tian, Anand Iyer, Madhu Gurumurthy, Mark Goldenson, Parashar Shah, MK Blake, Hongkun Yu, Anthony Urbanowicz, Jennimaria Palomaki, Chrisantha Fernando, Kevin Brooks, Ken Durden, Harsh Mehta, Nikola Momchev, Elahe Rahimtoroghi, Maria Georgaki, Amit Raul, Sebastian Ruder, Morgan Redshaw, Jinhyuk Lee, Komal Jalan, Dinghua Li, Ginger Perng, Blake Hechtman, Parker Schuh, Milad Nasr, Mia Chen, Kieran Milan, Vladimir Mikulik, Trevor Strohman, Juliana Franco, Tim Green, Demis Hassabis, Koray Kavukcuoglu, Jeffrey Dean, and Oriol Vinyals. 2023. Gemini: A family of highly capable multimodal models. *Preprint*, arXiv:2312.11805.

Hugo Touvron, Thibaut Lavril, Gautier Izacard, Xavier Martinet, Marie-Anne Lachaux, Timothée Lacroix, Baptiste Rozière, Naman Goyal, Eric Hambro, Faisal Azhar, Aurelien Rodriguez, Armand Joulin, Edouard Grave, and Guillaume Lample. 2023. Llama: Open and efficient foundation language models. *Preprint*, arXiv:2302.13971.

Alex Wang, Amanpreet Singh, Julian Michael, Felix Hill, Omer Levy, and Samuel Bowman. 2018. GLUE: A multi-task benchmark and analysis platform for natural language understanding. In *Proceedings of the 2018 EMNLP Workshop BlackboxNLP: Analyzing and Interpreting Neural Networks for NLP*, pages 353–355, Brussels, Belgium. Association for Computational Linguistics.

Longyue Wang, Zefeng Du, Donghuai Liu, Deng Cai,

Dian Yu, Haiyun Jiang, Yan Wang, Leyang Cui, Shuming Shi, and Zhaopeng Tu. 2023. Disco-bench: A discourse-aware evaluation benchmark for language modelling. *Preprint*, arXiv:2307.08074.

Alex Warstadt, Amanpreet Singh, and Samuel R Bowman. 2019. Neural network acceptability judgments. *Transactions of the Association for Computational Linguistics*, 7:625–641.

Jason Wei, Maarten Bosma, Vincent Zhao, Kelvin Guu, Adams Wei Yu, Brian Lester, Nan Du, Andrew M. Dai, and Quoc V Le. 2022a. Finetuned language models are zero-shot learners. In *International Conference on Learning Representations*.

Jason Wei, Yi Tay, Rishi Bommasani, Colin Raffel, Barret Zoph, Sebastian Borgeaud, Dani Yogatama, Maarten Bosma, Denny Zhou, Donald Metzler, Ed H. Chi, Tatsunori Hashimoto, Oriol Vinyals, Percy Liang, Jeff Dean, and William Fedus. 2022b. Emergent abilities of large language models. *Transactions on Machine Learning Research*. Survey Certification.

Adina Williams, Nikita Nangia, and Samuel Bowman. 2018. A broad-coverage challenge corpus for sentence understanding through inference. In *Proceedings of the 2018 Conference of the North American Chapter of the Association for Computational Linguistics: Human Language Technologies, Volume 1 (Long Papers)*, pages 1112–1122, New Orleans, Louisiana. Association for Computational Linguistics.

Thomas Wolf, Lysandre Debut, Victor Sanh, Julien Chaumond, Clement Delangue, Anthony Moi, Pierric Cistac, Tim Rault, Rémi Louf, Morgan Funtowicz, et al. 2019. Huggingface's transformers: State-of-the-art natural language processing. *arXiv preprint arXiv:1910.03771*.

Chuhan Wu, Fangzhao Wu, Tao Qi, and Yongfeng Huang. 2021. Hi-transformer: Hierarchical interactive transformer for efficient and effective long document modeling. In *Proceedings of the 59th Annual Meeting of the Association for Computational Linguistics and the 11th International Joint Conference on Natural Language Processing (Volume 2: Short Papers)*, pages 848–853, Online. Association for Computational Linguistics.

Felix Wu, Kwangyoun Kim, Shinji Watanabe, Kyu J Han, Ryan McDonald, Kilian Q Weinberger, and Yoav Artzi. 2023. Wav2seq: Pre-training speech-to-text encoder-decoder models using pseudo languages. In *ICASSP 2023-2023 IEEE International Conference on Acoustics, Speech and Signal Processing (ICASSP)*, pages 1–5. IEEE.

Linting Xue, Noah Constant, Adam Roberts, Mihir Kale, Rami Al-Rfou, Aditya Siddhant, Aditya Barua, and Colin Raffel. 2021. mT5: A massively multilingual pre-trained text-to-text transformer. In *Proceedings of the 2021 Conference of the North American Chapter of the Association for Computational Linguistics: Human Language Technologies*, pages 483–498, Online. Association for Computational Linguistics.

Ziyi Yang, Yinfei Yang, Daniel Cer, Jax Law, and Eric Darve. 2021. Universal sentence representation learning with conditional masked language model. In *Proceedings of the 2021 Conference on Empirical Methods in Natural Language Processing*, pages 6216–6228, Online and Punta Cana, Dominican Republic. Association for Computational Linguistics.

Shaoyun Yu, Chanyuan Gu, Kexin Huang, and Ping Li. 2024. Predicting the next sentence (not word) in large language models: What model-brain alignment tells us about discourse comprehension. *Science Advances*, 10(21):eadn7744.

Xiaohua Zhai, Alexander Kolesnikov, Neil Houlsby, and Lucas Beyer. 2022. Scaling vision transformers. In *CVPR*.

Jingqing Zhang, Yao Zhao, Mohammad Saleh, and Peter Liu. 2020. Pegasus: Pre-training with extracted gap-sentences for abstractive summarization. In *International Conference on Machine Learning*, pages 11328–11339. PMLR.

Chao Zhao, Tenghao Huang, Somnath Basu Roy Chowdhury, Muthu Kumar Chandrasekaran, Kathleen McKeown, and Snigdha Chaturvedi. 2022. Read top news first: A document reordering approach for multi-document news summarization. *ArXiv*, abs/2203.10254.

Lianmin Zheng, Wei-Lin Chiang, Ying Sheng, Tianle Li, Siyuan Zhuang, Zhanghao Wu, Yonghao Zhuang, Zhuohan Li, Zi Lin, Eric Xing, et al. 2023. Lmsys-chat-1m: A large-scale real-world llm conversation dataset. *arXiv preprint arXiv:2309.11998*.

Ahmet Üstün, Viraat Aryabumi, Zheng-Xin Yong, Wei-Yin Ko, Daniel D'souza, Gbemileke Onilude, Neel Bhandari, Shivalika Singh, Hui-Lee Ooi, Amr Kayid, Freddie Vargus, Phil Blunsom, Shayne Longpre, Niklas Muennighoff, Marzieh Fadaee, Julia Kreutzer, and Sara Hooker. 2024. Aya model: An instruction finetuned open-access multilingual language model. *Preprint*, arXiv:2402.07827.

A Challenges in replicating T5

A.1 Our speculations

We recognize that both DEPTH and T5 CPT models quickly reach a significantly lower reconstruction loss than their FS counterparts. While the original T5's reached a final training loss of ≈ 0.75 (with 512k steps of batch size 128 with packing) (Raffel et al., 2020), our training loss reached ≈ 0.8 (after 800k steps of batch size 200 without packing). We propose the following ideas to explain this gap:

1. The baseline model from which CPT models are initialized is trained on 1T tokens. This is $\approx 20\times$ greater than the amount of tokens we used to train FS models.

2. Our examples never consist of the later text in long documents. By truncating text after 512 tokens, our FS models might miss out on valuable text to train on.

3. Our training examples consists of $\approx 2\times$ fewer tokens (on average) than examples the original T5 was trained on. Furthermore, there is much greater variance in example lengths in our pre-training experiments. These factors may impact our models' learning dynamics (e.g., learning effective positional representations given the presence of irregular padding patterns).

4. The T5 baseline plot was reported using a masking probability of 0.15, which is $2\times$ lower than the one we used. Our higher masking probability makes the reconstruction task more challenging.

5. T5 models using the T5x framework use aggressively high learning rates, which can lead to a different, and perhaps more effective training dynamics than the ones we found in our FS experiments. Using such high learning rates in our settings caused our models to diverge.

A.2 Example packing

Given our choice of avoiding example-packing, we found that we were not able to pre-train T5 with the same hyper-parameters used in (Raffel et al., 2020). Specifically, we found that with a batch size of 128 and a learning rate of $1e^{-2}$, our model consistently diverged. This issue persisted with a learning rate of $1e^{-3}$. To stabilize our loss given the absence of packing, we used a lower maximum learning rate ($1e^{-4}$), which is in line with those used to pre-train BERT, SLM, and PMI. On the other hand, we see that given the same training parameters (i.e., learning rate and batch size), pre-training with packing can converge at a high learning rate (see Figure 7).

We speculate that packing acts in a similar way to increasing the batch size during training. The model is exposed to loss on a greater amount of tokens in each optimization step, and is therefore able to generalize even with a larger learning rate.

One possible side effect of avoiding example-packing is the truncation of long examples (examples are not dynamically chunked, so every token past the context limit of 512 is ignored). We empirically find that while T5 suffers greatly from no packing, DEPTH is able to train effectively despite these limitations.

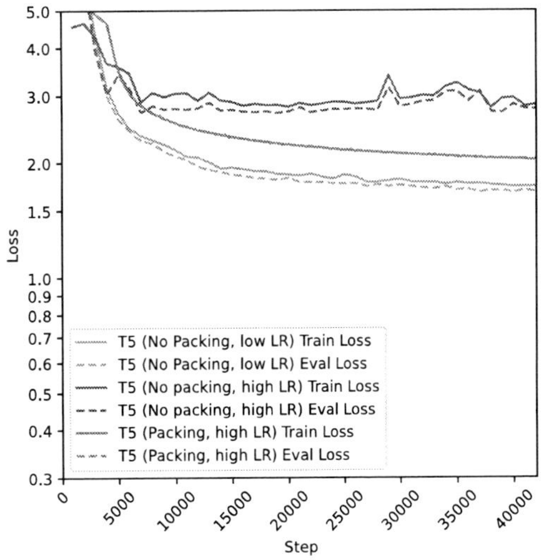

Figure 7: Exploration of packing and learning rates when pre-training T5 models. "High LR" corresponds to a learning rate of $1e^{-2}$, while "Low LR" corresponds to a learning rate of $1e^{-4}$.

B DEPTH loss decomposition

When we decompose DEPTH's losses in the FS setting, we find that sentence loss is consistently lower than reconstruction loss, but plateus early on into training. The overall loss is dominated by the reconstruction loss, reflected by overlapping lines in Figure 8. In the CPT setting (Figure 9), we find that both of DEPTH's losses plateu sooner, and that the sentence loss is approximately equal (though with higher fluctuations) to the reconstruction loss.

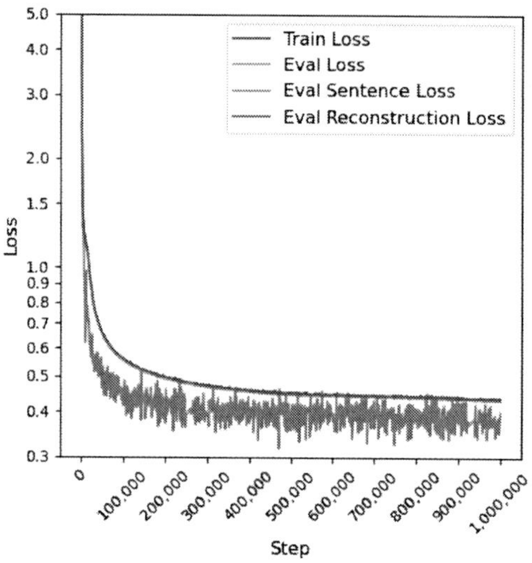

Figure 8: Decomposition of from-scratch pre losses (validation) for DEPTH.

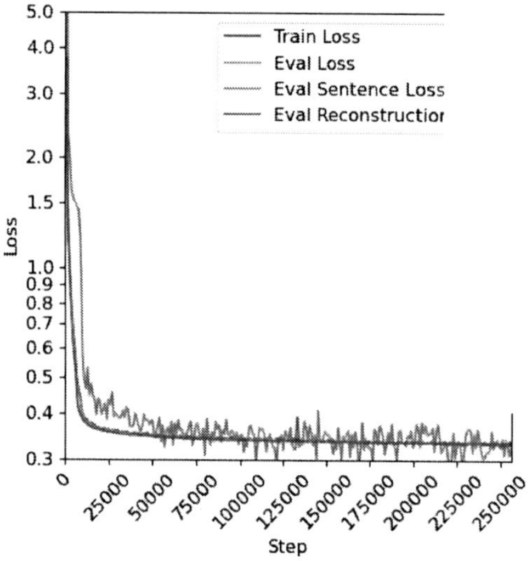

Figure 9: Decomposition of continuous pre-training losses (validation) for DEPTH

We note that DEPTH's loss over sentence tokens in the FC setting, is close to that which the DEPTH-CPT achieved (both in the range of 0.3-0.4, where the more examples are shuffled, the higher the sentence loss). In practice, given comperable ratios of shuffling sentences, CPT DEPTH outperforms FS DEPTH in predicting the next sentence accurately during pre-training ($\approx 1\% - 3\%$ higher given a fixed shuffling ratio). We speculate that the better representations for non-sentence tokens in the CPT setting is the reason for this performance boost.

B.1 Weight of sentence loss

We explored the impact of increasing the weight of the sentence loss during DEPTH pre-training. Our "Baseline" run is the DEPTH model we reported on in the main body of the paper. In our "Sentence Weight 1x" run, our loss is composed of the average loss over sentence tokens plus the average loss over non-sentence tokens (as opposed to the average loss over all tokens). This formulation places increased weight on sentence tokens, since there are significantly fewer sentence tokens than non-sentence tokens. In the "Sentence Weight 5x" run, we weighed the sentence loss $5\times$ more than reconstruction loss.

We found that increasing the weight of this loss had minimal impact on the model's accuracy in predicting sentence tokens, and adversely harmed the model's loss (see Figure 10).

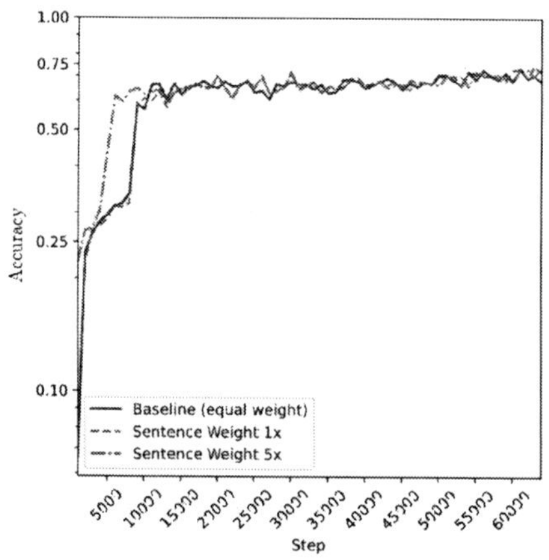

Figure 10: We explore the impact of weighing sentence loss more than reconstruction loss, and find that it has minimal impact beyond early stages of pre-training.

C Computational resources

We utilize 4 A40 GPUs, and 64 CPUs for training. We use a batch size of 200, since it helps us achieve much better GPU memory utilization. We leverage 16 CPUs for each GPU in order to increase the data loading time to accommodate for DEPTH's more-complex corruption method, and to allow effective optimizer offloading with DeepSpeed Zero2 (Rajbhandari et al., 2020).

D Pre-training considerations

D.1 Pre-training scale

In Table 2 below we show the relative magnitude of DEPTH's pre-training. Specifically, we compare the number of observed tokens and optimization steps of our T5 and DEPTH models to comparably sized models (such as SLM, BERT, and RoBERTa). We highlight that the models we independently pre-trained (bottom 4 rows of the table) observed far fewer tokens than comparable LMs.

D.2 Pre-training data

The rationale behind selecting C4 extends beyond its sheer volume and diversity. Given DEPTH's architectural roots in the T5 model, which was originally pre-trained on C4, leveraging the same dataset facilitates a direct comparison of the enhancements our model introduces. This baseline compatibility is crucial for isolating the effects of our architectural and methodological innovations on the model's performance. Furthermore, C4 is a subset of both Dolma (Soldaini et al., 2024) and RedPajama (Computer, 2023). These datasets were used to train the most capable fully-open-source LMs (with released data) to date: OLMO (Groeneveld et al., 2024) and LLama (Touvron et al., 2023) respectively. This suggests that C4 is an effective component in pre-training effective LMs, and offers multiple additional datasets components that would be new to our model for future training. Finally, Muennighoff et al. (2023) suggest that pre-training over the same data up to $4\times$ still improves model performance, while (Raffel et al., 2020)'s model has not completed even one full iteration over the C4 dataset. This hints at the viability of continuing to pre-train T5 on the same dataset it was already pre-trained on.

E Error Analysis

We select randomly select 30 examples from each task in DiscoEval, and manually inspect the nature of our models' errors. For example, in the SP task, we were interested in observing if a model tended to misunderstand clues from pronouns or transitions. For both DC and SP, we were also counted the number of examples where a human might find the LLM's answer reasonable (given the human-perceived coherence of the example).

E.1 Sentence Position

Consistent with the macro-level results from our DiscoEval fine-tuning experiments, DEPTH generally performs better in FS than T5. However, in the CPT setting, while DEPTH shows better reasoning in some cases, T5-CPT outperforms it, particularly on simpler tasks like SP-Wiki and SP-Rocstory, likely benefiting from more consistent pretraining. DEPTH's greater number of reasonable mistakes indicates its strength in engaging with complex discourse structures, but pronoun resolution and transition errors remain areas for further improvement.

Given the 30 examples we've sampled, we categorize the types of errors our models tend to make. An error type is a reason by which a person might be able to infer the correct label. If the model predicts incorrectly given an "obvious" hint (e.g. introducing an entity that is referenced via a pronoun), then we categorize the error type based on that hint. In Table 3 we show the counts of error types that each model made on each subset of SP.

E.2 Discourse Coherence

We found that in the Discourse Coherence (DC) subset, both models were strictly incorrect by predicting poorly formatted outputs. Each of the poorly formatted predictions was incorrect (e.g., if the model predicted "cooherent" instead of "coherent", the correct label was "incoherent"). We analyze the ratio of these types of predictions on DC in Table 4. Further, we find that in DC-Chat, both models tend to make errors that a human might find reasonable. This implies that the augmentation on the input example (i.e., replacing one if the sentences in the paragraph with another one) did not adversely impact the example's coherence. Strangely, we found that FS models predicted more correct outputs than their CPT counterparts. This may be the result of selecting a too small a sample-size of examples to analyze.

F GLUE results

In this section we show the full results from our downstream experiments on GLUE tasks. Table 5 is reflected in the top row (FS) of Figure 4, while Table 6 is reflected in the bottom row (CPT) of figure 4. Consistent with our hypothesis, we found that both DEPTH and T5 improve across downstream tasks as a function of the pre-training steps they've

Model	Tokens	Steps	Batch Size	# Params	Learning Rate
SLM-1M	$125B$	$1M$	256	$\approx 110M$	$1.5e^{-4}$
SLM-3M	$375B$	$3M$	256	$\approx 110M$	$1.5e^{-4}$
BERT-Base	$137B$	$1M$	256	$\approx 110M$	$1e^{-4}$
BERT-Large	$137B$	$1M$	256	$\approx 340M$	$1e^{-4}$
RoBERTa-Base	$2.2T$	$500k$	8000	$\approx 110M$	$1e^{-4}$
CONPONO (*)	-	$256k$	256	$\approx 110M$	$1e^{-4}$
T5-Base	$1T$	$1M$	2048	$\approx 220M$	$1e^{-2}$
T5-FS	$58.6B$	$1M$	200	$\approx 220M$	$1e^{-4}$
T5-CPT (*)	$15B$	$256k$	200	$\approx 220M$	$1e^{-4}$
DEPTH-FS	$48.9B$	$1M$	200	$\approx 220M$	$1e^{-4}$
DEPTH-CPT (*)	$12.5B$	$256k$	200	$\approx 220M$	$1e^{-4}$

Table 2: Hyper-parameters of comparable models to DEPTH. We show published hyper-parameters in the top rows of the table, and the models we train ourselves in the bottom of the table. We mark all models initialized from publically released pre-training models with (*). Note that CONPONO did not report the number of tokens it pre-trained on, so we exclude that value from the table above.

Dataset	Model	0	1	2	3	4
SP-Wiki CPT	T5	0.57	0.07	0.23	0.13	0.07
	DEPTH	0.57	0.03	0.23	0.2	0.03
SP-Wiki FS	T5	0.57	0.07	0.23	0.13	0.07
	DEPTH	0.57	0.03	0.23	0.2	0.03
SP-Arxiv CPT	T5	0.63	0.07	0.2	0.1	0
	DEPTH	0.57	0.13	0.2	0.1	0
SP-Arxiv FS	T5	0.37	0.23	0.3	0.07	0.03
	DEPTH	0.43	0.1	0.3	0.23	0
SP-Rocstory CPT	T5	0.77	0.07	0.1	0.07	0
	DEPTH	0.57	0.13	0.2	0.1	0
SP-Rocstory FS	T5	0.47	0.2	0.27	0.07	0
	DEPTH	0.6	0.2	0.13	0.07	0

Table 3: Approximate ratio of prediction types for SP-Wiki, SP-Arxiv, and SP-Rocstory across T5 and DEPTH models in FS and CPT settings. There are 30 total examples. Each prediction over these examples is categorized into one of 5 prediction types: 0 - Correct prediction, 1 - Incorrect (hint from transitions), 2 - Incorrect (hint from pronoun), 3 - Incorrect (reasonable error), 4 - Incorrect (hint from punctuation).

taken. While DEPTH outperforms T5 across all tasks is the FS setting, it did not reach the scores of Raffel et al. (2020)'s T5 model. In the CPT setting, T5 and DEPTH perform quite comparably. In fact, in the penultimate checkpoint (128k) we found that DEPTH outperformed T5 on all tasks except for CoLA.

G DiscoEval results

In this section we show the full results from our downstream experiments on discourse tasks from the DiscoEval benchmark. In Table 7, we show the full results of our models in the FS setting, while in Table 8 we show the full results of our models in the CPT setting. These tables reflect the top and bottom row of Figure 5 respectively.

Dataset	Model	0	1	2
DC-Wiki-FS	T5	0.87	0.32	0.00
	DEPTH	0.87	0.13	0.00
DC-Wiki-CPT	T5	0.80	0.08	0.00
	DEPTH	0.83	0.08	0.00
DC-Chat-FS	T5	0.60	0.42	0.17
	DEPTH	0.63	0.35	0.23
DC-Chat-CPT	T5	0.83	0.30	0.10
	DEPTH	0.77	0.29	0.07

Table 4: Prediction types for models and dataset splits. 0: Correct predictions (Type 0), 1: Poorly formatted predictions (Type 1), 2: Reasonable errors (Type 2).

In the FS setting, we found that DEPTH's wins over T5 are even more pronounced in DiscoEval than they were in GLUE. Specifically, T5 struggles to learn discourse tasks (especially SP) during early stages of pre-training. On the other hand, DEPTH was highly effective in discourse tasks already from early pre-training checkpoints. In the CPT setting, we found that DEPTH still outperformed T5, despite the fact that the original checkpoint was pre-trained substantially with a different objective.

Model	CoLA	SST-2	MNLI	
			Matched	*Mismatched*
T5-Base @ 0 (Test)	12.3	80.62	68.02	68.0
T5-Base @ 1M (Test)	53.84	92.68	84.24	84.57
T5-Base @ 1M (Val)	53.98	94.73	87.28	87.1
T5 @ 2k	8.62	80.08	52.54	52.3
DEPTH @ 2k	8.67	78.52	57.07	58.14
T5 @ 4k	6.23	80.66	53.16	53.89
DEPTH @ 4k	7.75	80.08	59.31	59.62
T5 @ 8k	4.66	82.23	54.33	54.62
DEPTH @ 8k	6.93	79.69	58.92	59.73
T5 @ 16k	8.99	80.96	54.1	54.1
DEPTH @ 16k	10.94	81.25	62.79	61.46
T5 @ 32k	10.72	81.64	55.18	55.6
DEPTH @ 32k	7.73	82.81	71.23	72.7
T5 @ 64k	6.86	82.42	57.68	60.88
DEPTH @ 64k	27.78	86.72	73.84	76.05
T5 @ 128k	12.85	83.2	69.61	69.82
DEPTH @ 128k	38.01	88.87	77.5	78.06
T5 @ 256k	11.78	85.94	72.82	73.39
DEPTH @ 256k	45.57	91.31	79.45	80.07
T5 @ 512k	19.96	86.52	74.22	74.26
DEPTH @ 512k	47.14	91.11	80.42	81.43
T5 @ 1M	29.35	88.77	74.53	75.37
DEPTH @ 1M	45.91	91.41	81.0	81.96

Table 5: GLUE benchmark results for From Scratch (FS). Note that the first two rows are reported by Raffel et al., 2019, while all later rows are the best reported results on the validation set across 3 attempted learning rates.

H NI results

In the from-scratch setting (Figure 6a and Table 9), we observe that DEPTH outperforms T5 in the NI benchmark, with a notable leap in performance between steps 16k and 32k. This indicates that DEPTH's pre-training objective is more effective at learning representations that are beneficial for the NI task. However, at steps 2k, 8k, and 16k, DEPTH underperforms compared to T5, suggesting that the benefits of DEPTH's pre-training objective may not be immediately apparent in the early stages of training.

However, in the continuously pre-trained setting (Figure 6b and Table 10), we find that DEPTH's pre-training harms downstream performance compared to T5. Additionally, we observe that CPT models are less sensitive to learning rate and can train effectively across a wider range of learning rates, with the exception of DEPTH in the early stages of CPT, where it is adapting to a task that differs from its initial pre-training. This robustness to learning rate is a positive property that the FS models did not exhibit, likely due to limitations in training scale (e.g., small batch size, avoiding packing, and training on fewer tokens overall). Furthermore, early in the CPT process, DEPTH's performance is somewhat unstable, possibly due to the domain shift from T5's pre-training task to DEPTH's pre-training task. Interestingly, lower learning rates perform worse for DEPTH after CPT, suggesting that the model needs to adjust its representations more substantially to adapt to the downstream task.

Model	CoLA	SST-2	MNLI	
			Matched	*Mismatched*
T5-Base @ 1M (Test)	53.84	92.68	84.24	84.57
T5-Base @ 1M (Val)	53.98	94.73	87.28	87.1
T5 @ 2k	57.41	95.02	86.93	87.06
DEPTH @ 2k	53.93	94.34	86.38	86.2
T5 @ 4k	55.18	95.02	87.4	87.34
DEPTH @ 4k	47.11	94.34	87.14	87.01
T5 @ 8k	55.35	95.21	87.47	87.31
DEPTH @ 8k	50.67	94.43	86.62	86.52
T5 @ 16k	54.75	95.7	86.91	86.67
DEPTH @ 16k	52.65	94.34	86.62	86.67
T5 @ 32k	54.95	95.21	86.64	86.06
DEPTH @ 32k	53.79	94.63	86.95	87.02
T5 @ 64k	54.77	95.21	86.96	86.93
DEPTH @ 64k	52.95	94.14	86.65	86.91
T5 @ 128k	58.62	95.21	86.79	86.67
DEPTH @ 128k	56.21	95.61	87.42	87.64
T5 @ 256k	57.62	95.21	87.27	87.22
DEPTH @ 256k	56.78	95.02	86.86	86.45

Table 6: GLUE benchmark results for Continuous Pre-Training (CPT). As in the FS setting, we report our results on the validation set after a hyper-parameter sweep over 3 learning rates.

Model		SP		DC	
	Arxiv	*Wiki*	*Rocstory*	*Chat*	*Wiki*
Baseline T5 @ 1M	52.76	51.07	70.58	68.99	92.09
T5 @ 2k	21.0	20.9	21.2	55.18	53.59
DEPTH @ 2k	34.81	40.19	51.51	55.27	53.2
T5 @ 4k	20.4	21.4	20.9	57.18	55.37
DEPTH @ 4k	35.72	40.38	52.03	56.49	54.74
T5 @ 8k	20.6	20.9	21.0	57.42	54.57
DEPTH @ 8k	36.43	40.14	51.25	57.03	54.69
T5 @ 16k	21.4	22.0	21.24	57.62	55.18
DEPTH @ 16k	36.47	40.33	53.13	57.52	55.44
T5 @ 32k	21.75	21.75	20.63	57.62	56.1
DEPTH @ 32k	38.04	44.26	54.05	58.5	57.37
T5 @ 64k	21.92	21.53	21.24	57.23	57.01
DEPTH @ 64k	42.24	45.85	55.96	60.94	72.58
T5 @ 128k	21.09	33.96	42.63	60.16	60.01
DEPTH @ 128k	45.0	47.71	59.57	64.65	78.0
T5 @ 256k	22.85	37.92	44.85	58.89	61.91
DEPTH @ 256k	48.68	48.93	61.33	65.33	81.69
T5 @ 512k	26.61	41.97	52.29	61.33	60.89
DEPTH @ 512k	52.59	51.66	65.92	66.85	83.81
T5 @ 1M	28.54	43.22	50.98	61.13	65.48
DEPTH @ 1M	52.39	50.07	63.89	67.92	84.52

Table 7: DiscoEval Downstream Full Training (FS) Results

Model	SP			DC	
	Arxiv	Wiki	Rocstory	Wiki	Chat
T5 @ 2k	62.26	51.9	74.83	92.09	71.44
DEPTH @ 2k	44.14	49.34	74.78	89.99	70.46
T5 @ 4k	61.33	52.39	74.98	91.72	74.27
DEPTH @ 4k	56.62	51.2	67.65	91.46	72.02
T5 @ 8k	63.63	52.03	77.0	92.33	73.1
DEPTH @ 8k	55.03	51.56	71.02	91.99	71.97
T5 @ 16k	60.94	51.78	76.49	91.53	74.71
DEPTH @ 16k	58.86	52.08	76.15	92.63	72.71
T5 @ 32k	60.69	52.22	75.61	92.33	74.02
DEPTH @ 32k	59.35	53.27	78.08	92.48	72.85
T5 @ 64k	58.96	52.25	76.07	92.58	73.73
DEPTH @ 64k	58.57	52.95	76.1	92.58	73.24
T5 @ 128k	60.13	51.03	75.76	91.14	73.44
DEPTH @ 128k	70.56	54.77	82.42	92.53	73.96
T5 @ 256k	59.03	52.66	66.77	92.31	72.22
DEPTH @ 256k	67.07	53.0	76.71	92.07	72.9

Table 8: DiscoEval Downstream Continuous Pre-Training (CPT) Results

Model	Step	RougeL
Baseline T5	1M	42.48
T5	2k	8.36
DEPTH	2k	10.92
T5	4k	10.11
DEPTH	4k	11.03
T5	8k	10.15
DEPTH	8k	9.06
T5	16k	10.82
DEPTH	16k	10.43
T5	32k	10.68
DEPTH	32k	23.51
T5	64k	12.89
DEPTH	64k	30.23
T5	128k	18.24
DEPTH	128k	32.24
T5	256k	26.36
DEPTH	256k	32.63
T5	512k	28.05
DEPTH	512k	34.72
T5	1M	29.6
DEPTH	1M	33.8

Table 9: NI benchmark results for From Scratch (FS) pre-training. The first row reports the performance of the baseline T5 model, while all later rows show the best reported results on the validation set across 3 attempted learning rates.

Model	Step	NI RougeL
T5	2k	41.96
DEPTH	2k	39.15
T5	4k	42.72
DEPTH	4k	37.85
T5	8k	42.83
DEPTH	8k	38.04
T5	16k	42.88
DEPTH	16k	38.19
T5	32k	43.56
DEPTH	32k	37.79
T5	64k	43.06
DEPTH	64k	38.99
T5	128k	42.58
DEPTH	128k	39.19
T5	256k	43.29
DEPTH	256k	37.86

Table 10: NI benchmark results for Continuous Pre-Training (CPT). All rows show the best reported results on the validation set across 3 attempted learning rates.

Vocabulary-level Memory Efficiency for Language Model Fine-tuning

Miles Williams and **Nikolaos Aletras**
University of Sheffield
{mwilliams15, n.aletras}@sheffield.ac.uk

Abstract

The extensive memory footprint of language model (LM) fine-tuning poses a challenge for both researchers and practitioners. LMs use an embedding matrix to represent extensive vocabularies, forming a substantial proportion of the model parameters. While previous work towards memory-efficient fine-tuning has focused on minimizing the number of trainable parameters, reducing the memory footprint of the embedding matrix has yet to be explored. We first demonstrate that a significant proportion of the vocabulary remains unused during fine-tuning. We then propose a simple yet effective approach that leverages this finding to minimize memory usage. We show that our approach provides substantial reductions in memory usage across a wide range of models and tasks. Notably, our approach does not impact downstream task performance, while allowing more efficient use of computational resources.[1]

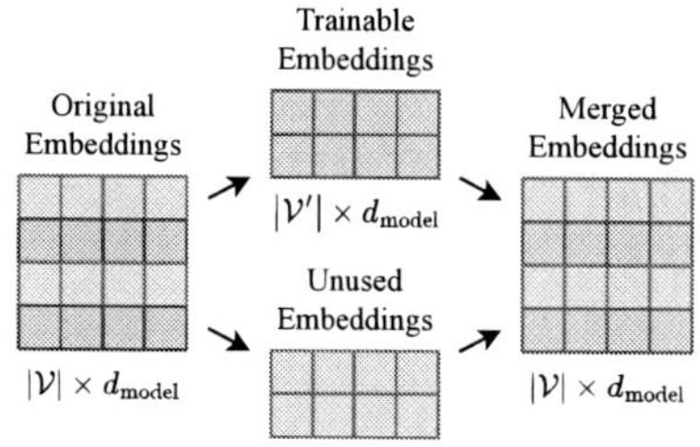

Figure 1: Memory-efficient language model fine-tuning with Partial Embedding Matrix Adaptation (PEMA).

1 Introduction

Language models (LMs) (Chung et al., 2022; Touvron et al., 2023; Warner et al., 2024) form the foundation of contemporary natural language processing (NLP), however they require extensive computational resources to train (Kaplan et al., 2020; Hoffmann et al., 2022). This is contrary to the democratization of NLP, exacerbating economic inequalities and hindering inclusivity (Schwartz et al., 2020; Weidinger et al., 2022). Consequently, there is a growing focus towards developing efficient methods for LM training and fine-tuning (Treviso et al., 2023; Lialin et al., 2023).

The memory footprint of LMs is a major challenge for their application. Storing model parameters requires extensive amounts of memory, constraining the size and architecture of the model (Paleyes et al., 2022). This problem is especially prominent during training as gradients and optimizer states must also be retained (Kingma and Ba, 2017). This can be problematic when using consumer hardware or facing an academic budget (Izsak et al., 2021; Ciosici and Derczynski, 2022).

LMs ordinarily use fixed vocabularies to derive vector representations from text, known as word embeddings. Each element of the vocabulary has a corresponding word embedding, which collectively form an embedding matrix within the LM. The size of the embedding matrix scales with both the vocabulary size and embedding dimension, comprising a substantial proportion of the model parameters (Table 5, Appendix A). This proportion is usually even greater for multilingual LMs, which benefit from larger vocabularies (Conneau et al., 2020; Liang et al., 2023). However, we hypothesize that a significant proportion of LM vocabulary remains unused during fine-tuning on many downstream tasks.

In this paper, we first demonstrate that our hypothesis holds for a variety of downstream tasks, with only a small subset of vocabulary used. We then propose a method to reduce memory usage during fine-tuning by excluding unused embeddings. Finally, we empirically demonstrate the memory savings from our approach across a range of models and tasks. Notably, our approach does not impact downstream task performance and is orthogonal to many existing LM memory efficiency techniques.

[1] https://github.com/mlsw/partial-embedding-matrix-adaptation

Proceedings of the 10th Workshop on Representation Learning for NLP (RepL4NLP-2025), pages 26–37
May 4, 2025

2 Related Work

Tokenization. Transformer LMs (Vaswani et al., 2017) typically adopt subword tokenization (Schuster and Nakajima, 2012; Sennrich et al., 2016) to encode text using a finite vocabulary. The use of large subword vocabularies enables improved task performance (Gallé, 2019), inference efficiency (Tay et al., 2022), and multilingual performance (Liang et al., 2023). Conversely, character or byte level tokenization can be used (Clark et al., 2022; Xue et al., 2022), reducing the size of the embedding matrix at the cost of increasing the sequence length.

Reducing embedding parameters. To reduce the size of the embedding matrix, LMs can be trained with embedding factorization (Sun et al., 2020; Lan et al., 2020), albeit with slightly lower task performance. Alternatively, embeddings can be generated from hash functions (Sankar et al., 2021; Xue and Aletras, 2022; Cohn et al., 2023), although this may harm performance due to the many-to-one mapping from tokens to embeddings.

Multilingual vocabulary trimming. The closest work to our own is Abdaoui et al. (2020), which creates smaller multilingual LMs by permanently reducing the number of supported languages. This can harm performance as the removed vocabulary may later be required for a downstream task. Moreover, selecting which vocabulary to remove requires the computationally expensive processing of a large corpus. Ushio et al. (2023) further examine the performance impact of permanently removing LM vocabulary either before or after fine-tuning. However, the same fundamental limitations persist.

Parameter-efficient fine-tuning. PEFT methods, such as adapters (Houlsby et al., 2019), soft prompts (Lester et al., 2021; Li and Liang, 2021), ladder side-tuning (Sung et al., 2022), and low-rank adaptation (Hu et al., 2022), effectively adapt LMs by fine-tuning only a small number of parameters. However, these methods still require all LM parameters to be held in accelerator memory.

Offloading. To minimize accelerator (e.g. GPU) memory usage, LM parameters can be held in separate (e.g. CPU) memory until needed (Pudipeddi et al., 2020; Ren et al., 2021). However, this approach substantially increases inference latency.

Model compression. In Appendix B, we discuss a variety of orthogonal LM compression methods, such as quantization, pruning, and distillation.

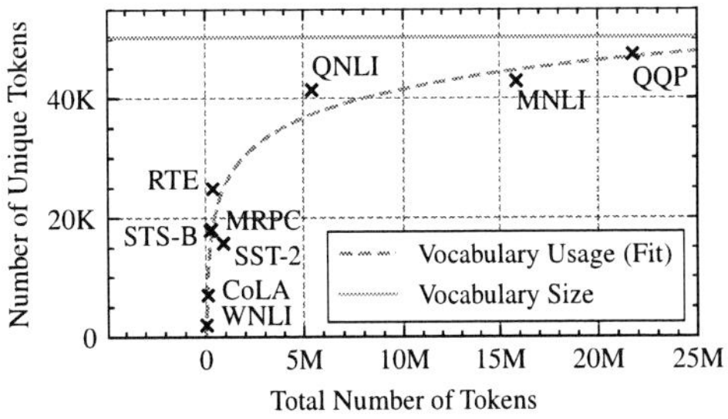

Figure 2: The trend in vocabulary use for the datasets in GLUE when using the vocabulary from GPT-2.

#	Token
49,990	natureconservancy
50,072	;;;;;;;;;;;;
50,160	PsyNetMessage
50,174	rawdownloadcloneembedreportprint
50,243	SolidGoldMagikarp

Table 1: Five examples of tokens from the GPT-2 vocabulary that do not occur within English Wikipedia.

3 Vocabulary Usage Analysis

To empirically assess the level of vocabulary usage during fine-tuning, we first examine the popular GLUE benchmark (Wang et al., 2019). This comprises a series of tasks that are varied in both size and domain (Appendix C). For tokenization, we use the subword vocabulary from GPT-2, which was later adopted by models including RoBERTa (Liu et al., 2019), BART (Lewis et al., 2020), GPT-3 (Brown et al., 2020), and OPT (Zhang et al., 2022).

Figure 2 illustrates the relationship between unique tokens and total tokens in each of the GLUE datasets. Notably, six out of nine datasets fail to use more than half of the vocabulary. Moreover, the smallest dataset, WNLI, uses less than 4%. Interestingly, we observe that the GLUE datasets follow a trend resembling Heaps' Law (Heaps, 1978). This states that as the size of a corpus grows, there are diminishing gains in new vocabulary. However, our use of a finite subword vocabulary means that the trend is asymptotic to the vocabulary size.

Separately, the statistical construction of subword vocabularies can reflect anomalies in their training data, creating tokens that may never be used. To examine the extent of the issue, we identify such tokens by evaluating a processed dump of English Wikipedia, comprising over 20GB of text. Peculiarly, we identify nearly 200 anomalous tokens without a single occurrence (see Table 1).[2]

[2]We refer readers interested in such anomalous tokens to Rumbelow and Watkins (2023) and Land and Bartolo (2024).

4 Partial Embedding Matrix Adaptation

Our empirical analysis (Section 3) suggests that many fine-tuning datasets only use a fraction of LM vocabulary. We leverage this insight to propose Partial Embedding Matrix Adaptation (PEMA), a method that achieves substantial memory savings by selecting only the minimum subset of word embeddings needed for fine-tuning. Notably, this does not impact task performance, as unused word embeddings are not updated during backpropagation.

Preliminaries. Let each token in the vocabulary $\{w_1, \ldots, w_k\}$ be denoted by a unique integer i such that $\mathcal{V} = \{i \in \mathbb{N} \mid i \leq k\}$. The embedding matrix $E \in \mathbb{R}^{|\mathcal{V}| \times d}$ is then used to project each token to a corresponding d-dimensional vector.

Before fine-tuning. Suppose we have fine-tuning dataset $D \in \mathcal{V}^{m \times n}$ where m is the number of examples and n is the length of each example. We compute the partial vocabulary $\mathcal{V}' \subset \mathcal{V}$ consisting of *only* the tokens in D. As the elements of $\mathcal{V}'$ are not necessarily consecutive integers, we define an arbitrary mapping $f\colon \mathcal{V}' \to \{i \in \mathbb{N} \mid i \leq |\mathcal{V}'|\}$. We then construct the partial embedding matrix $E' \in \mathbb{R}^{|\mathcal{V}'| \times d}$ with entries $E'[:, f(i)] = E[:, i]$ for all $i \in \mathcal{V}'$. That is, E' retains only embedding vectors corresponding to tokens in $\mathcal{V}'$. To adapt D for the partial vocabulary $\mathcal{V}'$, we create an intermediary dataset D' where each entry $D'[i, j] = f(D[i, j])$. Finally, we use D' and E' in place of D and E.

After fine-tuning. Following fine-tuning, our partial embedding matrix E' holds the newly learned embeddings for the partial vocabulary. However, we do not wish to keep only the partial vocabulary, as this would limit future use of the model (i.e. tasks with different vocabulary). Therefore, we merge the newly learned embeddings into the original embedding matrix (stored on-disk). More formally, we update E such that $E[:, f^{-1}(i)] = E'[:, i]$ for all $i \in \mathcal{V}'$. This ensures that the model remains structurally identical, with embeddings for the complete vocabulary.

5 Experimental Setup

Datasets. To offer a fair selection of datasets, we follow existing PEFT literature (Houlsby et al., 2019; Hu et al., 2022; Sung et al., 2022; Zhang et al., 2023) and focus our evaluation on the popular GLUE benchmark. We additionally employ XNLI (Conneau et al., 2018) to assess the performance of our approach with multilingual data. Complete data sources and implementation details are listed in Appendix C and Appendix D, respectively.

Models. Similarly, we select a variety of popular models used in existing work. However, we place an emphasis on having a variety of vocabularies (Table 5, Appendix A). For monolingual models, we use BERT (Devlin et al., 2019), RoBERTa (Liu et al., 2019), and DeBERTaV3 (He et al., 2023). For multilingual models, we use mBERT (Devlin et al., 2019), XLM-RoBERTa (Conneau et al., 2020), and XLM-V (Liang et al., 2023). To evaluate the performance of distilled models, we also use the available distilled counterparts: DistilBERT, DistilRoBERTa, and DistilmBERT (Sanh et al., 2020a). For a fair comparison between models, we consistently select the base size ($d_{\text{model}} = 768$).

Memory efficiency metrics. Following convention in the PEFT literature (Houlsby et al., 2019; Hu et al., 2022; Ben Zaken et al., 2022), we report memory efficiency in terms of model parameters. This is advantageous as it avoids confounding factors such as weight precision, optimizer choice, software implementation, and batch size.

6 Results

Larger vocabularies see more memory savings. Table 2 presents the reduction in parameters for each model across the GLUE benchmark. Following our expectations from Section 3, we generally observe that as vocabulary sizes increase (Table 5, Appendix A), so do the potential memory savings. For example, an average reduction in embedding parameters of 47.3% is achieved for BERT, 52.1% for RoBERTa, and 72.4% for DeBERTaV3.

Memory savings vary between datasets. In line with our expectations from Section 3, the memory savings vary substantially between datasets. For BERT, the embedding matrix can be reduced by 94.3% for the smallest dataset (WNLI), yet only 11.5% for the largest (QQP). We demonstrate that downstream task performance remains consistent across models and datasets in Appendix E.

Distilled models substantially benefit. Considering the distilled models, we observe that they all achieve an identical reduction in embedding parameters to their original counterparts. This is because they use the same vocabulary and embedding size (Sanh et al., 2020a). However, they offer substan-

Model	CoLA	MNLI	MRPC	QNLI	QQP	RTE	SST-2	STS-B	WNLI	Mean
				Reduction in Embedding Parameters (%)						
DistilBERT	80.1	14.8	54.9	13.1	11.5	41.5	57.9	57.2	94.3	47.3
DistilRoBERTa	86.1	14.8	64.0	17.7	5.9	51.6	68.6	64.4	96.0	52.1
DistilmBERT	94.9	76.9	88.2	73.8	72.7	85.0	91.9	88.8	98.4	85.6
BERT	80.1	14.8	54.9	13.1	11.5	41.5	57.9	57.2	94.3	47.3
RoBERTa	86.1	14.8	64.0	17.7	5.9	51.6	68.6	64.4	96.0	52.1
DeBERTaV3	95.0	44.3	85.7	47.1	28.5	79.0	87.5	85.9	98.6	72.4
mBERT	94.9	76.9	88.2	73.8	72.7	85.0	91.9	88.8	98.4	85.6
XLM-RoBERTa	97.8	88.8	94.9	87.6	85.4	93.3	96.3	94.9	99.3	93.1
XLM-V	99.3	93.2	98.0	92.8	90.5	97.1	98.3	98.0	99.8	96.3
				Reduction in Model Parameters (%)						
DistilBERT	28.0	5.2	19.2	4.6	4.0	14.5	20.3	20.0	33.0	16.5
DistilRoBERTa	40.5	7.0	30.1	8.3	2.8	24.3	32.3	30.3	45.1	24.5
DistilmBERT	64.4	52.2	59.9	50.1	49.3	57.7	62.3	60.2	66.8	58.1
BERT	17.1	3.2	11.8	2.8	2.5	8.9	12.4	12.2	20.2	10.1
RoBERTa	26.7	4.6	19.8	5.5	1.8	16.0	21.2	19.9	29.7	16.1
DeBERTaV3	50.7	23.6	45.7	25.1	15.2	42.1	46.7	45.8	52.6	38.6
mBERT	49.0	39.7	45.5	38.1	37.5	43.9	47.4	45.8	50.8	44.2
XLM-RoBERTa	67.5	61.3	65.5	60.5	59.0	64.4	66.5	65.5	68.5	64.3
XLM-V	88.3	82.9	87.2	82.6	80.5	86.4	87.5	87.2	88.8	85.7

Table 2: The reduction in embedding and model parameters (%) for each model across the GLUE benchmark.

Size	CoLA	MNLI	MRPC	QNLI	QQP	RTE	SST-2	STS-B	WNLI	Mean
XSmall	46.7	21.8	42.2	23.2	14.0	38.8	43.1	42.3	48.5	35.6
Small	93.4	43.6	84.3	46.3	28.0	77.7	86.1	84.5	97.0	71.2
Base	93.4	43.6	84.3	46.3	28.0	77.7	86.1	84.5	97.0	71.2
Large	124.6	58.1	112.4	61.8	37.3	103.6	114.8	112.7	129.4	95.0

Table 3: The reduction in model parameters (millions) for each size of DeBERTaV3 across the GLUE benchmark.

tially higher overall savings, as there are fewer parameters allocated to the transformer layers.

Memory savings scale with model size. Table 3 presents the reduction in model parameters for each model from the DeBERTaV3 family. We observe that this reduction continues to increase with model size. On average, the extra small size is reduced by 35.6M parameters, while the large size is reduced by 95.0M parameters. Although the same fixed-size vocabulary is shared across models, the embedding dimension continues to grow (Table 6, Appendix A), offering further memory savings. The exception to this is the small and base sizes, where the only difference is the number of layers.

Multilingual models achieve extreme savings. Unsurprisingly, multilingual models demonstrate extreme memory savings across the monolingual GLUE benchmark. On average, a reduction in model parameters of 44.2% is achieved for mBERT, 64.3% for XLM-RoBERTa, and 85.7% for XLM-V. Table 4 presents the reduction in parameters for the multilingual models when fine-tuning on different subsets of XNLI. Even when fine-tuning on all fifteen languages, these models still demonstrate substantial memory savings from 23.0% to 58.4%.

Model	en	en-de	en-zh	All
	Reduction in Embedding Parameters (%)			
DistilmBERT	77.1	71.7	73.0	44.6
mBERT	77.1	71.7	73.0	44.6
XLM-RoBERTa	89.2	86.0	84.4	56.9
XLM-V	93.6	90.0	90.0	65.7
	Reduction in Model Parameters (%)			
DistilmBERT	52.3	48.6	49.6	30.3
mBERT	39.8	37.0	37.7	23.0
XLM-RoBERTa	61.6	59.4	58.3	39.3
XLM-V	83.2	80.0	80.0	58.4

Table 4: The reduction in parameters across different subsets of XNLI, in addition to all fifteen languages.

7 Conclusion

In this paper, we identified that many fine-tuning datasets do not use the majority of LM vocabulary. We then proposed Partial Embedding Matrix Adaptation (PEMA), a simple yet effective approach to minimize LM memory use during fine-tuning, that is orthogonal to many existing methods. Finally, we empirically demonstrated that our approach offers substantial memory savings across a variety of popular tasks and models, without compromising performance. As future work, we are interested in adapting our approach for the output embedding matrix to offer further memory savings.

Limitations

Processing the fine-tuning dataset to assess vocabulary usage incurs a runtime cost. However, we observe that this cost is negligible. We provide a detailed analysis of this matter in Appendix F.

Ethical Considerations

Our approach improves the memory efficiency of LM fine-tuning, therefore facilitating the use of less powerful hardware. Although we hope that this can reduce the environmental footprint of LM fine-tuning, we acknowledge that it could be used to support the fine-tuning of even larger LMs. We also recognize the dual-use nature of LMs and concede that efforts towards improving efficiency, including our own, can lower the barrier to entry for their misuse (Weidinger et al., 2022).

Acknowledgments

We are sincerely grateful to Nafise Sadat Moosavi, Huiyin Xue, Atsuki Yamaguchi, and the anonymous reviewers for their invaluable feedback. MW is supported by the Centre for Doctoral Training in Speech and Language Technologies (SLT) and their Applications funded by UK Research and Innovation grant EP/S023062/1.

References

Amine Abdaoui, Camille Pradel, and Grégoire Sigel. 2020. Load what you need: Smaller versions of mutililingual BERT. In *Proceedings of SustaiNLP: Workshop on Simple and Efficient Natural Language Processing*, pages 119–123, Online. Association for Computational Linguistics.

Elad Ben Zaken, Yoav Goldberg, and Shauli Ravfogel. 2022. BitFit: Simple parameter-efficient fine-tuning for transformer-based masked language-models. In *Proceedings of the 60th Annual Meeting of the Association for Computational Linguistics (Volume 2: Short Papers)*, pages 1–9, Dublin, Ireland. Association for Computational Linguistics.

Yelysei Bondarenko, Markus Nagel, and Tijmen Blankevoort. 2021. Understanding and overcoming the challenges of efficient transformer quantization. In *Proceedings of the 2021 Conference on Empirical Methods in Natural Language Processing*, pages 7947–7969, Online and Punta Cana, Dominican Republic. Association for Computational Linguistics.

Tom Brown, Benjamin Mann, Nick Ryder, Melanie Subbiah, Jared D Kaplan, Prafulla Dhariwal, Arvind Neelakantan, Pranav Shyam, Girish Sastry, Amanda Askell, Sandhini Agarwal, Ariel Herbert-Voss, Gretchen Krueger, Tom Henighan, Rewon Child, Aditya Ramesh, Daniel Ziegler, Jeffrey Wu, Clemens Winter, and 12 others. 2020. Language models are few-shot learners. In *Advances in Neural Information Processing Systems*, volume 33, pages 1877–1901. Curran Associates, Inc.

Daniel Cer, Mona Diab, Eneko Agirre, Iñigo Lopez-Gazpio, and Lucia Specia. 2017. SemEval-2017 task 1: Semantic textual similarity multilingual and crosslingual focused evaluation. In *Proceedings of the 11th International Workshop on Semantic Evaluation (SemEval-2017)*, pages 1–14, Vancouver, Canada. Association for Computational Linguistics.

Hyung Won Chung, Le Hou, Shayne Longpre, Barret Zoph, Yi Tay, William Fedus, Yunxuan Li, Xuezhi Wang, Mostafa Dehghani, Siddhartha Brahma, Albert Webson, Shixiang Shane Gu, Zhuyun Dai, Mirac Suzgun, Xinyun Chen, Aakanksha Chowdhery, Alex Castro-Ros, Marie Pellat, Kevin Robinson, and 16 others. 2022. Scaling instruction-finetuned language models. *Preprint*, arXiv:2210.11416.

Manuel R. Ciosici and Leon Derczynski. 2022. Training a T5 using lab-sized resources. *Preprint*, arXiv:2208.12097.

Jonathan H. Clark, Dan Garrette, Iulia Turc, and John Wieting. 2022. Canine: Pre-training an efficient tokenization-free encoder for language representation. *Transactions of the Association for Computational Linguistics*, 10:73–91.

Gabrielle Cohn, Rishika Agarwal, Deepanshu Gupta, and Siddharth Patwardhan. 2023. EELBERT: Tiny models through dynamic embeddings. In *Proceedings of the 2023 Conference on Empirical Methods in Natural Language Processing: Industry Track*, pages 451–459, Singapore. Association for Computational Linguistics.

Alexis Conneau, Kartikay Khandelwal, Naman Goyal, Vishrav Chaudhary, Guillaume Wenzek, Francisco Guzmán, Edouard Grave, Myle Ott, Luke Zettlemoyer, and Veselin Stoyanov. 2020. Unsupervised cross-lingual representation learning at scale. In *Proceedings of the 58th Annual Meeting of the Association for Computational Linguistics*, pages 8440–8451, Online. Association for Computational Linguistics.

Alexis Conneau, Ruty Rinott, Guillaume Lample, Adina Williams, Samuel Bowman, Holger Schwenk, and Veselin Stoyanov. 2018. XNLI: Evaluating cross-lingual sentence representations. In *Proceedings of the 2018 Conference on Empirical Methods in Natural Language Processing*, pages 2475–2485, Brussels, Belgium. Association for Computational Linguistics.

Ido Dagan, Oren Glickman, and Bernardo Magnini. 2006. The pascal recognising textual entailment challenge. In *Machine Learning Challenges. Evaluating Predictive Uncertainty, Visual Object Classification, and Recognising Tectual Entailment*, pages 177–190, Berlin, Heidelberg. Springer Berlin Heidelberg.

Tim Dettmers, Mike Lewis, Younes Belkada, and Luke Zettlemoyer. 2022. GPT3.int8(): 8-bit matrix multiplication for transformers at scale. In *Advances in Neural Information Processing Systems*.

Jacob Devlin, Ming-Wei Chang, Kenton Lee, and Kristina Toutanova. 2019. BERT: Pre-training of deep bidirectional transformers for language understanding. In *Proceedings of the 2019 Conference of the North American Chapter of the Association for Computational Linguistics: Human Language Technologies, Volume 1 (Long and Short Papers)*, pages 4171–4186, Minneapolis, Minnesota. Association for Computational Linguistics.

William B. Dolan and Chris Brockett. 2005. Automatically constructing a corpus of sentential paraphrases. In *Proceedings of the Third International Workshop on Paraphrasing (IWP2005)*.

Elias Frantar and Dan Alistarh. 2023. SparseGPT: Massive language models can be accurately pruned in one-shot. In *Proceedings of the 40th International Conference on Machine Learning*, volume 202 of *Proceedings of Machine Learning Research*, pages 10323–10337. PMLR.

Elias Frantar, Saleh Ashkboos, Torsten Hoefler, and Dan Alistarh. 2023. OPTQ: Accurate quantization for generative pre-trained transformers. In *The Eleventh International Conference on Learning Representations*.

Matthias Gallé. 2019. Investigating the effectiveness of BPE: The power of shorter sequences. In *Proceedings of the 2019 Conference on Empirical Methods in Natural Language Processing and the 9th International Joint Conference on Natural Language Processing (EMNLP-IJCNLP)*, pages 1375–1381, Hong Kong, China. Association for Computational Linguistics.

Pengcheng He, Jianfeng Gao, and Weizhu Chen. 2023. DeBERTaV3: Improving DeBERTa using ELECTRA-style pre-training with gradient-disentangled embedding sharing. In *The Eleventh International Conference on Learning Representations*.

Harold Stanley Heaps. 1978. *Information Retrieval: Computational and Theoretical Aspects*. Library and information science series. Academic Press.

Geoffrey Hinton, Oriol Vinyals, and Jeffrey Dean. 2015. Distilling the knowledge in a neural network. In *NIPS Deep Learning and Representation Learning Workshop*.

Jordan Hoffmann, Sebastian Borgeaud, Arthur Mensch, Elena Buchatskaya, Trevor Cai, Eliza Rutherford, Diego de Las Casas, Lisa Anne Hendricks, Johannes Welbl, Aidan Clark, Thomas Hennigan, Eric Noland, Katherine Millican, George van den Driessche, Bogdan Damoc, Aurelia Guy, Simon Osindero, Karén Simonyan, Erich Elsen, and 3 others. 2022. An empirical analysis of compute-optimal large language model training. In *Advances in Neural Information Processing Systems*, volume 35, pages 30016–30030. Curran Associates, Inc.

Neil Houlsby, Andrei Giurgiu, Stanislaw Jastrzebski, Bruna Morrone, Quentin De Laroussilhe, Andrea Gesmundo, Mona Attariyan, and Sylvain Gelly. 2019. Parameter-efficient transfer learning for NLP. In *Proceedings of the 36th International Conference on Machine Learning*, volume 97 of *Proceedings of Machine Learning Research*, pages 2790–2799. PMLR.

Edward J Hu, yelong shen, Phillip Wallis, Zeyuan Allen-Zhu, Yuanzhi Li, Shean Wang, Lu Wang, and Weizhu Chen. 2022. LoRA: Low-rank adaptation of large language models. In *International Conference on Learning Representations*.

Shankar Iyer, Nikhil Dandekar, Kornél Csernai, and 1 others. 2017. First Quora dataset release: Question pairs.

Peter Izsak, Moshe Berchansky, and Omer Levy. 2021. How to train BERT with an academic budget. In *Proceedings of the 2021 Conference on Empirical Methods in Natural Language Processing*, pages 10644–10652, Online and Punta Cana, Dominican Republic. Association for Computational Linguistics.

Jared Kaplan, Sam McCandlish, Tom Henighan, Tom B. Brown, Benjamin Chess, Rewon Child, Scott Gray, Alec Radford, Jeffrey Wu, and Dario Amodei. 2020. Scaling laws for neural language models. *Preprint*, arXiv:2001.08361.

Diederik P. Kingma and Jimmy Ba. 2017. Adam: A method for stochastic optimization. *Preprint*, arXiv:1412.6980.

Eldar Kurtic, Daniel Campos, Tuan Nguyen, Elias Frantar, Mark Kurtz, Benjamin Fineran, Michael Goin, and Dan Alistarh. 2022. The optimal BERT surgeon: Scalable and accurate second-order pruning for large language models. In *Proceedings of the 2022 Conference on Empirical Methods in Natural Language Processing*, pages 4163–4181, Abu Dhabi, United Arab Emirates. Association for Computational Linguistics.

Eldar Kurtic, Torsten Hoefler, and Dan Alistarh. 2024. How to prune your language model: Recovering accuracy on the "sparsity may cry" benchmark. In *Conference on Parsimony and Learning*, volume 234 of *Proceedings of Machine Learning Research*, pages 542–553. PMLR.

Zhenzhong Lan, Mingda Chen, Sebastian Goodman, Kevin Gimpel, Piyush Sharma, and Radu Soricut. 2020. ALBERT: A lite bert for self-supervised learning of language representations. In *International Conference on Learning Representations*.

Sander Land and Max Bartolo. 2024. Fishing for magikarp: Automatically detecting under-trained tokens in large language models. In *Proceedings of the 2024 Conference on Empirical Methods in Natural Language Processing*, pages 11631–11646, Miami, Florida, USA. Association for Computational Linguistics.

Yann LeCun, John Denker, and Sara Solla. 1989. Optimal brain damage. In *Advances in Neural Information Processing Systems*, volume 2. Morgan-Kaufmann.

Brian Lester, Rami Al-Rfou, and Noah Constant. 2021. The power of scale for parameter-efficient prompt tuning. In *Proceedings of the 2021 Conference on Empirical Methods in Natural Language Processing*, pages 3045–3059, Online and Punta Cana, Dominican Republic. Association for Computational Linguistics.

Hector J. Levesque, Ernest Davis, and Leora Morgenstern. 2012. The Winograd schema challenge. In *Proceedings of the Thirteenth International Conference on Principles of Knowledge Representation and Reasoning*, KR'12, pages 552–561. AAAI Press.

Mike Lewis, Yinhan Liu, Naman Goyal, Marjan Ghazvininejad, Abdelrahman Mohamed, Omer Levy, Veselin Stoyanov, and Luke Zettlemoyer. 2020. BART: Denoising sequence-to-sequence pre-training for natural language generation, translation, and comprehension. In *Proceedings of the 58th Annual Meeting of the Association for Computational Linguistics*, pages 7871–7880, Online. Association for Computational Linguistics.

Quentin Lhoest, Albert Villanova del Moral, Yacine Jernite, Abhishek Thakur, Patrick von Platen, Suraj Patil, Julien Chaumond, Mariama Drame, Julien Plu, Lewis Tunstall, Joe Davison, Mario Šaško, Gunjan Chhablani, Bhavitvya Malik, Simon Brandeis, Teven Le Scao, Victor Sanh, Canwen Xu, Nicolas Patry, and 13 others. 2021. Datasets: A community library for natural language processing. In *Proceedings of the 2021 Conference on Empirical Methods in Natural Language Processing: System Demonstrations*, pages 175–184, Online and Punta Cana, Dominican Republic. Association for Computational Linguistics.

Xiang Lisa Li and Percy Liang. 2021. Prefix-tuning: Optimizing continuous prompts for generation. In *Proceedings of the 59th Annual Meeting of the Association for Computational Linguistics and the 11th International Joint Conference on Natural Language Processing (Volume 1: Long Papers)*, pages 4582–4597, Online. Association for Computational Linguistics.

Vladislav Lialin, Vijeta Deshpande, and Anna Rumshisky. 2023. Scaling down to scale up: A guide to parameter-efficient fine-tuning. *Preprint*, arXiv:2303.15647.

Davis Liang, Hila Gonen, Yuning Mao, Rui Hou, Naman Goyal, Marjan Ghazvininejad, Luke Zettlemoyer, and Madian Khabsa. 2023. XLM-V: Overcoming the vocabulary bottleneck in multilingual masked language models. In *Proceedings of the 2023 Conference on Empirical Methods in Natural Language Processing*, pages 13142–13152, Singapore. Association for Computational Linguistics.

Yinhan Liu, Myle Ott, Naman Goyal, Jingfei Du, Mandar Joshi, Danqi Chen, Omer Levy, Mike Lewis, Luke Zettlemoyer, and Veselin Stoyanov. 2019. RoBERTa: A robustly optimized BERT pretraining approach. *Preprint*, arXiv:1907.11692.

Andrei Paleyes, Raoul-Gabriel Urma, and Neil D. Lawrence. 2022. Challenges in deploying machine learning: A survey of case studies. *ACM Comput. Surv.*, 55(6).

Adam Paszke, Sam Gross, Francisco Massa, Adam Lerer, James Bradbury, Gregory Chanan, Trevor Killeen, Zeming Lin, Natalia Gimelshein, Luca Antiga, Alban Desmaison, Andreas Kopf, Edward Yang, Zachary DeVito, Martin Raison, Alykhan Tejani, Sasank Chilamkurthy, Benoit Steiner, Lu Fang, and 2 others. 2019. PyTorch: An imperative style, high-performance deep learning library. In *Advances in Neural Information Processing Systems*, volume 32. Curran Associates, Inc.

Bharadwaj Pudipeddi, Maral Mesmakhosroshahi, Jinwen Xi, and Sujeeth Bharadwaj. 2020. Training large neural networks with constant memory using a new execution algorithm. *Preprint*, arXiv:2002.05645.

Pranav Rajpurkar, Jian Zhang, Konstantin Lopyrev, and Percy Liang. 2016. SQuAD: 100,000+ questions for machine comprehension of text. In *Proceedings of the 2016 Conference on Empirical Methods in Natural Language Processing*, pages 2383–2392, Austin, Texas. Association for Computational Linguistics.

Jie Ren, Samyam Rajbhandari, Reza Yazdani Aminabadi, Olatunji Ruwase, Shuangyan Yang, Minjia Zhang, Dong Li, and Yuxiong He. 2021. ZeRO-Offload: Democratizing billion-scale model training. In *2021 USENIX Annual Technical Conference (USENIX ATC 21)*, pages 551–564. USENIX Association.

Jessica Rumbelow and Matthew Watkins. 2023. SolidGoldMagikarp (plus, prompt generation).

Victor Sanh, Lysandre Debut, Julien Chaumond, and Thomas Wolf. 2020a. DistilBERT, a distilled version of BERT: smaller, faster, cheaper and lighter. *Preprint*, arXiv:1910.01108.

Victor Sanh, Thomas Wolf, and Alexander Rush. 2020b. Movement pruning: Adaptive sparsity by fine-tuning. In *Advances in Neural Information Processing Systems*, volume 33, pages 20378–20389. Curran Associates, Inc.

Chinnadhurai Sankar, Sujith Ravi, and Zornitsa Kozareva. 2021. ProFormer: Towards on-device LSH projection based transformers. In *Proceedings of the 16th Conference of the European Chapter of the Association for Computational Linguistics: Main Volume*, pages 2823–2828, Online. Association for Computational Linguistics.

Mike Schuster and Kaisuke Nakajima. 2012. Japanese and Korean voice search. In *2012 IEEE International Conference on Acoustics, Speech and Signal Processing (ICASSP)*, pages 5149–5152.

Roy Schwartz, Jesse Dodge, Noah A. Smith, and Oren Etzioni. 2020. Green AI. *Commun. ACM*, 63(12):54–63.

Rico Sennrich, Barry Haddow, and Alexandra Birch. 2016. Neural machine translation of rare words with subword units. In *Proceedings of the 54th Annual Meeting of the Association for Computational Linguistics (Volume 1: Long Papers)*, pages 1715–1725, Berlin, Germany. Association for Computational Linguistics.

Sheng Shen, Zhen Dong, Jiayu Ye, Linjian Ma, Zhewei Yao, Amir Gholami, Michael W. Mahoney, and Kurt Keutzer. 2020. Q-BERT: Hessian based ultra low precision quantization of bert. *Proceedings of the AAAI Conference on Artificial Intelligence*, 34(05):8815–8821.

Pranaydeep Singh and Els Lefever. 2022. When the student becomes the master: Learning better and smaller monolingual models from mBERT. In *Proceedings of the 29th International Conference on Computational Linguistics*, pages 4434–4441, Gyeongju, Republic of Korea. International Committee on Computational Linguistics.

Richard Socher, Alex Perelygin, Jean Wu, Jason Chuang, Christopher D. Manning, Andrew Ng, and Christopher Potts. 2013. Recursive deep models for semantic compositionality over a sentiment treebank. In *Proceedings of the 2013 Conference on Empirical Methods in Natural Language Processing*, pages 1631–1642, Seattle, Washington, USA. Association for Computational Linguistics.

Zhiqing Sun, Hongkun Yu, Xiaodan Song, Renjie Liu, Yiming Yang, and Denny Zhou. 2020. MobileBERT: a compact task-agnostic BERT for resource-limited devices. In *Proceedings of the 58th Annual Meeting of the Association for Computational Linguistics*, pages 2158–2170, Online. Association for Computational Linguistics.

Yi-Lin Sung, Jaemin Cho, and Mohit Bansal. 2022. LST: Ladder side-tuning for parameter and memory efficient transfer learning. In *Advances in Neural Information Processing Systems*, volume 35, pages 12991–13005. Curran Associates, Inc.

Yi Tay, Mostafa Dehghani, Dara Bahri, and Donald Metzler. 2022. Efficient transformers: A survey. *ACM Comput. Surv.*, 55(6).

Hugo Touvron, Thibaut Lavril, Gautier Izacard, Xavier Martinet, Marie-Anne Lachaux, Timothée Lacroix, Baptiste Rozière, Naman Goyal, Eric Hambro, Faisal Azhar, Aurelien Rodriguez, Armand Joulin, Edouard Grave, and Guillaume Lample. 2023. LLaMA: Open and efficient foundation language models. *Preprint*, arXiv:2302.13971.

Marcos Treviso, Ji-Ung Lee, Tianchu Ji, Betty van Aken, Qingqing Cao, Manuel R. Ciosici, Michael Hassid, Kenneth Heafield, Sara Hooker, Colin Raffel, Pedro H. Martins, André F. T. Martins, Jessica Zosa Forde, Peter Milder, Edwin Simpson, Noam Slonim, Jesse Dodge, Emma Strubell, Niranjan Balasubramanian, and 3 others. 2023. Efficient methods for natural language processing: A survey. *Transactions of the Association for Computational Linguistics*, 11:826–860.

Asahi Ushio, Yi Zhou, and Jose Camacho-Collados. 2023. Efficient multilingual language model compression through vocabulary trimming. In *Findings of the Association for Computational Linguistics: EMNLP 2023*, pages 14725–14739, Singapore. Association for Computational Linguistics.

Ashish Vaswani, Noam Shazeer, Niki Parmar, Jakob Uszkoreit, Llion Jones, Aidan N Gomez, Ł ukasz Kaiser, and Illia Polosukhin. 2017. Attention is all you need. In *Advances in Neural Information Processing Systems*, volume 30. Curran Associates, Inc.

Alex Wang, Amanpreet Singh, Julian Michael, Felix Hill, Omer Levy, and Samuel R. Bowman. 2019. GLUE: A multi-task benchmark and analysis platform for natural language understanding. In *International Conference on Learning Representations.*

Benjamin Warner, Antoine Chaffin, Benjamin Clavié, Orion Weller, Oskar Hallström, Said Taghadouini, Alexis Gallagher, Raja Biswas, Faisal Ladhak, Tom Aarsen, Nathan Cooper, Griffin Adams, Jeremy Howard, and Iacopo Poli. 2024. Smarter, better, faster, longer: A modern bidirectional encoder for fast, memory efficient, and long context finetuning and inference. *Preprint*, arXiv:2412.13663.

Alex Warstadt, Amanpreet Singh, and Samuel R. Bowman. 2019. Neural network acceptability judgments. *Transactions of the Association for Computational Linguistics*, 7:625–641.

Laura Weidinger, Jonathan Uesato, Maribeth Rauh, Conor Griffin, Po-Sen Huang, John Mellor, Amelia Glaese, Myra Cheng, Borja Balle, Atoosa Kasirzadeh, Courtney Biles, Sasha Brown, Zac Kenton, Will Hawkins, Tom Stepleton, Abeba Birhane, Lisa Anne Hendricks, Laura Rimell, William Isaac, and 4 others. 2022. Taxonomy of risks posed by language models. In *Proceedings of the 2022 ACM Conference on Fairness, Accountability, and Transparency*, FAccT '22, page 214–229, New York, NY, USA. Association for Computing Machinery.

Adina Williams, Nikita Nangia, and Samuel Bowman. 2018. A broad-coverage challenge corpus for sentence understanding through inference. In *Proceedings of the 2018 Conference of the North American Chapter of the Association for Computational Linguistics: Human Language Technologies, Volume 1 (Long Papers)*, pages 1112–1122, New Orleans, Louisiana. Association for Computational Linguistics.

Thomas Wolf, Lysandre Debut, Victor Sanh, Julien Chaumond, Clement Delangue, Anthony Moi, Pierric Cistac, Tim Rault, Remi Louf, Morgan Funtowicz, Joe Davison, Sam Shleifer, Patrick von Platen, Clara Ma, Yacine Jernite, Julien Plu, Canwen Xu, Teven Le Scao, Sylvain Gugger, and 3 others. 2020. Transformers: State-of-the-art natural language processing. In *Proceedings of the 2020 Conference on Empirical Methods in Natural Language Processing: System Demonstrations*, pages 38–45, Online. Association for Computational Linguistics.

Huiyin Xue and Nikolaos Aletras. 2022. HashFormers: Towards vocabulary-independent pre-trained transformers. In *Proceedings of the 2022 Conference on Empirical Methods in Natural Language Processing*, pages 7862–7874, Abu Dhabi, United Arab Emirates. Association for Computational Linguistics.

Linting Xue, Aditya Barua, Noah Constant, Rami Al-Rfou, Sharan Narang, Mihir Kale, Adam Roberts, and Colin Raffel. 2022. ByT5: Towards a token-free future with pre-trained byte-to-byte models. *Transactions of the Association for Computational Linguistics*, 10:291–306.

Zhewei Yao, Reza Yazdani Aminabadi, Minjia Zhang, Xiaoxia Wu, Conglong Li, and Yuxiong He. 2022. ZeroQuant: Efficient and affordable post-training quantization for large-scale transformers. In *Advances in Neural Information Processing Systems*, volume 35, pages 27168–27183. Curran Associates, Inc.

Ofir Zafrir, Guy Boudoukh, Peter Izsak, and Moshe Wasserblat. 2019. Q8BERT: Quantized 8bit bert. In *2019 Fifth Workshop on Energy Efficient Machine Learning and Cognitive Computing - NeurIPS Edition (EMC2-NIPS)*, pages 36–39.

Qingru Zhang, Minshuo Chen, Alexander Bukharin, Pengcheng He, Yu Cheng, Weizhu Chen, and Tuo Zhao. 2023. Adaptive budget allocation for parameter-efficient fine-tuning. In *The Eleventh International Conference on Learning Representations*.

Susan Zhang, Stephen Roller, Naman Goyal, Mikel Artetxe, Moya Chen, Shuohui Chen, Christopher Dewan, Mona Diab, Xian Li, Xi Victoria Lin, Todor Mihaylov, Myle Ott, Sam Shleifer, Kurt Shuster, Daniel Simig, Punit Singh Koura, Anjali Sridhar, Tianlu Wang, and Luke Zettlemoyer. 2022. OPT: Open pre-trained transformer language models. *Preprint*, arXiv:2205.01068.

Sanqiang Zhao, Raghav Gupta, Yang Song, and Denny Zhou. 2021. Extremely small BERT models from mixed-vocabulary training. In *Proceedings of the 16th Conference of the European Chapter of the Association for Computational Linguistics: Main Volume*, pages 2753–2759, Online. Association for Computational Linguistics.

Yi Zhou, Jose Camacho-Collados, and Danushka Bollegala. 2023. A predictive factor analysis of social biases and task-performance in pretrained masked language models. In *Proceedings of the 2023 Conference on Empirical Methods in Natural Language Processing*, pages 11082–11100, Singapore. Association for Computational Linguistics.

A Language Model Vocabulary Sizes

Table 5 presents the vocabulary sizes ($|\mathcal{V}|$) for the models used in our experiments, as identified by the Hugging Face Hub. We also report the number of embedding parameters (N_{emb}), the number of model parameters (N), and the overall proportion of embedding parameters (N_{emb}/N). These metrics are also presented in Table 6 for each size of DeBERTa, in addition to model hyperparameters.

Model	$\lvert\mathcal{V}\rvert$	N_{emb}	N	N_{emb}/N
DistilBERT	28,996	22.3M	65.8M	33.9%
DistilRoBERTa	50,265	38.6M	82.1M	47.0%
DistilmBERT	119,547	91.8M	135.3M	67.8%
BERT	28,996	22.3M	108.3M	20.6%
RoBERTa	50,265	38.6M	124.6M	31.0%
DeBERTaV3	128,100	98.4M	184.4M	53.3%
mBERT	119,547	91.8M	177.9M	51.6%
XLM-RoBERTa	250,002	192.0M	278.0M	69.1%
XLM-V	901,629	692.5M	778.5M	88.9%

Table 5: The vocabulary size and allocation of parameters for each of the models used in our experiments. In all cases, we select the base model size ($d_{\text{model}} = 768$).

Size	l	h	d_{model}	N_{emb}	N	N_{emb}/N
XSmall	12	6	384	49.2M	70.8M	69.4%
Small	6	12	768	98.4M	141.9M	69.3%
Base	12	12	768	98.4M	184.4M	53.3%
Large	24	16	1024	131.2M	435.1M	30.2%

Table 6: The DeBERTaV3 (He et al., 2023) family of models. Columns l, h, and d_{model} show the number of hidden layers, number of attention heads, and hidden embedding size, respectively.

B Language Model Compression

Supplementary to our discussion of related work (Section 2), we additionally discuss the relation to variety of popular LM compression approaches. We emphasize that these methods are orthogonal to our proposed approach.

Knowledge distillation. Knowledge distillation (Hinton et al., 2015) aims to achieve comparable performance by training a smaller model using the predictions from a larger model. This approach has been successfully applied to LMs (Sanh et al., 2020a; Sun et al., 2020). It can also be used to train models with a smaller vocabulary than the original (Zhao et al., 2021; Singh and Lefever, 2022).

Pruning. Neural network pruning (LeCun et al., 1989) seeks to remove redundant weights while preserving performance. Existing approaches focus on pruning the linear and attention weights in LMs (Sanh et al., 2020b; Kurtic et al., 2022; Frantar and Alistarh, 2023). However, pruning the embedding matrix is widely avoided, as it can substantially harm performance (Kurtic et al., 2024).

Quantization. The aim of quantization is to represent neural network weights using lower precision, therefore reducing computational costs. Recent LM quantization efforts generally focus on quantizing the linear layers (Dettmers et al., 2022; Yao et al., 2022; Frantar et al., 2023). The embedding matrix can also be quantized (Zafrir et al., 2019; Bondarenko et al., 2021), although Shen et al. (2020) find that it is more sensitive to quantization.

C Datasets

In all cases, we use the publicly available version of each dataset available from Hugging Face (Lhoest et al., 2021). The GLUE benchmark comprises a diverse range of tasks, including linguistic acceptability (CoLA, Warstadt et al. 2019), sentiment analysis (SST-2, Socher et al. 2013), paraphrasing/sentence similarity (MRPC, Dolan and Brockett 2005; STS-B, Cer et al. 2017; QQP, Iyer et al. 2017), and natural language inference (RTE, Dagan et al. 2006; WNLI, Levesque et al. 2012; QNLI, Rajpurkar et al. 2016; MNLI, Williams et al. 2018). The number of examples per split in each dataset are listed in Table 7. The XNLI dataset (Conneau et al., 2018) extends MNLI to 15 languages: Arabic, Bulgarian, Chinese, English, French, German, Greek, Hindi, Russian, Spanish, Swahili, Thai, Turkish, Vietnamese, and Urdu.

D Implementation & Hardware

We implement our experiments using PyTorch (Paszke et al., 2019), Hugging Face Transformers (Wolf et al., 2020) and Hugging Face Datasets (Lhoest et al., 2021). Since downstream task performance is not relevant to this study, we do not perform hyperparameter tuning. Instead, we broadly follow the hyperparameters from Devlin et al. (2019), listed in Table 8.

We fine-tune all models using a single NVIDIA Tesla V100 (SXM2 32GB) GPU and Intel Xeon Gold 6138 CPU. For consistency, each model type is evaluated on the same physical hardware.

E Fine-tuning on GLUE

Table 10 presents the task performance for each model across the GLUE benchmark. We observe that the performance is largely identical, although there are occasional fluctuations where PEMA performs fractionally better or worse than the baseline. Finally, we note that XLM-RoBERTa and XLM-V both demonstrate very low performance on CoLA, although this issue has also been observed in other studies, e.g. Zhou et al. (2023).

F Runtime Impact

Table 9 presents the mean duration and standard deviation of applying PEMA to RoBERTa and the subsequent fine-tuning process. It also shows the proportion of time spent applying PEMA relative to fine-tuning. We observe that for five of the nine datasets in GLUE, applying PEMA takes less than half a second. For eight out of nine datasets, applying PEMA takes less than 1% of the fine-tuning duration. We note that the time taken to apply PEMA correlates with the size of the fine-tuning dataset (Figure 2). Overall, we note that the time taken to apply PEMA is generally fractional compared to the fine-tuning duration, even though we made no effort to optimize our implementation. As guidance for future optimization efforts, we note that the dataset processing operations in PEMA are trivially parallelizable.

Dataset	Train	Validation	Test	Total
CoLA	8,551	1,043	1,063	10,657
MNLI	392,702	19,647	19,643	431,992
MRPC	3,668	408	1,725	5,801
QNLI	104,743	5,463	5,463	115,669
QQP	363,846	40,430	390,965	795,241
RTE	2,490	277	3,000	5,767
SST-2	67,349	872	1,821	70,042
STS-B	5,749	1,500	1,379	8,628
WNLI	635	71	146	852

Table 7: The number of examples per split in each of the GLUE datasets.

Hyperparameter	GLUE	XNLI
Adam ϵ	1e-8	
Adam β_1	0.9	
Adam β_2	0.999	
Batch Size	32	
Dropout (Attention)	0.1	
Dropout (Hidden)	0.1	
Learning Rate (Peak)	2e-5, 7.5e-6 (XLM)	
Learning Rate Schedule	Linear	
Sequence Length	128	
Training Epochs	3	2

Table 8: The hyperparameters used for each set of experiments.

Dataset	PEMA	Fine-tuning	%
CoLA	$0.4_{0.0}$	$172.7_{0.9}$	0.2
MNLI	$8.8_{0.2}$	$7817.8_{16.6}$	0.1
MRPC	$0.3_{0.0}$	$78.7_{0.7}$	0.4
QNLI	$2.4_{0.0}$	$2092.8_{2.9}$	0.1
QQP	$13.3_{0.5}$	$7235.5_{4.9}$	0.2
RTE	$0.4_{0.0}$	$55.4_{0.6}$	0.7
SST-2	$1.2_{0.0}$	$1329.2_{0.3}$	0.1
STS-B	$0.4_{0.0}$	$118.7_{0.5}$	0.3
WNLI	$0.3_{0.0}$	$18.3_{0.8}$	1.4

Table 9: The mean duration (seconds) and standard deviation over five runs of applying PEMA to RoBERTa and fine-tuning on the GLUE datasets.

Model	PEMA	CoLA	MNLI	MRPC	QNLI	QQP	RTE	SST-2	STS-B	WNLI	Mean
DistilBERT	✗	49.3	82.2	84.2	88.5	86.7	59.6	90.5	86.5	49.3	$75.2_{1.5}$
	✓	49.3	82.2	84.2	88.6	86.7	59.6	90.5	86.5	49.3	$75.2_{1.5}$
DistilRoBERTa	✗	56.4	84.2	85.0	90.9	87.2	65.7	92.3	87.2	53.0	$78.0_{0.9}$
	✓	56.4	84.2	85.0	90.9	87.2	65.7	92.3	87.2	53.0	$78.0_{0.9}$
DistilmBERT	✗	29.7	78.3	81.8	86.7	85.8	60.9	89.1	84.4	48.2	$71.6_{0.3}$
	✓	29.6	78.3	81.8	86.7	85.8	60.9	89.2	84.4	48.2	$71.6_{0.4}$
BERT	✗	56.4	84.3	84.3	91.1	87.9	64.4	92.6	88.1	37.7	$76.3_{0.7}$
	✓	56.7	84.3	84.3	91.3	87.8	64.4	92.5	88.1	37.7	$76.3_{0.8}$
RoBERTa	✗	57.6	87.8	88.4	92.8	88.4	71.1	94.2	89.9	52.1	$80.3_{1.2}$
	✓	57.6	87.8	88.4	92.7	88.4	71.1	94.2	89.9	52.1	$80.3_{1.2}$
DeBERTaV3	✗	67.4	90.2	88.5	93.9	89.9	79.8	95.6	90.9	53.0	$83.2_{0.8}$
	✓	67.4	90.2	88.3	93.9	89.9	79.8	95.5	90.9	53.0	$83.2_{0.8}$
mBERT	✗	35.3	82.3	85.8	91.1	87.1	69.0	91.0	88.0	53.0	$75.8_{2.0}$
	✓	35.4	82.2	85.8	91.1	87.2	69.0	90.8	88.0	53.0	$75.8_{2.0}$
XLM-RoBERTa	✗	22.6	83.9	76.9	89.5	86.9	57.3	92.2	84.2	52.1	$71.7_{2.0}$
	✓	22.4	84.0	76.8	89.5	86.8	57.3	92.0	84.2	52.1	$71.7_{2.0}$
XLM-V	✗	0.0	84.5	68.8	89.6	86.7	54.1	91.8	80.8	55.2	$68.0_{0.6}$
	✓	0.0	84.5	68.8	89.6	86.7	54.1	91.6	80.8	55.2	$67.9_{0.6}$

Table 10: Results on the validation set for each task from GLUE. We present the mean performance over five different seeds, accompanied by the overall mean and standard deviation. We report Matthews correlation for CoLA, F1 for QQP, Spearman correlation for STS-B, and accuracy for the remaining tasks.

Prompt Tuning Can Simply Adapt Large Language Models to Text Encoders

Kaiyan Zhao, Qiyu Wu, Zhongtao Miao, Yoshimasa Tsuruoka
The University of Tokyo, Tokyo, Japan
{zhaokaiyan1006, qiyuw, mzt, yoshimasa-tsuruoka}@g.ecc.u-tokyo.ac.jp

Abstract

Recently, many works have been attempting to adapt Large Language Models (LLMs) for sentence embedding, with most of them fine-tuning LLMs towards the contrastive objective and enabling bi-directional attention for better performance, using LoRA to address the large model scale. In this work, we suggest that this adaptation can also be simply and effectively achieved using causal attention and with even fewer trainable parameters through soft prompt tuning, as an alternative to fine-tuning with LoRA and other methods with extra post-training tasks. Our method only optimizes a few learnable tokens while keeping the rest of the model frozen. Through experiments on a diverse set of evaluation tasks, we find that simply tuning only a few tokens can achieve a competitive performance with that of fine-tuning with LoRA. The percentage of trainable parameters can be reduced to less than 0.001%. Moreover, we also demonstrate that turning causal attention to bi-directional attention with or without extra post-training tasks does not provide additional benefit when soft prompt tuning is applied, suggesting that causal attention can be naturally used in decoder-only LLMs for sentence embedding adaptation.

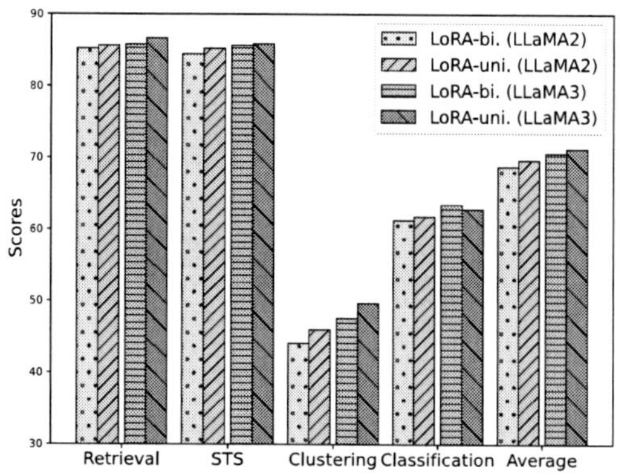

Figure 1: Comparison of LoRA fine-tuning using bi-directional attention or uni-directional attention. Extra post-training task is solely applied to LoRA-bi. Simply fine-tuning with LoRA-uni. shows strong performances. Refer to Table 1 for detailed results.

1 Introduction

Sentence embedding compresses the semantic meaning of sentences into fixed-size vectors in a shared space (Conneau et al., 2017; Wu et al., 2018; Reimers and Gurevych, 2019). Conventional sentence embedding models are typically built on an encoder-only architecture trained with Contrastive Learning (CL) (van den Oord et al., 2018), where the distance between semantically similar sentences are pulled closer and dissimilar ones are pushed farther (Gao et al., 2021; Wu et al., 2022; Chuang et al., 2022; Jiang et al., 2022a). On the other hand, scaled-up Large Language Models (LLMs) in the decoder-only architecture have dominated various downstream tasks with very large-scale parameters and training data (OpenAI, 2022; Touvron et al., 2023a,b; OpenAI, 2023). However, the use of LLMs on sentence embedding still remains challenging, given the fact that decoder-only LLMs are pre-trained to generate continuous texts instead of semantically meaningful vectors (Jiang et al., 2023).

To this end, numerous recent methods attempt to adapt LLMs for sentence embedding, e.g., CL-based fine-tuning (Jiang et al., 2023; Li and Li, 2023), attention mechanism manipulation (Li and Li, 2024), instruction tuning (Muennighoff et al., 2024), with some approaches employing the combinations thereof. Among these efforts, LLM2Vec (BehnamGhader et al., 2024) stands out as a promising method, employing a three-step approach: (1) enabling bi-directional attention, (2) using Masked Next Token Prediction (MNTP) (Lv et al., 2023) to effectively adapt LLMs to bi-directional attention, and (3) fine-tuning with CL, as shown in the upper part of Figure 2.

Proceedings of the 10th Workshop on Representation Learning for NLP (RepL4NLP-2025), pages 38–50
May 4, 2025 ©2025 Association for Computational Linguistics

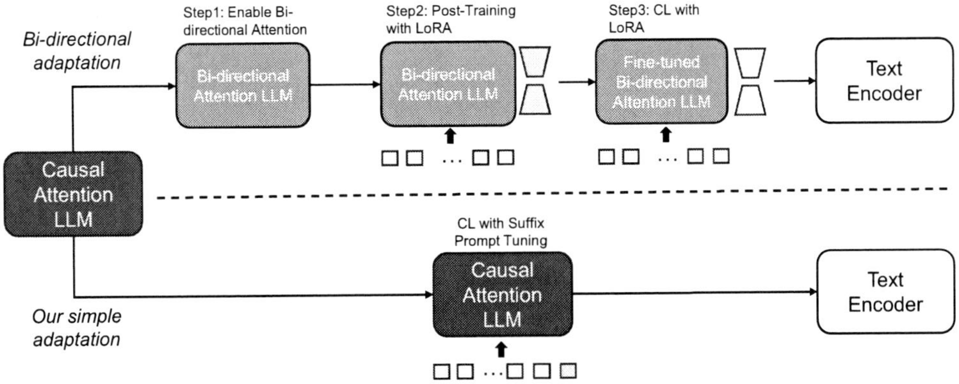

Figure 2: Upper: Conventional three-step methods of turning LLMs into text encoders. We refer to tasks performed before fine-tuning under the CL objective as post-training tasks. Lower: Our simple method which naturally maintains causal attention by appending trainable soft prompts into the input.

However, given the large-scale parameters of LLMs, performing these three steps, especially the latter two, can be computationally inefficient. To address this, Low-Rank Adaptation (LoRA) (Hu et al., 2022) is commonly employed in the aforementioned works to enable more efficient fine-tuning by reducing the number of trainable parameters while maintaining performance.

Given the additional post-training efforts required by LLM2Vec, we begin questioning whether it is possible to naturally maintain causal attention in LLMs for sentence embedding. To explore this, we compare LoRA under bi-directional attention with post-training to directly LoRA under uni-directional attention without post-training on the same dataset, and the results are shown in Figure 1. Interestingly, our results reveal that simply fine-tuning LLMs with LoRA consistently yields strong performances across the four evaluated tasks. Based on these findings, we seek answers to the following two questions: (1) Is bi-directional attention with additional post-training necessary for the adaptation? (2) Is there a simpler adaptation method with minimum modification of the original LLM?

We first investigate the adaptation of LLMs for sentence embedding with even fewer trainable parameters by employing soft prompt tuning (Lester et al., 2021; Li and Liang, 2021; Liu et al., 2022). We introduce SPT (**S**uffix **P**rompt **T**uning based Adaptation of LLMs for Sentence Embedding), a straightforward yet effective alternative to adapt LLMs for sentence embedding. The use of soft prompt tuning in this scenario is non-trivial. Specifically, we append trainable tokens to the inputs, allowing them to attend to all the input tokens due to the causal attention in the decoder-only LLMs, as illustrated in the lower part of Figure 2. Notably, as our approach only optimizes the parameters within the additional soft prompt tokens, it is flexible enough to reduce the amount of trainable parameters to just a few tokens[1]. The percentage of trainable parameters with our approach is less than 0.001%, which is a percentage unreachable by LoRA, even when setting the rank r to 1. Experimental results on retrieval, Semantic Textual Similarities (STS), clustering, and classification tasks reveal that training with only a few tokens can yield comparable or even superior performance to LoRA-based fine-tuning.

Additionally, we thoroughly analyze the impact of bi-directional attention and extra post-training tasks, finding that regardless of the pooling method or attention mechanism used, causal attention without post-training consistently delivers better performance when SPT is applied.

In summary, the contribution of this work includes:

- We propose a simple method that adapts LLMs to text encoders without requiring extra adjustment for bi-directional attention, which is applied in previous methods.
- We investigate the utilization of suffix prompt

[1]The amount of one trainable token varies according to different models, e.g., 768 for OPT and 4096 for LLaMA.

tuning other than LoRA fine-tuning for the adaptation, providing the flexibility to further reduce the trainable parameters.

2 Related Works

2.1 Turning LLMs into Text Encoders

Current methods for adapting LLMs into text encoders can be mainly categorized into two types based on the attention mechanism they use.

w/ Causal Attention. Since most LLMs are pre-trained with casual attention, it is natural to keep this mechanism for sentence representation, using the output of the last input token as sentence embedding. Jiang et al. (2023) make the first attempt to adapt LLMs for sentence embedding. They propose PromptEOL, which utilizes the prompt *This sentence: "[text]" means in one word:"* to generate sentence embedding. Li and Li (2023) later extend this prompt-based method on LLaMA2 using angle optimization to address the gradient vanishing problem in CL. In our work, we also prioritize the natural use of causal attention, while aiming for a simple but effective approach.

w/ Bidirectional Attention On the other hand, some methods transform the causal attention into bi-directional attention for better representation ability. Li and Li (2024) observe that an LLM's sentence representation ability with causal attention initially improves across layers but begins to degrade after reaching a critical turning point (a particular layer). By modifying the layers after the turning point to use bi-directional attention, the LLM improves its sentence encoding ability. BehnamGhader et al. (2024) introduce a three-step pipeline for converting LLMs into text encoders, including enabling bi-directional attention, masked next token prediction (MNTP) and CL-based fine-tuning. MNTP, which requires the model to predict the masked token based solely on the tokens before it, is applied to help LLMs adapt to bi-directional attention. GRITLM (Muennighoff et al., 2024), which utilizes instruction tuning, applies bidirectional attention for embedding tasks and causal attention for generation tasks. However, these methods often require more complex design, potential post-training tasks and rely on much bigger datasets, which is far from simple. To this end, we propose a more efficient and effective method to easily adapt LLMs for high-quality sentence embedding based on causal attention.

2.2 Soft Prompt Tuning in LLMs

Prompts normally refer to the physical tokens additionally provided to the model towards specific tasks (Brown et al., 2020; Zhou et al., 2022; Ouyang et al., 2024). Soft prompt tuning (Lester et al., 2021; Li and Liang, 2021; Liu et al., 2022), which provides virtual tokens (continuous vectors) prepended to the input texts, offers an efficient alternative for fine-tuning LMs. Soft prompt tuning can mitigate overfitting by freezing the model's parameters and updating only the parameters within the soft prompts. Recent works continue to seek for more efficient prompt tuning methods with even fewer parameters (Shi and Lipani, 2024). In the field of sentence embedding, Jiang et al. (2022b) incorporate soft prompts into each layer of the transformer encoder. In contrast, we focus on decoder-only causal attention LLMs and append soft prompts exclusively into the input embedding layer for better efficiency.

3 Methods

CL has become the common practice for learning sentence embeddings with pre-trained LMs (Gao et al., 2021; Wu et al., 2022; Zhao et al., 2024; Miao et al., 2024). It is performed with one anchor sentence, one positive instance and multiple negative instances. Given a sentence X_i, it can be tokenized into $x_1, x_2, ..., x_{|X_i|}$, where $|\cdot|$ denotes the number of tokens in X_i. Our method, SPT, is simple and straightforward. It additionally appends a soft prompt, namely, a few trainable tokens $p = \{p_1, p_2, ..., p_k\}$, to the sentence X_i. This constructs the input as $x_1, x_2, ..., x_{|X_i|}, p_1, p_2, ..., p_k$. Here, k is the length of the soft prompt and the trainable parameters in the soft prompt equal to `[k, hidden_size]`.

Similar to existing methods, the text encoder then transforms X_i into a fixed size dense vector $\mathbf{h}_i$. We use the output of the appended soft prompt for sentence embedding when $k = 1$, and the output of the last soft prompt token p_k as the sentence embedding when $k > 1$.

Our training objective is consistent with previous works. The main idea of CL is to pull the distance between the representation of anchor sentence $\mathbf{h}_i$ and its positive example's representation $\mathbf{h}_i^+$ close while keeping $\mathbf{h}_i$ and other negative examples' representations far away. Moreover, hard negatives (Kalantidis et al., 2020), which are instances that are particularly challenging for models to distinguish from the anchor sentence, are usually adopted to improve CL. We also use the training objective with the aforementioned ideas, as follows:

$$l_i = -\log \frac{e^{sim(\mathbf{h}_i,\mathbf{h}_i^+)/\tau}}{\sum_{j=1}^{N}(e^{sim(\mathbf{h}_i,\mathbf{h}_j^+)/\tau}+e^{sim(\mathbf{h}_i,\mathbf{h}_j^-)/\tau})}, \quad (1)$$

where $sim(\cdot,\cdot)$ is a similarity metric, N is the size of a mini-batch, and τ is the temperature parameter. $\mathbf{h}_i^-$ is the representation of hard negative X_i^- for anchor sentence X_i. The training objective remains the same for LLMs with or without post-training tasks.

4 Experiments

4.1 Experimental Setup

In order to demonstrate the effectiveness of SPT, we conduct experiments across models of three different sizes: base, 7B and 8B. Specifically, for base size models, we choose OPT-125M[2] (Zhang et al., 2022) while for 7B models, LLaMA2-7B[3] (Touvron et al., 2023b) serves as our backbone model. Finally, for 8B models, we select LLaMA3-8B[4]. All of them are decoder-only auto-regressive models whose `hidden_size` is 768 for OPT-125M and 4096 for LLaMA2-7B and LLaMA3-8B. Following (BehnamGhader et al., 2024), we set MNTP as the post-training task.

4.2 Implementation Details

The training dataset we use is the NLI dataset[5] from Gao et al. (2021), which is a supervised dataset containing one positive example and one hard negative example for each anchor sentence with about 275k data examples in total. We use cosine similarity as the similarity metric and τ is set to 0.05 in Equation 1. For SPT, all of our models are trained for one epoch, with evaluation on the development set of STS-B (Cer et al., 2017) and SICK-R (Marelli et al., 2014) conducted every 125 steps to find the best checkpoint. Batch size is set to 32 for all models. Learning rate is grid-searched from {0.02, 0.01, 0.005, 0.001}. Weight decay is set to 0.01 with AdamW optimizer (Loshchilov and Hutter, 2017) implemented for all models. The input sequence length is set to 32 following Gao et al. (2021). All of our experiments for SPT are conducted on one A100 80GB GPU.

[2]https://huggingface.co/facebook/opt-125m

[3]https://huggingface.co/meta-llama/llama-2-7b-chat-hf

[4]https://huggingface.co/meta-llama/Meta-Llama-3-8B

[5]https://huggingface.co/datasets/princeton-nlp/datasets-for-simcse/resolve/main/nli_for_simcse.csv

4.3 Evaluation Tasks

We evaluate our models across a diverse set of tasks, including retrieval, Semantic Textual Similarity (STS), clustering and classification. Considering the input length of the NLI training dataset, we prioritize relatively shorter datasets for evaluation.

Retrieval tasks require the model to identify the most relevant sentence among a large set of documents for a specific given query sentence. The tested model will first transform the query sentences and documents into embeddings and then find the most relevant ones based on metrics such as cosine similarity. We choose the QuoraRetrieval dataset (DataCanary et al., 2017) from the MTEB benchmark (Muennighoff et al., 2023) to evaluate the retrieval performance of our models and report the nDCG@10 metric.

STS tasks evaluate the model's sentence representation ability by calculating the cosine similarity for the two given sentences after transforming them into embeddings. We utilize the SentEval (Conneau and Kiela, 2018) toolkit which includes STS12-16 (Agirre et al., 2012, 2013, 2014, 2015, 2016), STS-B (Cer et al., 2017) and SICK-R (Marelli et al., 2014). Spearman's correlation scores are reported for STS tasks.

Clustering tasks evaluate the models' ability to group sentences based on their semantic similarity, typically across different domains. The model assigns sentences to clusters such that similar sentences are grouped together, without relying on pre-defined labels. To assess our models' clustering performance, we specifically select the Twenty Newsgroup Clustering dataset (Mitchell, 1997) from MTEB and report the Validity Measure (V-measure) metric.

Classification tasks involve training an additional classifier layer on top of the tested model to evaluate its ability to correctly categorize input sentences into predefined classes. In our experiments, we specifically choose the Tweet Sentiment Extraction Classification dataset (Maggie et al., 2020) from MTEB. This task requires the model to identify and classify the sentiment (e.g., positive, negative, neutral) of tweets. Accuracy is reported as the evaluation metric.

4.4 Baselines

We choose several strong baselines and compare them with our models based on the four kinds of evaluation tasks. For base size models, we first choose SimCSE (Gao et al., 2021) as a commonly used encoder-only sentence embedder. Besides, we fully fine-tune OPT-125M under CL objective as a baseline. For larger size models, we first choose LLM2Vec (BehnamGhader et al., 2024) as the SOTA model. Notice that LLM2Vec is post-trained with MNTP and further fine-tuned on a larger dataset, E5 (Wang et al., 2024), using LoRA with an input sequence length of 128. The E5 dataset contains about 1.5m training examples (much bigger than 275k NLI) from different data sources such as retrieval, QA, and ranking. Due to limited computational resources and to ensure a fairer comparison between LLM2Vec and our models, we reproduce LLM2Vec with MNTP post-training using our NLI dataset by initiating from the released checkpoint[6]. Finally, we also fine-tune LLaMA models under CL with LoRA as a general baseline. We specifically set γ=16 and α=32, following settings introduced in BehnamGhader et al. (2024). Implementation details of baselines can be found in Appendix A.1.

4.5 Experimental Results

The performance of various models on four different evaluation tasks is shown in Table 1. We report results using a fixed seed=42 in our main experiments. Details of trainable parameters for each model can be found in Appendix A.2, while full results of seven STS tasks are shown in Appendix A.3.

In Table 1, models-bi. refers to models trained with bi-directional attention after post-training tasks while models-uni indicates those trained on causal attention without additional post-training tasks. The LoRA-bi. equals to LLM2Vec fine-tuned on the same NLI dataset as other models. Except for LoRA-bi., where mean pooling is used as suggested in BehnamGhader et al. (2024), all the other models use the output of the last token as sentence embedding. We will discuss the effect of different pooling methods in Section 5.1. For our SPT, we report two variants for each model: one with a soft prompt length of 1, representing the fewest trainable parameters, and the other with the optimal soft prompt length that achieves the best performance. The process for determining the best length will be discussed in Section 5.2.

Upon observing the results of base size models, we find that the best average score for the four evaluated tasks is given by the fully fine-tuned OPT-125M under CL. While encoder-only models like SimCSE outperform decoder-only models in the traditional STS task, decoder-only models excel SimCSE especially in retrieval and clustering tasks. As for our SPT, it demonstrates competitive performance with SimCSE even with a soft prompt length of just 1, with only a 0.33 point difference in the average scores. Extending the soft prompt length to 16 further narrows the gap (0.2 average performance differences) between our model and the fully fine-tuned OPT-125M under CL, despite our model updating just 0.0098% of the total parameters, compared to 100% in the fully fine-tuned model. Note that the best scores for both retrieval and classification tasks are from our SPT, with a soft prompt length of 16. From the first part of Table 1, we can see that uni-directional models show strong performance at the base size.

As for larger 7B and 8B models, we first focus on the first six rows and observe that the best average performance is achieved by our SPT in uni-directional attention without extra post-training tasks for both LLaMA2-7B and LLaMA3-8B with optimal soft prompt lengths. Their performances consistently outperform the reproduced LLM2Vec models fine-tuned on the NLI dataset (referred as LoRA-bi. in Table 1). Notably, our SPT on LLaMA2-7B with k=16 achieves the highest classification accuracy while SPT on LLaMA3-8B with k=5 delivers the best scores in retrieval, STS and classification across all four tasks. Importantly, SPT with the optimal soft prompt length requires significantly fewer trainable parameters than other baselines, underscoring the effectiveness and efficiency of our approach. Moreover, as observed in the base-sized models, even with just one trainable token (4096 parameters), SPT greatly improves LLMs' sentence embedding capabilities, trailing LoRA-based fine-tuned models by only about 1 point in average score. To this end, simply fine-tuning LLMs using SPT results in comparable or even better performances compared to fine-tuning with more trainable parameters and models with MNTP post-training.

[6]https://huggingface.co/McGill-NLP/LLM2Vec-Llama-2-7b-chat-hf-mntp

Model	Params%	Retrieval	STS	Clustering	Classification	avg.
		Base models (≤ 125M)				
SimCSE	100%	79.62	**81.57**	34.86	59.73	63.95
OPT w/o fine-tuning	0%	18.65	14.23	9.63	43.57	21.52
OPT w/ fine-tuning	100%	81.33	79.69	**39.46**	59.53	**65.00**
OPT w/ SPT (ours)						
-k=1	0.000613%	80.32	78.06	36.61	59.50	63.62
-k=16	0.009812%	**81.39**	78.71	39.21	**59.84**	64.79
		LLaMA2-7B				
w/o fine-tuning	0%	52.93	35.48	11.69	48.39	37.12
LoRA-uni.	0.59%	85.64	**85.24**	**45.97**	61.79	69.66
LoRA-bi.	0.59%	85.24	84.43	44.07	61.30	68.76
SPT-uni. (ours)						
k=1	0.000061%	85.10	83.60	43.25	62.31	68.57
k=16	0.000973%	85.34	84.93	45.74	**62.77**	**69.70**
SPT-bi. (ours)						
-k=1	0.000061%	85.07	83.87	44.07	62.12	68.78
-k=16	0.000973%	**86.01**	84.34	45.48	62.20	69.51
		LLaMA3-8B				
w/o fine-tuning	0%	48.04	28.33	21.91	44.87	35.79
LoRA-uni.	0.56%	86.65	85.87	49.63	62.81	71.24
LoRA-bi.	0.56%	85.78	85.65	47.54	63.46	70.61
SPT-uni. (ours)						
-k=1	0.000051%	85.20	84.32	48.25	62.55	70.08
-k=5	0.000255%	**87.18**	**86.00**	**49.98**	**63.75**	**71.73**
SPT-bi. (ours)						
-k=1	0.000051%	85.47	84.55	48.08	62.34	70.11
-k=5	0.000255%	87.06	85.59	49.37	63.07	71.27

Table 1: Different models' performance on four different evaluation tasks. **Params%** stands for the percentage of trainable parameters in each model. Models-bi. refers to models trained with bi-directional attention after post-training tasks, while models-uni. indicates uni-directional attention models without post-training tasks. LoRA-bi. here equals to LLM2Vec trained on the NLI dataset. We highlight the best result for each task in bold and the second-best result with an underline in each section of the table. Except for results of SimCSE, which are quoted from its paper, other results are from our own implementation.

Next, we focus on the last three rows for LLaMA2-7B and LLaMA3-8B in Table 1. To better demonstrate the advantages of naturally using causal attention, we implement SPT on bi-directional models post-trained with MNTP, referred to as SPT-bi.. In these variants, bi-directional attention is employed during post-training and fine-tuning. Comparing SPT-uni. and SPT-bi., we observe that post-training with MNTP and enabling bi-directional attention does not provide additional benefits over the natural use of causal attention without MNTP training. SPT with only a few trainable tokens on models with MNTP still achieves strong performance, particularly when the soft prompt length k is set to 1. In this case, bi-directional attention with MNTP post-training shows a slightly higher average score than the uni-directional model without MNTP, but the increase is minimal (0.2 for LLaMA2-7B and 0.03 for LLaMA3-8B). However, the better average scores are consistently achieved by SPT w/o MNTP for both LLaMA2-7B and LLaMA3-8B when setting k to the optimal length. Considering the significant extra training efforts required of post-training tasks for LLMs, we move on to discuss the necessity of applying post-training tasks for turning LLMs into text encoders in Section 5.1.

5 Discussion

5.1 Do We Really Need Bi-directional with MNTP Post-training?

In this section, we explore the usage of MNTP post-training, which is designed to help LLMs effectively get adapted to the bi-directional attention mechanism. Notably, enabling bi-directional attention allows us to prepend soft prompts to the input layer. We specifically select LLaMA2-7B and report different variants' performances on the STS task. We compare them based on the attention mechanism, the soft prompt position and the

Methods	Attention	Soft Prompt Length	Soft Prompt Position	Pooling Method	avg STS Scores
			LLaMA2-7B		
	bi	1	append	EOSP	82.74
SPT w/o MNTP	bi	16	append	EOSP	83.77
	bi	10	append	Mean	83.59
	bi	1	prepend	SOSP	82.09
SPT w/o MNTP	bi	20	prepend	SOSP	83.56
	bi	16	prepend	Mean	83.41
	bi	1	append	EOSP	83.87
SPT w/ MNTP	bi	16	append	EOSP	84.34
	bi	16	append	Mean	84.22
	bi	1	prepend	SOSP	83.03
SPT w/ MNTP	bi	10	prepend	SOSP	<u>84.56</u>
	bi	16	prepend	Mean	84.32
	uni	1	append	EOSP	83.60
SPT w/o MNTP	uni	16	append	EOSP	**84.93**
	uni	20	append	Mean	84.60

Table 2: Comparison of models with different attention mechanisms, soft prompt positions and pooling methods. EOSP refers to the end token of soft prompt while SOSP indicates the start token of soft prompt. Mean stands for the average pooling for all soft prompts. Best and second-best scores are highlighted in bold and with underline.

pooling method.

We present the average results of seven STS tasks in Table 2, reporting outcomes for both k=1 and the optimal searched k. For the optimal length k, we also include results from different pooling methods: the output of the last soft prompt token for appending (referred to as EOSP), the output of the first token for prepending (SOSP), and the average pooling of all soft prompts for both appending and prepending (Mean). Notice that the optimal k may vary across different pooling methods.

We first examine the bi-directional models in Table 2 and observe that models with MNTP consistently outperform those without MNTP across different soft prompt positions and pooling methods, a trend that demonstrates the benefits brought by post-training tasks for bi-directional models. However, when compared to our SPT with causal attention and without MNTP post-training, the highest STS score across various soft prompt lengths, positions, and pooling methods is still achieved by our simpler approach. Despite the gains brought by post-training, our results show that SPT with causal attention, without the need for MNTP post-training, can still achieve superior performance on key tasks like STS. This highlights the simplicity of leveraging causal attention naturally, offering competitive results without the added complexity and computational cost of MNTP post-training. Thus, while MNTP enhances bi-directional models, the simplicity and effectiveness of our approach make it a strong alternative for sentence embedding tasks.

5.2 Search for the Optimal Length k

In this section, we explore the effect of the length k for the soft prompts. We range k from {1, 2, 5, 10, 16, 20} and test them with OPT-125m, LLaMA2-7B and LLaMA3-8B on the seven STS tasks. We particularly evaluate the best settings, where causal attention is preserved and soft prompts are appended with no MNTP post-training. As shown in Figure 3 and discussed in former sections, average pooling on soft prompt tokens yields a slightly worse performance compared to using the output of the last token. For both OPT-125m and LLaMA2-7B, the best performance on STS is achieved at k=16, while for LLaMA3-8B, the optimal length is found at k=5. However, when k exceeds a certain threshold, the performance deteriorates, which is a consistent observation as noted by Li and Liang (2021). We will introduce a possible solution on how to involve more trainable parameters in Section 5.3.

5.3 More Trainable Parameters

As discussed in the aforementioned section, the performance of SPT hits its limit when the prompt length k exceeds a particular threshold. However, it is possible to implement more trainable tokens through a variant of soft prompt tuning, which is p-tuning v2 (Liu et al., 2022). Instead of only inserting trainable tokens into the input embedding layer, p-tuning v2 introduces more trainable parameters by inserting trainable tokens into each layer of the model. We specifically choose LLaMA2-7B for p-tuning v2 implementation and evaluate its

Model	Params%	Retrieval	STS	Clustering	Classification	avg.
		LLaMA2-7B				
LoRA-bi.	0.59%	85.24	84.43	44.07	61.30	68.76
LoRA-uni.						
r=1 †	0.04%	85.19	84.86	<u>46.02</u>	60.88	69.24
r=16	0.59%	**85.64**	<u>85.24</u>	45.97	61.79	69.66
SPT-uni. (ours)						
k=1	0.000061%	85.10	83.60	43.25	62.31	68.57
k=16	0.000973%	85.34	84.93	45.74	<u>62.77</u>	<u>69.70</u>
SPT v2-uni. (ours)						
k=1	0.004%	85.39	84.95	45.74	62.50	69.65
k=10	0.039%	<u>85.58</u>	**85.29**	**47.66**	**63.15**	**70.42**

Table 3: Evaluation results of SPT v2. All the models are trained on the same NLI dataset. Models-bi. refers to models trained with bi-directional attention after post-training tasks, while models-uni indicates uni-directional attention models without post-training tasks. The best and second-best results are highlighted in bold and with underline, respectively. To ensure a fair comparison with a similar number of trainable parameters, we reproduced LoRA with r=1†.

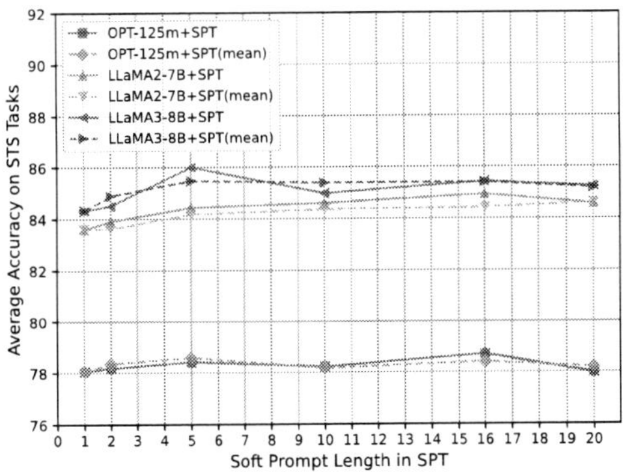

Figure 3: Performance on the STS tasks of models with different pooling methods and k values.

performance on four evaluation tasks. The results are shown in Table 3.

Notice that the official implementation of p-tuning v2[7] achieves this by prepending tokens to the `past_key_values` (one token for key and one token for value in each layer), so the actual number of trainable parameters would be `[2, num_layers, k, hidden_size]`. This method does not alter the number of input tokens. Since we maintain causal attention, we follow Liu et al. (2022) and prepend soft prompts to each layer, while still using the output of the last token as sentence embedding.

As shown in Table 3, by increasing the number of trainable parameters, our SPT v2 models outperform all other baselines fine-tuned on the same NLI dataset. Notably, our SPT v2 with k=10 achieves the best performance in three out of the four evaluated tasks, even surpassing the strong LoRA-based fine-tuned models. We reproduced LoRA with r=1, as it has nearly the same number of trainable parameters as our SPT v2 with k=10. These results demonstrate that implementing p-tuning v2 with SPT can achieve higher performance than LoRA-based fine-tuning, while requiring fewer trainable parameters. This highlights the simplicity and effectiveness of our approach in optimizing model performance with minimal parameter overhead.

6 Conclusion

In this work, we first investigate a simple method to adapt LLMs for sentence embedding by tuning a few learnable tokens. We append trainable tokens to the inputs and utilize the output of the last one as the sentence embedding. Our approach can achieve the adaptation with less than 0.001% trainable parameters, which is unattainable with LoRA. Experimental results on various tasks demonstrate that only a few tokens with our approach can achieve competitive performance with fine-tuning with LoRA. Moreover, we also find that directly using causal attention in decoder-only LLMs is capable of adapting them for sentence embedding. Specifically, our simple method with causal attention outperforms bi-directional attention baselines with extra post-training tasks, offering insights on the adaptation of LLMs for sentence embedding.

[7]https://github.com/THUDM/P-tuning-v2

Limitations

In this work, we demonstrate the effectiveness of using soft prompts for sentence representation in LLMs. However, whether this kind of adaptation works in other tasks remains unclear. The optimal soft prompt length relies on various factors, including the training dataset and model size, which require extra searches. Also, the multilingual scenario could be taken into consideration.

Ethics Statement

This paper aims at adapting LLMs for sentence representation with low cost. All the data and models we used are publicly open-sourced and contain no privacy-related ones. We agree to the license and privacy policy of the corresponding models and datasets. We try to make a positive contribution to the community. Our work does not introduce ethical biases as well. We use ChatGPT to check the grammar in our writing.

Acknowledgment

Kaiyan Zhao was supported by JST SPRING, Grant Number JPMJSP2108.

References

Eneko Agirre, Carmen Banea, Claire Cardie, Daniel Cer, Mona Diab, Aitor Gonzalez-Agirre, Weiwei Guo, Iñigo Lopez-Gazpio, Montse Maritxalar, Rada Mihalcea, German Rigau, Larraitz Uria, and Janyce Wiebe. 2015. SemEval-2015 task 2: Semantic textual similarity, English, Spanish and pilot on interpretability. In *Proceedings of the 9th International Workshop on Semantic Evaluation (SemEval 2015)*, pages 252–263, Denver, Colorado. Association for Computational Linguistics.

Eneko Agirre, Carmen Banea, Claire Cardie, Daniel Cer, Mona Diab, Aitor Gonzalez-Agirre, Weiwei Guo, Rada Mihalcea, German Rigau, and Janyce Wiebe. 2014. SemEval-2014 task 10: Multilingual semantic textual similarity. In *Proceedings of the 8th International Workshop on Semantic Evaluation (SemEval 2014)*, pages 81–91, Dublin, Ireland. Association for Computational Linguistics.

Eneko Agirre, Carmen Banea, Daniel Cer, Mona Diab, Aitor Gonzalez-Agirre, Rada Mihalcea, German Rigau, and Janyce Wiebe. 2016. SemEval-2016 task 1: Semantic textual similarity, monolingual and cross-lingual evaluation. In *Proceedings of the 10th International Workshop on Semantic Evaluation (SemEval-2016)*, pages 497–511, San Diego, California. Association for Computational Linguistics.

Eneko Agirre, Daniel Cer, Mona Diab, and Aitor Gonzalez-Agirre. 2012. SemEval-2012 task 6: A pilot on semantic textual similarity. In **SEM 2012: The First Joint Conference on Lexical and Computational Semantics – Volume 1: Proceedings of the main conference and the shared task, and Volume 2: Proceedings of the Sixth International Workshop on Semantic Evaluation (SemEval 2012)*, pages 385–393, Montréal, Canada. Association for Computational Linguistics.

Eneko Agirre, Daniel Cer, Mona Diab, Aitor Gonzalez-Agirre, and Weiwei Guo. 2013. *SEM 2013 shared task: Semantic textual similarity. In *Second Joint Conference on Lexical and Computational Semantics (*SEM), Volume 1: Proceedings of the Main Conference and the Shared Task: Semantic Textual Similarity*, pages 32–43, Atlanta, Georgia, USA. Association for Computational Linguistics.

Parishad BehnamGhader, Vaibhav Adlakha, Marius Mosbach, Dzmitry Bahdanau, Nicolas Chapados, and Siva Reddy. 2024. LLM2vec: Large language models are secretly powerful text encoders. In *First Conference on Language Modeling*.

Tom Brown, Benjamin Mann, Nick Ryder, Melanie Subbiah, Jared D Kaplan, Prafulla Dhariwal, Arvind Neelakantan, Pranav Shyam, Girish Sastry, Amanda Askell, Sandhini Agarwal, Ariel Herbert-Voss, Gretchen Krueger, Tom Henighan, Rewon Child, Aditya Ramesh, Daniel Ziegler, Jeffrey Wu, Clemens Winter, Chris Hesse, Mark Chen, Eric Sigler, Mateusz Litwin, Scott Gray, Benjamin Chess, Jack Clark, Christopher Berner, Sam McCandlish, Alec Radford, Ilya Sutskever, and Dario Amodei. 2020. Language models are few-shot learners. In *Advances in Neural Information Processing Systems*, volume 33, pages 1877–1901. Curran Associates, Inc.

Daniel Cer, Mona Diab, Eneko Agirre, Iñigo Lopez-Gazpio, and Lucia Specia. 2017. SemEval-2017 task 1: Semantic textual similarity multilingual and crosslingual focused evaluation. In *Proceedings of the 11th International Workshop on Semantic Evaluation (SemEval-2017)*, pages 1–14, Vancouver, Canada. Association for Computational Linguistics.

Yung-Sung Chuang, Rumen Dangovski, Hongyin Luo, Yang Zhang, Shiyu Chang, Marin Soljacic, Shang-Wen Li, Scott Yih, Yoon Kim, and James Glass. 2022. DiffCSE: Difference-based contrastive learning for sentence embeddings. In *Proceedings of the 2022 Conference of the North American Chapter of the Association for Computational Linguistics: Human Language Technologies*, pages 4207–4218, Seattle, United States. Association for Computational Linguistics.

Alexis Conneau and Douwe Kiela. 2018. SentEval: An evaluation toolkit for universal sentence representations. In *Proceedings of the Eleventh International Conference on Language Resources and Evaluation (LREC 2018)*, Miyazaki, Japan. European Language Resources Association (ELRA).

Alexis Conneau, Douwe Kiela, Holger Schwenk, Loïc Barrault, and Antoine Bordes. 2017. Supervised learning of universal sentence representations from natural language inference data. In *Proceedings of the 2017 Conference on Empirical Methods in Natural Language Processing*, pages 670–680, Copenhagen, Denmark. Association for Computational Linguistics.

DataCanary, hilfialkaff, Jiang Lili, Risdal Meg, Dandekar Nikhil, and tomtung. 2017. Quora question pairs.

Tianyu Gao, Xingcheng Yao, and Danqi Chen. 2021. Simcse: Simple contrastive learning of sentence embeddings. In *Conference on Empirical Methods in Natural Language Processing*.

Edward J Hu, Yelong Shen, Phillip Wallis, Zeyuan Allen-Zhu, Yuanzhi Li, Shean Wang, Lu Wang, and Weizhu Chen. 2022. LoRA: Low-rank adaptation of large language models. In *International Conference on Learning Representations*.

Ting Jiang, Shaohan Huang, Zhongzhi Luan, Deqing Wang, and Fuzhen Zhuang. 2023. Scaling sentence embeddings with large language models. *Preprint*, arXiv:2307.16645.

Ting Jiang, Jian Jiao, Shaohan Huang, Zihan Zhang, Deqing Wang, Fuzhen Zhuang, Furu Wei, Haizhen Huang, Denvy Deng, and Qi Zhang. 2022a. PromptBERT: Improving BERT sentence embeddings with prompts. In *Proceedings of the 2022 Conference on Empirical Methods in Natural Language Processing*, pages 8826–8837, Abu Dhabi, United Arab Emirates. Association for Computational Linguistics.

Yuxin Jiang, Linhan Zhang, and Wei Wang. 2022b. Improved universal sentence embeddings with prompt-based contrastive learning and energy-based learning. In *Findings of the Association for Computational Linguistics: EMNLP 2022*, pages 3021–3035, Abu Dhabi, United Arab Emirates. Association for Computational Linguistics.

Yannis Kalantidis, Mert Bulent Sariyildiz, Noe Pion, Philippe Weinzaepfel, and Diane Larlus. 2020. Hard negative mixing for contrastive learning. *Advances in Neural Information Processing Systems*, 33:21798–21809.

Brian Lester, Rami Al-Rfou, and Noah Constant. 2021. The power of scale for parameter-efficient prompt tuning. In *Proceedings of the 2021 Conference on Empirical Methods in Natural Language Processing*, pages 3045–3059, Online and Punta Cana, Dominican Republic. Association for Computational Linguistics.

Xiang Lisa Li and Percy Liang. 2021. Prefix-tuning: Optimizing continuous prompts for generation. In *Proceedings of the 59th Annual Meeting of the Association for Computational Linguistics and the 11th International Joint Conference on Natural Language Processing (Volume 1: Long Papers)*, pages 4582–4597, Online. Association for Computational Linguistics.

Xianming Li and Jing Li. 2023. Angle-optimized text embeddings. *Preprint*, arXiv:2309.12871.

Xianming Li and Jing Li. 2024. BeLLM: Backward dependency enhanced large language model for sentence embeddings. In *Proceedings of the 2024 Conference of the North American Chapter of the Association for Computational Linguistics: Human Language Technologies (Volume 1: Long Papers)*, pages 792–804, Mexico City, Mexico. Association for Computational Linguistics.

Xiao Liu, Kaixuan Ji, Yicheng Fu, Weng Tam, Zhengxiao Du, Zhilin Yang, and Jie Tang. 2022. P-tuning: Prompt tuning can be comparable to fine-tuning across scales and tasks. In *Proceedings of the 60th Annual Meeting of the Association for Computational Linguistics (Volume 2: Short Papers)*, pages 61–68, Dublin, Ireland. Association for Computational Linguistics.

Ilya Loshchilov and Frank Hutter. 2017. Decoupled weight decay regularization. In *International Conference on Learning Representations*.

Ang Lv, Kaiyi Zhang, Shufang Xie, Quan Tu, Yuhan Chen, Ji-Rong Wen, and Rui Yan. 2023. Are we falling in a middle-intelligence trap? an analysis and mitigation of the reversal curse. *arXiv preprint arXiv:2311.07468*.

Maggie, Culliton Phil, and Chen Wei. 2020. Tweet sentiment extraction.

Marco Marelli, Stefano Menini, Marco Baroni, Luisa Bentivogli, Raffaella Bernardi, and Roberto Zamparelli. 2014. A SICK cure for the evaluation of compositional distributional semantic models. In *Proceedings of the Ninth International Conference on Language Resources and Evaluation (LREC'14)*, pages 216–223, Reykjavik, Iceland. European Language Resources Association (ELRA).

Zhongtao Miao, Qiyu Wu, Kaiyan Zhao, Zilong Wu, and Yoshimasa Tsuruoka. 2024. Enhancing cross-lingual sentence embedding for low-resource languages with word alignment. In *Findings of the Association for Computational Linguistics: NAACL 2024*, pages 3225–3236, Mexico City, Mexico. Association for Computational Linguistics.

Tom Mitchell. 1997. Twenty Newsgroups. UCI Machine Learning Repository. DOI: https://doi.org/10.24432/C5C323.

Niklas Muennighoff, Hongjin Su, Liang Wang, Nan Yang, Furu Wei, Tao Yu, Amanpreet Singh, and Douwe Kiela. 2024. Generative representational instruction tuning. *arXiv preprint arXiv:2402.09906*.

Niklas Muennighoff, Nouamane Tazi, Loic Magne, and Nils Reimers. 2023. MTEB: Massive text embedding benchmark. In *Proceedings of the 17th Conference of the European Chapter of the Association for Computational Linguistics*, pages 2014–2037, Dubrovnik, Croatia. Association for Computational Linguistics.

OpenAI. 2022. Introducing chatgpt. `https://openai.com/blog/chatgpt`.

OpenAI. 2023. Gpt-4 technical report.

Liangyang Ouyang, Ruicong Liu, Yifei Huang, Ryosuke Furuta, and Yoichi Sato. 2024. Actionvos: Actions as prompts for video object segmentation. *arXiv preprint arXiv:2407.07402*.

Nils Reimers and Iryna Gurevych. 2019. Sentence-bert: Sentence embeddings using siamese bert-networks. In *Conference on Empirical Methods in Natural Language Processing*.

Zhengxiang Shi and Aldo Lipani. 2024. Dept: Decomposed prompt tuning for parameter-efficient finetuning. In *International Conference on Learning Representations*.

Hugo Touvron, Thibaut Lavril, Gautier Izacard, Xavier Martinet, Marie-Anne Lachaux, Timothée Lacroix, Baptiste Rozière, Naman Goyal, Eric Hambro, Faisal Azhar, Aurelien Rodriguez, Armand Joulin, Edouard Grave, and Guillaume Lample. 2023a. Llama: Open and efficient foundation language models. *ArXiv*, abs/2302.13971.

Hugo Touvron, Louis Martin, Kevin R. Stone, Peter Albert, Amjad Almahairi, Yasmine Babaei, Nikolay Bashlykov, Soumya Batra, Prajjwal Bhargava, Shruti Bhosale, Daniel M. Bikel, Lukas Blecher, Cristian Cantón Ferrer, Moya Chen, Guillem Cucurull, David Esiobu, Jude Fernandes, Jeremy Fu, Wenyin Fu, Brian Fuller, Cynthia Gao, Vedanuj Goswami, Naman Goyal, Anthony S. Hartshorn, Saghar Hosseini, Rui Hou, Hakan Inan, Marcin Kardas, Viktor Kerkez, Madian Khabsa, Isabel M. Kloumann, A. V. Korenev, Punit Singh Koura, Marie-Anne Lachaux, Thibaut Lavril, Jenya Lee, Diana Liskovich, Yinghai Lu, Yuning Mao, Xavier Martinet, Todor Mihaylov, Pushkar Mishra, Igor Molybog, Yixin Nie, Andrew Poulton, Jeremy Reizenstein, Rashi Rungta, Kalyan Saladi, Alan Schelten, Ruan Silva, Eric Michael Smith, R. Subramanian, Xia Tan, Binh Tang, Ross Taylor, Adina Williams, Jian Xiang Kuan, Puxin Xu, Zhengxu Yan, Iliyan Zarov, Yuchen Zhang, Angela Fan, Melanie Kambadur, Sharan Narang, Aurelien Rodriguez, Robert Stojnic, Sergey Edunov, and Thomas Scialom. 2023b. Llama 2: Open foundation and fine-tuned chat models. *ArXiv*, abs/2307.09288.

Aäron van den Oord, Yazhe Li, and Oriol Vinyals. 2018. Representation learning with contrastive predictive coding. *ArXiv*, abs/1807.03748.

Liang Wang, Nan Yang, Xiaolong Huang, Binxing Jiao, Linjun Yang, Daxin Jiang, Rangan Majumder, and Furu Wei. 2024. Text embeddings by weakly-supervised contrastive pre-training. *Preprint*, arXiv:2212.03533.

Ledell Wu, Adam Fisch, Sumit Chopra, Keith Adams, Antoine Bordes, and Jason Weston. 2018. Starspace: Embed all the things! In *Proceedings of the AAAI conference on artificial intelligence*, volume 32.

Qiyu Wu, Chongyang Tao, Tao Shen, Can Xu, Xiubo Geng, and Daxin Jiang. 2022. PCL: Peer-contrastive learning with diverse augmentations for unsupervised sentence embeddings. In *Proceedings of the 2022 Conference on Empirical Methods in Natural Language Processing*, pages 12052–12066, Abu Dhabi, United Arab Emirates. Association for Computational Linguistics.

Susan Zhang, Stephen Roller, Naman Goyal, Mikel Artetxe, Moya Chen, Shuohui Chen, Christopher Dewan, Mona T. Diab, Xian Li, Xi Victoria Lin, Todor Mihaylov, Myle Ott, Sam Shleifer, Kurt Shuster, Daniel Simig, Punit Singh Koura, Anjali Sridhar, Tianlu Wang, and Luke Zettlemoyer. 2022. Opt: Open pre-trained transformer language models. *ArXiv*, abs/2205.01068.

Kaiyan Zhao, Qiyu Wu, Xin-Qiang Cai, and Yoshimasa Tsuruoka. 2024. Leveraging multi-lingual positive instances in contrastive learning to improve sentence embedding. In *Proceedings of the 18th Conference of the European Chapter of the Association for Computational Linguistics (Volume 1: Long Papers)*, pages 976–991, St. Julian's, Malta. Association for Computational Linguistics.

Kaiyang Zhou, Jingkang Yang, Chen Change Loy, and Ziwei Liu. 2022. Learning to prompt for vision-language models. *International Journal of Computer Vision*, 130(9):2337–2348.

A Appendix

A.1 Baseline Implementation Details

We introduce the implementation details for baseline reproduction in this section. For baselines directly fine-tuned with Low-Rank Adaptation (LoRA), we follow the implementation introduced in Jiang et al. (2023), with the modification of changing the batch size to 32 and evaluating the model every 125 steps on the development set (compared to 50 steps in the original paper). α is consistently set to 16. We do not include the proposed PromptEOL method in Jiang et al. (2023) for a fairer comparison and utilize the output of the last input token as the sentence embedding. The baseline reproduction is carried out on two A100 80GB GPUs.

For other baselines with Masked Next Token Prediction (MNTP) post-training, we initiate the models from the released checkpoint, while training with SPT follows the settings introduced in Section 4.2.

A.2 Details of Trainable Parameters

We count the trainable parameters based on PEFT library [8]. The number of trainable parameters, total parameters and the percentage of trainable parameters for each model are shown in Table 4. The hidden state size for OPT-125M and LLaMA is 768 and 4096, respectively.

Model	**Trainable Param**	**Total Param**	**Percentage**
OPT-125M + CL	125239296	125239296	100%
OPT-125M + SPT, k=1	768	125240064	0.00061%
OPT-125M + SPT, k=16	12288	125251584	0.0098%
LLaMA2 + LoRA r=1	2498560	6740914176	0.04%
LLaMA2 + LoRA r=16	39976960	6778392576	0.59%
LLaMA2 + LLM2Vec r=16	39976960	6778392576	0.59%
LLaMA2 + SPT, k=1	4096	6738419712	0.000061%
LLaMA2 + SPT, k=2	8192	6738423808	0.00012%
LLaMA2 + SPT, k=5	20480	6738436096	0.0003%
LLaMA2 + SPT, k=10	40960	6738456576	0.00061%
LLaMA2 + SPT, k=16	65536	6738481152	0.00097%
LLaMA2 + SPT, k=20	81920	6738497536	0.0012%
LLaMA2 + SPT v2, k=1	262144	6738677760	0.004%
LLaMA2 + SPT v2, k=10	2621440	6741037056	0.04%
LLaMA3 + LoRA, r=16	45088768	8075350016	0.56%
LLaMA3 + LLM2Vec, r=16	45088768	8075350016	0.56%
LLaMA3 + SPT, k=1	4096	8030265344	0.000051%
LLaMA3 + SPT, k=2	8192	8030269440	0.00001%
LLaMA3 + SPT, k=5	20480	8030281728	0.00026%
LLaMA3 + SPT, k=10	40960	8030302208	0.00051%
LLaMA3 + SPT, k=16	65536	8030326784	0.0008%
LLaMA3 + SPT, k=20	81920	8030343168	0.001%

Table 4: Comparison of trainable parameters.

[8] https://huggingface.co/docs/peft/main/en/index

A.3 Full STS Results

We show full results on seven STS tasks in Table 5.

Model	STS12	STS13	STS14	STS15	STS16	STS-B	SICK-R	avg.
				Base models (≤ 125M)				
SimCSE	75.30	84.67	80.19	85.40	80.82	84.25	80.39	81.57
OPT w/o fine-tuning †	7.47	9.48	8.30	19.63	22.45	7.40	24.91	14.23
OPT w/ fine-tuning	73.80	81.97	77.58	83.42	79.50	83.05	78.51	79.69
OPT w/ SPT, k=1 **(ours)**	71.72	80.92	74.66	82.77	79.87	81.41	75.09	78.06
OPT w/ SPT, k=16 **(ours)**	73.43	81.03	75.57	82.73	79.26	82.33	76.60	78.71
				LLaMA2-7B				
w/o fine-tuning †	22.30	30.92	27.10	38.92	52.95	33.66	42.54	35.48
LoRA w/o MNTP, r=16	78.29	89.11	84.26	88.97	85.36	87.83	82.34	85.24
LoRA w/ MNTP (LLM2Vec, NLI)	78.01	87.96	83.06	88.45	85.51	87.57	80.44	85.24
SPT w/o MNTP, k=1 **(ours)**	75.46	87.91	82.84	87.00	84.66	87.15	80.16	83.60
SPT w/o MNTP, k=16 **(ours)**	76.53	89.12	83.26	89.21	85.21	88.34	82.86	84.93
SPT w/ MNTP, k=1 **(ours)**	76.60	87.70	81.97	88.38	84.07	87.35	81.00	83.87
SPT w/ MNTP, k=16 **(ours)**	76.13	88.54	82.69	88.82	85.12	87.80	81.29	84.34
				LLaMA3-8B				
w/o fine-tuning †	10.35	38.69	24.72	34.55	37.46	23.07	29.49	28.33
LoRA w/o MNTP, r=16	79.04	89.66	85.95	89.41	85.96	88.54	82.57	85.87
LoRA w/ MNTP (LLM2Vec, NLI)	78.59	89.67	85.40	89.83	85.16	88.41	82.46	85.65
SPT w/o MNTP, k=1 **(ours)**	75.20	88.79	83.60	88.60	84.15	87.82	82.05	84.32
SPT w/o MNTP, k=5 **(ours)**	78.61	90.23	85.10	89.53	86.87	89.33	82.38	86.00
SPT w/ MNTP, k=1 **(ours)**	76.59	88.11	84.16	88.97	85.16	87.03	81.87	84.55
SPT w/ MNTP, k=5 **(ours)**	78.74	89.63	84.72	89.30	86.04	87.92	82.81	85.59

Table 5: Full results of seven STS tasks. † marks models without further training, for which we take the output of last input token as sentence embedding. Results with * are quoted from the MTEB leaderboard (Muennighoff et al., 2023). Results of SimCSE is quoted from its paper.

Cross-Modal Learning for Music-to-Music-Video Description Generation

Zhuoyuan Mao[1] **Mengjie Zhao**[1] **Qiyu Wu**[1] **Zhi Zhong**[1]
Wei-Hsiang Liao[2] **Hiromi Wakaki**[1] **Yuki Mitsufuji**[1,2]
[1]Sony Group Corporation [2]Sony AI
{zhuoyuan.mao, mengjie.zhao, qiyu.wu, zhi.zhong
weihsiang.liao, hiromi.wakaki, yuhki.mitsufuji}@sony.com

Abstract

Music-to-music-video generation is a challenging task due to the intrinsic differences between the music and video modalities. The advent of powerful text-to-video diffusion models has opened a promising pathway for music-video (MV) generation by first addressing the music-to-MV description task and subsequently leveraging these models for video generation. In this study, we focus on the MV description generation task and propose a comprehensive pipeline encompassing training data construction and multimodal model fine-tuning. We fine-tune existing pre-trained multimodal models on our newly constructed music-to-MV description dataset based on the Music4All dataset, which integrates both musical and visual information. Our experimental results demonstrate that music representations can be effectively mapped to textual domains, enabling the generation of meaningful MV description directly from music inputs. We also identify key components in the dataset construction pipeline that critically impact the quality of MV description and highlight specific musical attributes that warrant greater focus for improved MV description generation.

1 Introduction

Generating a music-video (MV) to match a given piece of music is a challenging task due to the inherent differences between the music and video modalities. Despite the challenges, MV generation holds significant potential for enhancing the music experience by providing a visual narrative that aligns with the music's tone, style, and mood, offering a more immersive and engaging way for audiences to connect with the music. Compared to generating music or audio from a given video (Tian et al., 2024; Kang et al., 2024), the reverse task is more complex, as the video modality typically conveys richer spatial and temporal information than music. However, with the advent of text-to-video diffusion models (Yang et al., 2024; Polyak et al., 2024; Kong et al., 2024), videos can now be generated from textual descriptions. This development enables MV generation to be divided into two subtasks: (1) music-to-MV description generation and (2) MV description-to-MV generation. As illustrated in Fig. 1, MV descriptions can be further refined using large language models (LLMs) like GPT (OpenAI, 2023) to fit specific text-to-video models (Khachatryan et al., 2023). *In this study, we focus on the first task: generating MV descriptions from music.*

To this end, we propose a practical pipeline for data construction and model training to generate meaningful MV descriptions based on music inputs. Additionally, we explore methods to enhance the alignment of the generated descriptions to the given music. Specifically, we investigate the impact of various data sources—such as music, music genre tags, MV type tags, and lyrics understanding text—on the quality of the generated MV descriptions when fine-tuning multimodal LLMs like NExT-GPT (Wu et al., 2024). As shown in Fig. 1, our approach first leverages existing music understanding models (Zhao et al., 2024; Mao et al., 2025) to extract lyrics understanding text. We then fine-tune a multimodal LLM to process these diverse inputs and generate MV descriptions. The training data is constructed from gold-standard MVs, incorporating music-related information to enhance the connection between music and the generated descriptions. Unlike prior studies on MV generation, such as ViPE (Shahmohammadi et al., 2023), which focused solely on lyrics as input, our work emphasizes leveraging multiple modalities and evaluates the effectiveness of various combinations of input data in connecting multimodal representations for MV description generation.

To facilitate this study, we construct a music-to-MV description training and evaluation dataset using the Music4All dataset (Santana et al., 2020).

Proceedings of the 10th Workshop on Representation Learning for NLP (RepL4NLP-2025), pages 51–58
May 4, 2025

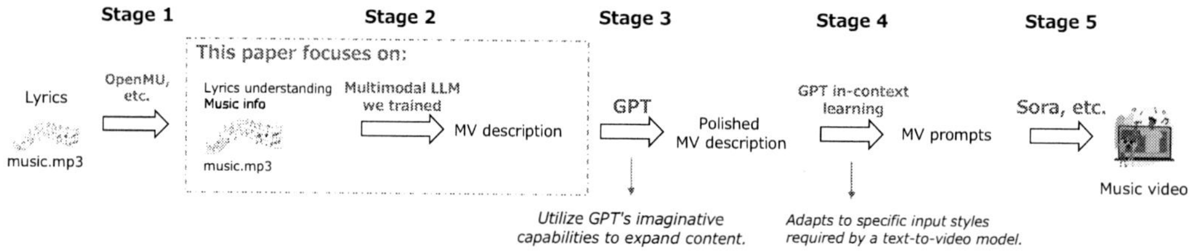

Figure 1: **Pipeline of music-to-MV generation.** We focus on multimodal model training of Stage 2 in this study.

Empirical results on the NExT-GPT baseline and multimodal LLMs fine-tuned with our dataset demonstrate that meaningful MV descriptions can be generated from music and music-related textual inputs after multimodal fine-tuning. An ablation study on different combinations of input sources, including music, music genre tags, MV type tags, and lyrics understanding text, reveals that music and MV type tags are key components for high-quality MV description generation. While music genre tags and lyrics understanding text also contribute positively, they can be used interchangeably. Our findings can contribute to future study on enhancing MV descriptions and temporal alignment between music, lyrics, and the generated MV.

2 Proposed Method

In this section, we present the pipeline proposed for training a multimodal LLM specifically tailored to the music-to-MV description generation task. For the first time, our pipeline incorporates a broader range of musical information beyond lyrics as inputs, aiming to enrich the holistic understanding of the music. Additionally, we introduce strategies to ensure the generated MV descriptions are more closely aligned with the musical inputs. The curated dataset is then utilized to fine-tune a multimodal LLM for performing the MV description generation task.

2.1 Data Construction

This section outlines our proposed pipeline for constructing training and evaluation datasets for the music-to-MV description generation task.

2.1.1 MV Datasets

We construct our datasets based on the Music4All dataset (Santana et al., 2020), which comprises approximately 100k music clips paired with corresponding MVs and enriched with metadata such as energy, valence, and genre. To enhance the dataset, we leverage the OpenMU model (Zhao et al., 2024) to generate lyrics understanding text for all music clips in Music4All. This process effectively interprets the lyrics for each piece of music, providing concise textual information related to the lyrics. Additionally, we filter out MVs that consist solely of static images rather than actual video footage. After filtering, the final dataset includes $56,446$ samples, $55,000$ for training and $1,446$ for testing.

2.1.2 Construction of Input Data for Music and Associated Information

After preparing the training and evaluation splits of music clips, MVs, lyrics understanding text, and metadata from the Music4All dataset, we curate various data types as inputs for the MV description generation task. To incorporate richer musical information across different modalities, we include music genre tags and lyrics understanding text as inputs in addition to the music clips. Moreover, to refine the output MV descriptions and make the task less open-ended, we specify the style of the output by providing MV type tags. These tags are assigned to the MV clips using GPT-4o mini (OpenAI, 2023) and include ten category candidates: Live Performance, Lyric Video, Animation, Story Narrative, Artistic/Abstract, Dance Performance, Behind-the-Scenes, Nature/Scenic, Static/Dynamic Picture Montage, and Cinematic Drama.[1]

As shown in Fig. 2, the four types of inputs are used to train the multimodal LLM, guided by a fixed instruction: "Generate a concise video prompt that captures the essence of the MV, incorporating the music's tone, style, and lyrical themes. The prompt should reflect the specified MV type and align with the music genre to ensure stylistic coherence for guiding a text-to-video model."

2.1.3 Construction of Output Data for MV Description

The output MV descriptions should provide rich content detailing the visual elements of the MV

[1]Generated based on suggestions from GPT-4o mini.

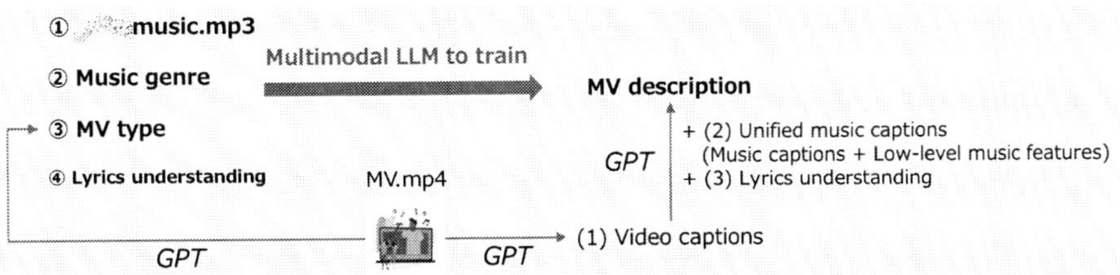

Input:
① **Music:** <Audio>
② **Music Genre:** Underground Hip Hop
③ **MV Type (The type or style of MV to create):** Artistic/Abstract, Cinematic Drama
④ **Lyrics Understanding:** I think the song is about being optimistic in a "world of riffraff". It's about the mess that the world is in, but he still tries to be positive and do something about it, and he's asking everyone else to do the same. He says that everyone should be "bleeding or healing" instead of just "eating all our feelings with guilt after the fact". We should do something instead of just feeling bad about everything that's wrong in the world. ...

Instruction:
Generate a concise video prompt that captures the essence of the MV, incorporating the music's tone, style, and lyrical themes. The prompt should reflect the specified MV type and align with the music genre to ensure stylistic coherence for guiding a text-to-video model.

Output (MV description):
Overview
A mesmerizing journey through duality and introspection unfolds in this surreal music video. The brisk tempo mirrors the energetic yet contemplative soundscape, navigating between rich harmonies and softer reflective moments. The thoughtful interplay of organic and geometric visuals, complemented by shifting color tones, creates an immersive experience that invites deeper engagement with themes of transformation and optimism amidst chaos.

Frame-by-frame Breakdown
1. **Blurred Reflection**: Begin with a soft, abstract blur, setting an enigmatic tone that hints at duality.
2. **Obscured Humanity**: Introduce a warm, human form partially hidden, symbolizing vulnerability and connection.
...

Figure 2: Process for creating music-to-MV description training datasets (top) and an example of utilizing the generated data to train music-to-text LLMs (bottom).

while remaining closely tied to musical features, such as tempo, downbeats, and high-level characteristics like the mood conveyed by the music. To achieve this, we first utilize GPT-4o mini to caption MV clips and extract relevant visual contexts. Next, we refine these captions using GPT-4o mini again, integrating key musical features, including music captions, low-level musical attributes, and lyrics understanding. Music captions and lyrics understanding texts are generated using the OpenMU music understanding model, while low-level musical features are extracted with open-source tools (Böck et al., 2016), following the methodology of LLark (Gardner et al., 2024). The constructed MV description dataset includes two main components: an overview and a frame-by-frame breakdown, with frame captions extracted at two-second intervals for each 30-second MV clip. Examples of music captions, low-level music features, and a complete version of an MV description are provided in Appendix A.

2.2 Multimodal Model Training

We utilize NExT-GPT (Wu et al., 2024), an any-to-any multimodal training framework, to fine-tune our model using the constructed music-to-MV description datasets. Following NExT-GPT's methodology, the fine-tuning process is divided into multiple stages. In the first stage, we fine-tune only the adaptor between the ImageBind (Girdhar et al., 2023) encoder and the Vicuna LLM (Zheng et al., 2023) utilizing the music captioning task. In the second stage, we simultaneously fine-tune the adaptor and apply LoRA (Hu et al., 2022) fine-tuning to Vicuna with the constructed music-to-MV description dataset. As illustrated in Fig. 2, the input data including the music clip is sequentially formatted, followed by a fixed instruction. The model is trained to generate MV descriptions comprising an overall summary and frame-by-frame breakdowns. We fine-tune for 5 and 2 epochs in the first and second stages, respectively, utilizing a learning rate of 1e−4 and a batch size of 2. Training is conducted on 2 NVIDIA A6000 GPUs. For LoRA, the rank and alpha are both set to 32, following NExT-GPT.

Model	BLEU-1	BLEU	ROUGE-P	ROUGE-R	ROUGE-F1	BERT-P	BERT-R	BERT-F1
Baseline								
NExT-GPT (Wu et al., 2024)	8.3	0.2	20.7	9.2	11.8	80.9	76.5	78.6
Main results								
①+②+③+④	**42.9**	**14.6**	**22.9**	**23.2**	**22.7**	**87.4**	**86.4**	**86.9**
Ablation study								
②+③+④	42.5	14.4	22.4	22.8	22.3	87.2	86.2	86.7
①+②+③	**43.6**	**14.7**	**23.0**	**23.5**	**22.9**	**87.4**	**86.7**	**87.0**
①+③+④	**42.8**	**14.5**	**22.8**	**23.2**	**22.7**	**87.3**	**86.4**	**86.9**
①+②+④	42.2	14.1	21.7	22.5	21.8	86.9	86.2	86.5
②+③	41.8	14.0	21.8	22.4	21.8	87.2	86.1	86.6
①+③	42.4	14.4	22.3	22.8	22.2	87.2	86.2	86.6
①+④	41.3	13.8	21.4	22.4	21.6	86.8	86.0	86.4
Sanity check (w/o inputs, solely w/ instructions during inference)								
①+②+③+④	39.3	13.2	20.2	22.5	21.0	85.8	85.6	85.7
①+④	39.7	12.5	20.3	20.8	20.3	86.1	85.6	85.9

Table 1: Results of MV description generation on the Music4All dataset. We provide BLEU-1 and BLEU-4 scores for BLEU, along with precision, recall, and F1 scores for both ROUGE-L and BERT-score. ①, ②, ③, and ④ represent music, music genre tags, MV type tags, and lyrics understanding text, respectively. The top three values in each metric are highlighted in **bold**.

3 Evaluation

Using the 1,446 test samples from our constructed dataset, we evaluate the generated MV descriptions with BLEU (Papineni et al., 2002), ROUGE-L (Lin, 2004), and BERT-score (Zhang et al., 2020), considering different combinations of inputs: ① music, ② music genre tags, ③ MV type tags, and ④ lyrics understanding text. Additionally, we present several MV frames generated by Text2Video-Zero (Khachatryan et al., 2023) to test the feasibility of the entire proposed MV generation pipeline in Appendix B, using the ground-truth MV descriptions annotated by us as input.

3.1 Main Results

As shown in Table 1, our proposed pipeline for music-to-MV description generation achieves significant improvements over the NExT-GPT baseline after fine-tuning for a specific music domain. This demonstrates that, with the proposed datasets and pipeline, music can be effectively mapped to the text domain. Comparing the main results with sanity checks that remove all inputs during inference (leaving only a fixed instruction), we observe that our carefully designed inputs for music-related information substantially contribute to the quality of the generated MV descriptions. Interestingly, after training, the model can generate reasonable MV descriptions even without any inputs, suggesting that the NExT-GPT model successfully adapts to the MV description generation downstream task.

3.2 Ablation Study

Through an ablation study exploring different combinations of data sources, we find that settings ①+②+③ and ①+③+④ achieve comparable or even slightly better performance to the full data combination (①+②+③+④). This suggests that the contributions of music genre tags (②) and lyrics understanding text (④) are interchangeable, without providing additional benefits when used together. Observing the results of ①+③, we note that music genre tags (②) and lyrics understanding (④) positively impact the results and are not redundant inputs. When comparing the top three performing settings (①+②+③, ①+③+④, and ①+②+③+④) with the combinations ②+③+④ and ①+②+④, we observe a significant performance drop. This highlights the importance of including both music (①) and MV type tags (③). Seeing the results of ①+④, the simultaneous inclusion of music genre tags (②) and MV type tags (③) yields consistent improvement across all metrics. Moreover, the results of ②+③ demonstrate that even with simple tags for music and MV, the model can generate reasonable MV descriptions, suggesting future opportunities to enhance the model's performance by leveraging finer-grained features such as temporal alignment between lyrics and musical waves.

4 Conclusion

In this study, we explored data construction and multimodal training pipelines for the music-to-MV description task, with the goal of building robust base models for the broader music-to-MV generation task. Our results on the constructed Music4All dataset highlight key data sources that significantly impact the quality of MV descriptions. Future work could extend our proposed dataset construction pipeline to additional music domains. Additionally, exploring more effective methods to align MV descriptions or MVs with the corresponding music could pave the way for improved performance in this challenging task.

Limitations

The proposed approach has several limitations: (1) The pipeline was evaluated on a single constructed dataset. Testing on additional datasets could strengthen the claims made in this paper. (2) The pipeline focuses on converting music into MV descriptions for MV generation tasks, but relying solely on text descriptions may overlook important information necessary for effective MV generation. (3) Inputs were limited to music, music genre tags, MV type tags, and lyrics understanding text, while other features that could significantly enhance MV descriptions may not have been considered. (4) The data construction pipeline depends on LLMs for captioning, and the choice of LLMs could influence the quality of the generated MV descriptions.

Ethical Considerations

In this study, we utilized only publicly available datasets and models to fine-tune the music-to-MV description generation task, ensuring no copyright issues. While our experiments focused on MV description generation, it is important to acknowledge that the fine-tuned models may produce potentially risky hallucinations. Users should use the generated content with caution, understand the risks associated with LLM-generated outputs, and implement content safety checks as post-processing. Although debiasing fine-tuning could help address these issues, it falls outside the scope of this work. Additionally, caution is needed when using text-to-video models based on the generated MV descriptions, ensuring that no illegal content, such as unauthorized human identities or privacy violations, is included.

References

Sebastian Böck, Filip Korzeniowski, Jan Schlüter, Florian Krebs, and Gerhard Widmer. 2016. madmom: A new python audio and music signal processing library. In *Proceedings of the 2016 ACM Conference on Multimedia Conference, MM 2016, Amsterdam, The Netherlands, October 15-19, 2016*, pages 1174–1178. ACM.

Joshua Patrick Gardner, Simon Durand, Daniel Stoller, and Rachel M. Bittner. 2024. Llark: A multimodal instruction-following language model for music. In *Forty-first International Conference on Machine Learning, ICML 2024, Vienna, Austria, July 21-27, 2024*. OpenReview.net.

Rohit Girdhar, Alaaeldin El-Nouby, Zhuang Liu, Mannat Singh, Kalyan Vasudev Alwala, Armand Joulin, and Ishan Misra. 2023. Imagebind one embedding space to bind them all. In *IEEE/CVF Conference on Computer Vision and Pattern Recognition, CVPR 2023, Vancouver, BC, Canada, June 17-24, 2023*, pages 15180–15190. IEEE.

Edward J. Hu, Yelong Shen, Phillip Wallis, Zeyuan Allen-Zhu, Yuanzhi Li, Shean Wang, Lu Wang, and Weizhu Chen. 2022. Lora: Low-rank adaptation of large language models. In *The Tenth International Conference on Learning Representations, ICLR 2022, Virtual Event, April 25-29, 2022*. OpenReview.net.

Jaeyong Kang, Soujanya Poria, and Dorien Herremans. 2024. Video2music: Suitable music generation from videos using an affective multimodal transformer model. *Expert Syst. Appl.*, 249:123640.

Levon Khachatryan, Andranik Movsisyan, Vahram Tadevosyan, Roberto Henschel, Zhangyang Wang, Shant Navasardyan, and Humphrey Shi. 2023. Text2video-zero: Text-to-image diffusion models are zero-shot video generators. In *IEEE/CVF International Conference on Computer Vision, ICCV 2023, Paris, France, October 1-6, 2023*, pages 15908–15918. IEEE.

Weijie Kong, Qi Tian, Zijian Zhang, Rox Min, Zuozhuo Dai, Jin Zhou, Jiangfeng Xiong, Xin Li, Bo Wu, Jianwei Zhang, Kathrina Wu, Qin Lin, Junkun Yuan, Yanxin Long, Aladdin Wang, Andong Wang, Changlin Li, Duojun Huang, Fang Yang, Hao Tan, Hongmei Wang, Jacob Song, Jiawang Bai, Jianbing Wu, Jinbao Xue, Joey Wang, Kai Wang, Mengyang Liu, Pengyu Li, Shuai Li, Weiyan Wang, Wenqing Yu, Xinchi Deng, Yang Li, Yi Chen, Yutao Cui, Yuanbo Peng, Zhentao Yu, Zhiyu He, Zhiyong Xu, Zixiang Zhou, Zunnan Xu, Yangyu Tao, Qinglin Lu, Songtao Liu, Daquan Zhou, Hongfa Wang, Yong Yang, Di Wang, Yuhong Liu, Jie Jiang, and Caesar Zhong. 2024. Hunyuanvideo: A systematic framework for large video generative models. *CoRR*, abs/2412.03603.

Chin-Yew Lin. 2004. ROUGE: A package for automatic evaluation of summaries. In *Text Summarization Branches Out*, pages 74–81, Barcelona, Spain. Association for Computational Linguistics.

Zhuoyuan Mao, Mengjie Zhao, Qiyu Wu, Hiromi Wakaki, and Yuki Mitsufuji. 2025. Deepresonance:

Enhancing multimodal music understanding via music-centric multi-way instruction tuning. *CoRR*, abs/2502.12623.

OpenAI. 2023. GPT-4 technical report. *CoRR*, abs/2303.08774.

Kishore Papineni, Salim Roukos, Todd Ward, and Wei-Jing Zhu. 2002. Bleu: a method for automatic evaluation of machine translation. In *Proceedings of the 40th Annual Meeting of the Association for Computational Linguistics*, pages 311–318, Philadelphia, Pennsylvania, USA. Association for Computational Linguistics.

Adam Polyak, Amit Zohar, Andrew Brown, Andros Tjandra, Animesh Sinha, Ann Lee, Apoorv Vyas, Bowen Shi, Chih-Yao Ma, Ching-Yao Chuang, David Yan, Dhruv Choudhary, Dingkang Wang, Geet Sethi, Guan Pang, Haoyu Ma, Ishan Misra, Ji Hou, Jialiang Wang, Kiran Jagadeesh, Kunpeng Li, Luxin Zhang, Mannat Singh, Mary Williamson, Matt Le, Matthew Yu, Mitesh Kumar Singh, Peizhao Zhang, Peter Vajda, Quentin Duval, Rohit Girdhar, Roshan Sumbaly, Sai Saketh Rambhatla, Sam S. Tsai, Samaneh Azadi, Samyak Datta, Sanyuan Chen, Sean Bell, Sharadh Ramaswamy, Shelly Sheynin, Siddharth Bhattacharya, Simran Motwani, Tao Xu, Tianhe Li, Tingbo Hou, Wei-Ning Hsu, Xi Yin, Xiaoliang Dai, Yaniv Taigman, Yaqiao Luo, Yen-Cheng Liu, Yi-Chiao Wu, Yue Zhao, Yuval Kirstain, Zecheng He, Zijian He, Albert Pumarola, Ali K. Thabet, Artsiom Sanakoyeu, Arun Mallya, Baishan Guo, Boris Araya, Breena Kerr, Carleigh Wood, Ce Liu, Cen Peng, Dmitry Vengertsev, Edgar Schönfeld, Elliot Blanchard, Felix Juefei-Xu, Fraylie Nord, Jeff Liang, John Hoffman, Jonas Kohler, Kaolin Fire, Karthik Sivakumar, Lawrence Chen, Licheng Yu, Luya Gao, Markos Georgopoulos, Rashel Moritz, Sara K. Sampson, Shikai Li, Simone Parmeggiani, Steve Fine, Tara Fowler, Vladan Petrovic, and Yuming Du. 2024. Movie gen: A cast of media foundation models. *CoRR*, abs/2410.13720.

Igor André Pegoraro Santana, Fabio Pinhelli, Juliano Donini, Leonardo Gabiato Catharin, Rafael Biazus Mangolin, Yandre Maldonado e Gomes da Costa, Valéria Delisandra Feltrim, and Marcos Aurélio Domingues. 2020. Music4all: A new music database and its applications. In *2020 International Conference on Systems, Signals and Image Processing, IWSSIP 2020, Niterói, Brazil, July 1-3, 2020*, pages 399–404. IEEE.

Hassan Shahmohammadi, Adhiraj Ghosh, and Hendrik Lensch. 2023. ViPE: Visualise pretty-much everything. In *Proceedings of the 2023 Conference on Empirical Methods in Natural Language Processing*, pages 5477–5494, Singapore. Association for Computational Linguistics.

Zeyue Tian, Zhaoyang Liu, Ruibin Yuan, Jiahao Pan, Xiaoqiang Huang, Qifeng Liu, Xu Tan, Qifeng Chen, Wei Xue, and Yike Guo. 2024. Vidmuse: A simple video-to-music generation framework with long-short-term modeling. *CoRR*, abs/2406.04321.

Shengqiong Wu, Hao Fei, Leigang Qu, Wei Ji, and Tat-Seng Chua. 2024. Next-gpt: Any-to-any multimodal LLM. In *Forty-first International Conference on Machine Learning, ICML 2024, Vienna, Austria, July 21-27, 2024*. OpenReview.net.

Zhuoyi Yang, Jiayan Teng, Wendi Zheng, Ming Ding, Shiyu Huang, Jiazheng Xu, Yuanming Yang, Wenyi Hong, Xiaohan Zhang, Guanyu Feng, Da Yin, Xiaotao Gu, Yuxuan Zhang, Weihan Wang, Yean Cheng, Ting Liu, Bin Xu, Yuxiao Dong, and Jie Tang. 2024. Cogvideox: Text-to-video diffusion models with an expert transformer. *CoRR*, abs/2408.06072.

Tianyi Zhang, Varsha Kishore, Felix Wu, Kilian Q. Weinberger, and Yoav Artzi. 2020. Bertscore: Evaluating text generation with BERT. In *8th International Conference on Learning Representations, ICLR 2020, Addis Ababa, Ethiopia, April 26-30, 2020*. OpenReview.net.

Mengjie Zhao, Zhi Zhong, Zhuoyuan Mao, Shiqi Yang, Wei-Hsiang Liao, Shusuke Takahashi, Hiromi Wakaki, and Yuki Mitsufuji. 2024. Openmu: Your swiss army knife for music understanding. *CoRR*, abs/2410.15573.

Lianmin Zheng, Wei-Lin Chiang, Ying Sheng, Siyuan Zhuang, Zhanghao Wu, Yonghao Zhuang, Zi Lin, Zhuohan Li, Dacheng Li, Eric P. Xing, Hao Zhang, Joseph E. Gonzalez, and Ion Stoica. 2023. Judging llm-as-a-judge with mt-bench and chatbot arena. In *Advances in Neural Information Processing Systems 36: Annual Conference on Neural Information Processing Systems 2023, NeurIPS 2023, New Orleans, LA, USA, December 10 - 16, 2023*.

A Examples of How to Construct MV Description

We first extract low-level music features, including tempo, key, downbeats, and chords, using the open-source tool madmom (Böck et al., 2016). Based on these features and the textual captions of each music piece, we employ GPT-4o mini[2] to generate unified music captions that seamlessly integrate all the musical information into natural, coherent sentences, as illustrated in Figure 3. Subsequently, we prompt GPT-4o mini again to construct MV descriptions by combining the video captions of each gold-standard MV, the unified music captions, and the lyrics understanding text (see Figure 2). The resulting MV descriptions incorporate both visual and musical content, making them better suited for reconstructing the original MV.

B Generating Video Frames using MV Description

Figure 5 showcases frames generated by the Text2Video-Zero (Khachatryan et al., 2023) model using the gold-standard MV description example provided in Figure 4. When compared to the original MV frames, we observe that even with only textual descriptions, the text-to-video model can produce content closely aligned with the intended visuals, such as the abstract geometric shapes in frames #3 to #5 and the mirrored sky in frames #6 and #7. This demonstrates the feasibility of our proposed pipeline for MV generation, as illustrated in Figure 1. However, challenges remain, particularly in accurately generating complex elements like multi-layered imagery and human faces using current text-to-video models. Addressing these limitations will be crucial for future advancements in this domain.

[2]https://platform.openai.com/docs/models#gpt-4o-mini

Input: Music captions, low-level music features

Music captions: The music clip features a very fast tempo with medium energy, creating a sense of urgency in the rhythm. It has a low valence, conveying a somber or melancholic mood. The overall danceability is moderate, suggesting a balance between movement and reflection in the music. The combination of the brisk tempo, medium energy, and low valence gives the clip a unique sense of momentum tempered with emotional depth.

Low-level music features: {'tempo': [[85.71428571428571, 0.31086550309221533], [43.16546762589928, 0.16042116950818738], [171.42857142857142, 0.12771306118557813], [57.142857142857146, 0.0782649741917839], [64.51612903225806, 0.07135607527230461], [127.65957446808511, 0.065676126308472], [51.724137931034484, 0.04765587930734781], [68.96551724137932, 0.04586137274352434], [113.20754716981132, 0.03241035380095120 4], [250.0, 0.030369918652813157], [49.18032786885246, 0.029405565936822024]], 'chords': [[0.0, 3.1, 'D#:maj'], [3.1, 4.7, 'A#:maj'], [4.7, 5.800000000000001, 'F:maj'], [5.800000000000001, 8.700000000000001, 'G:min'], [8.700000000000001, 11.0, 'F:maj'], [11.0, 13.200000000000001, 'D#:maj'], [13.200000000000001, 14.3, 'G:min'], [14.3, 16.3, 'A#:maj'], [16.3, 16.900000000000002, 'F:maj'], [16.900000000000002, 18.5, 'G:min'], [18.5, 19.1, 'A#:maj'], [19.1, 19.900000000000002, 'D#:maj'], [19.900000000000002, 20.400000000000002, 'A#:maj'], [20.400000000000002, 21.900000000000002, 'C:maj'], [21.900000000000002, 22.8, 'G:min'], [22.8, 25.200000000000003, 'D#:maj'], [25.200000000000003, 27.900000000000002, 'A#:maj'], [27.900000000000002, 30.000000000000004, 'G:min']], 'downbeats': [[0.11, 1.0], [0.81, 2.0], [1.54, 3.0], [2.21, 4.0], [2.91, 1.0], [3.6, 2.0], [4.34, 3.0], [5.0, 4.0], [5.69, 1.0], [6.39, 2.0], [7.12, 3.0], [7.79, 4.0], [8.49, 1.0], [9.18, 2.0], [9.91, 3.0], [10.58, 4.0], [11.28, 1.0], [11.98, 2.0], [12.7, 3.0], [13.37, 4.0], [14.07, 1.0], [14.77, 2.0], [15.5, 3.0], [16.16, 4.0], [16.86, 1.0], [17.56, 2.0], [18.27, 3.0], [18.95, 4.0], [19.65, 1.0], [20.35, 2.0], [21.08, 3.0], [21.74, 4.0], [22.44, 1.0], [23.14, 2.0], [23.85, 3.0], [24.53, 4.0], [25.23, 1.0], [25.93, 2.0], [26.65, 3.0], [27.33, 4.0], [28.02, 1.0], [28.72, 2.0], [29.45, 3.0]], 'key': [[0.0026776420418173075, 0.5507075190544128, 0.0008813949534669518, 0.006849234458059 0725, 0.0008653984405100346, 0.04045381024479866, 0.015051022171974182, 0.0028856105636805296, 0.0017399969510734081, 0.008495241403579712, 0.006829794496297836, 0.002278234576806426, 0.0019952855072915554, 0.003142772009596 2286, 0.0035238098353147507, 0.04947231337428093, 0.0013390464009717107, 0.014915909618139267, 0.003726801136508584, 0.002005897229537368, 0.0014139574486762285, 0.0013369121588766575, 0.2761196196079254, 0.001292902510613203]]}

Model: GPT-4o mini
Output: Unified music captions

The music clip unfolds with a brisk tempo, distinctively fast but balanced with a medium energy that fuels a palpable sense of urgency throughout its rhythm. This intensity carries a somber undertone, reflective in the music's low valence, leading listeners through a contemplative journey amid its forward momentum.

The harmonic structure pivots through a series of rich chords—beginning with the striking resonance of D#:maj, transitioning through A#:maj and F:maj, before settling into the darker reflections of G:min. This progression adds depth, embodying a landscape that evokes both movement and introspection. The interchange of these chords facilitates a pivotal emotional exploration, enhancing the track's melancholic essence while maintaining a danceable character, where reflection subtly intersperses with kinetic energy.

Synchronization of downbeats adds to the sense of drive, propelling the listener forward while imbuing each moment with a tender fragility. It creates a nuanced interplay between urgency and contemplation, inviting engagement without overwhelming the senses. In its entirety, the composition weaves a narrative that balances the frenetic pace of existence with the weight of emotional contemplation, crafting an immersive atmosphere where movement and melancholy coexist harmoniously.

Figure 3: An example of music caption, low-level features and generated unified music captions.

Input: (1) Video captions, (2) Unified Music Captions, (3) Lyrics understanding
Model: GPT-4o mini
Output: Video description

Overview
A mesmerizing journey through duality and introspection unfolds in this surreal music video. The brisk tempo mirrors the energetic yet contemplative soundscape, navigating between rich harmonies and softer reflective moments. The thoughtful interplay of organic and geometric visuals, complemented by shifting color tones, creates an immersive experience that invites deeper engagement with themes of transformation and optimism amidst chaos.

Frame-by-frame Breakdown
1. **Blurred Reflection**: Begin with a soft, abstract blur, setting an enigmatic tone that hints at duality.
2. **Obscured Humanity**: Introduce a warm, human form partially hidden, symbolizing vulnerability and connection.
3. **Geometric Chaos**: Shift to darker visuals with floating geometric shapes, suggesting tension and direction.
4. **Radiant Lines**: Bright red lines burst forth, enhancing the dynamic energy of the visual progression.
5. **Intricate Motion**: More complex red layers emerge, indicating escalating movement and urgency.
6. **Dreamlike Nature**: Transition to mirrored greenery, evoking serenity and a connection to the Earth.
7. **Skyward Contemplation**: Move towards the calmness of a mirrored sky, fostering reflection and peace.
8. **Whimsical Objects**: Introduce artistic mobile-like structures in soft tones, providing a sense of wonder.
9. **Intimate Textures**: Zoom in on reflective surfaces, deepening the intimate atmosphere within the narrative.
10. **Layered Complexity**: Explore deeper reflections and shadows, suggesting hidden depths beneath the surface.
11. **Earthy Symmetry**: Return to natural settings with earthy tones, enhancing organic beauty and exploration.
12. **Grounding Focus**: Highlight rich textures of the ground, reinforcing connection to nature.
13. **Endless Horizons**: Present a symmetrical sky view, connoting endless possibilities through mirroring.
14. **Tranquil Warmth**: A warm horizon emphasizes a feeling of openness and tranquility.
15. **Reflective Closure**: Conclude with a blend of organic shapes and warm tones, inviting contemplation on the journey within the video.

This concise frame-by-frame breakdown supports a nuanced visualization that evokes the music's balance of urgency and reflection, mirroring the overarching themes expressed through lyrics.

Figure 4: An example of a full MV description.

- **Original frames from MV:**

- **Frames generated by Text2video-Zero based on the MV description:**

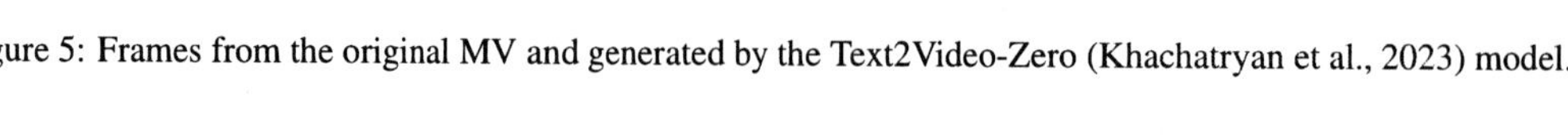

Figure 5: Frames from the original MV and generated by the Text2Video-Zero (Khachatryan et al., 2023) model.

A Comparative Study of Learning Paradigms in Large Language Models via Intrinsic Dimension

Saahith Janapati
University of Virginia
jax4zk@virginia.edu

Yangfeng Ji
University of Virginia
yj3fs@virginia.edu

Abstract

The performance of Large Language Models (LLMs) on natural language tasks can be improved through both supervised fine-tuning (SFT) and in-context learning (ICL), which operate via distinct mechanisms. SFT updates the model's weights by minimizing loss on training data, whereas ICL leverages task demonstrations embedded in the prompt, without changing the model's parameters. This study investigates the effects of these learning paradigms on the hidden representations of LLMs using Intrinsic Dimension (ID). We use ID to estimate the number of degrees of freedom between representations extracted from LLMs as they perform specific natural language tasks. We first explore how the ID of LLM representations evolves during SFT and how it varies due to the number of demonstrations in ICL. We then compare the IDs induced by SFT and ICL and find that ICL consistently induces a higher ID compared to SFT, suggesting that representations generated during ICL reside in higher dimensional manifolds in the embedding space. [1]

1 Introduction

Large Language Models (LLMs) have transformed the field of Natural Language Processing through their general natural language understanding capabilities, which can be applied to a broad range of tasks. The performance of an LLM on a specific task can be improved through two primary learning paradigms: supervised fine-tuning (SFT) and in-context learning (ICL). SFT adapts pretrained models to specific tasks by updating their parameters, while ICL requires no parameter updates, relying instead on task-specific demonstrations within the model's context window. Despite their widespread success, how these methods influence a model's internal representation space is still not fully understood.

Intrinsic dimension (ID) is a useful metric for assessing the geometric complexity of a model's representations. It quantifies the number of degrees of freedom in the representation space, serving as a measure of the complexity of the underlying manifolds where the embeddings reside.

In this work, we analyze the intrinsic dimension (ID) of hidden representations across model layers during task execution under both supervised fine-tuning (SFT) and in-context learning (ICL). Specifically, we explore:

- How fine-tuning duration influences ID of representations on both training and validation data.
- How the number of demonstrations used in ICL affects ID of representations.

Our findings reveal that (1) the ID sometimes decreases during the early stages of fine-tuning but generally increases in the later stages, and (2) the ID increases initially with more demonstrations in ICL, then either plateaus or decreases as the number of demonstrations continues to rise.

We then conduct experiments directly comparing the intrinsic dimensions of ICL and fine-tuning across several models and datasets. We find that the intrinsic dimensions of representations from fine-tuned models are generally lower than those from models using ICL, even though the fine-tuned models achieve higher accuracy than the ICL models. Additionally, our results suggest that ID may serve as a practical heuristic for selecting the optimal number of demonstrations in ICL to maximize performance while minimizing input length. These findings shed light on the differing impacts that the two learning paradigms have on the representation space of LLMs.

[1] Code is available at the following GitHub repo.

Proceedings of the 10th Workshop on Representation Learning for NLP (RepL4NLP-2025), pages 59–86
May 4, 2025

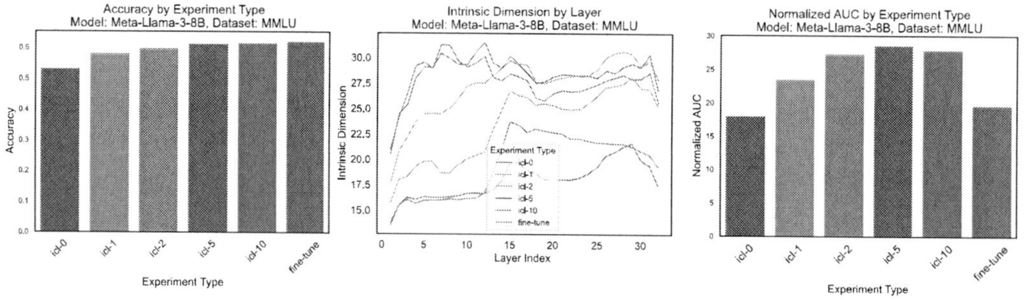

Figure 1: Accuracy, intrinsic dimension, and normalized AUC for the Llama-3-8B model on the MMLU dataset. (a) Fine-tuning achieves the highest accuracy. (b) ICL produces intermediate representations with higher intrinsic dimensions across model layers compared to zero-shot (ICL-0) and fine-tuned models. (c) Normalized AUC increases with the number of demonstrations in ICL, while fine-tuned models exhibit lower AUC.

2 Background

2.1 Decoder Transformer Architecture

LLMs are built on the Transformer decoder architecture, which processes token sequences through a series of Transformer layers. In each layer, token representations are updated via self-attention that considers only the preceding tokens from the previous layer, progressively encoding information for the next-token prediction task. The final layer then uses the representation of the last token to predict the next token in the sequence. In this work, we analyze the intrinsic dimension of the representations corresponding to the last token of sequences where LLMs are prompted to perform specific natural language tasks.

2.2 Intrinsic Dimension Estimation

Intrinsic dimension (ID) refers to the minimal number of variables required to capture the essential structure of high-dimensional data. Although modern neural networks operate in high-dimensional spaces (e.g., the hidden representations of Llama-3-8B span 4096 dimensions), the representations corresponding to a specific dataset or task often lie on a manifold of much lower dimension. This occurs because the network disentangles and extracts the most relevant lower-dimensional features needed to complete the task.

According to the manifold hypothesis, real-world data typically resides on a low-dimensional manifold (Goodfellow, 2016). Therefore, to effectively solve tasks—such as next-token prediction—neural networks must learn representations that align with this low-dimensional structure. Consequently, the intrinsic dimension of data representations provides unique insight into the complexity of the representation spaces constructed across the layers of a neural network.

In this work, we estimate the intrinsic dimension (ID) of our representations using the **TwoNN estimator**, as introduced by Facco et al. (2017). We chose this method because of its simplicity, computational efficiency, and robustness when handling datasets with non-uniform densities and high-dimensional curvature—common challenges in neural network representations.

The TwoNN estimator operates on a set of points by computing the distances to each point's first (r_1) and second (r_2) nearest neighbors. For a given point x, the ratio

$$\mu = \frac{r_2}{r_1}$$

is calculated. The intrinsic dimension d is then derived from the empirical cumulative distribution function (CDF) of μ. Specifically, the log-linear relationship between $\log(\mu)$ and $\log\big(1 - F_{\text{emp}}(\mu)\big)$, where $F_{\text{emp}}(\mu)$ is the empirical CDF, is used to estimate d:

$$d = -\frac{\log\big(1 - F_{\text{emp}}(\mu)\big)}{\log(\mu)}$$

The TwoNN estimator has been successfully applied in several prior works analyzing the intrinsic dimension of neural network representations, including Sharma and Kaplan (2022), Ansuini et al. (2019), Valeriani et al. (2024), and specifically in large language models (LLMs) by Cheng et al. (2023) and Lee et al. (2024). We also validate the correlation between the TwoNN estimator and another widely used intrinsic dimension estimator—the Maximum Likelihood Estimator introduced by

Levina and Bickel (2004)—in Appendix F as a sanity check.

3 Related Works

3.1 Supervised Fine-Tuning in LLMs

Pre-trained LLMs can be quickly adapted to improve performance on natural language tasks through supervised fine-tuning, which updates the model's parameters via gradient descent on task-specific training examples.

Aghajanyan et al. (2020) show that fine-tuning large language models often requires updating only a low-dimensional subspace of parameters to achieve near-optimal performance. (Note that their work focuses on the intrinsic dimension of the parameter space, whereas our work examines the intrinsic dimension of the representation space.) Building on this, Hu et al. (2021) introduce Low-Rank Adaptation (LoRA), a method that injects low-rank matrices into the weight matrices for fine-tuning instead of updating all parameters. We employ LoRA for all our fine-tuning experiments.

3.2 In-Context Learning

Introduced in GPT-3 by Brown (2020), ICL (or few-shot learning) refers to the ability of LLMs to learn to perform a task in a single forward pass, using (input, output) pairs embedded in a prompt.

Dai et al. (2022) provides evidence that ICL operates as implicit meta-optimization, where GPT models perform a gradient-like update via attention mechanisms during the forward pass. This suggests that ICL replicates fine-tuning behavior; specifically, they demonstrate that attention outputs and weights are updated in a direction similar to that of fine-tuning.

Xie et al. (2021) explain in-context learning as implicit Bayesian inference, where large language models infer latent document-level concepts during pretraining. These inferred concepts are then leveraged at test time to solve tasks based on the input-output examples provided in prompts.

Expanding the ICL paradigm to long-context models, Agarwal et al. (2024) studied many-shot ICL, in which hundreds or thousands of task examples are used to improve the performance of frontier models. Their work finds that an increasing number of demonstrations generally improves model performance on a variety of complex tasks, such as mathematical problem-solving.

3.3 Intrinsic Dimension in Deep Learning

Ansuini et al. (2019) investigated the intrinsic dimensionality (ID) of data representations across various convolutional neural networks (CNNs) for image classification. They observed a consistent "hunchback" pattern in ID evolution—an initial increase in the early layers followed by a progressive decrease in later layers.

Valeriani et al. (2024) extended this analysis to protein language models and image transformers, finding that the evolution of representations across layers of these models is also marked by distinct phases of ID growth and compression.

Yin et al. (2024) explore the use of Local Intrinsic Dimension (LID) to detect untruthful outputs from LLMs. Their study reveals that truthful outputs typically exhibit lower LIDs compared to hallucinated ones, suggesting that LID can serve as a signal for truthfulness in LLM generations. They also identify a positive relationship between the ID of data representations and validation performance during fine-tuning.

Cheng et al. (2023) demonstrate that intrinsic dimension correlates with fine-tuning ease and perplexity, with low-dimensional representations enabling faster task adaptation. Moreover, they find that ID values are consistent across model sizes, supporting the manifold hypothesis and suggesting that LLMs trained on similar data recover comparable intrinsic dimensions.

Of particular relevance to our study is the concurrent work of Doimo et al. (2024), which examines the internal representations of LLMs solving tasks from the MMLU dataset using both ICL and SFT. Their analysis reveals that ICL forms semantic clusters in the early layers, while SFT sharpens these clusters in later layers for task-specific answers. Moreover, they observe that intrinsic dimension (ID) increases with a higher number of demonstrations in ICL, and that SFT generally induces a higher ID compared to ICL. In contrast, our findings indicate that beyond a certain range of ICL demonstrations, ID may plateau or even decrease, and that SFT consistently induces a lower ID than ICL.

To our knowledge, our work is the first to systematically analyze and compare intrinsic dimension across the two learning paradigms for numerous datasets and models. We further provide in-depth analyses of how ID is affected by various factors within each paradigm, such as the number of gradient steps in SFT and the number of demonstrations in ICL.

3.4 Intrinsic Dimension and Neural Network Scaling Laws

Sharma and Kaplan (2022) propose that the power-law scaling of neural network performance is rooted in the intrinsic dimensionality (ID) of the data manifold. They empirically demonstrate that the ID of learned representations, particularly in the final hidden layer, directly relates to the scaling exponent. Their theory, predicting a scaling exponent of approximately $\alpha \approx 4/d$ (where d is ID), suggests that neural networks achieve efficient scaling by effectively performing regression on a lower-dimensional data manifold, thus linking model capacity to the data's inherent complexity.

4 Methods

We perform experiments using subsets from the following datasets: AG News (Zhang et al., 2015), CoLA (Warstadt et al., 2018), CommonsenseQA (Talmor et al., 2018), MMLU (Hendrycks et al., 2020), MultiNLI (Williams et al., 2017), QNLI (Wang, 2018), QQP (Wang et al., 2017), and SST2 (Socher et al., 2013).

For these experiments, we utilize the following open-source LLMs: Llama-3-8B (Dubey et al., 2024), Llama-2-13b, Llama-2-7b (Touvron et al., 2023), and Mistral-7B-v0.3 (Jiang et al., 2023), running them on 6 NVIDIA A6000s.

For each dataset, we created a training set of 1000 examples and a validation set of 5000 examples. We use the 5000 validation examples to ensure stability of the TwoNN estimator. Details regarding dataset creation can be found in Appendix G. Details of split generations and prompt templates are provided in Appendix G.

We calculate the accuracy of model responses using the logit probabilities assigned to the tokens corresponding to the possible answers for each question. We mark a response as correct if the probability corresponding to the first token of the correct answer label is the highest.

4.1 Computing Intrinsic Dimension

In both Supervised Fine-Tuning (SFT) and In-Context Learning (ICL) paradigms, a language model receives an input sequence of tokens and is tasked with generating an output sequence that answers the given prompt. To quantify the intrinsic dimensionality (ID) of a model's representations for a given dataset, we extract the hidden state activations at each layer of the LLM. Specifically, we focus on the activations corresponding to the **last token of each input sequence** in the dataset. For a model with L layers and a dataset containing N input sequences, this process yields L sets of hidden state representations. Each set corresponds to a specific layer and comprises N representation vectors (one for each input sequence in the dataset). Subsequently, we compute the intrinsic dimension (ID) for each of these L sets of N vectors. This provides us with an ID estimate for the representation space at each layer. By plotting the Layer Index against the corresponding ID estimates, we construct what we term the **Intrinsic Dimension Curve**.

To derive a single, aggregated metric that encapsulates the intrinsic dimensionality across all layers of a model, we calculate the **Normalized Area Under the Curve (AUC)** of the Intrinsic Dimension Curve, defined as follows:

$$\text{Normalized AUC} = \frac{1}{L}\sum_{i=1}^{L-1}\frac{1}{2}\left(\text{ID}_i + \text{ID}_{i+1}\right)$$

In this equation, ID_i denotes the intrinsic dimension estimate at layer i. The formula employs the trapezoidal rule for numerical integration to approximate the area beneath the Intrinsic Dimension Curve. The normalization by L (the number of layers) enables fair comparisons of intrinsic dimensionality across models with varying depths.

5 Dynamics of ID during Supervised Fine-Tuning

5.1 Supervised Fine-Tuning Experimental Setup

To investigate the impact of supervised fine-tuning at a granular level, we conduct experiments using the 8 datasets discussed in Section 4 and the Llama-3-8B and Llama-2-13B models.

Using the training split for each of the datasets, we perform LoRA fine-tuning on the query, key, value, and output projection matrices of attention heads across all layers of the model. For all models, we fine-tune with a batch size of 16 for 15 epochs. For all fine-tuning runs, we use LoRA hyperparameters of $r = 64$, lora_alpha $= 16$, lora_dropout $= 0.1$, no LoRA bias, and a learning rate of $1e^{-4}$.

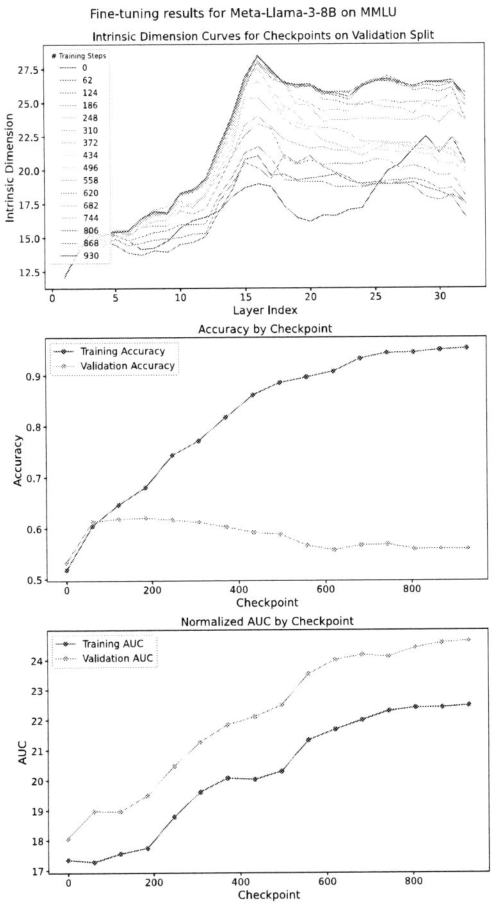

Figure 2: Fine-tuning results for Meta-Llama-3-8B on the MMLU dataset. (a) Intrinsic Dimension curves on the validation split increase across training steps. (b) Training accuracy improves steadily, while validation accuracy plateaus. (c) Normalized AUC for training and validation sets increases throughout fine-tuning.

During the fine-tuning process for a specific model and dataset, we save a checkpoint of the model after every epoch (~62 gradient update steps). For each checkpoint, we evaluate the model's accuracy and measure the intrinsic dimension (ID) of the hidden representations on prompts from the training and validation splits for the dataset.

5.2 Intrinsic Dimension Generally Increases Through Fine-Tuning

As depicted in Figure 2c, we find that ID of representations corresponding to both training data and validation data sometimes decreases during the initial stages of fine-tuning, but then generally increases as fine-tuning progresses.

We also observe larger changes in ID values for later layers of the models, despite LoRA adaptation being applied on all the layers with the same configuration (Figure 2a).

Additionally, we find that the AUC values of the model on the training set and validation set are often highly correlated with each other during the training process (Figure 2c). Experimental results for all models and datasets can be found in Appendix B.

Prior work by Yin et al. (2024) found that on Question-Answering datasets, intrinsic dimension of representations is correlated with validation performance and can therefore be used as a heuristic to select final checkpoints. In general, we do not find this trend to hold on the datasets and models we tested. In fact, as shown in Figure 13, large increases in validation accuracy sometimes coincide with drops in ID on both the training and validation datasets.

6 Relationship of ID in ICL with Different Numbers of Shots

6.1 In-Context Learning Experimental Setup

To investigate the impact of ICL on the ID of model representations, we conduct experiments using the Llama-3-8B and Llama-2-13B models. The datasets included in our evaluation are CommonsenseQA, MMLU, and QNLI.

We evaluate ICL performance using various values of k, where k denotes the number of demonstrations in the ICL prompt. The values considered are $k \in \{0, 1, 2, 5, 10, 12, 14, 16, 18, 20\}$. Note that $k = 0$ serves as a baseline, representing the model's performance in the absence of both ICL and SFT.

For each k and dataset, we generate 5000 ICL prompts (one for each element of the validation split of the dataset). Each ICL prompt includes k unique demonstrations, or (input, output) pairs, randomly sampled from the training set. While we ensure that demonstrations within a single prompt are unique, they may be reused across different prompts.

6.2 ID Has a Non-Linear Relationship with Number of Demonstrations

We observe that ID values across layers can fluctuate until a threshold value of k (typically around 5 to 10 for most model configurations), after which

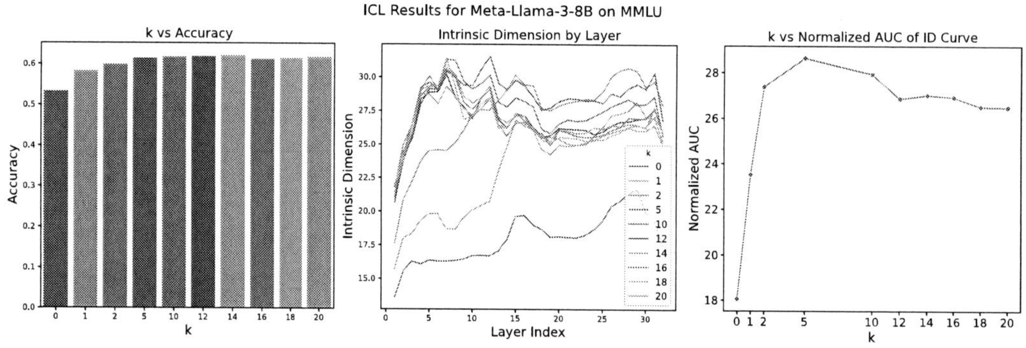

Figure 3: (ICL) results for Meta-Llama-3-8B model on MMLU dataset. (a) Accuracy increases, then plateaus as number of demonstrations increases (b) Intrinsic Dimension (ID) curves for different values of k. (c) Normalized AUC of the ID curves peaks at k=5, which also aligns with saturation of accuracy.

they either plateau or steadily decrease for larger values of k (see Figure 3c). Results for all model and dataset configurations are provided in Appendix A. This observation extends the findings of Doimo et al. (2024), who found that ID increased as k was varied from 0, 1, 2, and 5, by demonstrating that beyond a certain number of demonstrations, the trend can reverse.

We observe that across most (model, dataset) combinations, the shapes of the intrinsic dimension (ID) curves correlate strongly with each other for $k \geq 2$.

Due to our procedure of selecting demonstrations with replacement, we suspected that the plateau in ID for larger values of k might be caused by a greater number of demonstrations shared across prompts. We hypothesized that shared demonstrations could make representations corresponding to these prompts artificially similar, thereby skewing ID results. To test this, we performed additional experiments using a larger number of dataset elements from the CommonsenseQA, QNLI, and AG News datasets, which contain enough training elements to ensure that demonstrations are not reused in prompts for more than one element of the validation set. We observed the same trend—an increase followed by a general plateau in the ID—suggesting that the plateau is likely not due to the reuse of demonstrations among the prompts. Full results for this experiment can be found in Appendix D.

Furthermore, we find that peaks in the k versus AUC relationship align with peak (or near-peak) accuracy in 5 out of the 6 ICL experiments we conducted. Thus, the k value corresponding to the peak ID may serve as a practical indicator of the optimal number of demonstrations to use for ICL, maximizing performance while minimizing input length.

One hypothesis for why ID plateaus or slightly decreases as k increases is that more demonstrations allow the model to more effectively capture the underlying task conveyed by the demonstrations, causing representations corresponding to different inputs to become more similar. This idea is supported by previous theoretical analysis of ICL by Xie et al. (2021), which posits that a greater number of demonstrations helps the model more effectively infer the latent concept across demonstrations.

Finally, we find that across most experiments, accuracy either steadily increases or plateaus with higher numbers of demonstrations (Figure 3a).

7 Comparing Intrinsic Dimension of In-Context Learning and Supervised Fine-Tuning

7.1 Experiment Setup for Comparative Analysis

We conduct a series of experiments to directly compare the ID curves obtained from both SFT and ICL, following similar setups as discussed in Sections 5 and 6. For the fine-tuning experiments in this section, we train for only 4 epochs and measure the accuracy and ID solely at the final checkpoint. This choice is motivated by the observation in Section 5 that models tend to overfit beyond 4 epochs across the tested datasets.

For the ICL experiments, we consider values of $k \in \{0, 1, 2, 5, 10\}$ for the number of demonstra-

Dataset	ICL-0	ICL-1	ICL-2	ICL-5	ICL-10	Finetune 1K
SST-2	0.685	0.633	0.731	0.807	0.832	**0.944**
CoLA	0.720	0.723	0.735	0.746	0.742	**0.750**
QNLI	0.517	0.513	0.555	0.590	0.585	**0.761**
QQP	0.417	0.462	0.485	0.508	0.519	**0.707**
MNLI	0.374	0.367	0.387	0.414	0.431	**0.676**
AGNews	0.638	0.573	0.712	0.772	0.809	**0.881**
CommonsenseQA	0.199	0.375	0.417	0.470	0.492	**0.500**
MMLU	0.449	0.488	0.511	0.524	0.531	**0.542**

Table 1: Average accuracy results for Datasets across ICL and SFT settings. SFT obtains the highest average accuracy for all datasets. Accuracy increases and then plateaus for higher number of demonstrations.

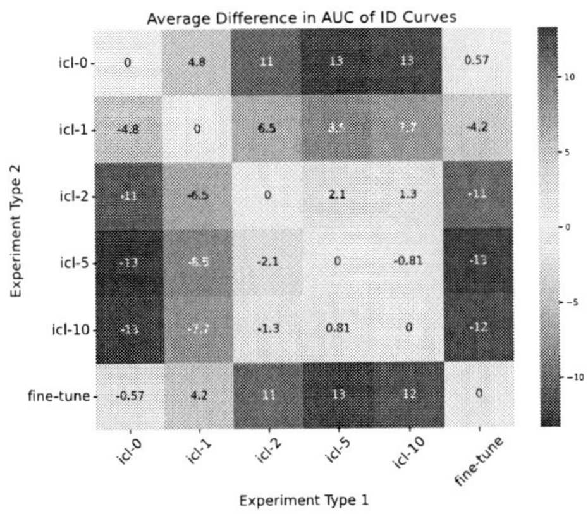

Figure 4: Heatmap showing the average differences in normalized AUC of ID curves between pairs of learning paradigms. Each value represents the average difference (Experiment Type 1 - Experiment Type 2), computed across all (model, dataset) pairs.

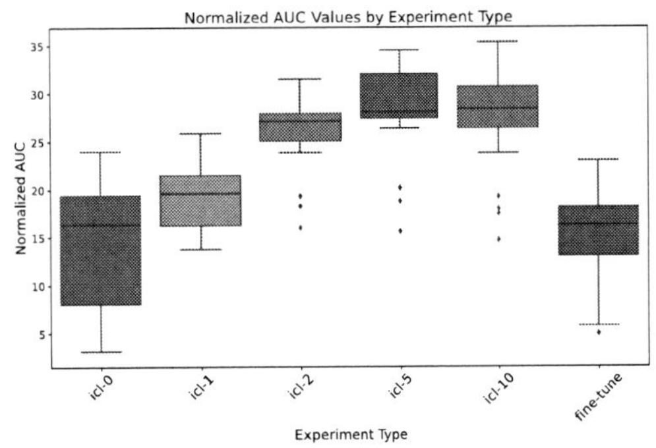

Figure 5: Boxplot displaying the distribution of normalized AUC values for different learning paradigms. Each point corresponds to the normalized AUC value for a (model, dataset) pair. The median normalized AUC peaks with 5-shot ICL, while values for SFT are closer to the 0-shot baseline (icl-0).

tions. These values are popular in practice, and our previous experiments in Section 6 indicate that ID curves tend to plateau when $k \geq 10$. We perform these experiments on all 8 datasets and 4 models discussed in Section 4.

7.2 In-context Learning Induces Higher IDs Compared to Fine-Tuning

We find that across all datasets and models, ICL prompts with $k \geq 5$ consistently induces higher intrinsic dimensions (IDs) across all layers compared to both SFT and 0-shot prompts (see Figures 1b and 1c). This contrasts with the findings of Doimo et al. (2024), who find that SFT models often induces higher ID than models performing ICL.

We also find that the ID values of models fine-tuned with 1000 samples tend to remain similar to the original ID of the baseline model on a zero-shot prompt (designated by icl-0). We present a heatmap displaying the average differences in normalized AUC between learning paradigms in Figure 4, and a boxplot depicting the distribution of normalized AUC values for the different paradigms in Figure 5.

7.3 Analysis of Intrinsic Dimension Curves

7.3.1 Differing Shapes of Intrinsic Dimension Curves

We observe that the exact shape of the Intrinsic Dimension curves is highly dependent on the dataset. For some datasets, such as AG News, we observe a consistent "hunchback" shape, where the ID initially increases and then is progressively lower in the later layers of the model across all models and learning paradigms (Figure 36). This shape has been reported by previous work (Yin et al., 2024) in QA datasets. However, this pattern does not consistently hold across all models, datasets, and learning paradigms. For example, on the QQP dataset, we

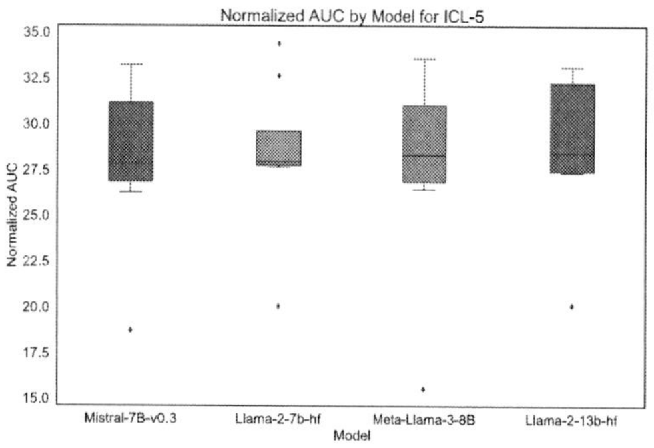

Figure 6: Boxplot displaying the distribution of normalized AUC values across datasets for each model in the ICL-5 shot setting. Each point corresponds to a (model, dataset) pair. The ID values lie in a narrow range, highlighting similarity in representation spaces across models.

do not observe a consistent hunchback shape for icl-0, icl-1, or fine-tuning learning paradigms (Figure 33). In contrast, prior work has shown that Convolutional Neural Networks (Ansuini et al., 2019), as well as Image Generation Transformers such as ImageGPT and Protein Language Models (Valeriani et al., 2024), exhibit consistent Intrinsic Dimension patterns across their layers for inputs of their respective data modalities. This difference suggests that LLMs encode data into more diverse manifolds in their representation space, potentially reflecting their generality and the complexity of their learning tasks compared to other neural networks.

We also find that, within a specific learning paradigm, the range of normalized AUC values across datasets is similar for the four different models we tested, despite the fact that these models come from different families and have different embedding dimensions (e.g., Llama-2-13b has a hidden dimension of 5120, while the other three models have hidden dimensions of 4096). Figure 6 depicts the range of normalized AUC values for the ICL-5 learning paradigm and shows that all values fall within a range of 20. We view this as evidence that different models may be generating representations with similar geometric complexity for a specific dataset, despite differences in model size or pre-training schemes. Similar boxplots for normalized AUC values from other experiments are included in Appendix B.2. These findings are in agreement with results from Cheng et al. (2023), which show that LLMs of different sizes and families create representations with similar ID values for a variety of text corpora.

7.4 Comparing Performance of Different Learning Paradigms

We found that models fine-tuned with 1k samples obtained the highest accuracy, while models performing ICL with 10 samples followed closely. This observation suggests that intrinsic dimension (ID) may not be directly related to accuracy: although fine-tuning with 1k samples yields ID values that remain closer to the baseline model, ICL models exhibit higher IDs yet achieve substantially lower accuracies. See Table 1 for the average performance of each learning paradigm across the models and datasets tested.

8 Summary

We present a detailed analysis of the intrinsic dimension (ID) induced by the SFT and ICL learning paradigms. Our experiments reveal that the normalized AUC of ID curves sometimes decreases during the initial stages of SFT but generally increases during the later stages.

Additionally, we observe that the normalized AUC of ID curves in ICL initially increases for small values of k (the number of demonstrations) but plateaus or slightly decreases as k increases further. Notably, the k value corresponding to the highest normalized AUC also achieves peak (or near-peak) accuracy, suggesting that ID may serve as a useful indicator for selecting the optimal number of demonstrations during ICL.

Finally, our direct comparison of ID curves from ICL and SFT reveals that representations generated during ICL consistently yield higher ID curves compared to those from SFT on 1k samples, even though SFT with 1k samples achieves the highest overall performance. This analysis provides evidence that the two learning paradigms induce distinct representational structures in the embedding space, with ICL representations occupying higher-dimensional manifolds.

9 Limitations

In this study, we limit our analysis to models with sizes between 7B and 13B parameters. Future work may extend this investigation to models of different sizes. We also focus on datasets defined by narrowly focused tasks and do not consider datasets with long-form answers. Due to computational constraints, we perform fine-tuning only using LoRA adapters and do not explore the impacts of full fine-tuning on intrinsic dimension.

References

Rishabh Agarwal, Avi Singh, Lei M Zhang, Bernd Bohnet, Stephanie Chan, Ankesh Anand, Zaheer Abbas, Azade Nova, John D Co-Reyes, Eric Chu, et al. 2024. Many-shot in-context learning. *arXiv preprint arXiv:2404.11018*.

Armen Aghajanyan, Luke Zettlemoyer, and Sonal Gupta. 2020. Intrinsic dimensionality explains the effectiveness of language model fine-tuning. *arXiv preprint arXiv:2012.13255*.

Alessio Ansuini, Alessandro Laio, Jakob H Macke, and Davide Zoccolan. 2019. Intrinsic dimension of data representations in deep neural networks. *Advances in Neural Information Processing Systems*, 32.

Stephen Bach, Victor Sanh, Zheng Xin Yong, Albert Webson, Colin Raffel, Nihal V. Nayak, Abheesht Sharma, Taewoon Kim, M Saiful Bari, Thibault Fevry, Zaid Alyafeai, Manan Dey, Andrea Santilli, Zhiqing Sun, Srulik Ben-david, Canwen Xu, Gunjan Chhablani, Han Wang, Jason Fries, Maged Alshaibani, Shanya Sharma, Urmish Thakker, Khalid Almubarak, Xiangru Tang, Dragomir Radev, Mike Tian-jian Jiang, and Alexander Rush. 2022. PromptSource: An integrated development environment and repository for natural language prompts. In *Proceedings of the 60th Annual Meeting of the Association for Computational Linguistics: System Demonstrations*, pages 93–104, Dublin, Ireland. Association for Computational Linguistics.

Tom B Brown. 2020. Language models are few-shot learners. *arXiv preprint arXiv:2005.14165*.

Emily Cheng, Corentin Kervadec, and Marco Baroni. 2023. Bridging information-theoretic and geometric compression in language models. *arXiv preprint arXiv:2310.13620*.

Damai Dai, Yutao Sun, Li Dong, Yaru Hao, Shuming Ma, Zhifang Sui, and Furu Wei. 2022. Why can gpt learn in-context? language models implicitly perform gradient descent as meta-optimizers. *arXiv preprint arXiv:2212.10559*.

Diego Doimo, Alessandro Serra, Alessio Ansuini, and Alberto Cazzaniga. 2024. The representation landscape of few-shot learning and fine-tuning in large language models. *arXiv preprint arXiv:2409.03662*.

Abhimanyu Dubey, Abhinav Jauhri, Abhinav Pandey, Abhishek Kadian, Ahmad Al-Dahle, Aiesha Letman, Akhil Mathur, Alan Schelten, Amy Yang, Angela Fan, et al. 2024. The llama 3 herd of models. *arXiv preprint arXiv:2407.21783*.

Elena Facco, Maria d'Errico, Alex Rodriguez, and Alessandro Laio. 2017. Estimating the intrinsic dimension of datasets by a minimal neighborhood information. *Scientific reports*, 7(1):12140.

Ian Goodfellow. 2016. Deep learning.

Dan Hendrycks, Collin Burns, Steven Basart, Andy Zou, Mantas Mazeika, Dawn Song, and Jacob Steinhardt. 2020. Measuring massive multitask language understanding. *arXiv preprint arXiv:2009.03300*.

Edward J Hu, Yelong Shen, Phillip Wallis, Zeyuan Allen-Zhu, Yuanzhi Li, Shean Wang, Lu Wang, and Weizhu Chen. 2021. Lora: Low-rank adaptation of large language models. *arXiv preprint arXiv:2106.09685*.

Albert Q Jiang, Alexandre Sablayrolles, Arthur Mensch, Chris Bamford, Devendra Singh Chaplot, Diego de las Casas, Florian Bressand, Gianna Lengyel, Guillaume Lample, Lucile Saulnier, et al. 2023. Mistral 7b. *arXiv preprint arXiv:2310.06825*.

Jin Hwa Lee, Thomas Jiralerspong, Lei Yu, Yoshua Bengio, and Emily Cheng. 2024. Geometric signatures of compositionality across a language model's lifetime. *arXiv preprint arXiv:2410.01444*.

Elizaveta Levina and Peter Bickel. 2004. Maximum likelihood estimation of intrinsic dimension. *Advances in neural information processing systems*, 17.

Utkarsh Sharma and Jared Kaplan. 2022. Scaling laws from the data manifold dimension. *Journal of Machine Learning Research*, 23(9):1–34.

Richard Socher, Alex Perelygin, Jean Wu, Jason Chuang, Christopher D Manning, Andrew Y Ng, and Christopher Potts. 2013. Recursive deep models for semantic compositionality over a sentiment treebank. In *Proceedings of the 2013 conference on empirical methods in natural language processing*, pages 1631–1642.

Alon Talmor, Jonathan Herzig, Nicholas Lourie, and Jonathan Berant. 2018. Commonsenseqa: A question answering challenge targeting commonsense knowledge. *arXiv preprint arXiv:1811.00937*.

Hugo Touvron, Louis Martin, Kevin Stone, Peter Albert, Amjad Almahairi, Yasmine Babaei, Nikolay Bashlykov, Soumya Batra, Prajjwal Bhargava, Shruti Bhosale, et al. 2023. Llama 2: Open foundation and fine-tuned chat models. *arXiv preprint arXiv:2307.09288*.

Lucrezia Valeriani, Diego Doimo, Francesca Cuturello, Alessandro Laio, Alessio Ansuini, and Alberto Cazzaniga. 2024. The geometry of hidden representations of large transformer models. *Advances in Neural Information Processing Systems*, 36.

Alex Wang. 2018. Glue: A multi-task benchmark and analysis platform for natural language understanding. *arXiv preprint arXiv:1804.07461*.

Zhiguo Wang, Wael Hamza, and Radu Florian. 2017. Bilateral multi-perspective matching for natural language sentences. *arXiv preprint arXiv:1702.03814*.

Alex Warstadt, Amanpreet Singh, and Samuel R Bowman. 2018. Neural network acceptability judgments. *arXiv preprint arXiv:1805.12471*.

Adina Williams, Nikita Nangia, and Samuel R Bowman. 2017. A broad-coverage challenge corpus for sentence understanding through inference. *arXiv preprint arXiv:1704.05426*.

Sang Michael Xie, Aditi Raghunathan, Percy Liang, and Tengyu Ma. 2021. An explanation of in-context learning as implicit bayesian inference. *arXiv preprint arXiv:2111.02080*.

Fan Yin, Jayanth Srinivasa, and Kai-Wei Chang. 2024. Characterizing truthfulness in large language model generations with local intrinsic dimension. *arXiv preprint arXiv:2402.18048*.

Xiang Zhang, Junbo Zhao, and Yann LeCun. 2015. Character-level convolutional networks for text classification. *Advances in neural information processing systems*, 28.

A In-Context Learning Experiments

A.1 Llama-3-8B In-Context Learning Experiments

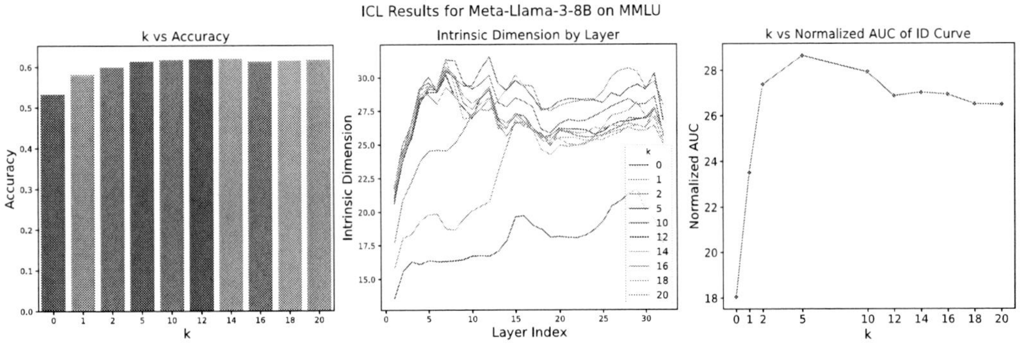

Figure 7: ICL Experiment Results for Meta-Llama-3-8B on MMLU

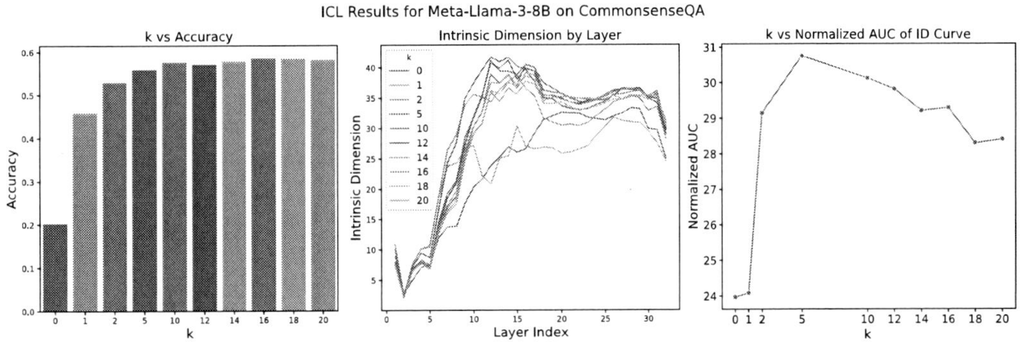

Figure 8: ICL Experiment Results for Meta-Llama-3-8B on CommonsenseQA

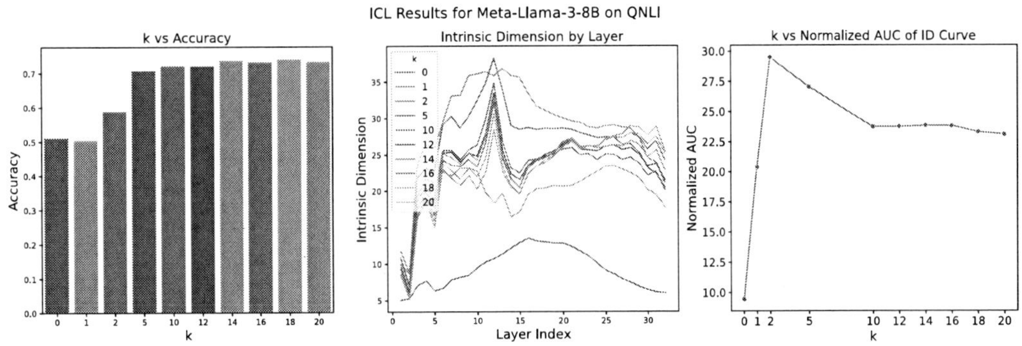

Figure 9: ICL Experiment Results for Meta-Llama-3-8B on QNLI

A.2 Llama-2-13b In-Context Learning Experiments

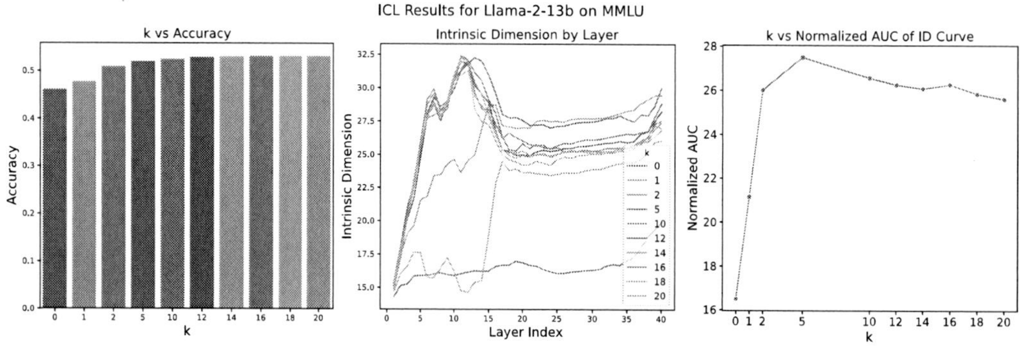

Figure 10: ICL Experiment Results for Llama-2-13b on MMLU

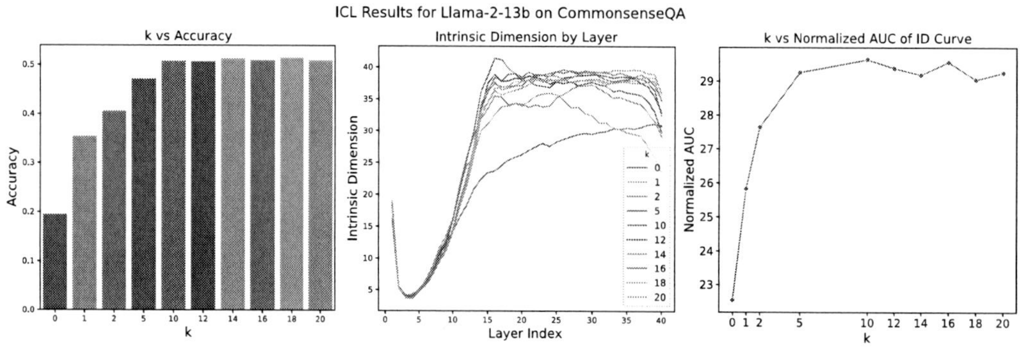

Figure 11: ICL Experiment Results for Llama-2-13b on CommonsenseQA

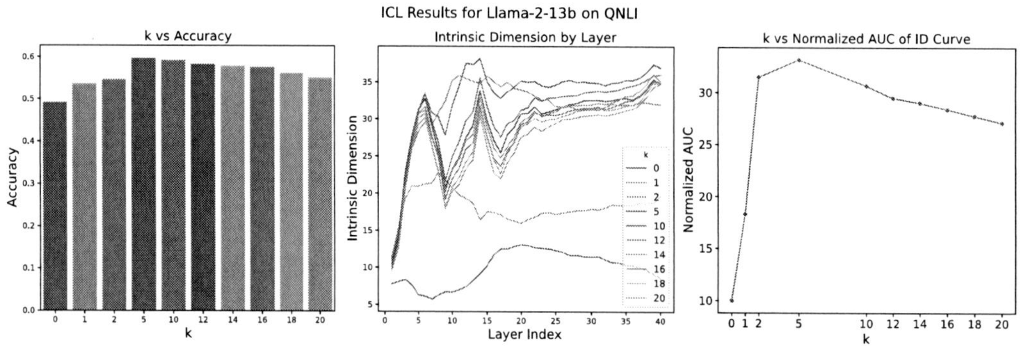

Figure 12: ICL Experiment Results for Llama-2-13b on QNLI

B Supervised Fine-Tuning Experiments

B.1 Supervised Fine-Tuning Results for Llama-3-8B

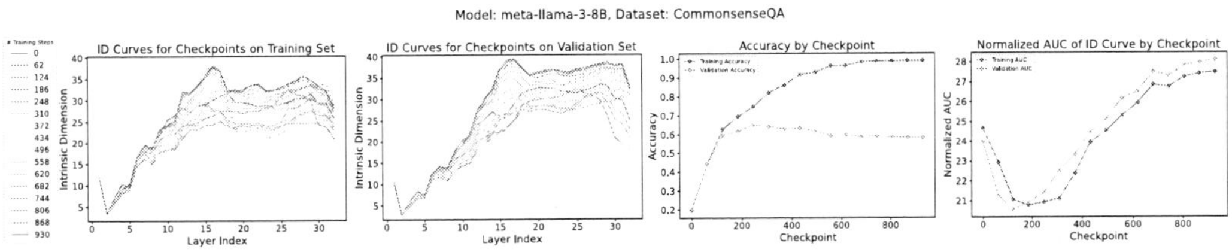

Figure 13: Supervised Fine-Tuning Results for Llama-3-8B on Commonsense QA

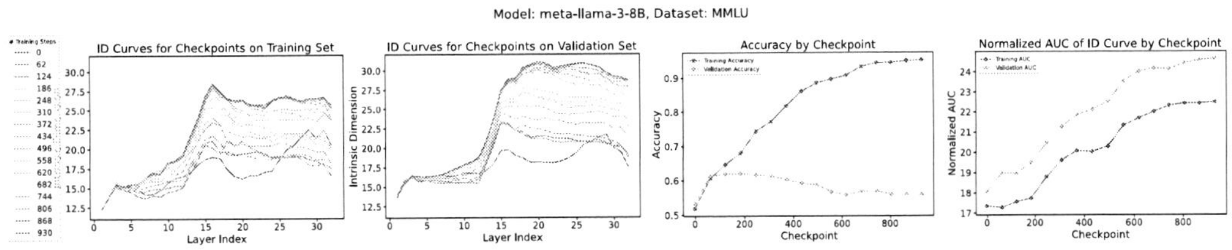

Figure 14: Supervised Fine-Tuning Results for Llama-3-8B on MMLU

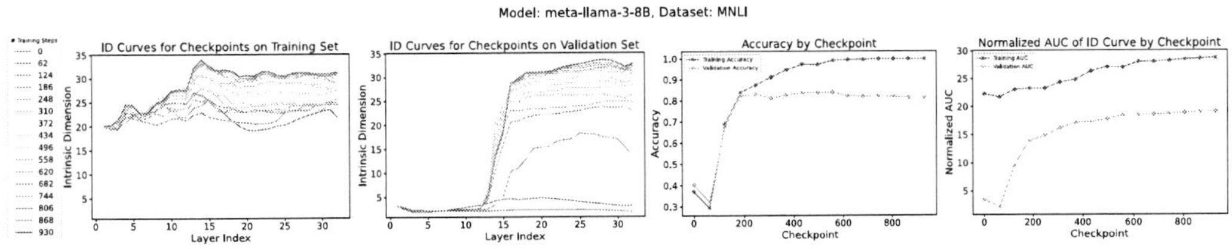

Figure 15: Supervised Fine-Tuning Results for Llama-3-8B on MNLI

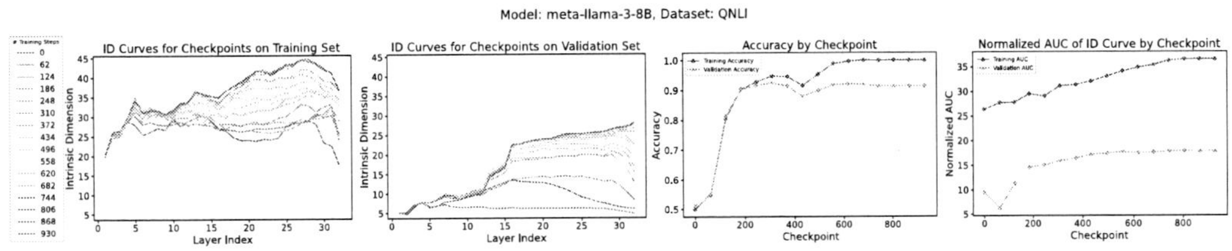

Figure 16: Supervised Fine-Tuning Results for Llama-3-8B on QNLI

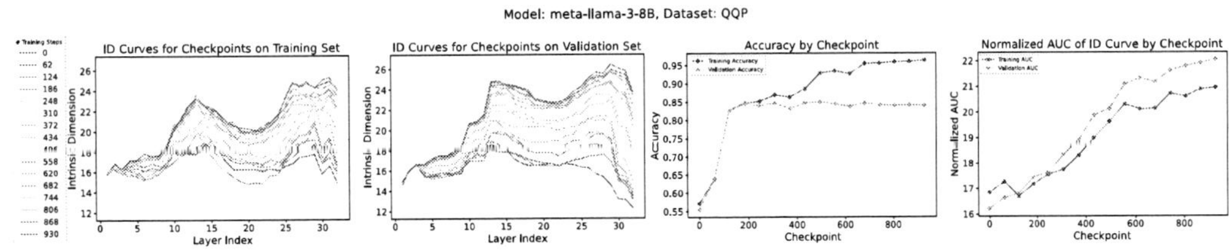

Figure 17: Supervised Fine-Tuning Results for Llama-3-8B on QQP

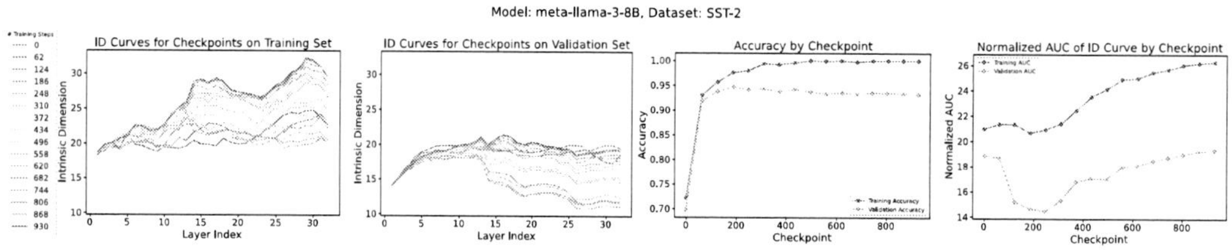

Figure 18: Supervised Fine-Tuning Results for Llama-3-8B on SST-2

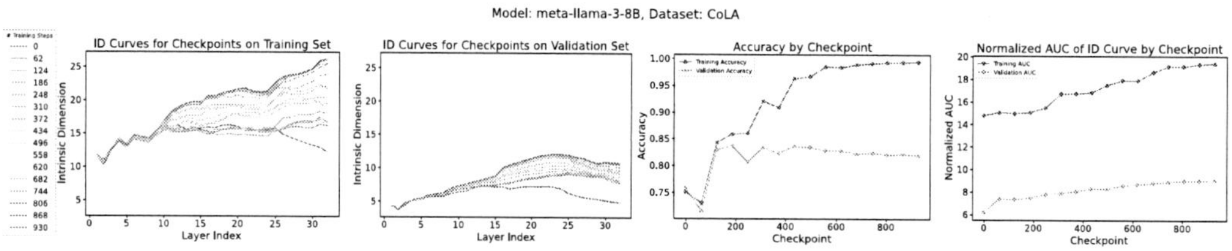

Figure 19: Supervised Fine-Tuning Results for Llama-3-8B on CoLA

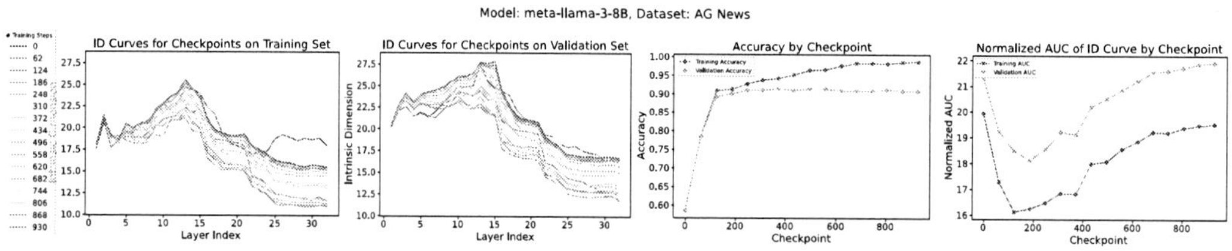

Figure 20: Supervised Fine-Tuning Results for Llama-3-8B on AG News

B.2 Supervised Fine-Tuning Results for Llama-2-13B

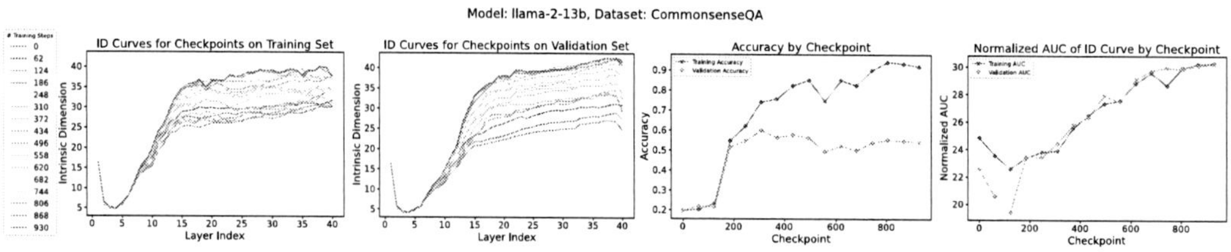

Figure 21: Supervised Fine-Tuning Results for Llama-2-13B on Commonsense QA

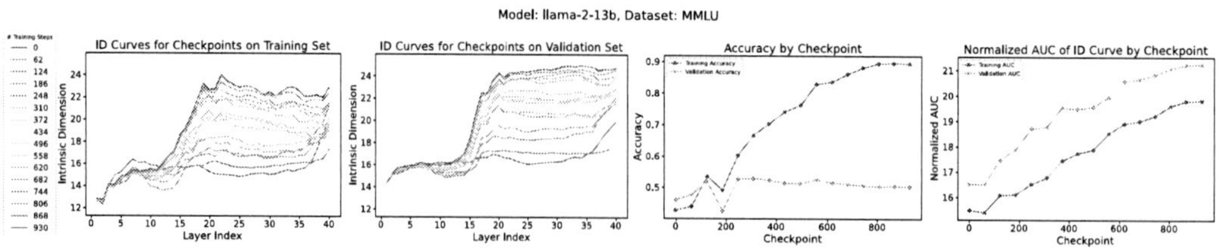

Figure 22: Supervised Fine-Tuning Results for Llama-2-13B on MMLU

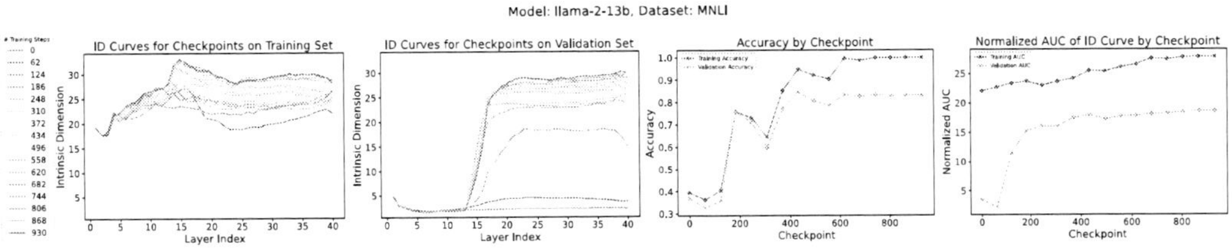

Figure 23: Supervised Fine-Tuning Results for Llama-2-13B on MNLI

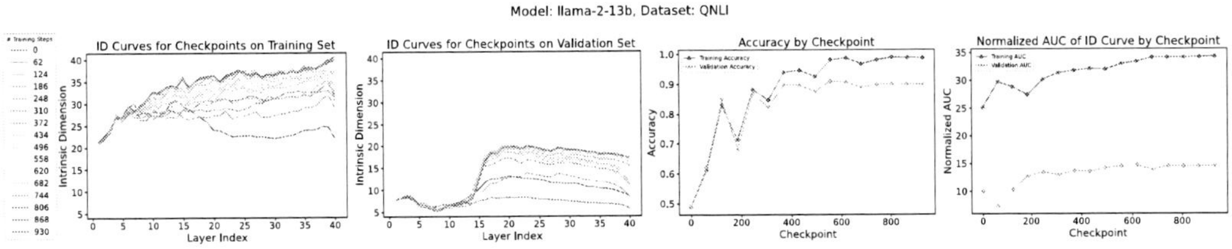

Figure 24: Supervised Fine-Tuning Results for Llama-2-13B on QNLI

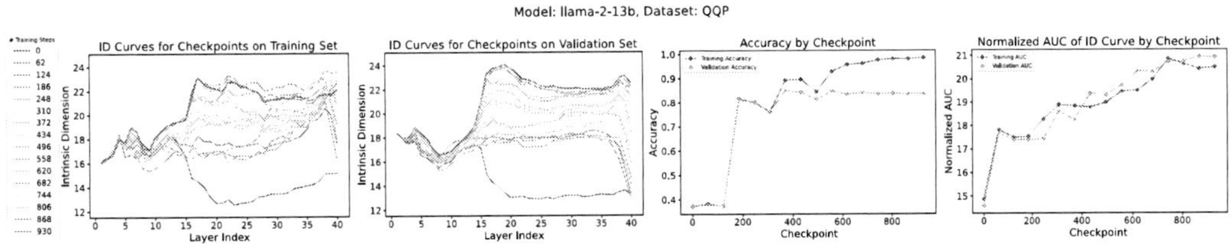

Figure 25: Supervised Fine-Tuning Results for Llama-2-13B on QQP

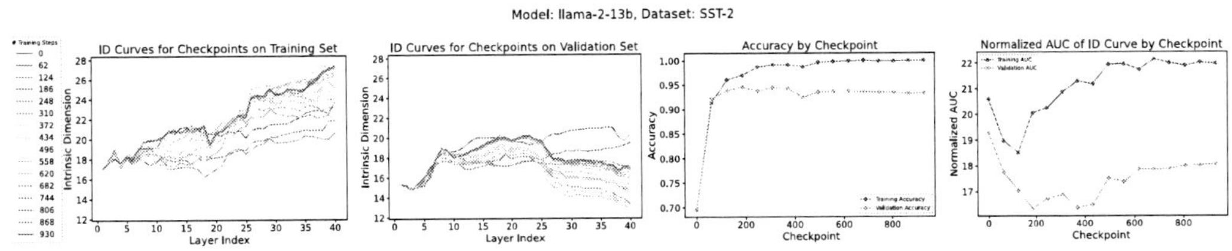

Figure 26: Supervised Fine-Tuning Results for Llama-2-13B on SST-2

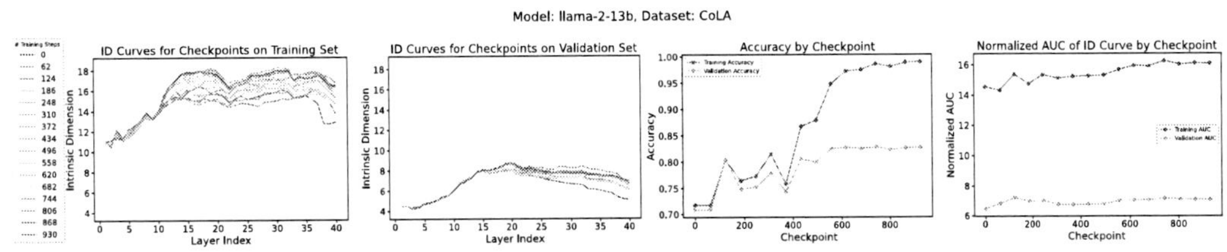

Figure 27: Supervised Fine-Tuning Results for Llama-2-13B on CoLA

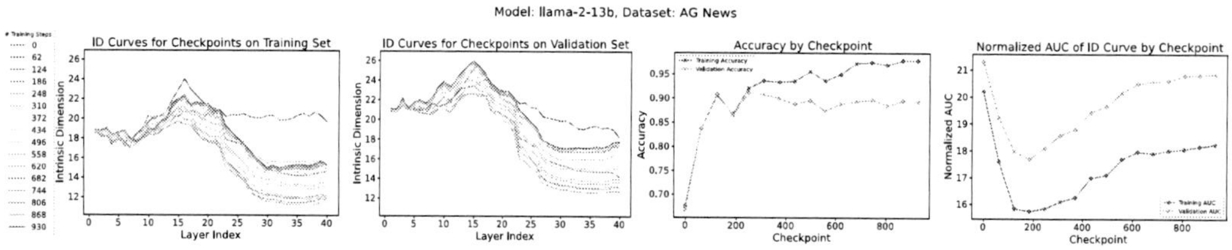

Figure 28: Supervised Fine-Tuning Results for Llama-2-13B on AG News

C Comparisons of Supervised Fine-Tuning and In-Context Learning

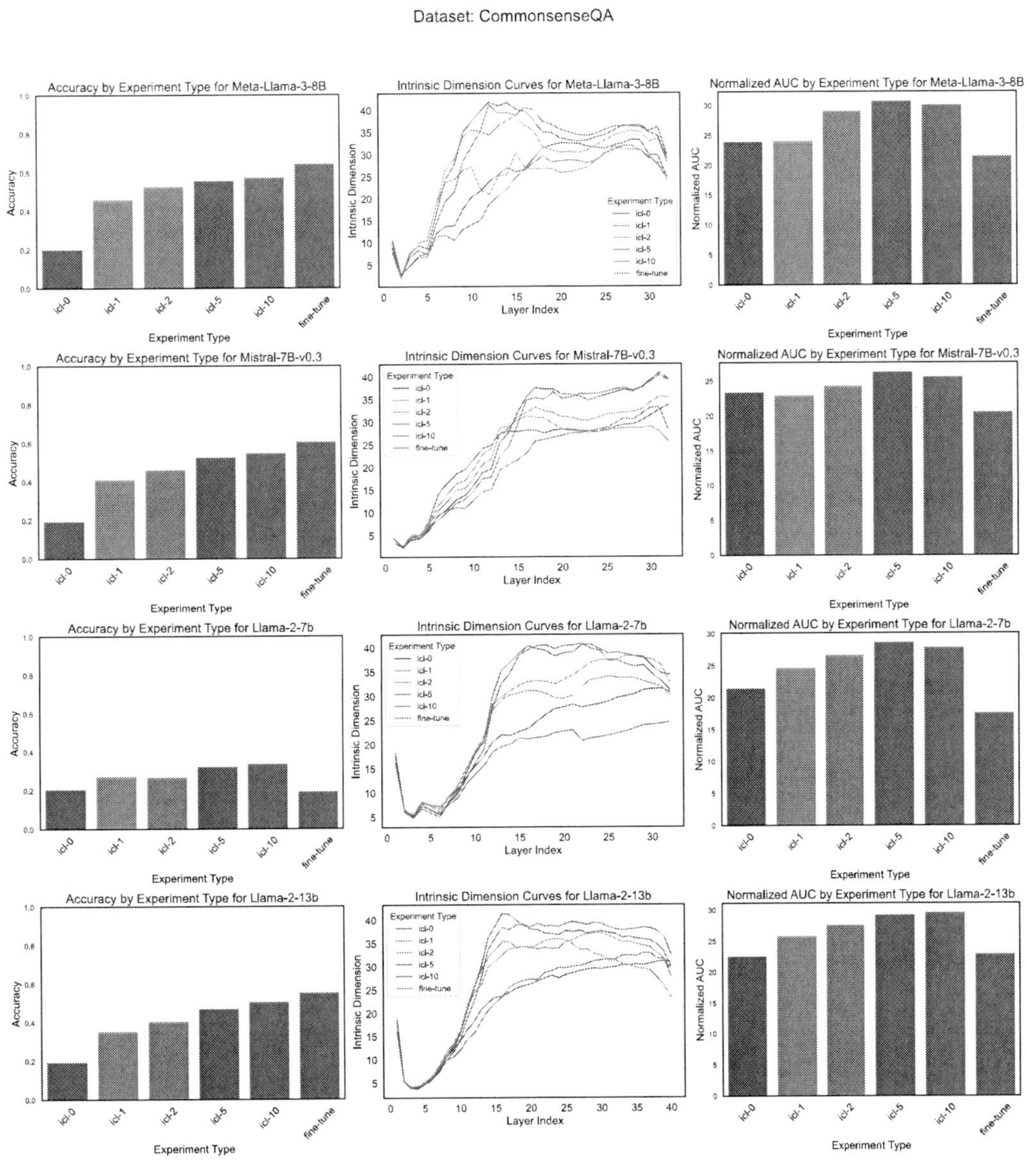

Figure 29: Comparison of Experimental Results for Commonsense QA

Dataset: MMLU

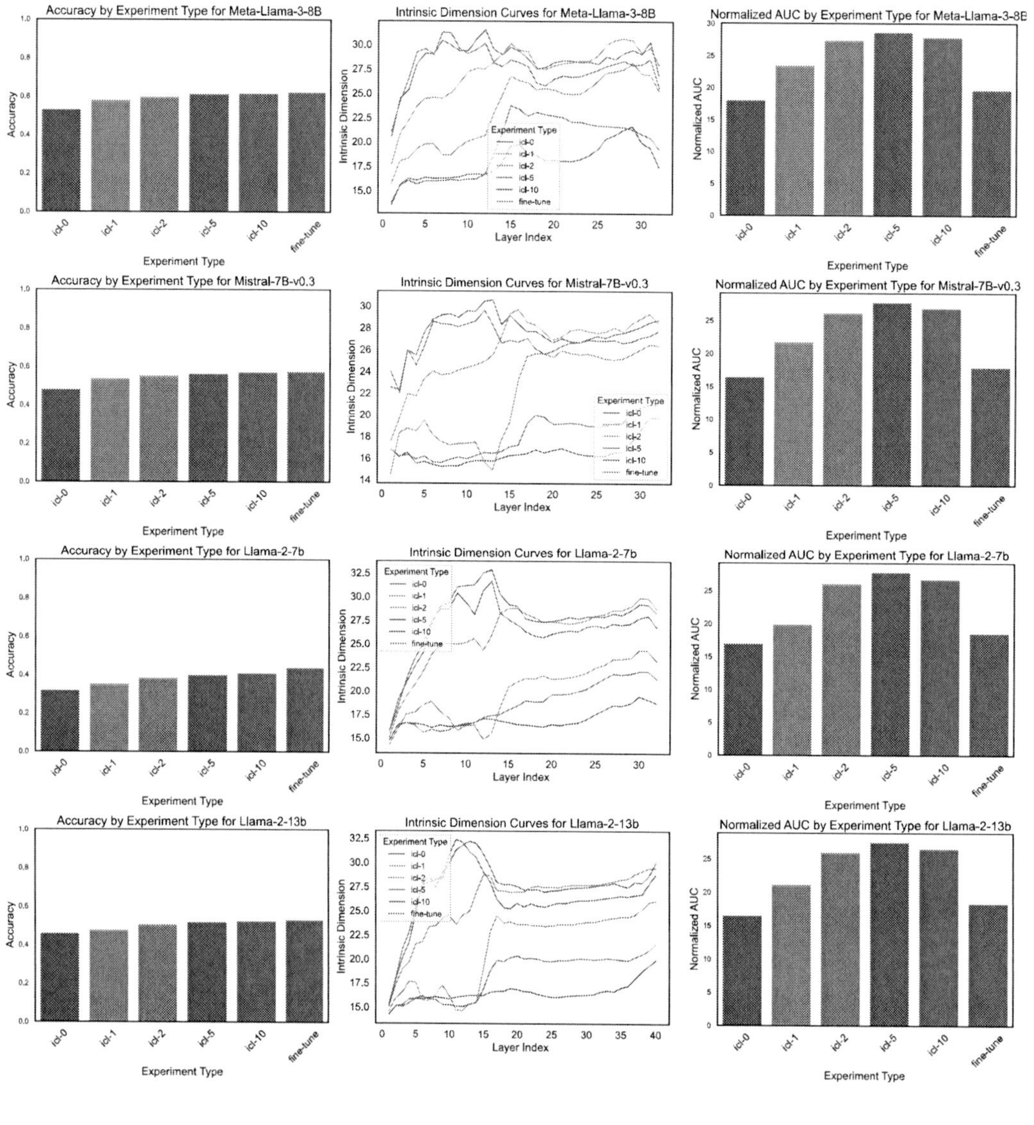

Figure 30: Comparison of Experimental Results for MMLU

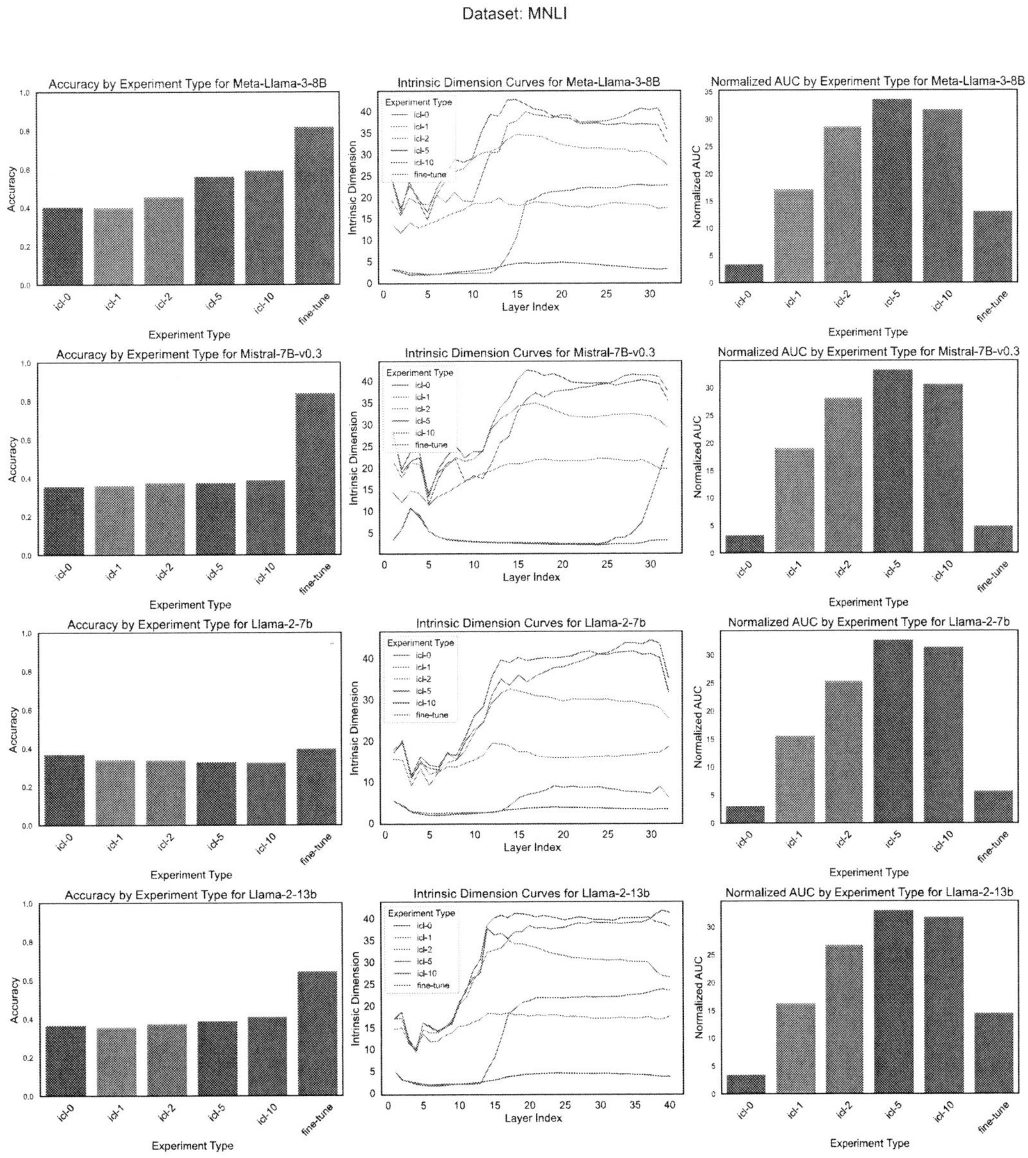

Figure 31: Comparison of Experimental Results for MNLI

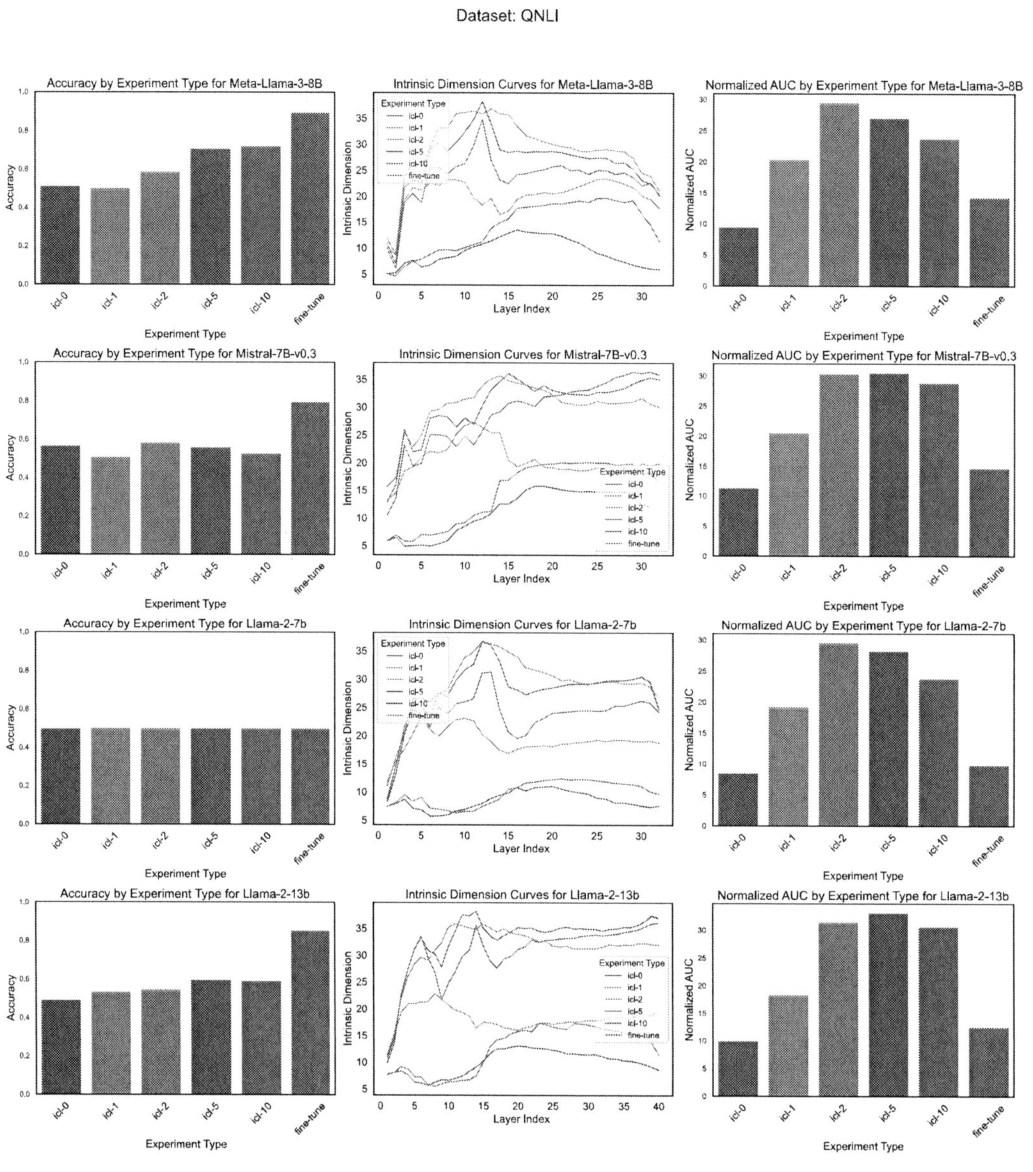

Figure 32: Comparison of Experimental Results for QNLI

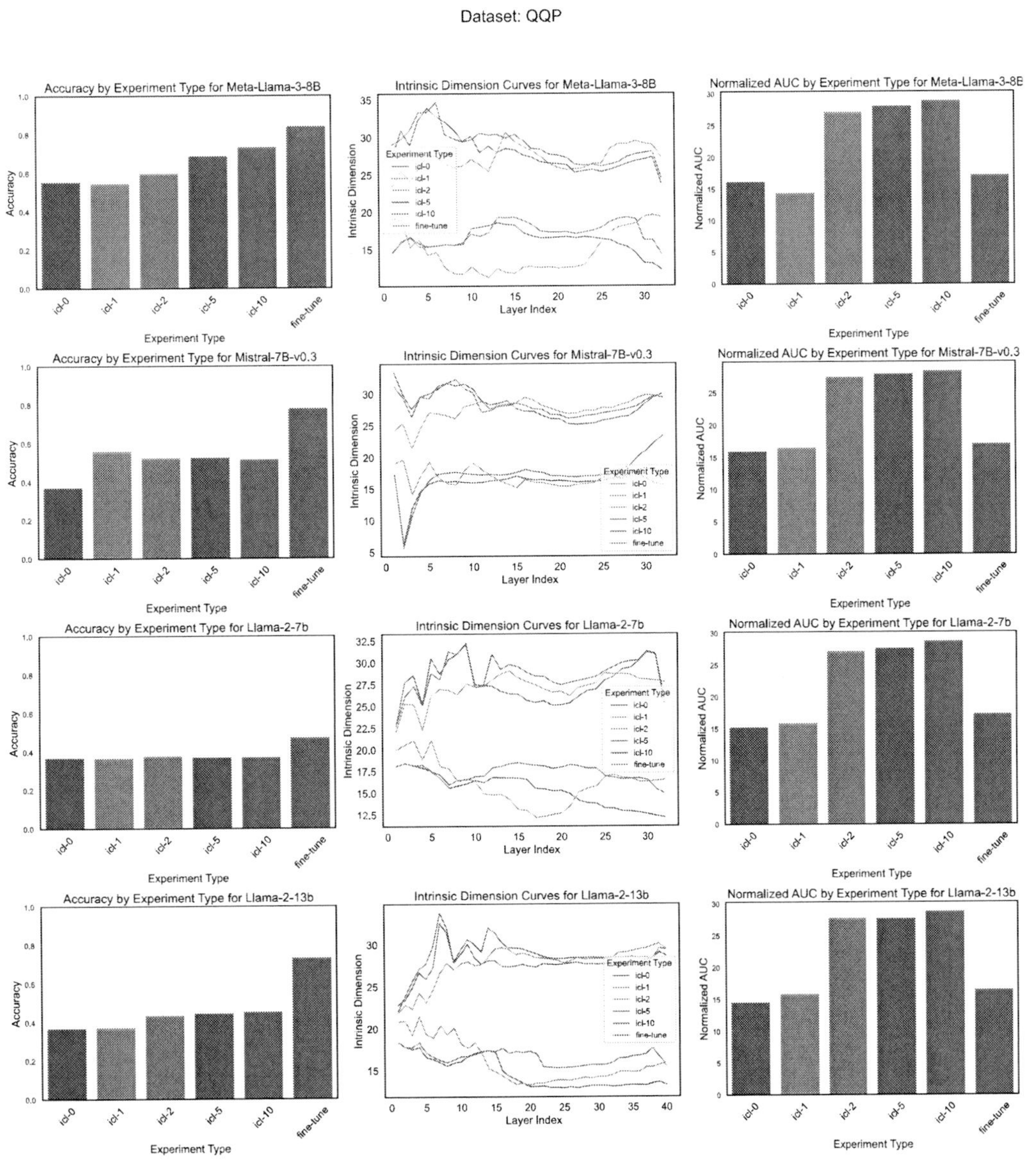

Figure 33: Comparison of Experimental Results for QQP

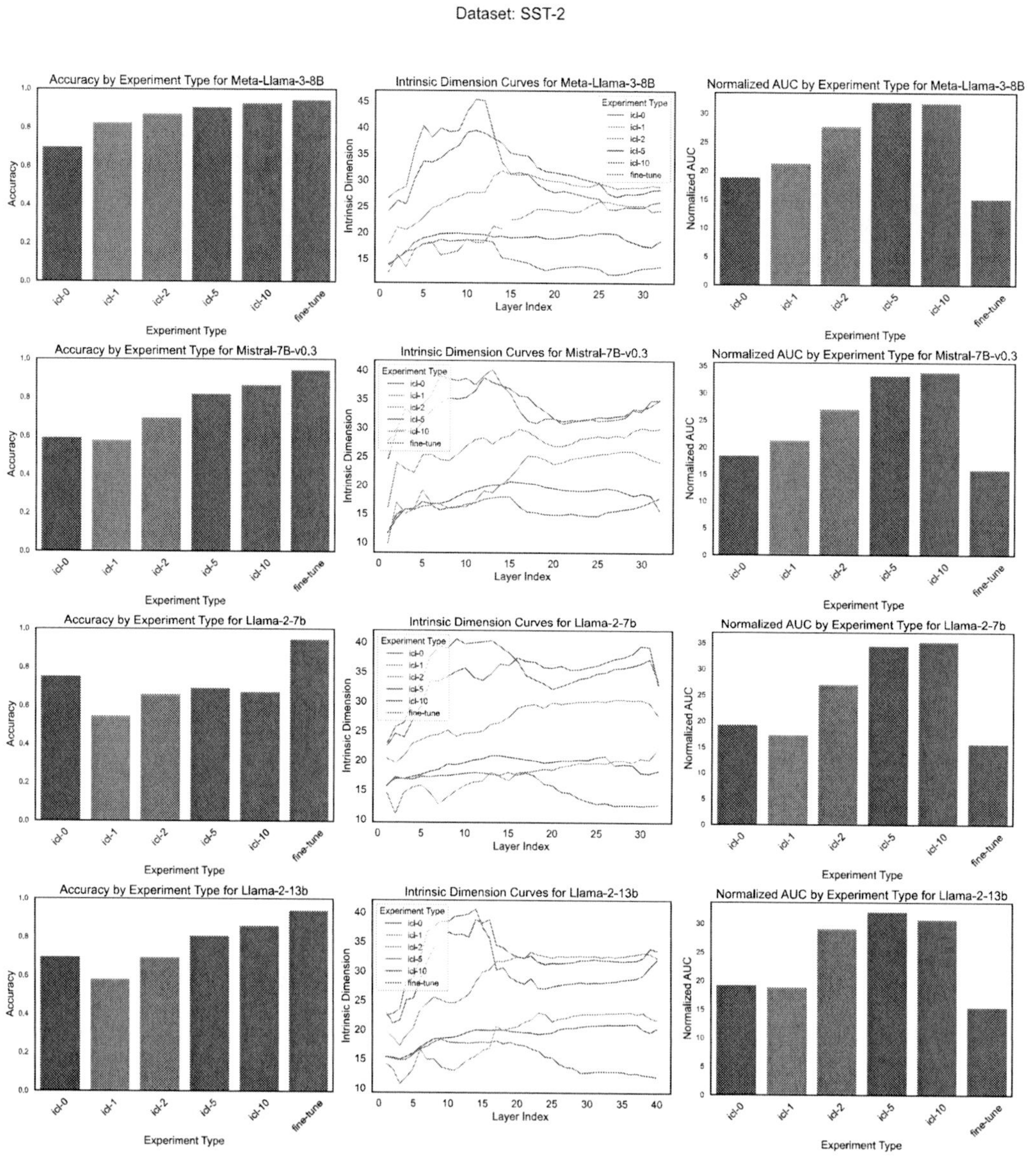

Figure 34: Comparison of Experimental Results for SST-2

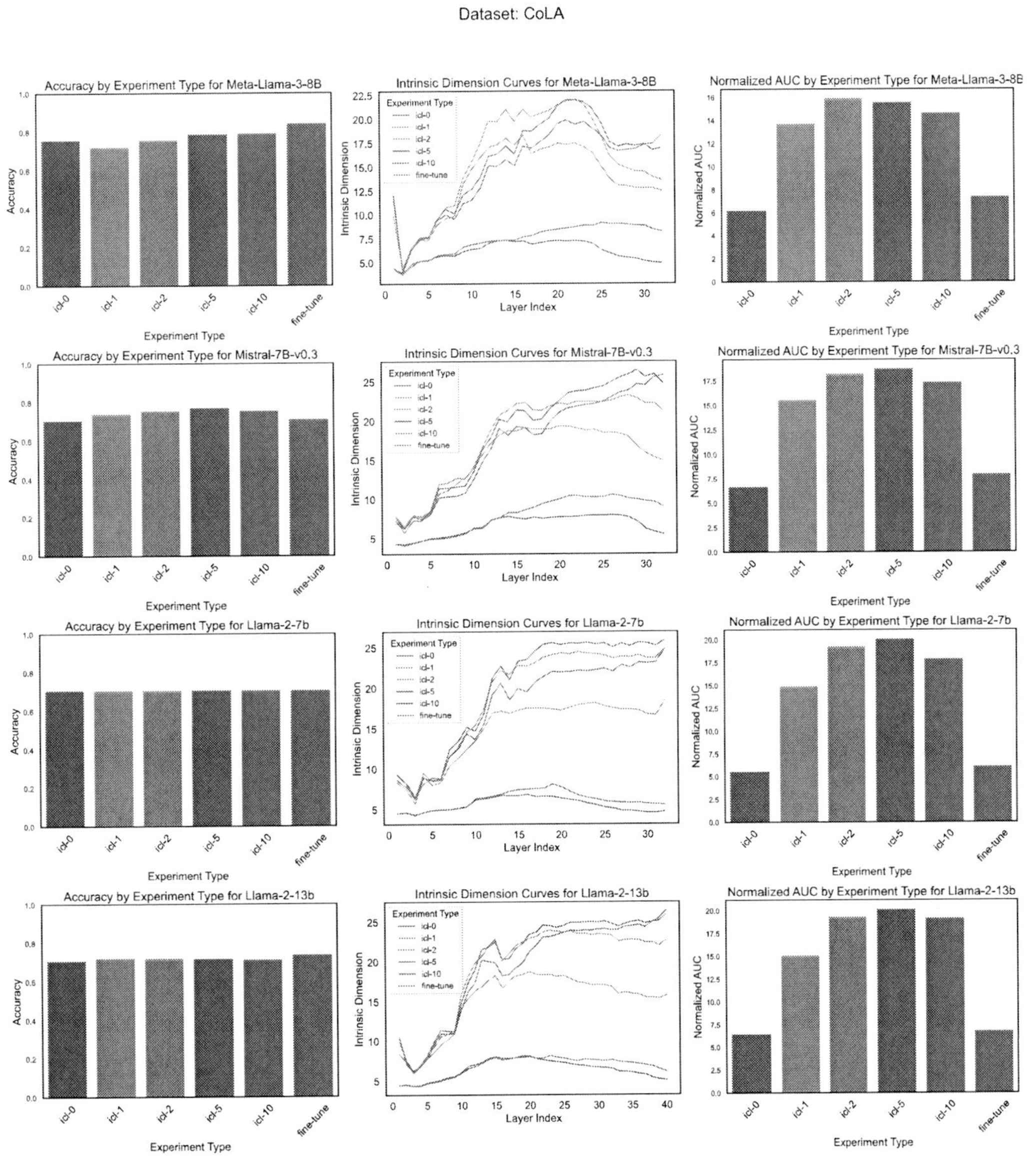

Figure 35: Comparison of Experimental Results for CoLA

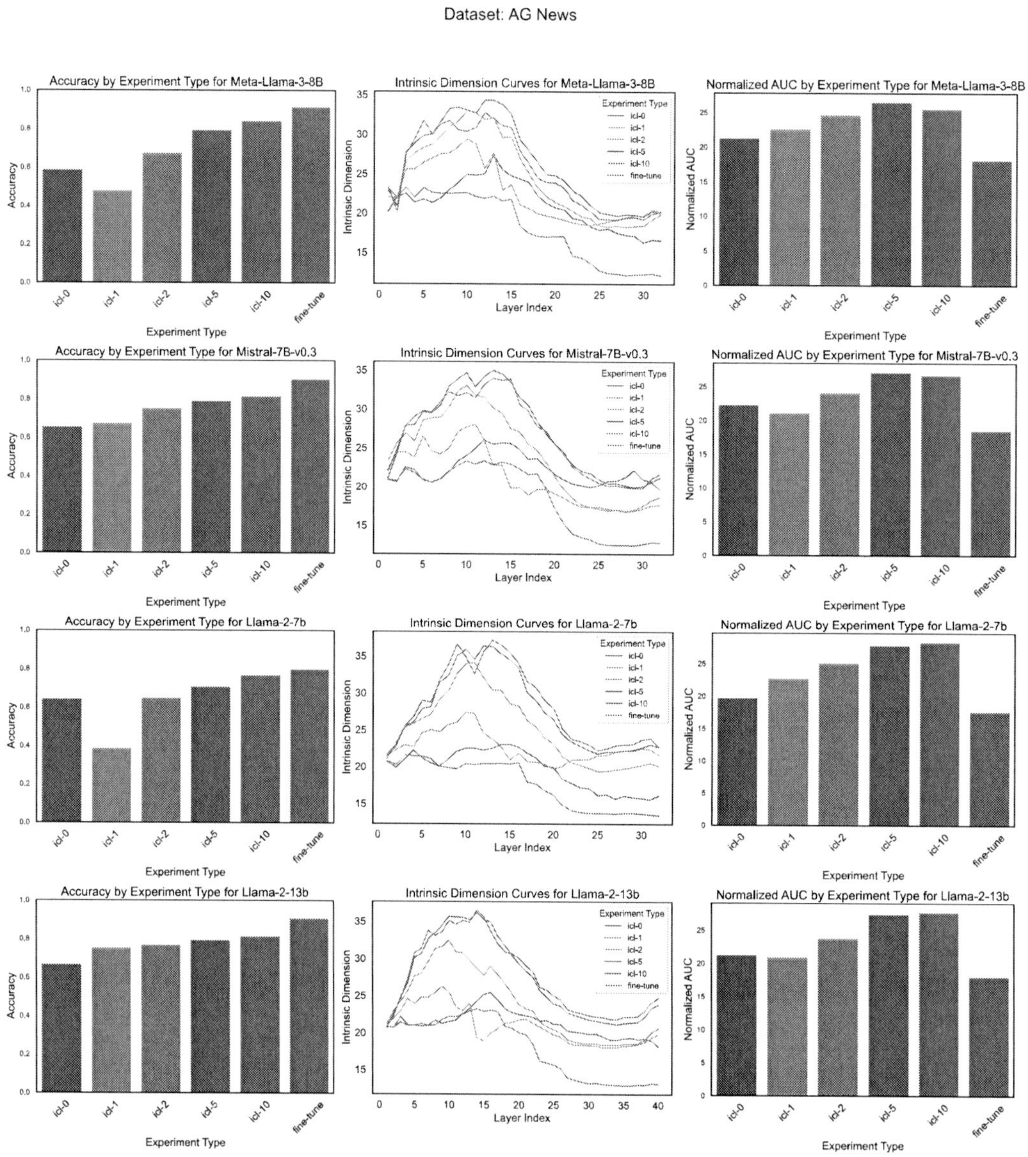

Figure 36: Comparison of Experimental Results for AG News

D ICL Experiment Results with Unique Demonstrations

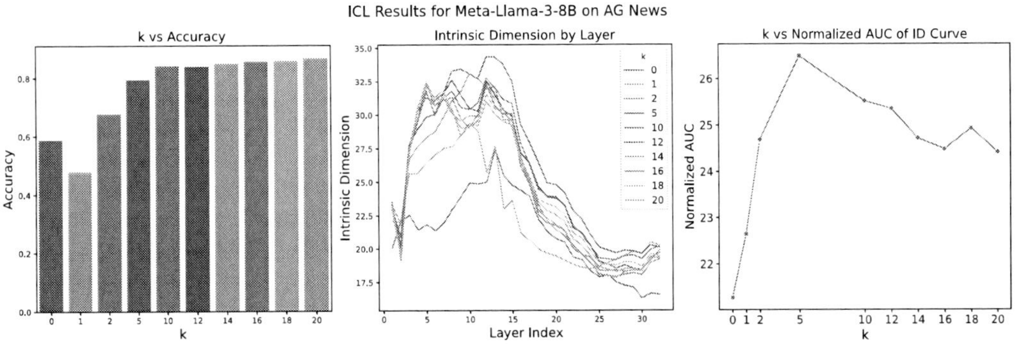

Figure 37: ICL Experiment Results with Unique Demonstrations on AGNews Dataset

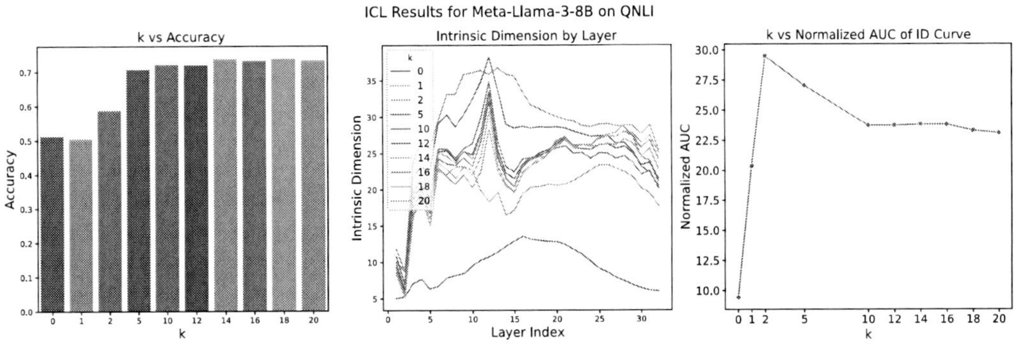

Figure 38: ICL Experiment Results with Unique Demonstrations on QNLI Dataset

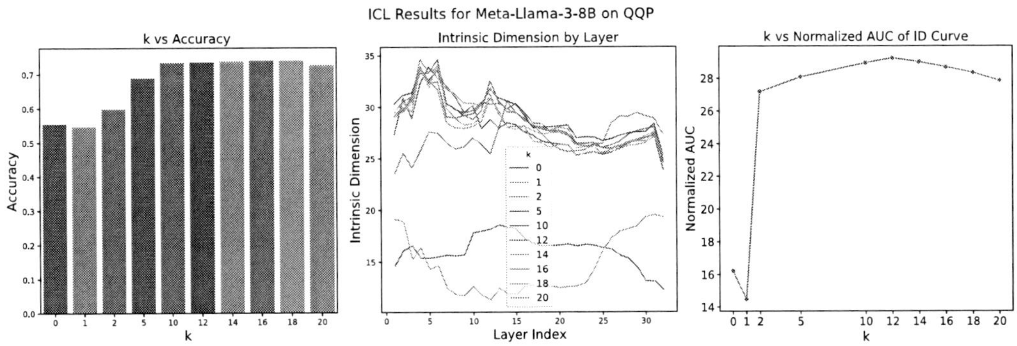

Figure 39: ICL Experiment Results with Unique Demonstrations on QQP Dataset

E Normalized AUC Boxplot by Model for All Learning Paradigms

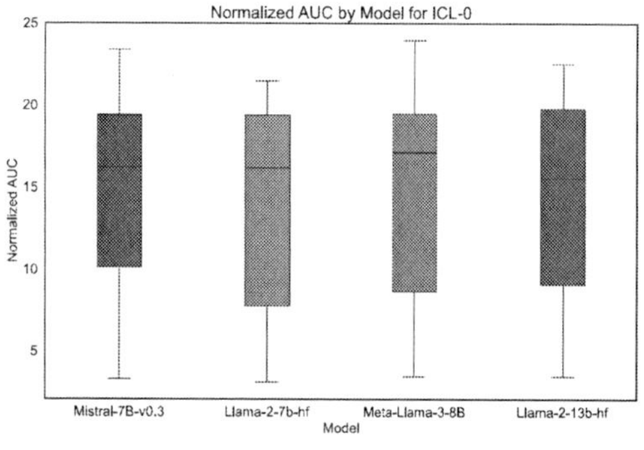

Figure 40: Normalized AUC by Model boxplot for ICL-0 experiments.

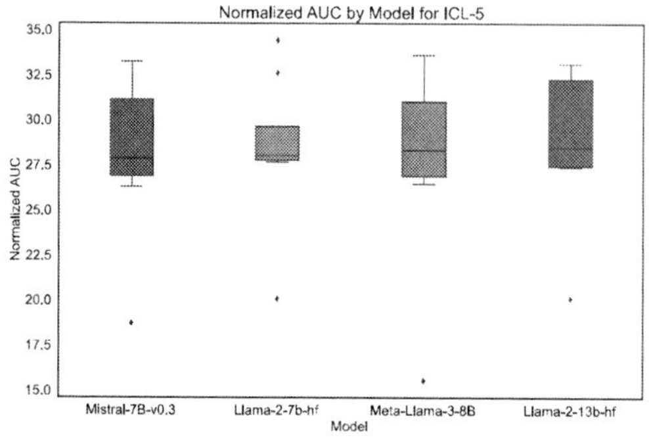

Figure 43: Normalized AUC by Model boxplot for ICL-5 experiments.

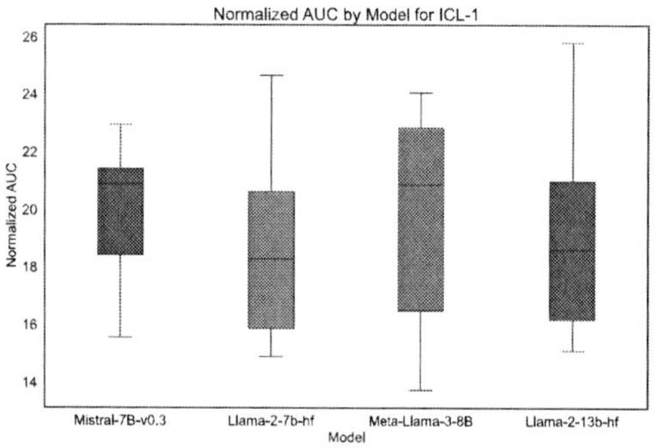

Figure 41: Normalized AUC by Model boxplot for ICL-1 experiments.

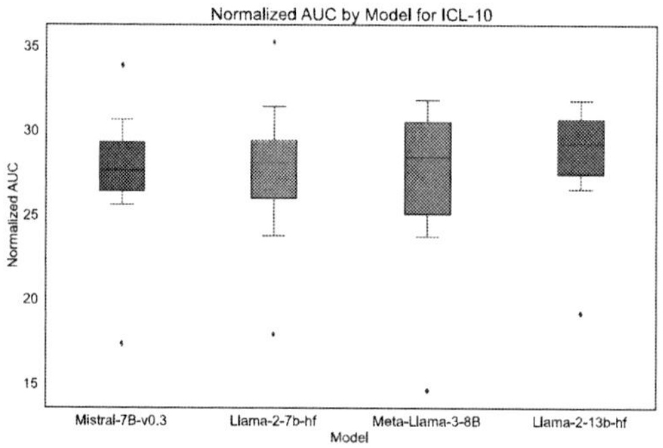

Figure 44: Normalized AUC by Model boxplot for ICL-10 experiments.

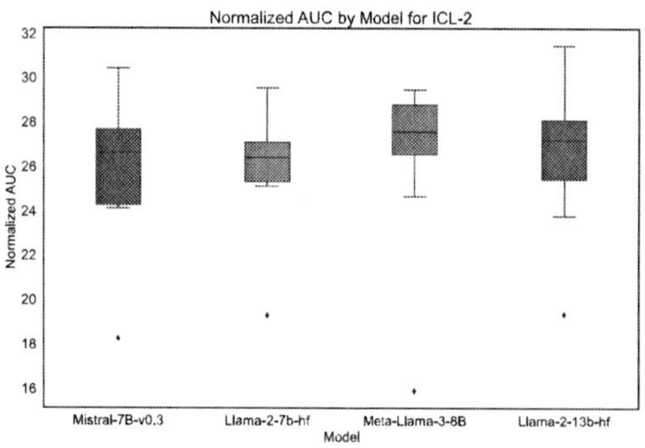

Figure 42: Normalized AUC by Model boxplot for ICL-2 experiments.

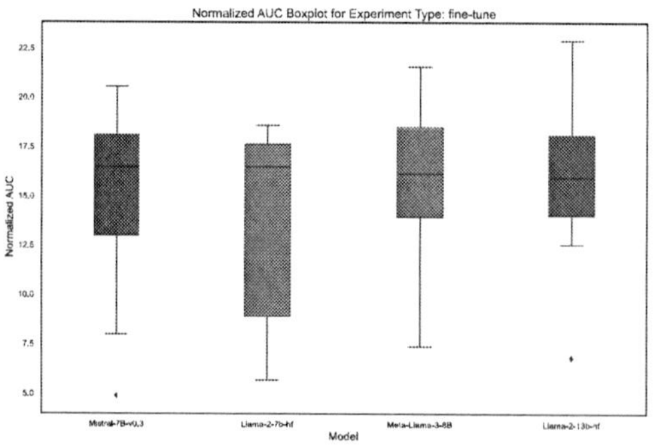

Figure 45: Normalized AUC by Model boxplot for SFT experiments.

F Validating the TwoNN Estimator with the MLE Estimator

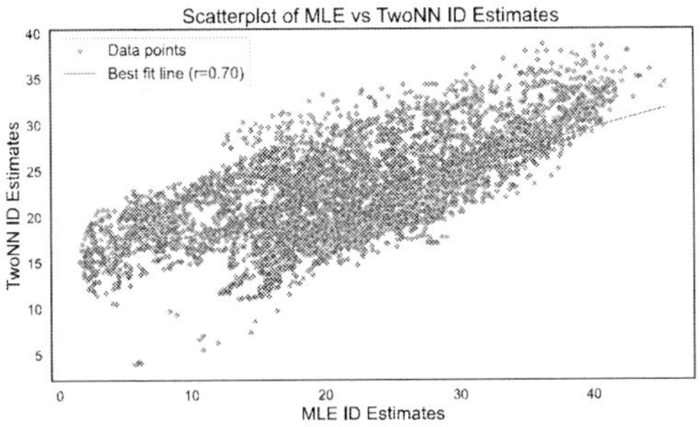

Figure 46: Scatterplot plotting ID estimation results for all experiments using the MLE and TwoNN Estimators.

To assess the validity of our intrinsic dimension estimator, we calculate the intrinsic dimension for different combinations of (learning paradigm, dataset, model, layer) using the TwoNN estimator and Maximum Likelihood Estimator (MLE) introduced by Levina and Bickel (2004). We use a neighborhood of size $k = 50$ when applying MLE. We find that the estimates from the two estimators are correlated with $r = 0.7$. While it is not possible to know the 'true' intrinsic dimensionality of the representations, high correlation between two separate estimators provides a sanity check for our choice of the TwoNN estimator.

G Dataset Generation Details

H Dataset Details

We include details about dataset generation below. We get prompts for all datasets except MMLU from the PromptSource library (Bach et al., 2022).

H.1 QNLI

Items for the training and validation splits in our QNLI experiments were taken from the official QNLI 'train' and 'validation' splits respectively.

Prompt Template:

```
Does that sentence have all you need to
    ↪ answer the question
    ↪ "{{question}}"?
|||
{{answer_choices[label]}}
```

Labels: ['yes', 'no']

H.2 CommonsenseQA

Items for both the training and validation splits in our CommonsenseQA experiments were taken from the official CommonsenseQA 'train' split.

Prompt Template:

```
Given the following options, what do
    ↪ you think is the correct answer
    ↪ to the question below:

{{question}}

Options:
{% for letter, t in zip(answer_choices,
    ↪ choices.text) %}
- {{letter}}: {{t}}
{% endfor %} |||
{{answerKey}}
{% endif %}
```

Labels: ['A', 'B', 'C', 'D']

H.3 MMLU

Items for both the training and validation splits in our MMLU experiments were taken from the official MMLU 'test' split.

Prompt Template:

```
# generate input txt and output txt
letters = ['A', 'B', 'C', 'D']
choices = dataset_element['choices']

input_txt =
    ↪ f"{dataset_element['question']}\n\nA:
    ↪ {choices[0]}\nB:
    ↪ {choices[1]}\nC:
    ↪ {choices[2]}\nD:
    ↪ {choices[3]}\nAnswer:"

output_txt = letters[answer_idx]
combined = input_txt + output_txt
```

H.4 SST-2

Items for both the training and validation splits in our SST-2 experiments were taken from the official SST-2 'train' split.

Prompt Template:

```
{{sentence}}
Question: Was that sentence
    ↪ {{"positive"}} or
    ↪ {{"negative"}}? Answer: ||| {{
    ↪ answer_choices[label] }}
```

Labels: ['negative', 'positive']

H.5 CoLA

Items for both the training and validation splits in our CoLA experiments were taken from the official CoLA 'train' split.

Prompt Template:

```
Does the following sentence make sense
    ↪ and use correct English? Please
    ↪ answer {{"yes"}} or {{"no"}}.
{{sentence}}
|||
{{ answer_choices[label] }}
```

Labels: ['no', 'yes']

H.6 AGNews

Items for the training and validation splits in our AGNews experiments were taken from the official AGNews 'train' and 'validation' splits respectively.

Prompt Template:

```
What label best describes this news
    ↪ article?
{{text}} |||
{{answer_choices[label] }}
```

Labels: ['World politics', 'Sports', 'Business', 'Science and technology']

H.7 MNLI

Items for the training and validation splits in our MNLI experiments were taken from the official MNLI 'train' and 'validation_matched' splits respectively.

Prompt Template:

```
{{premise}} Are we justified in saying
    ↪ that "{{hypothesis}}"? Yes, no,
    ↪ or maybe? ||| {{
    ↪ answer_choices[label] }}
```

Labels: ['Yes', 'Maybe', 'No']

H.8 QQP

Items for the training and validation splits in our QQP experiments were taken from the official QQP 'train' and 'validation' splits respectively.

Prompt Template:

```
I'm an administrator on the website
    ↪ Quora. There are two posts, one
    ↪ that asks "{{question1}}" and
    ↪ another that asks
    ↪ "{{question2}}". I can merge
    ↪ questions if they are asking the
    ↪ same thing. Can I merge these
    ↪ two questions? ||| {{
    ↪ answer_choices[label] }}
```

Labels: ['no', 'yes']

Choose Your Words Wisely: Domain-adaptive Masking Makes Language Models Learn Faster

Vanshpreet S. Kohli
IIIT Hyderabad
vanshpreet.k@research.iiit.ac.in

Aaron Monis
IIIT Hyderabad
aaron.monis@students.iiit.ac.in

Radhika Mamidi
IIIT Hyderabad
radhika.mamidi@iiit.ac.in

Abstract

Foundational Language Models perform significantly better on downstream tasks in specialised domains (such as law, computer science, and medical science) upon being further pre-trained on extensive domain-specific corpora, but this continual pre-training incurs heavy computational costs. Indeed, some of the most performant specialised language models such as BioBERT incur even higher computing costs during domain-specific training than the pre-training cost of the foundational models they are initialised from. In this paper, we argue that much of the extended pre-training is redundant, with models seemingly wasting valuable resources re-learning lexical and semantic patterns already well-represented in their foundational models such as BERT, T5 and GPT. Focusing on Masked Language Models, we introduce a novel domain-specific masking strategy that is designed to facilitate continual learning while minimizing the training cost. Using this approach, we train and present a BERT-based model trained on a biomedical corpus that matches or surpasses traditionally trained biomedical language models in performance across several downstream classification tasks while incurring up to 11 times lower training costs.

1 Introduction

Rapid advancements in Large Language Models (LLMs) (OpenAI, 2024, Touvron et al., 2023) have resulted in an increased focus on their capabilities in specialised domains like biology, law and computer science (Lai et al., 2024, Chen et al., 2024). The significance of foundational models like BERT, T5, GPT and LLaMa for application in such fields is particularly evident from the multitude of models based on them – such as LegalBERT (Chalkidis et al., 2020), SciFive (Phan et al., 2021), BioGPT (Luo et al., 2022) and PMC-LLaMa (Wu et al., 2023) – delivering state-of-the-art results on benchmarks in their respective domains. Given the vast amount of training data available for continual pre-training across various fields, existing literature shows that further pre-training foundational language models on a domain-specific corpus yields better model performance across downstream tasks (Gururangan et al., 2020, Rongali et al., 2021). However, pre-training language models can be resource-prohibitive, both in terms of monetary cost and time spent on training. This is especially true for large, parameter-dense language models like LLaMa (Touvron et al., 2023), which are not only significantly more expensive to train further, but also exhibit much smaller improvements in downstream performance per unit of compute spent (Chen et al., 2024).

It is therefore worthwhile to attempt to leverage the capabilities of contemporary foundational language models for tasks across such domains without expending exorbitant computing resources on diminishing returns. In this paper, we present a novel strategy for continual/mixed-domain pre-training that emphasises selecting relevant (as opposed to random) training samples to maximise compute efficiency. We test our strategy in the biomedical domain by further pre-training BERT on a corpus of PubMed abstracts, mirroring the selection of architecture and pre-training corpora of BioBERT (Lee et al., 2020), one of the most popular biomedical language models. In our testing over 8 Named Entity Recognition (NER) tasks, the resultant model significantly outperforms BioBERT-v1.0 at two-thirds of the compute cost, and performs similarly to BioBERT-v1.1 at about one-eleventh of its compute cost.

2 Related Works

2.1 Biomedical Language Models

The vast majority of domain-adapted language models employ the transformer architecture

Proceedings of the 10th Workshop on Representation Learning for NLP (RepL4NLP-2025), pages 87–91

(Vaswani, 2017), either as encoder layers (like BERT), decoder layers (like GPT) or a combination of the two (like T5). The two most popular strategies to train domain-specific language models are: **1.** pre-training from scratch on a corpus relevant to the domain, and **2.** further pre-training a foundational model on the corpus. The former approach has generally been shown to yield better results when large corpora are available for training, because such models use a vocabulary relevant to their corpus instead of inheriting the vocabulary from a general-domain model (Gu et al., 2021). However, experiments from the likes of Chalkidis et al. (2020) and Lee et al. (2020) demonstrate that the latter approach yields competitive results while requiring significantly less training due to the transfer of learning from their foundational models.

Of the architectures discussed above, the versatility of encoder representations in downstream tasks makes BERT-like models vastly popular for domain adaptation. This is particularly true in the biomedical domain which is littered with models like SciBERT (Beltagy et al., 2019), BioBERT, BioLinkBERT (Yasunaga et al., 2022), DistilBioBERT (Rohanian et al., 2022), PubMedBERT and so on. Indeed, among the 8 tasks we test our model on, the current State-Of-The-Art (SOTA) results[1] are claimed by a non–BERT-style model only for two of the tasks.

2.2 Curriculum Learning

In a curriculum learning setting (Bengio et al., 2009), training samples are presented to a model not arbitrarily, but in an "easy-to-difficult" order, where the method for ranking the difficulty of samples depends on the model and task involved. This framework is designed to better simulate human cognition, wherein humans learn complex concepts more easily after having learnt basic ones. Recent studies indicate that employing this approach demonstrably accelerates convergence compared to random presentation of samples in many settings (Roy et al., 2024, Jarca et al., 2024, Tang et al., 2024).

We approach domain-adaptation of a foundational language model as an analogous task to curriculum learning. We posit that since the model has already been trained on a general ("easy") corpus and must now be trained in a specific ("difficult") domain, we can apply the same curriculum learning principle of curating training samples such that they specifically facilitate domain-specific learning. To the best of our knowledge, this approach has not thus far been tested or reported on.

[1]sourced from https://paperswithcode.com/sota

3 Methodology

We begin by creating a biomedical corpus consisting of PubMed abstracts publicly available at https://pubmed.ncbi.nlm.nih.gov/download/, amounting to about 9.4GB of text. Leveraging the linguistic difficulty criterion and subsequent curriculum generation approach introduced by Lee et al. (2022), who claim that frequently occuring words that have many connections in a large knowledge graph are easier to learn, we build a set S of "basic" concepts – i.e. the n concepts with the most connections in a large-scale knowledge graph that occur in the corpus above a threshold frequency f. Iterating through all the elements s_i of S, we add s_i and every concept in ConceptNet within k hops of s_i to a new set C, which acts as a "curriculum" consisting of relevant concepts. Following manual assessment of the curriculum generated, we settled on using $f = 200,000$, $n = 5,000$ and $k = 5$.

For our purposes, despite the availability of biomedical knowledge graphs like BIKG (Geleta et al., 2021) and BIOS (Yu et al., 2022), we chose to use the general-domain ConceptNet (Speer et al., 2017) as the knowledge graph. We did not assess the overlap between these specific knowledge graphs and our corpus, and could not be certain that their usage would not be counterproductive given that BERT's vocabulary itself is not tailored towards biomedical terms. Moreover, this makes our approach easier to generalise for other domains without pre-existing large knowledge graphs. Nonetheless, we recognise that the use of domain-specific knowledge graphs for concept extraction, wherever available, is worth investigating in future studies.

Since this curriculum includes general-domain concepts already represented well in BERT, we iterate once over BERT's corpus (Wikipedia + BooksCorpus), identify concepts occuring more than $f/3$ times and remove them from C. Note that this cutoff frequency has been scaled down with respect to the threshold frequency used for the PubMed corpus above to account for the difference in sizes between the corpora. We then iterate through C and remove any concepts that do not occur at all in the PubMed corpus, ensuring that

Dataset	Entity type	No. of annotations
NCBI Disease	Disease	6,881
BC5CDR	Disease	12,694
BC5CDR	Drug/Chem.	15,411
BC4CHEMD	Drug/Chem.	79,842
BC2GM	Gene/Protein	20,703
JNLPBA	Gene/Protein	35,460
LINNAEUS	Species	4,077
Species-800	Species	3,708

Table 1: Statistics of the biomedical NER datasets.

the concepts now contained in C are relevant to the biomedical domain.

We then initialize our model from the publicly available BERT-base checkpoint, and train it for Masked Language Modeling (MLM) over our corpus. Past studies indicate that the difference between using cased and uncased models to warm-start biomedical language models is minimal with no clear advantage for either (Lee et al., 2020, Gu et al., 2021, and it is beyond the scope of our current experiment to test and compare the two. For our purposes, we use the uncased version of the model.

Differing from the likes of BERT and BioBERT that randomly mask 15% of the tokens in each batch, we mask only the tokens that form a concept within the previously curated curriculum C while ensuring that no more than 20% of the tokens in any batch are masked. As concepts can span multiple tokens, we follow Lee et al. (2022)'s Whole Concept Masking (WCM) strategy such that all the tokens comprising a single concept are simultaneously masked. As is the standard, we replace 80% of the masked concepts with a mask token, replace another 10% with a random token and do not replace the remaining 10%. Since existing literature shows minimal gains from calculating the Next Sentence Prediction (NSP) loss (Liu et al., 2019), we chose to omit it; MLM was our sole pre-training objective.

4 Experimental Setup

4.1 Pre-training

We trained the model for 200K steps on four NVIDIA RTX 6000 GPUs, using PyTorch's DistributedDataParallel to share the load across the GPUs. The batch size was fixed at 256 and the maximum sequence length was set to 256, resulting in 65,536 tokens per training iteration. This equates to 33% lower compute compared to BioBERT-v1.0 trained on the same corpus (98,304 tokens per iteration and 200K iterations), and 91% lower compute than BioBERT-v1.1, which was trained on the same corpus[2] for 1.2M training steps and additionally trained on full-length PubMed Central articles ($\sim$3 times the corpus size of PubMed Abstracts) for 270K steps. Note that the computational overhead caused by curriculum generation is minimal compared to model training, as it only requires iterating over two corpora and a section of one knowledge graph.

4.2 Fine-tuning

With NER being a fundamental task for text mining, we focus our limited testing on commonly used NER benchmarks. We fine-tune and evaluate our model on 8 tasks: BC2GM (Smith et al., 2008), BC4CHEMD (Krallinger et al., 2015), BC5CDR-Chemical (Li et al., 2016), BC5CDR-Disease (Li et al., 2016), JNLPBA (Collier et al., 2004), LINNAEUS (Gerner et al., 2010), NCBI Disease (Doğan et al., 2014) and Species-800 (Pafilis et al., 2013). We use pre-processed versions of the respective datasets released by Rohanian et al. (2022). Some specifications for the datasets are listed in Table 1. Following the setup described in the BioBERT paper, we use a learning rate of 5e-5 and train for 25 epochs per dataset. We leave testing this approach in other tasks – such as Question Answering, Relation Extraction as well as other NER tasks – for future studies.

5 Results

The results obtained by our model relative to BERT, BioBERT-v1.0, BioBERT-v1.1 and the current SOTA[3] are shown in Table 2. We consider these to be the most apt comparisons to showcase because BERT is the baseline we train upon, and BioBERT most closely reflects what our model's performance would be if it had been trained using regular MLM. The models delivering the SOTA results are, for the most part, more resource-intensive to train or are tailored towards Biomedical NER tasks as opposed to being general-purpose biomedical transformers. Nevertheless, we consider their performance to be relevant benchmarks and include them in this comparison.

[2] our corpus is collected from the same source but is larger as a virtue of being more up-to-date

[3] to the best of our knowledge

Task/Model	SOTA	BERT	BioBERT-v1.0	BioBERT-v1.1	Ours
BC2GM	*86.97*	81.79	82.54	<u>84.72</u>	**85.43**
BC4CHEMD	*94.39*	90.04	<u>91.26</u>	**92.36**	90.23
BC5CDR-Chemistry	*94.88*	91.16	92.64	**93.47**	<u>93.25</u>
BC5CDR-Disease	*88.50*	82.41	<u>86.2</u>	**87.15**	85.49
JNLPBA	*82.0*	74.94	76.65	<u>77.49</u>	**79.29**
LINNAEUS	*92.7*	87.6	88.13	<u>88.24</u>	**89.23**
NCBI Disease	*89.71*	85.63	87.38	**89.71**	<u>87.92</u>
Species-800	*82.44*	71.63	73.08	<u>74.06</u>	**75.20**

Table 2: Performance comparison across different models (F1 scores). The best result other than the SOTA (*italicised*) is in **bold**, and the second-best is <u>underlined</u>.

Our model outperforms BioBERT-v1.0 in three-fourths of the tasks and, despite significantly less training on a much smaller corpus, outperforms BioBERT-v1.1 in half of the tasks, demonstrating the effectiveness of our training-sample-curation strategy.

Limitations and Future Work

We acknowledge that being a short extended abstract, this paper does not present a full comprehensive study detailing the impact of our strategy. Our aim in presenting our preliminary experiment and findings is to incite further research into this idea from the broader NLP community, encouraging exploration of this approach with different parameters, domains, corpora, model sizes, training steps, model architectures and so on.

Ethics statement

The authors have no competing interests to declare that are relevant to the contents of this article. All the datasets and models accessed as part of this study were sourced from publicly available archives and checkpoints.

References

Iz Beltagy, Kyle Lo, and Arman Cohan. 2019. Scibert: A pretrained language model for scientific text. *arXiv preprint arXiv:1903.10676*.

Yoshua Bengio, Jérôme Louradour, Ronan Collobert, and Jason Weston. 2009. Curriculum learning. In *Proceedings of the 26th annual international conference on machine learning*, pages 41–48.

Ilias Chalkidis, Manos Fergadiotis, Prodromos Malakasiotis, Nikolaos Aletras, and Ion Androutsopoulos. 2020. Legal-bert: The muppets straight out of law school. *arXiv preprint arXiv:2010.02559*.

Qingyu Chen, Yan Hu, Xueqing Peng, Qianqian Xie, Qiao Jin, Aidan Gilson, Maxwell B. Singer, Xuguang Ai, Po-Ting Lai, Zhizheng Wang, Vipina Kuttichi Keloth, Kalpana Raja, Jiming Huang, Huan He, Fongci Lin, Jingcheng Du, Rui Zhang, W. Jim Zheng, Ron A. Adelman, Zhiyong Lu, and Hua Xu. 2024. A systematic evaluation of large language models for biomedical natural language processing: benchmarks, baselines, and recommendations. *Preprint*, arXiv:2305.16326.

Nigel Collier, Tomoko Ohta, Yoshimasa Tsuruoka, Yuka Tateisi, and Jin-Dong Kim. 2004. Introduction to the bio-entity recognition task at jnlpba. In *Proceedings of the International Joint Workshop on Natural Language Processing in Biomedicine and its Applications (NLPBA/BioNLP)*, pages 73–78.

Rezarta Islamaj Doğan, Robert Leaman, and Zhiyong Lu. 2014. Ncbi disease corpus: a resource for disease name recognition and concept normalization. *Journal of biomedical informatics*, 47:1–10.

David Geleta, Andriy Nikolov, Gavin Edwards, Anna Gogleva, Richard Jackson, Erik Jansson, Andrej Lamov, Sebastian Nilsson, Marina Pettersson, Vladimir Poroshin, Benedek Rozemberczki, Timothy Scrivener, Michaël Ughetto, and Eliseo Papa. 2021. Biological insights knowledge graph: an integrated knowledge graph to support drug development. *bioRxiv*.

Martin Gerner, Goran Nenadic, and Casey M Bergman. 2010. Linnaeus: a species name identification system for biomedical literature. *BMC bioinformatics*, 11:1–17.

Yu Gu, Robert Tinn, Hao Cheng, Michael Lucas, Naoto Usuyama, Xiaodong Liu, Tristan Naumann, Jianfeng Gao, and Hoifung Poon. 2021. Domain-specific language model pretraining for biomedical natural language processing. *ACM Transactions on Computing for Healthcare*, 3(1):1–23.

Suchin Gururangan, Ana Marasović, Swabha Swayamdipta, Kyle Lo, Iz Beltagy, Doug Downey, and Noah A. Smith. 2020. Don't stop pretraining: Adapt language models to domains and tasks. *Preprint*, arXiv:2004.10964.

Andrei Jarca, Florinel-Alin Croitoru, and Radu Tudor Ionescu. 2024. Cbm: Curriculum by masking. *Preprint*, arXiv:2407.05193.

Martin Krallinger, Obdulia Rabal, Florian Leitner, Miguel Vazquez, David Salgado, Zhiyong Lu, Robert Leaman, Yanan Lu, Donghong Ji, Daniel M Lowe, et al. 2015. The chemdner corpus of chemicals and drugs and its annotation principles. *Journal of cheminformatics*, 7:1–17.

Jinqi Lai, Wensheng Gan, Jiayang Wu, Zhenlian Qi, and Philip S. Yu. 2024. Large language models in law: A survey. *AI Open*, 5:181–196.

Jinhyuk Lee, Wonjin Yoon, Sungdong Kim, Donghyeon Kim, Sunkyu Kim, Chan Ho So, and Jaewoo Kang. 2020. Biobert: a pre-trained biomedical language representation model for biomedical text mining. *Bioinformatics*, 36(4):1234–1240.

Mingyu Lee, Jun-Hyung Park, Junho Kim, Kang-Min Kim, and SangKeun Lee. 2022. Efficient pre-training of masked language model via concept-based curriculum masking. *arXiv preprint arXiv:2212.07617*.

Jiao Li, Yueping Sun, Robin J Johnson, Daniela Sciaky, Chih-Hsuan Wei, Robert Leaman, Allan Peter Davis, Carolyn J Mattingly, Thomas C Wiegers, and Zhiyong Lu. 2016. Biocreative v cdr task corpus: a resource for chemical disease relation extraction. *Database*, 2016.

Yinhan Liu, Myle Ott, Naman Goyal, Jingfei Du, Mandar Joshi, Danqi Chen, Omer Levy, Mike Lewis, Luke Zettlemoyer, and Veselin Stoyanov. 2019. Roberta: A robustly optimized bert pretraining approach. *Preprint*, arXiv:1907.11692.

Renqian Luo, Liai Sun, Yingce Xia, Tao Qin, Sheng Zhang, Hoifung Poon, and Tie-Yan Liu. 2022. Biogpt: generative pre-trained transformer for biomedical text generation and mining. *Briefings in bioinformatics*, 23(6):bbac409.

OpenAI. 2024. Gpt-4 technical report. *Preprint*, arXiv:2303.08774.

Evangelos Pafilis, Sune P Frankild, Lucia Fanini, Sarah Faulwetter, Christina Pavloudi, Aikaterini Vasileiadou, Christos Arvanitidis, and Lars Juhl Jensen. 2013. The species and organisms resources for fast and accurate identification of taxonomic names in text. *PloS one*, 8(6):e65390.

Long N. Phan, James T. Anibal, Hieu Tran, Shaurya Chanana, Erol Bahadroglu, Alec Peltekian, and Grégoire Altan-Bonnet. 2021. Scifive: a text-to-text transformer model for biomedical literature. *Preprint*, arXiv:2106.03598.

Omid Rohanian, Mohammadmahdi Nouriborji, Samaneh Kouchaki, and David A. Clifton. 2022. On the effectiveness of compact biomedical transformers. *Preprint*, arXiv:2209.03182.

Subendhu Rongali, Abhyuday Jagannatha, Bhanu Pratap Singh Rawat, and Hong Yu. 2021. Continual domain-tuning for pretrained language models. *Preprint*, arXiv:2004.02288.

Soumyadeep Roy, Shamik Sural, and Niloy Ganguly. 2024. *Unlocking Efficiency: Adaptive Masking for Gene Transformer Models*. IOS Press.

Larry Smith, Lorraine K Tanabe, Rie Johnson nee Ando, Cheng-Ju Kuo, I-Fang Chung, Chun-Nan Hsu, Yu-Shi Lin, Roman Klinger, Christoph M Friedrich, Kuzman Ganchev, et al. 2008. Overview of biocreative ii gene mention recognition. *Genome biology*, 9:1–19.

Robyn Speer, Joshua Chin, and Catherine Havasi. 2017. Conceptnet 5.5: An open multilingual graph of general knowledge. In *Proceedings of the AAAI conference on artificial intelligence*, volume 31.

Yao Tang, Zhihui Xie, Zichuan Lin, Deheng Ye, and Shuai Li. 2024. Learning versatile skills with curriculum masking. *Preprint*, arXiv:2410.17744.

Hugo Touvron, Thibaut Lavril, Gautier Izacard, Xavier Martinet, Marie-Anne Lachaux, Timothée Lacroix, Baptiste Rozière, Naman Goyal, Eric Hambro, Faisal Azhar, Aurelien Rodriguez, Armand Joulin, Edouard Grave, and Guillaume Lample. 2023. Llama: Open and efficient foundation language models. *Preprint*, arXiv:2302.13971.

A Vaswani. 2017. Attention is all you need. *Advances in Neural Information Processing Systems*.

Chaoyi Wu, Weixiong Lin, Xiaoman Zhang, Ya Zhang, Yanfeng Wang, and Weidi Xie. 2023. Pmc-llama: Towards building open-source language models for medicine. *Preprint*, arXiv:2304.14454.

Michihiro Yasunaga, Jure Leskovec, and Percy Liang. 2022. Linkbert: Pretraining language models with document links. *Preprint*, arXiv:2203.15827.

Sheng Yu, Zheng Yuan, Jun Xia, Shengxuan Luo, Huaiyuan Ying, Sihang Zeng, Jingyi Ren, Hongyi Yuan, Zhengyun Zhao, Yucong Lin, Keming Lu, Jing Wang, Yutao Xie, and Heung-Yeung Shum. 2022. Bios: An algorithmically generated biomedical knowledge graph. *Preprint*, arXiv:2203.09975.

Efficient Document-level Event Relation Extraction

Ruochen Li, Zimu Wang, Xinya Du
University of Texas at Dallas
{ruochen.li, zimu.wang, xinya.du}@utdallas.edu

Abstract

Event Relation Extraction (ERE) predicts temporal and causal relationships between events, playing a crucial role in constructing comprehensive event knowledge graphs. However, existing approaches based on pairwise comparisons often suffer from computational inefficiency, particularly at the document level, due to the quadratic operations required. Additionally, the predominance of unrelated events also leads to largely skewed data distributions. In this paper, we propose an innovative two-stage framework to tackle the challenges, consisting of a retriever to identify the related event pairs and a cross-encoder to classify the relationships between the retrieved pairs. Evaluations across representative benchmarks demonstrate our approach achieves better efficiency and significantly better performance. We also investigate leveraging event coreference chains for ERE and demonstrate their effectiveness.

1 Introduction

Event Relation Extraction (ERE) aims at identifying relationships between events, especially temporal and causal connections. As illustrated in Figure 1, given the original text and three event mentions of interest, an ERE model should detect and classify the temporal (e.g., *overlaps* and *before*) and causal (e.g., *cause*) relationships between them. ERE plays a pivotal role in the construction of event knowledge graphs (EKGs, Ma et al., 2022) and supports a variety of tasks, such as future event prediction (Lin et al., 2022), machine reading comprehension (Zhu et al., 2023), and multi-hop reasoning (Li et al., 2024).

ERE is challenging due to the event relation variety and the required comprehension (Liu et al., 2020b). For document-level ERE (DERE), the challenge intensifies, needing event disambiguation and connection across expansive narrative structures. Previous research has mainly focused on enriching event semantics (Wen and Ji, 2021; Tran Phu and Nguyen, 2021), or exploiting large language models (LLMs) (Peng et al., 2023a). Nevertheless, current research faces a unique challenge in inefficient learning and inference because the determination of relationships requires pairwise classification after iterating through *all event pairs* (Hu et al., 2023; Wang et al., 2024), which inherently exhibits quadratic time complexity. Additional training challenges arise due to the largely skewed data distribution, where most event pairs have no relation, becoming particularly critical for DERE with a broader scope of events and lengthy sources (Gao et al., 2023). However, this aspect has been overlooked in existing studies, and we are the first to investigate the efficiency issue in DERE with crucial yet unexplored temporal and causal relations.

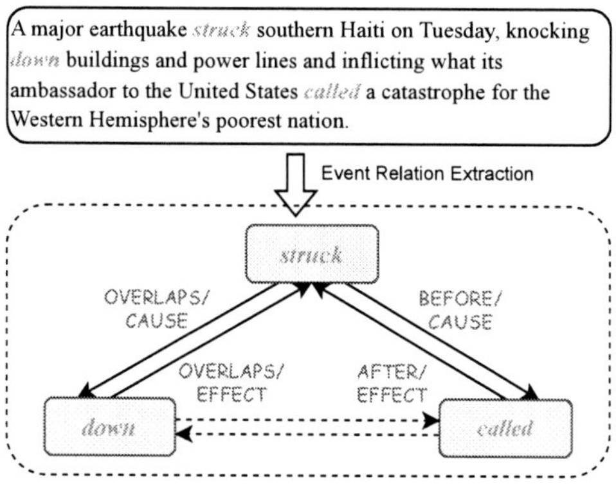

Figure 1: An example of ERE task with temporal and causal relations. The dashed lines indicate there are no event relations between the event mentions.

In this paper, we introduce a novel pruning-based two-stage paradigm for DERE (Figure 2). In the first stage of the framework, we employ a retriever model to efficiently sift through event mentions in latent embedding spaces and identify the related event pairs. Afterwards, a cross-encoder is fine-tuned for event relation prediction on the narrowed set of candidate pairs. This approach effectively prunes the candidate event pairs to tackle

Proceedings of the 10th Workshop on Representation Learning for NLP (RepL4NLP-2025), pages 92–99
May 4, 2025 ©2025 Association for Computational Linguistics

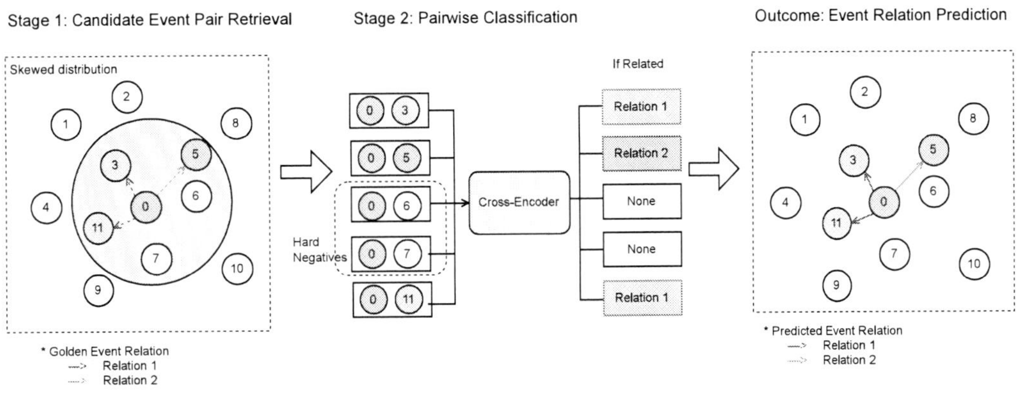

Figure 2: Overall architecture of the proposed pruning-based two-stage ERE framework. Stage 1 retrieves candidate event pairs, and then Stage 2 conducts the costly fine-grained event relation predictions on the retrieved pairs.

inefficiency and deals with the skewed distribution to enhance performance. Experimental results on Event StoryLine Corpus (ESC, Caselli and Vossen, 2017), Richer Event Description (RED, O'Gorman et al., 2016), and MAVEN-ERE (Wang et al., 2022) demonstrate significantly better performance and efficiency compared to representative baselines.

In summary, the key contributions of this paper are as follows: (1) We design a novel two-stage framework for DERE by pruning candidate event pairs to reduce computational complexity and mitigate the skewed distribution issue. (2) We conduct rigorous evaluations and ablation studies on DERE datasets with various retrievers and cross-encoders. (3) We conduct a comprehensive analysis, including time complexity, the effectiveness of encoding strategies and coreference chains, and the effect of retrieved candidate-pair count on performances.

2 Related Work

Recent progress of ERE has been made based on pre-trained language models (PLMs), utilizing semantic structures (Tran Phu and Nguyen, 2021; Hu et al., 2023), temporal clues (Wen and Ji, 2021), and external knowledge (Liu et al., 2020a; Cao et al., 2021) to enrich the event representations. Some other works leverage the high-order transitivity (Chen et al., 2022, 2023) and multi-task learning (Ning et al., 2018; Wang et al., 2022) to model the dependencies between different relation types. Some researchers further investigate the use of LLMs in ERE (Gao et al., 2023; Peng et al., 2023a,b; Wang et al., 2024). However, they often achieve this at the expense of computational efficiency when performing pairwise classifications, especially in document-level datasets (O'Gorman et al., 2016; Wang et al., 2022). While some recent work focus on improving the efficiency of entity coreference resolution (Lee et al., 2018; Held et al., 2021), they cannot be generalized to DERE because of the requirement for deeper semantic analysis and the existence of more specific relation types. In this paper, we inherit the ideas of pruning but design a more effective framework with a retriever model and a cross-encoder model.

3 Methodology

We formulate our DERE task as a multi-class classification problem. Formally, given a document D that contains multiple sentences and two event mentions e_h and e_t of interest, our goal is to predict the potential temporal (e.g., *before*) and causal (e.g., *cause*) relationships between them. Following the framework shown in Figure 2, we introduce the implementation of the retriever and cross-encoder models for training and inference in detail.

3.1 Candidate Event Pair Retrieval

The initial stage utilizes a retriever model (i.e., *bi-encoder*[1]) to efficiently represents event mentions in a latent embedding space to identify the event pairs likely to have a relation to improve efficiency and alleviate the skewed distribution problem. Formally, for two events e_h and e_t, the wrapped mentions are defined as the sentences containing them (s_h, s_t) with events wrapped by markers <m> and </m> for enhanced emphasis. With bi-encoder denoted as $Enc(\cdot)$, the representation of the events, $\mathbf{r}_h$ and $\mathbf{r}_t$, are encoded as:

$$\mathbf{r}_h = Enc(s_h) = Enc(\texttt{<s>}\ldots\texttt{<m>}e_h\texttt{</m>}\ldots\texttt{</s>}), \quad (1)$$

[1] Bi-encoders are a broad class of models that map the input and candidate responses separately into a common feature space where their similarity is measured (Huang et al., 2021).

$$\mathbf{r}_t = Enc(s_t) = Enc(\texttt{<s>}\ldots\texttt{<m>}e_t\texttt{</m>}\ldots\texttt{</s>}). \quad (2)$$

Afterwards, we select the top 5 event mentions most likely to form a relationship with each event. For fine-tuning, the task is regarded as binary classification over $\mathbf{r}_h \cdot \mathbf{r}_t$ with cross-entropy loss. This process is intended to direct the model's attention to the most significant elements of the event, thereby improving its ability to discern relevant event pairs.

3.2 Pairwise Classification

In the second stage, we conduct pairwise classification on the pruned candidate set with a cross-encoder, for which we employ both discriminative and generative models.

Discriminative Models. Given an input document D, we first obtain the hidden vectors in the last transformer layer. Then, for event mentions e_h and e_t, we compute the representations $\mathbf{r}_h$ and $\mathbf{r}_t$ by averaging the representation vectors of respect tokens. Finally, we form an overall representation vector $\mathbf{r}_{h\to t}$ by concatenating the two representations: $\mathbf{r}_{h\to t} = [\mathbf{r}_h; \mathbf{r}_t]$, and then feed it to a feed-forward neural network for relation classification.

Generative Models. The generative models utilize a Seq2Seq approach. An example is as follows:

> *Classify: Mention 1: The murder* <m> ***trial*** </m> *of a suspended female [...]* <sep> *Mention 2: The murder trial [...]* <m> ***shooting*** </m> *three co-workers [...]*

The design of the instruction starts from the word "*Classify:*". Then, we add the two sentences containing the events, separated by a special symbol <sep>, and we wrap the mentions with the markers <m> and </m>. <s> and </s> denote the sentence boundary. The output of the model is the specific event relationship between them.

All positive event pairs and *hard negatives*, i.e., the negatives retrieved in Stage 1, are used for training. We adopt this strategy because (1) the cross-encoder makes predictions on the outputs of the retriever, which are essential for its learning process; and (2) the retrieved event pairs are identified as related ones, making them ideal candidates for more expensive cross-comparison.

3.3 Inference

The inference process is distinct from training with additional strategies. Utilizing the trained retriever model, we retrieve a set of k events most likely to form a relationship with the given mention, regardless of whether it is fine-tuned, and then we use the cross-encoder to determine the specific relationship between them. Our approach prunes aggressively to improve efficiency. Stage 1 scales linearly, and retrieved event pairs are sent to the cross-encoder (Stage 2). In this case, the time of quadratic operation can be decreased significantly, and both the prediction and efficiency can be improved.

4 Experiments

4.1 Datasets and Experimental Setup

We conduct experiments on three well-established datasets: Event StoryLine Corpus (ESC, Caselli and Vossen, 2017), Richer Event Description (RED, O'Gorman et al., 2016), and MAVEN-ERE (Wang et al., 2022). For MAVEN-ERE, we follow previous work (Gao et al., 2023; Chen et al., 2024) to sample a subset. We report the precision (P), recall (R), and micro F1-score (F1) under (1) event pairs with relations following previous work, and (2) all event pairs, as it is closer to EKG construction.

We employ diverse retrievers (RoBERTa-Large, Liu et al., 2019) and S-BERT (Reimers and Gurevych, 2019)) and classifiers (RoBERTa-Large and T5-Large (Raffel et al., 2020)). The baseline models we compared are in Appendix A.

4.2 Experimental Results

Experimental results are depicted in Tables 1 and 2, from which we have the following observations:

Firstly, the introduce of retriever significantly enhances cross-encoder performance, with BERT and RoBERTa outperforming more complex models like LIP and RichGCN. GPT-3.5 does not outperform PLM-based approaches due to its zero-shot generative nature. Additionally, our retriever also outperforms random sampling as it is more closely aligned with the inference process. The hard negatives identified by the retriever are also more similar to positive ones, which are hard to differentiate.

Secondly, while all metrics increase simultaneously, the recall values increase more, particularly on ESC (increases two times) containing large negative samples. Simultaneously, the performance on non-negatives has significant increase; thus, the skewed distribution problem can be alleviated. The T5 model with the S-BERT retriever achieves the best performance on all datasets, demonstrating their superior capability in event relation classification and candidate event pair identification.

Retriever	Classifier	ESC P	ESC R	ESC F1	RED P	RED R	RED F1
Random	RoBERTa	78.4	85.2	81.7	81.2	86.2	83.6
	T5	86.1	85.7	85.9	86.8	89.9	88.3
RoBERTa	RoBERTa	77.2	86.9	81.8	82.7	87.5	85.0
RoBERTa (Fine-tuned)	RoBERTa	77.3	88.1	82.3	82.5	88.4	85.3
RoBERTa	T5	87.1	89.0	87.9	82.8	90.2	86.3
RoBERTa (Fine-tuned)	T5	85.8	90.3	88.0	87.5	90.1	88.8
S-BERT	RoBERTa	79.3	87.8	83.3	83.1	88.7	85.8
S-BERT (Fine-tuned)	RoBERTa	82.1	88.4	85.1	84.3	89.1	86.6
S-BERT	T5	88.9	90.6	89.7	90.6	91.2	90.9
S-BERT (Fine-tuned)	T5	89.2	92.5	**90.8***	93.5	91.9	**92.7***

Table 1: Performance comparison on the whole evaluation set. For the "Random" retriever, the negatives are randomly sampled to match our number of hard negatives. * designates statistical significance ($p < 0.05$).

Method	ESC P	ESC R	ESC F1	RED P	RED R	RED F1	MAVEN-ERE P	MAVEN-ERE R	MAVEN-ERE F1
BiLSTM	29.8	12.9	18.1	51.2	48.5	49.8	24.9	11.7	15.9
BERT	30.3	11.5	16.7	59.0	45.3	51.3	28.4	13.3	18.2
RoBERTa	31.9	14.4	21.5	61.3	48.7	54.3	28.6	12.7	17.6
LIP	36.2	23.5	28.2	64.8	57.6	61.0	–	–	–
T5	34.8	26.7	30.2	64.2	54.6	59.0	27.4	23.5	25.3
RichGCN	36.4	32.1	34.1	68.9	60.2	64.3	34.4	20.5	25.7
GPT-3.5	13.9	54.7	22.2	41.4	45.8	43.5	–	–	–
***Ours (Retriever + Classifier)**									
RoBERTa + RoBERTa	40.3	31.2	35.2	66.7	58.5	62.3	36.0	26.4	30.5
S-BERT + RoBERTa	40.6	34.2	37.1	76.9	59.5	67.1	36.2	26.9	32.0
RoBERTa + T5	41.4	33.6	37.0	70.9	75.5	**73.1**	40.4	33.5	31.9
S-BERT + T5	45.7	38.5	**41.8***	87.4	62.1	72.6*	36.8	29.5	**32.8***

Table 2: Performance comparison on all non-negative event pairs with different retrievers and classifiers.

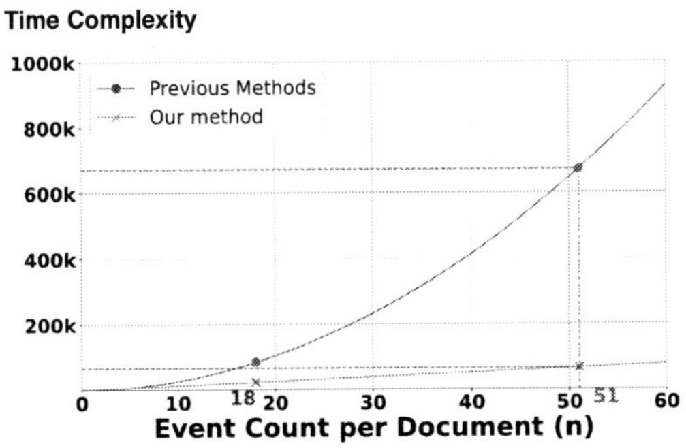

Figure 3: Inference time complexity comparison over *events per document* on ESC ($k = 5$).

Finally, after *fine-tuning* the retriever model, particularly S-BERT, the DERE performance can be further improved. Indeed, the fine-tuned retrievers significantly contribute to the overall performance and efficiency of DERE models. Our findings emphatically advocate for the integration of advanced retriever models as indispensable components of the DERE frameworks.

4.3 Additional Analysis

Time Complexity Analysis. For m documents with n events per document, conventional pairwise approaches exhibit a time complexity of $O(m * n^2)$. Our retriever narrows candidate pairs down to $k * n$ (k candidate per event), and it scales linearly with matrix multiplication in inference. To quantify the efficiency gains of our method, we compare the time complexity at inference time. Figure 3 illustrates the quadratic growth versus our method's linear growth. Average *(n=18)* and maximal *(n=51)* event count is highlighted, in which our approach reduces approximately 70% at inference time.

Retriever	Encoding	ESC P	ESC R	ESC F1	RED P	RED R	RED F1
	Trigger-only	73.2	77.0	75.1	81.3	79.8	80.5
RoBERTa	Wrapped*	85.8	90.3	**88.0**	87.5	90.1	**88.8**
	Graph-based	72.1	86.1	78.8	82.5	81.4	81.9
	Trigger-only	79.1	80.2	79.6	82.8	85.4	84.1
S-BERT	Wrapped*	89.2	92.5	**90.8**	93.5	91.9	**92.7**
	Graph-based	79.1	81.4	80.2	83.2	91.5	87.2

Table 3: Performance comparison using different encoding strategies for both stages on the ESC dataset.

Effectiveness of Encoding Strategies. Table 3 shows a comparative analysis of various encoding strategies. Our *wrapped encoding*, as formulated in Equation 2, effectively aids models in recognizing

k	P	R	F1
3	**91.4**	67.2	77.5
5	89.2	**92.5**	**90.8**
7	85.0	**93.2**	88.9
10	79.9	91.8	85.4
# EVENT	86.1	85.7	85.9

Table 4: Relationship between the number of top event pairs retrieved in Stage 1 (k) and Stage 2 performance.

Model	P	R	F1
Random (Retriever)	86.1	85.7	85.9
RoBERTa (Retriever)	85.8	90.3	88.0
+ *Coref Chain*	91.6	**90.8**	**91.2**
S-BERT (Retriever)	89.2	92.5	90.8
+ *Coref Chain*	**96.1**	86.5	**91.0**

Table 5: Impact of coreference chains on ESC.

and processing the relevant information within a rich textual landscape, whereas *trigger-only encoding*, formulated as: $\mathbf{r}_h = Enc(\texttt{<m>}e_h\texttt{</m>})$, misses some contextual nuances. Surprisingly, *graph-based encoding* (Nguyen and Grishman, 2018) with syntactic dependency trees does not improve the performance, which might be attributed to the noise introduced due to its high complexity.

Effect of Retrieved Candidate Count. We further investigate the impact of the number of candidates retrieved per event (k), where S-BERT retriever and T5 classifier are used on the ESC dataset. The results are shown in Table 4, where *# EVENT* denotes without retrievers. When $k = 3$, high precision is offset by low recall, suggesting that too few event pairs limit relation detection. $k = 5$ offers the best performance, striking a balance between capturing relevant relations and avoiding classification overload. As k increases beyond this point, while slowing the process by nature, more non-relevant pairs are also considered, making the classifier's training data more skewed as well, which detracts from the overall performance.

Effectiveness of Coreference Chains. Table 5 shows the experimental results after adding coreference chains information, which is defined as the event mentions referring to same events (Wang et al., 2022). The coreference chains are obtained from golden annotations and are incorporated as supplementary inputs. Experimental results show that the addition of coreference chains further enhance performance, regardless of which retriever is employed. Furthermore, the performance with the RoBERTa retriever gains more improvements, even outperforming S-BERT, possibly because RoBERTa are more proficient to leverage deep contextual insights from coreference chains.

4.4 Case Study

We further conduct a case study by sampling 50 event pairs that are mispredicted without the retriever but predicted correctly with the retriever model. We observe that the retriever model is particularly beneficial for *document-level* and *implicit* event relations because of the notable decrease in negative samples. As the following example:

> *A SAF spokesman denied the* ***attack*** *occurred. [...] did not explode,* ***fell*** *directly within the camp, [...]*

the events "***attack***" and "***fell***" span in separate sentences, and there are no causal clues (e.g., "cause" and "lead to") between them. Without the retrieval stage, the cross-encoders are unable to identify the relationship between them (i.e., ***attack*** is a precondition of ***fell***) because of the large proportion of negatives in the training set; however, with the cross-encoder trained on the samples retrieved by the retriever, the relationships between these samples are more likely to be recognized, alleviating the skewed distribution issue in DERE datasets.

5 Conclusion and Future Work

We for the first time introduce a novel two-stage framework for DERE, which improves both efficiency and model training. It first uses a retriever to identify event pairs, then a cross-encoder for event relation prediction. Experimental results on three representative datasets underscore the effectiveness of our method, which significantly improves both accuracy and efficiency compared to the baseline models. We further investigate the efficacy of different encoding strategies, and demonstrate the effectiveness of leveraging coreference chains in candidate event pair identification. In the future, we will adapt our method to more IE tasks (e.g., entity relation extraction), and verify its generalizability.

Limitations

Although our proposed two-stage framework performs well on DERE in terms of both overall performance and efficiency, it still has the following two limitations: (1) Due to the limitation of DERE datasets, we test the performance on the three most representative and wildly adopted datasets in other papers in this field. Future research demands the annotation of DERE datasets in other high-resource and low-resource languages to test the generalizability of our method. (2) For the second stage we employ the representative RoBERTa and T5 cross-encoders. More deliberated models or better prompting may yield better results, though they do not impact the conclusion of our experiments.

References

Pengfei Cao, Xinyu Zuo, Yubo Chen, Kang Liu, Jun Zhao, Yuguang Chen, and Weihua Peng. 2021. Knowledge-enriched event causality identification via latent structure induction networks. In *Proceedings of the 59th Annual Meeting of the Association for Computational Linguistics and the 11th International Joint Conference on Natural Language Processing (Volume 1: Long Papers)*, pages 4862–4872, Online. Association for Computational Linguistics.

Tommaso Caselli and Piek Vossen. 2017. The event StoryLine corpus: A new benchmark for causal and temporal relation extraction. In *Proceedings of the Events and Stories in the News Workshop*, pages 77–86, Vancouver, Canada. Association for Computational Linguistics.

Meiqi Chen, Yixin Cao, Kunquan Deng, Mukai Li, Kun Wang, Jing Shao, and Yan Zhang. 2022. ERGO: Event relational graph transformer for document-level event causality identification. In *Proceedings of the 29th International Conference on Computational Linguistics*, pages 2118–2128, Gyeongju, Republic of Korea. International Committee on Computational Linguistics.

Meiqi Chen, Yixin Cao, Yan Zhang, and Zhiwei Liu. 2023. CHEER: Centrality-aware high-order event reasoning network for document-level event causality identification. In *Proceedings of the 61st Annual Meeting of the Association for Computational Linguistics (Volume 1: Long Papers)*, pages 10804–10816, Toronto, Canada. Association for Computational Linguistics.

Meiqi Chen, Yubo Ma, Kaitao Song, Yixin Cao, Yan Zhang, and Dongsheng Li. 2024. Improving large language models in event relation logical prediction. In *Proceedings of the 62nd Annual Meeting of the Association for Computational Linguistics (Volume 1: Long Papers)*, pages 9451–9478, Bangkok, Thailand. Association for Computational Linguistics.

Fei Cheng and Yusuke Miyao. 2017. Classifying temporal relations by bidirectional LSTM over dependency paths. In *Proceedings of the 55th Annual Meeting of the Association for Computational Linguistics (Volume 2: Short Papers)*, pages 1–6, Vancouver, Canada. Association for Computational Linguistics.

Jacob Devlin, Ming-Wei Chang, Kenton Lee, and Kristina Toutanova. 2019. BERT: Pre-training of deep bidirectional transformers for language understanding. In *Proceedings of the 2019 Conference of the North American Chapter of the Association for Computational Linguistics: Human Language Technologies, Volume 1 (Long and Short Papers)*, pages 4171–4186, Minneapolis, Minnesota. Association for Computational Linguistics.

Jinglong Gao, Xiao Ding, Bing Qin, and Ting Liu. 2023. Is chatgpt a good causal reasoner? a comprehensive evaluation. *Preprint*, arXiv:2305.07375.

Lei Gao, Prafulla Kumar Choubey, and Ruihong Huang. 2019. Modeling document-level causal structures for event causal relation identification. In *Proceedings of the 2019 Conference of the North American Chapter of the Association for Computational Linguistics: Human Language Technologies, Volume 1 (Long and Short Papers)*, pages 1808–1817, Minneapolis, Minnesota. Association for Computational Linguistics.

William Held, Dan Iter, and Dan Jurafsky. 2021. Focus on what matters: Applying discourse coherence theory to cross document coreference. In *Proceedings of the 2021 Conference on Empirical Methods in Natural Language Processing*, pages 1406–1417, Online and Punta Cana, Dominican Republic. Association for Computational Linguistics.

Zhilei Hu, Zixuan Li, Xiaolong Jin, Long Bai, Saiping Guan, Jiafeng Guo, and Xueqi Cheng. 2023. Semantic structure enhanced event causality identification. In *Proceedings of the 61st Annual Meeting of the Association for Computational Linguistics (Volume 1: Long Papers)*, pages 10901–10913, Toronto, Canada. Association for Computational Linguistics.

Xin Huang, Chor Seng Tan, Yan Bin Ng, Wei Shi, Kheng Hui Yeo, Ridong Jiang, and Jung Jae Kim. 2021. Joint generation and bi-encoder for situated interactive multimodal conversations. In *AAAI 2021 DSTC9 Workshop*.

Kenton Lee, Luheng He, and Luke Zettlemoyer. 2018. Higher-order coreference resolution with coarse-to-fine inference. In *Proceedings of the 2018 Conference of the North American Chapter of the Association for Computational Linguistics: Human Language Technologies, Volume 2 (Short Papers)*, pages 687–692, New Orleans, Louisiana. Association for Computational Linguistics.

Ruosen Li, Zimu Wang, Son Quoc Tran, Lei Xia, and Xinya Du. 2024. Meqa: A benchmark for multi-hop event-centric question answering with explanations. In *Advances in Neural Information Processing Systems*, volume 37, pages 126835–126862. Curran Associates, Inc.

Li Lin, Yixin Cao, Lifu Huang, Shu'Ang Li, Xuming Hu, Lijie Wen, and Jianmin Wang. 2022. What makes the story forward? inferring commonsense explanations as prompts for future event generation. In *Proceedings of the 45th International ACM SIGIR Conference on Research and Development in*

Information Retrieval, SIGIR '22, page 1098–1109, New York, NY, USA. Association for Computing Machinery.

Jian Liu, Yubo Chen, and Jun Zhao. 2020a. Knowledge enhanced event causality identification with mention masking generalizations. In *Proceedings of the Twenty-Ninth International Joint Conference on Artificial Intelligence, IJCAI-20*, pages 3608–3614. International Joint Conferences on Artificial Intelligence Organization. Main track.

Kang Liu, Yubo Chen, Jian Liu, Xinyu Zuo, and Jun Zhao. 2020b. Extracting events and their relations from texts: A survey on recent research progress and challenges. *AI Open*, 1:22–39.

Yinhan Liu, Myle Ott, Naman Goyal, Jingfei Du, Mandar Joshi, Danqi Chen, Omer Levy, Mike Lewis, Luke Zettlemoyer, and Veselin Stoyanov. 2019. Roberta: A robustly optimized bert pretraining approach. *Preprint*, arXiv:1907.11692.

Yubo Ma, Zehao Wang, Mukai Li, Yixin Cao, Meiqi Chen, Xinze Li, Wenqi Sun, Kunquan Deng, Kun Wang, Aixin Sun, and Jing Shao. 2022. MMEKG: Multi-modal event knowledge graph towards universal representation across modalities. In *Proceedings of the 60th Annual Meeting of the Association for Computational Linguistics: System Demonstrations*, pages 231–239, Dublin, Ireland. Association for Computational Linguistics.

Thien Nguyen and Ralph Grishman. 2018. Graph convolutional networks with argument-aware pooling for event detection. In *Proceedings of the AAAI Conference on Artificial Intelligence*, volume 32.

Qiang Ning, Zhili Feng, Hao Wu, and Dan Roth. 2018. Joint reasoning for temporal and causal relations. In *Proceedings of the 56th Annual Meeting of the Association for Computational Linguistics (Volume 1: Long Papers)*, pages 2278–2288, Melbourne, Australia. Association for Computational Linguistics.

Tim O'Gorman, Kristin Wright-Bettner, and Martha Palmer. 2016. Richer event description: Integrating event coreference with temporal, causal and bridging annotation. In *Proceedings of the 2nd Workshop on Computing News Storylines (CNS 2016)*, pages 47–56, Austin, Texas. Association for Computational Linguistics.

Hao Peng, Xiaozhi Wang, Jianhui Chen, Weikai Li, Yunjia Qi, Zimu Wang, Zhili Wu, Kaisheng Zeng, Bin Xu, Lei Hou, and Juanzi Li. 2023a. When does in-context learning fall short and why? a study on specification-heavy tasks. *Preprint*, arXiv:2311.08993.

Hao Peng, Xiaozhi Wang, Feng Yao, Zimu Wang, Chuzhao Zhu, Kaisheng Zeng, Lei Hou, and Juanzi Li. 2023b. OmniEvent: A comprehensive, fair, and easy-to-use toolkit for event understanding. In *Proceedings of the 2023 Conference on Empirical Methods in Natural Language Processing: System Demonstrations*, pages 508–517, Singapore. Association for Computational Linguistics.

Colin Raffel, Noam Shazeer, Adam Roberts, Katherine Lee, Sharan Narang, Michael Matena, Yanqi Zhou, Wei Li, and Peter J. Liu. 2020. Exploring the limits of transfer learning with a unified text-to-text transformer. *Journal of Machine Learning Research*, 21(140):1–67.

Nils Reimers and Iryna Gurevych. 2019. Sentence-BERT: Sentence embeddings using Siamese BERT-networks. In *Proceedings of the 2019 Conference on Empirical Methods in Natural Language Processing and the 9th International Joint Conference on Natural Language Processing (EMNLP-IJCNLP)*, pages 3982–3992, Hong Kong, China. Association for Computational Linguistics.

Minh Tran Phu and Thien Huu Nguyen. 2021. Graph convolutional networks for event causality identification with rich document-level structures. In *Proceedings of the 2021 Conference of the North American Chapter of the Association for Computational Linguistics: Human Language Technologies*, pages 3480–3490, Online. Association for Computational Linguistics.

Xiaozhi Wang, Yulin Chen, Ning Ding, Hao Peng, Zimu Wang, Yankai Lin, Xu Han, Lei Hou, Juanzi Li, Zhiyuan Liu, Peng Li, and Jie Zhou. 2022. MAVEN-ERE: A unified large-scale dataset for event coreference, temporal, causal, and subevent relation extraction. In *Proceedings of the 2022 Conference on Empirical Methods in Natural Language Processing*, pages 926–941, Abu Dhabi, United Arab Emirates. Association for Computational Linguistics.

Zimu Wang, Lei Xia, Wei Wang, and Xinya Du. 2024. Document-level causal relation extraction with knowledge-guided binary question answering. In *Findings of the Association for Computational Linguistics: EMNLP 2024*, pages 16944–16955, Miami, Florida, USA. Association for Computational Linguistics.

Haoyang Wen and Heng Ji. 2021. Utilizing relative event time to enhance event-event temporal relation extraction. In *Proceedings of the 2021 Conference on Empirical Methods in Natural Language Processing*, pages 10431–10437, Online and Punta Cana, Dominican Republic. Association for Computational Linguistics.

Baiyan Zhang, Qin Chen, Jie Zhou, Jian Jin, and Liang He. 2024. Enhancing event causality identification with rationale and structure-aware causal question answering. *Preprint*, arXiv:2403.11129.

Jiazheng Zhu, Shaojuan Wu, Xiaowang Zhang, Yuexian Hou, and Zhiyong Feng. 2023. Causal intervention for mitigating name bias in machine reading comprehension. In *Findings of the Association for Computational Linguistics: ACL 2023*, pages 12837–12852, Toronto, Canada. Association for Computational Linguistics.

A Baseline Models

We compare our method against various baselines: **BiLSTM** (Cheng and Miyao, 2017) captures the dependency paths between events. **BERT** (Devlin et al., 2019) and **RoBERTa** (Liu et al., 2019) are transformer-based discriminative models, and **T5** (Raffel et al., 2020) is a transformer-based generative model. **LIP** (Gao et al., 2019) combines document structure with textual content, identifying nuanced event relations using structural patterns. **RichGCN** (Tran Phu and Nguyen, 2021) employs Graph Convolutional Networks to create interaction graphs. Zhang et al. (2024) employs **GPT-3.5** (`turbo-1106`) to enhance zero-shot prediction. All baselines (GPT excluded) conduct pairwise comparisons.

Investigating Adapters for Parameter-efficient Low-resource Automatic Speech Recognition

Ahnaf Mozib Samin[†§] **Shekhar Nayak**[§] **Andrea DeMarco**[†] **Claudia Borg**[†]
[†]Department of Artificial Intelligence, University of Malta, Malta
[§]University of Groningen, The Netherlands
{ahnaf.samin.22, andrea.demarco, claudia.borg}@um.edu.mt, s.nayak@rug.nl

Abstract

Recent years have witnessed the adoption of parameter-efficient adapters in pre-trained language models for natural language processing. Yet, their application in speech processing remains less studied. In this work, we explore the adapters for low-resource speech recognition, introducing a novel technique - ConvAdapt into pre-trained speech models. We investigate various aspects such as data requirements, transfer learning within adapters, and scaling of feed-forward layers in adapters. Our findings reveal that bottleneck adapters offer competitiveness with full fine-tuning with at least 10 hours of data, but they are not as effective in few-shot learning scenarios. Notably, ConvAdapt demonstrates improved performance in such cases. In addition, transfer learning in adapters shows promise, necessitating research in related languages. Furthermore, employing larger speech models for adapter-tuning surpasses fine-tuning with ample data, potentially due to reduced overfitting than fine-tuning.

1 Introduction

Automatic speech recognition (ASR) advancements have favored high-resource languages due to abundant data and computing power. However, over 7000 languages are low-resource or zero-resourced, raising concerns of extinction (Dunbar et al., 2021). Large pre-trained self-supervised speech models like Wav2vec 2.0 show promise in enhancing ASR for low-resource languages through fine-tuning with smaller datasets (Baevski et al., 2020). Fine-tuning such large and even multi-lingual models with a low-resource language data usually works well in practice but has its own limitations. It involves updating most of the model parameters which is inefficient, resource-intensive and storage-demanding. Moreover, it poses challenges in dealing with multiple tasks/languages, causing catastrophic forgetting and complex decision-making for choosing the task sequence (Pfeiffer et al., 2021).

Bottleneck adapters, initially introduced in computer vision (Rebuffi et al., 2017), consist of two-layer feed-forward networks inserted into large pre-trained models (Houlsby et al., 2019). This technique selectively updates adapter parameters while keeping the rest of the model frozen, effectively reducing trainable parameters. It facilitates task-specific adapter integration into pre-trained models, avoiding the need for full re-training and mitigating catastrophic forgetting (Pfeiffer et al., 2021).

While adapters have been well studied in natural language processing (NLP) literature (Houlsby et al., 2019), investigating adapters in the speech signal processing domain is relatively new. Bottleneck adapters are implemented for ASR with the Wav2vec 2.0 English base model (Thomas et al., 2022; Yue et al., 2024), MMS (Pratap et al., 2023), and Google Universal Speech Model (Zhang et al., 2023). These studies indicate that adapters perform on par with fine-tuning while being parameter efficient. Few studies explore bottleneck adapters for specialized tasks like multi-domain ASR modeling with Transformers (Lee et al., 2021), personalized speech recognition in a multi-turn dialog setting with Transducers (RNN-T) (Chang et al., 2023), atypical and accented speech recognition with RNN-T and Transformer Transducers (Tomanek et al., 2021). The latter one utilized residual connections within adapters. Different adapter-based approaches are compared for several speech processing tasks with three of the state-of-the-art pre-trained models (Chen et al., 2023a). The selection of different neural layers to insert the adapters is performed with a two-stage algorithm (Huang et al., 2023). While the prior works rely on bottleneck adapters, CHAPTER technique based on convolutional neural network (CNN) adapters are employed in HuBERT feature extractor on emotion and speaker tasks (Chen et al., 2023b). To the best

Proceedings of the 10th Workshop on Representation Learning for NLP (RepL4NLP-2025), pages 100–107
May 4, 2025

of our knowledge, no work leveraged convolutional nets as adapters by incorporating them into the contextual Transformer layers in the speech processing domain. Also, given the limited work on ASR modeling using adapters, there exist substantial research gaps that necessitate a comprehensive study of this method. It still remains an open question what the training data size must be for adapter-tuning to perform on par with complete fine-tuning for the low-resource ASR task since the prior work investigates the adapter-tuning for speech processing with only high-resource languages such as English, omitting the suitability of the approach for low-resource languages. Furthermore, the possibility of scaling the adapter modules or pre-training the adapters with a source language are not explored in the literature.

This study aims to address the aforementioned research gaps by conducting a comprehensive investigation of adapters for ASR, with a particular focus on the low-resource aspect. Through this research, we aim to reduce computational complexity while simultaneously maintaining ASR performance, ensuring the representation and preservation of low-resource languages in the field of speech technology. The contribution of this work is four-fold:

- Exploring the adapter-tuning approach for ASR across various resource-constrained scenarios, spanning from low-resource to medium/high-resource conditions in three diverse languages: English (West Germanic), Bengali (Indo-Aryan), and Maltese (Semitic). To this end, we propose a simple yet effective technique ConvAdapt for extreme low-resource parameter-efficient ASR. Notably, no prior research has explored the data requirements for adapter-based low-resource ASR, to the best of our knowledge.

- Leveraging the potential of multilingual, pre-trained self-supervised speech models, we incorporate adapters into state-of-the-art models, namely XLS-R (Babu et al., 2021) and MMS (Pratap et al., 2023). Additionally, we investigate whether employing a larger pre-trained model with a higher number of parameters enhances the performance of the adapter-tuning approach for ASR. Adapter performance for varied sizes of multi-lingual pre-trained models is not studied in the literature, to our knowledge.

- Exploring pre-training adapters on a source language and subsequently fine-tune them for the target language, enabling transfer learning within adapters for the first time.

- While bottleneck adapters with a two-layer feed-forward network are common in adapter architectures (Houlsby et al., 2019; Thomas et al., 2022), this study extends the adapter module by adding more fully connected layers and assesses their influence on performance across the three languages.

2 Integrating Adapters into Wav2vec 2.0

Figure 1 presents the architecture of the adapter-based Wav2vec 2.0 model. The core structure of Wav2vec 2.0 remains unchanged (Baevski et al., 2020), while each Transformer block includes two adapter modules. The process starts with raw input signal passing through a feature encoder, then entering the contextual network (Transformer). Each Transformer block consists of sub-modules like Multi-Head Self-Attention (MHSA) and feed-forward layer. Adapter modules are inserted after the MHSA and the feed-forward layer. There are two residual connections in each Transformer block. The model can contain N transformer blocks, with N being either 24 or 48, depending on the specific Wav2vec 2.0 model. A linear classifier (classification head) is added at the end of the network. During adapter-tuning, only adapter modules, normalization layers, and the head are trained while keeping the pre-trained backbone frozen, substantially reducing trainable parameters.

The bottleneck adapter architecture (FFAdapter), depicted on the upper right side of Figure 1, consists of two fully-connected feed-forward networks. The first layer acts as a down-sampler, projecting the Transformer model dimension to a lower inner dimension through down-projection. A GELU activation is added after that. The second layer functions as an up-sampler, projecting back to the original dimension. Both layers maintain an inner dimension of 256. A residual connection adds the second layer's output with the initial adapter input, processed through layer normalization to yield the final output.

Let the Transformer model representation be d_m and the representation from the second FC layer is f_m. Both d_m and the f_m have the same dimension of m. The output of the Add & Norm layer is

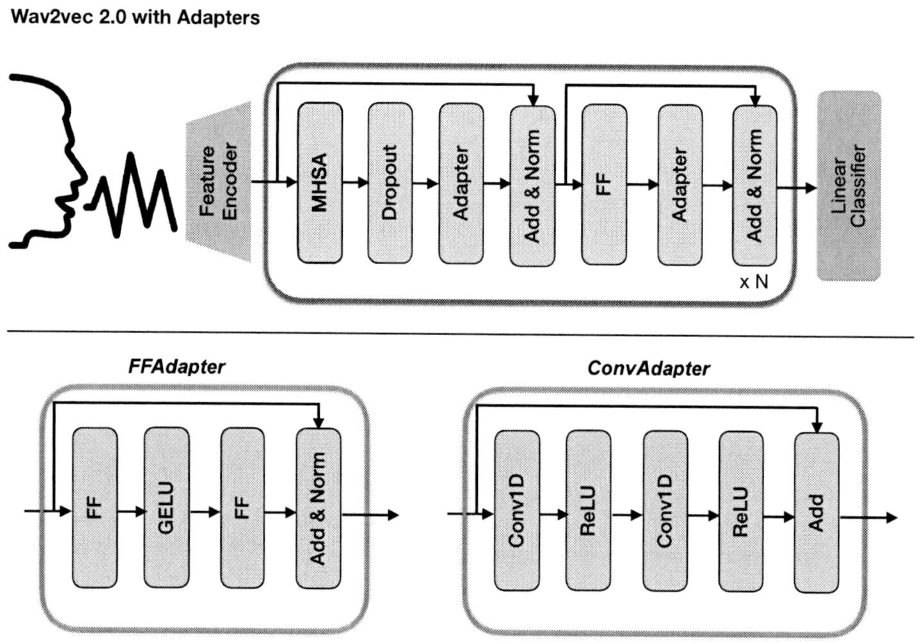

Figure 1: The upper figure depicts the Wav2vec 2.0 architecture with adapter modules. The bottom left figure shows the bottleneck adapter (FFAdapter), while the ConvAdapter is displayed on the bottom right. MHSA and FF represent multi-head self-attention and feed-forward layers, respectively.

computed as,

$$AdapterOutput = LayerNorm(d_m + f_m) \quad (1)$$

We propose the ConvAdapt technique by replacing the bottleneck adapters with CNN-based adapters while keeping them at the same position in the Transformer layers (See Figure 1). The latent representation from the MHSA/FF of the transformer is fed as input to the ConvAdapters after rearranging the tensors to avoid dimension mismatch. We employ two 1-dimensional convolutional layers, each followed by a rectified linear unit (ReLU). There are 1280 input channels and 1280 output channels, and both kernel size and stride are set to 1. The same padding is used. Finally, we rearrange the resultant tensors again to obtain the original dimension and add this to the adapter input through a residual connection.

3 Experiments

Datasets: We conduct the experiments on three languages: Bengali, Maltese, and English. The LibriSpeech corpus is used for English (Panayotov et al., 2015), the SUBAK.KO corpus for Bengali (Kibria et al., 2022), and a combination of datasets including CommonVoice, MASRI-HEADSET, MEP, Tube, MERLIN, and Parliament for Maltese (Ardila et al., 2020; Mena et al., 2020). Various subsets of data are created, ranging from 10 minutes to 50 hours, for analyzing data requirements. Besides the 10 minute, 1 hour and 10 hour subsets from LibriLight (Kahn et al., 2020), we add an additional 50 hour subset from the standard 100-hour English LibriSpeech subset. For Bengali, we create the subsets by randomly selecting samples from the 200-hour SUBAK.KO train set. We follow a similar random sampling approach for Maltese. To ensure standardized benchmarking, we utilize the LibriSpeech development (dev) and test sets, both containing *clean* and *other* subparts. The SUBAK.KO dataset includes standard dev and test sets with 20 hours of data each. Similarly, we utilize the standard Maltese dev and test sets, containing 1.5 hours and 2.3 hours of speech, respectively. The dataset details are summarized in Table 1.

Experimental setup: We choose two large pretrained cross-lingual models, namely XLS-R and MMS (Pratap et al., 2023; Babu et al., 2021). XLS-R has three variants with 0.3 billion (B), 1B, and 2B trainable parameters. We utilize MMS containing

Lang	Language Group	Datasets	train set length	dev set clean	dev set other	test set clean	test set other
BN	Indo-Aryan	SUBAK.KO (Kibria et al., 2022)	200.3	20.5	-	20.3	-
MT	Semitic	Common Voice (Ardila et al., 2020) MASRI-HEADSET (Mena et al., 2020) MEP Tube MERLIN Parlament	52.5	2.3	-	1.5	-
EN	West Germanic	LibriSpeech (Panayotov et al., 2015)	960.9	5.4	5.3	5.4	5.1

Table 1: The datasets are split into train, dev and test sets. BN, MT, and EN refer to Bengali, Maltese, and English, respectively. For English, each of dev and test sets has clean and other (noisy) versions.

1B parameters. Both fully fine-tuned and adapter-based ASR models are trained with a batch size of 4, accumulating gradients for two steps, max 150K steps, early stopping patience for 10K steps, and seed 100. The learning rates of 3e-5, 5e-5, and 5e-4 are used for complete fine-tuning, bottleneck adapter-tuning, and ConvAdapt, respectively. We use greedy search decoding leveraging connectionist temporal classification (CTC) to obtain the output characters (Graves et al., 2006).

Results: The comparison between fine-tuning and adapter-tuning reveals their distinct advantages depending on the dataset size (See Table 2). In extremely low-resource scenarios, like those with just 10 minutes or 1 hour of training data, fine-tuning significantly outperforms bottleneck adapter-tuning (FFAdapter) across languages and model sizes. This situation can be seen as few-shot learning due to the extremely limited labeled speech. However, in moderately low-resource conditions (at least 10 hours), bottleneck adapter-tuning performs competitive to fine-tuning while significantly reducing trainable parameters. We argue that, with less data, the fully connected feed-forward adapters cannot be properly trained and the subsequent modules in Transformer rely upon the output representations from adapter. For this reason, bottleneck adapters are not suitable for few-shot learning. To counter this issue, our proposed technique ConvAdapt is able to outperform bottleneck adapters in extremely low-resource cases while still under-performing than full fine-tuning. We hypothesize that due to sparse connectivity and weight sharing in convolutional nets as opposed to full connectivity in FF nets, ConvAdapter achieves superior performance than bottleneck adapters in few-shot scenarios with less data. As training data increases, however, the benefit of ConvAdapt over bottleneck adapters diminishes because fully connected weights in bottleneck adapters can be learned with sufficient amount of data.

From Table 2, it is evident that the fully fine-tuned XLS-R model with 2B parameters yields comparatively high WERs across different languages and training dataset sizes. The XLS-R 2B performance is consistently surpassed by smaller capacity fully fine-tuned XLS-R models (0.3B, 1B) and the MMS 1B model in all cases. Investigating further, we refer to (Babu et al., 2021), which explores fine-tuned XLS-R models on LibriSpeech. Though the authors argue that higher-capacity models could mitigate interference issue of pre-trained models and yield lower WERs, this remains unverified for the XLS-R 2B model with no results presented for this model.

In our work, we find that employing the bottleneck adapter-tuning approach enables the XLS-R with 2B parameters to achieve the lowest WERs across several dataset sizes except for the extremely low-resource ones e.g. 10 min or 1 hour. This finding is noteworthy since XLS-R 2B with bottleneck adapters not only improves performance but also reduces trainable parameters remarkably from 2B to 64M (almost 31 times reduction). We argue that adapters can function as regularizers in large pre-trained speech models by mitigating overfitting and

Train set size	Model	Adapter Type	# Params in adapters	Maltese		Bengali		English			
				FT	Adapter	FT	Adapter	FT clean	FT other	Adapter clean	Adapter other
10 min	XLS-R 0.3B	FF	26M	63.6	98.9	70.2	93.7	39.3	48.4	100.0	100.0
	XLS-R 1B	FF	64M	70.5	90.3	70.4	89.9	**36.1**	45.7	98.3	100.0
	XLS-R 2B	FF	64M	62.9	93.5	69.9	87.6	39.4	49.0	91.8	96.2
	MMS 1B	FF	64M	**60.5**	89.0	**64.2**	100.0	36.5	**43.4**	100.0	100.0
	XLS-R 1B	Conv	192M	70.5	76.7	70.4	76.5	**36.1**	45.7	43.3	54.2
1 hour	XLS-R 0.3B	FF	26M	**43.1**	65.4	46.2	63.4	16.7	25.5	86.0	92.2
	XLS-R 1B	FF	64M	48.1	63.4	**44.3**	56.9	**15.5**	24.9	38.2	53.3
	XLS-R 2B	FF	64M	43.9	98.2	47.5	66.2	17.9	27.6	24.2	36.3
	MMS 1B	FF	64M	43.5	61.9	**44.3**	58.5	16.1	**23.9**	34.9	49.4
	XLS-R 1B	Conv	192M	48.1	46.3	**44.3**	49.3	**15.5**	24.9	16.8	26.8
10 hours	XLS-R 0.3B	FF	26M	27.8	34.8	20.1	26.9	8.7	17.2	10.7	21.6
	XLS-R 1B	FF	64M	28.6	29.4	19.8	21.0	8.3	17.4	9.3	18.3
	XLS-R 2B	FF	64M	31.1	31.0	20.2	25.7	10.1	20.1	7.6	15.7
	MMS 1B	FF	64M	35.0	36.1	**18.8**	28.4	8.7	16.7	9.2	18.1
	XLS-R 1B	Conv	192M	28.6	**27.7**	19.8	24.2	8.3	17.4	**7.3**	**13.9**
20 hours	XLS-R 0.3B	FF	26M	26.0	28.2	15.2	17.4	7.1	16.3	8.0	19.8
	XLS-R 1B	FF	64M	26.2	26.5	18.6	25.0	7.1	18.2	6.8	16.7
	XLS-R 2B	FF	64M	28.2	**25.6**	**13.7**	15.8	7.4	18.2	**6.0**	14.9
	MMS 1B	FF	64M	26.5	30.2	13.9	18.0	7.5	16.5	7.5	16.2
	XLS-R 1B	Conv	192M	26.2	26.5	18.6	15.4	7.1	18.2	6.2	**14.7**
50 hours	XLS-R 0.3B	FF	26M	24.5	26.2	12.4	14.6	5.8	14.1	6.4	16.2
	XLS-R 1B	FF	64M	**21.1**	24.9	**10.9**	12.9	6.0	16.2	**5.1**	12.7
	XLS-R 2B	FF	64M	24.4	23.9	19.8	11.3	6.4	17.3	5.3	12.9
	MMS 1B	FF	64M	21.5	29.9	12.1	13.2	6.0	14.8	5.5	**12.6**
	XLS-R 1B	Conv	192M	**21.1**	25.2	**10.9**	12.6	6.0	16.2	**5.1**	12.8

Table 2: **Evaluation of full fine-tuning (FT) and adapter-tuning (bottleneck with FF and ConvAdapt approaches) with XLS-R and MMS models for low-resource ASR in terms of WERs (%).** Varied trainable parameters (0.3B, 1B, 2B) in pre-trained ASR models are explored. Maltese, Bengali, and English (LibriSpeech) are chosen, representing diverse language groups. Five training subsets ranging from 10 min to 50 hours are derived from corresponding datasets. Test set results are provided, and CTC-based greedy decoding is employed.

Language	ISO	XLS-R pre-training data
English	en	69493 hours
Maltese	mt	9120 hours
Bengali	bn	100 hours

Table 3: Number of hours of English, Maltese, and Bengali untranscribed speech data used for pre-training XLS-R (Babu et al., 2021).

effectively harnessing their potential.

Table 2 highlights that adapter-tuning provides the most benefits for English ASR, while Bengali ASR with adapters exhibits higher WERs across all dataset sizes. Notably, XLS-R underwent pre-training with 69,493 hours for English, 9,120 hours for Maltese, and only 100 hours for Bengali as shown in Table 3 (Babu et al., 2021). The subpar performance of adapter-tuning in Bengali might be attributed to its insufficient representation in the pre-trained XLS-R model (See Table 1). However, with increased Bengali labeled data (200 hours) for adapter-tuning, performance substantially improves over full fine-tuning (See Table 4).

For a mid-resource case (200 hours and 360 hours of training data), Table 4 illustrates that

Train dataset	Approach	dev set		test set	
		clean	other	clean	other
BN - 200 hrs	fine-tuning	18.8	-	16.3	-
	adapter-tuning	**8.1**	-	**6.9**	-
EN - 360 hrs	fine-tuning	6.4	17.9	5.8	15.7
	adapter-tuning	**3.5**	**9.4**	**3.7**	**9.4**

Table 4: Evaluation of fine-tuning and bottleneck adapter-tuning with XLS-R 2B for moderately large amount of data of 200 hours for Bengali (BN) and 360 hours for English (EN). Results are reported in terms of WERs (%).

Language	Transfer learning in adapters	dev set		test set	
		clean	other	clean	other
BN	No	**11.6**	-	**11.3**	-
	EN $\rightarrow$ BN	14.8	-	13.8	-
	MT $\rightarrow$ BN	14.5	-	13.6	-
MT	No	15.4	-	23.9	-
	BN $\rightarrow$ MT	**14.0**	-	**22.7**	-
	EN $\rightarrow$ MT	15.3	-	24.1	-
EN	No	5.0	12.7	5.3	12.9
	BN $\rightarrow$ EN	4.9	12.8	4.9	12.9
	MT $\rightarrow$ EN	**4.7**	**12.6**	**4.7**	**12.6**

Table 5: Bottleneck adapters in XLS-R 2B are pre-trained with a 50-hour source language dataset, then fine-tuned with an equivalent-sized target language dataset. The classification head dedicated to the source language is removed. WERs (%) on dev and test sets are reported. "Source language" $\rightarrow$ "target language" signifies knowledge transfer.

bottleneck adapter-tuning achieves notably lower WERs than fine-tuning for both Bengali and English, indicating its suitability for developing ASR models with a moderate to large amount of data. We underscore the significance of this finding for the speech processing community.

Pre-training the adapters with a source language shows a slight performance improvement for Maltese and English ASR, yet the Bengali ASR performance deteriorates when adapters are pre-trained with a source language (See Table 5). We hypothesize that initializing adapters with weights from a closely related source language could be advantageous.

The standard bottleneck adapter, widely used in computer vision and NLP, contains two FF layers. We investigate the impact of increasing the number of FF layers in each adapter block (See Figure 2), with an inner dimension of 256 and GELU activation after each FF layer. Our results show that using 6 FF layers in the adapter architecture yields optimal performance across all three languages. It is worth noting that increasing FF layers in adapters elevates the number of trainable parameters, such as from 64M for 2 FF layers to 102M for 6 FF layers, although not significantly.

4 Conclusion and Future Scope

This study presents a comprehensive analysis of parameter-efficient adapters for large pre-trained speech models. We find that bottleneck adapters are not suitable for few-shot learning, however, they perform competitive to full fine-tuning when at least 10 hours of data are available. Our proposed ConvAdapt technique in Transformer layers is simple yet effective to deal with extremely low-resource cases. In mid-to-high resource scenarios, bottleneck adapter-tuning surpasses the widely used full fine-tuning technique, signifying its considerable impact in the field. Leveraging higher-capacity models like XLS-R 2B significantly improves adapter-based tuning, countering the overfitting challenge posed by large pre-trained models during full fine-tuning. Impressively, adapters

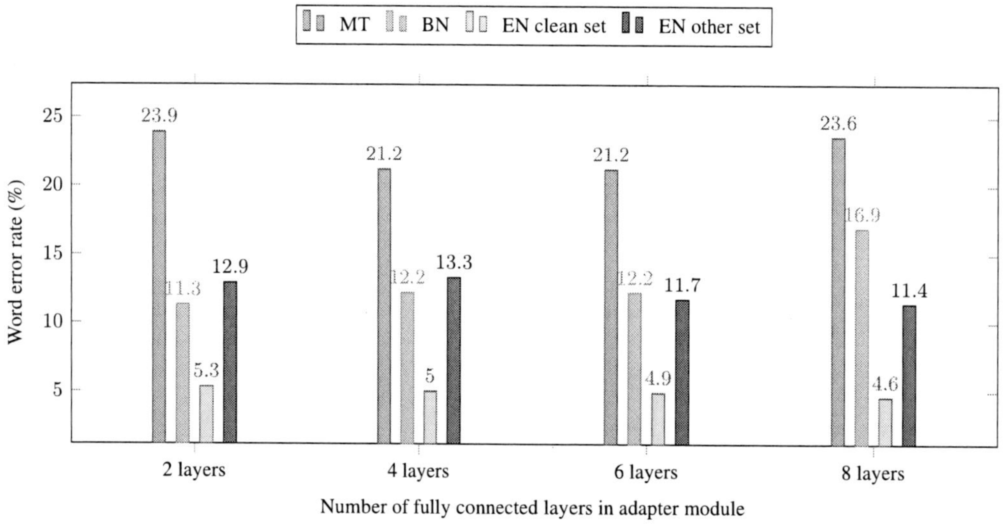

Figure 2: Impact of increasing the number of FC layers in each bottleneck adapter, inserted into XLS-R 2B.

achieve strong performance with merely 2.96% of total trainable parameters. The approach proves better for languages with ample pre-training data. Moreover, transfer learning within adapters benefits Maltese and English, but not Bengali potentially due to the lower amount of Bengali data used in pre-training. Scaling adapters with six feed-forward layers is optimal for all three languages.

We believe that our intriguing findings on adapter-tuning showing remarkable potential for both low-resource and mid/high-resource ASR would encourage more research into this direction. Future work includes exploring transfer learning in adapters with closely-related languages and performing multiple tasks using a single encoder.

5 Limitations

While this work provides novel findings applying adapters for ASR, there exist some limitations. In our experiments with pre-training adapters on the source language and then finetuning on the target language, we use three languages (Bengali, Maltese, and English) that derive from distinct language groups. However, using closely-related language pairs, more performance gain is expected as observed in different studies on transfer learning (Baevski et al., 2020). Due to the limited scope, we restrict this experiment to only the selected three languages in this paper and leave it for future studies.

Acknowledgments

Work supported by the Language and Communication Technologies program of the Erasmus+ project of the European Commission.

References

Rosana Ardila, Megan Branson, Kelly Davis, Michael Kohler, Josh Meyer, Michael Henretty, Reuben Morais, Lindsay Saunders, Francis Tyers, and Gregor Weber. 2020. Common voice: A massively-multilingual speech corpus. In *Proceedings of the Twelfth Language Resources and Evaluation Conference*, pages 4218–4222, Marseille, France. European Language Resources Association.

Arun Babu, Changhan Wang, Andros Tjandra, Kushal Lakhotia, Qiantong Xu, Naman Goyal, Kritika Singh, Patrick von Platen, Yatharth Saraf, Juan Pino, et al. 2021. Xls-r: Self-supervised cross-lingual speech representation learning at scale. *Interspeech*.

Alexei Baevski, Yuhao Zhou, Abdelrahman Mohamed, and Michael Auli. 2020. wav2vec 2.0: A framework for self-supervised learning of speech representations. *Advances in neural information processing systems*, 33:12449–12460.

Feng-Ju Chang, Thejaswi Muniyappa, Kanthashree Mysore Sathyendra, Kai Wei, Grant P. Strimel, and Ross McGowan. 2023. Dialog act guided contextual adapter for personalized speech recognition. In *ICASSP 2023 - 2023 IEEE International Conference on Acoustics, Speech and Signal Processing (ICASSP)*, pages 1–5.

Zih-Ching Chen, Chin-Lun Fu, Chih-Ying Liu, Shang-Wen Daniel Li, and Hung-yi Lee. 2023a. Exploring efficient-tuning methods in self-supervised speech models. In *2022 IEEE Spoken Language Technology Workshop (SLT)*, pages 1120–1127. IEEE.

Zih-Ching Chen, Yu-Shun Sung, and Hung-yi Lee. 2023b. Chapter: Exploiting convolutional neural network adapters for self-supervised speech models. In *2023 IEEE International Conference on Acoustics, Speech, and Signal Processing Workshops (ICASSPW)*, pages 1–5. IEEE.

Ewan Dunbar, Mathieu Bernard, Nicolas Hamilakis, Tu Anh Nguyen, Maureen de Seyssel, Patricia Rozé, Morgane Rivière, Eugene Kharitonov, and Emmanuel Dupoux. 2021. The zero resource speech challenge 2021: Spoken language modelling. In *Interspeech 2021-Conference of the International Speech Communication Association*.

Alex Graves, Santiago Fernández, Faustino Gomez, and Jürgen Schmidhuber. 2006. Connectionist temporal classification: labelling unsegmented sequence data with recurrent neural networks. In *Proceedings of the 23rd international conference on Machine learning*, pages 369–376.

Neil Houlsby, Andrei Giurgiu, Stanislaw Jastrzebski, Bruna Morrone, Quentin De Laroussilhe, Andrea Gesmundo, Mona Attariyan, and Sylvain Gelly. 2019. Parameter-efficient transfer learning for nlp. In *International Conference on Machine Learning*, pages 2790–2799. PMLR.

Junwei Huang, Karthik Ganesan, Soumi Maiti, Young Min Kim, Xuankai Chang, Paul Liang, and Shinji Watanabe. 2023. Findadaptnet: Find and insert adapters by learned layer importance. In *ICASSP 2023 - 2023 IEEE International Conference on Acoustics, Speech and Signal Processing (ICASSP)*, pages 1–5.

Jacob Kahn, Morgane Rivière, Weiyi Zheng, Evgeny Kharitonov, Qiantong Xu, Pierre-Emmanuel Mazaré, Julien Karadayi, Vitaliy Liptchinsky, Ronan Collobert, Christian Fuegen, et al. 2020. Libri-light: A benchmark for asr with limited or no supervision. In *ICASSP 2020-2020 IEEE International Conference on Acoustics, Speech and Signal Processing (ICASSP)*, pages 7669–7673. IEEE.

Shafkat Kibria, Ahnaf Mozib Samin, M Humayon Kobir, M Shahidur Rahman, M Reza Selim, and M Zafar Iqbal. 2022. Bangladeshi bangla speech corpus for automatic speech recognition research. *Speech Communication*, 136:84–97.

Taewoo Lee, Min-Joong Lee, Tae Gyoon Kang, Seokyeoung Jung, Minseok Kwon, Yeona Hong, Jungin Lee, Kyoung-Gu Woo, Ho-Gyeong Kim, Jiseung Jeong, et al. 2021. Adaptable multi-domain language model for transformer asr. In *ICASSP 2021-2021 IEEE International Conference on Acoustics, Speech and Signal Processing (ICASSP)*, pages 7358–7362. IEEE.

Carlos Daniel Hernandez Mena, Albert Gatt, Andrea DeMarco, Claudia Borg, Lonneke van der Plas, Amanda Muscat, and Ian Padovani. 2020. Masri-headset: A maltese corpus for speech recognition. In *Proceedings of the Twelfth Language Resources and Evaluation Conference*, pages 6381–6388.

Vassil Panayotov, Guoguo Chen, Daniel Povey, and Sanjeev Khudanpur. 2015. Librispeech: An asr corpus based on public domain audio books. In *2015 IEEE International Conference on Acoustics, Speech and Signal Processing (ICASSP)*, pages 5206–5210.

Jonas Pfeiffer, Aishwarya Kamath, Andreas Rücklé, Kyunghyun Cho, and Iryna Gurevych. 2021. Adapterfusion: Non-destructive task composition for transfer learning. In *16th Conference of the European Chapter of the Associationfor Computational Linguistics, EACL 2021*, pages 487–503. Association for Computational Linguistics (ACL).

Vineel Pratap, Andros Tjandra, Bowen Shi, Paden Tomasello, Arun Babu, Sayani Kundu, Ali Elkahky, Zhaoheng Ni, Apoorv Vyas, Maryam Fazel-Zarandi, et al. 2023. Scaling speech technology to 1,000+ languages. *arXiv preprint arXiv:2305.13516*.

Sylvestre-Alvise Rebuffi, Hakan Bilen, and Andrea Vedaldi. 2017. Learning multiple visual domains with residual adapters. *Advances in neural information processing systems*, 30.

Bethan Thomas, Samuel Kessler, and Salah Karout. 2022. Efficient adapter transfer of self-supervised speech models for automatic speech recognition. In *ICASSP 2022-2022 IEEE International Conference on Acoustics, Speech and Signal Processing (ICASSP)*, pages 7102–7106. IEEE.

Katrin Tomanek, Vicky Zayats, Dirk Padfield, Kara Vaillancourt, and Fadi Biadsy. 2021. Residual adapters for parameter-efficient asr adaptation to atypical and accented speech. In *Proceedings of the 2021 Conference on Empirical Methods in Natural Language Processing*, pages 6751–6760.

Xianghu Yue, Xiaoxue Gao, Xinyuan Qian, and Haizhou Li. 2024. Adapting pre-trained self-supervised learning model for speech recognition with light-weight adapters. *Electronics*, 13(1):190.

Yu Zhang, Wei Han, James Qin, Yongqiang Wang, Ankur Bapna, Zhehuai Chen, Nanxin Chen, Bo Li, Vera Axelrod, Gary Wang, et al. 2023. Google usm: Scaling automatic speech recognition beyond 100 languages. *arXiv preprint arXiv:2303.01037*.

Reverse Probing: Evaluating Knowledge Transfer via Finetuned Task Embeddings for Coreference Resolution

Tatiana Anikina[1,2,*], **Arne Binder**[1,*], **David Harbecke**[1], **Stalin Varanasi**[1,2],
Leonhard Hennig[1], **Simon Ostermann**[1,2], **Sebastian Möller**[1,3], and **Josef van Genabith**[1,2]
[1]German Research Centre for Artificial Intelligence, Saarbrücken
[2]Saarland Informatics Campus, Saarbrücken
[3]Technische Universität Berlin, Berlin
tatiana.anikina@dfki.de

Abstract

In this work, we reimagine classical probing to evaluate knowledge transfer from simple source to more complex target tasks. Instead of probing frozen representations from a complex source task on diverse simple target probing tasks (as usually done in probing), we explore the effectiveness of embeddings from multiple simple source tasks on a single target task. We select coreference resolution, a linguistically complex problem that requires contextual understanding, as the focus target task, and we test the usefulness of embeddings from comparably simpler tasks such as paraphrase detection, named entity recognition, and relation extraction. Through systematic experiments, we evaluate the impact of individual and combined task embeddings.

Our findings reveal that task embeddings vary significantly in utility for coreference resolution, with semantic similarity tasks (e.g., paraphrase detection) proving most beneficial. Additionally, representations from intermediate layers of fine-tuned models often outperform those from final layers. Combining embeddings from multiple tasks consistently improves performance, with attention-based aggregation yielding substantial gains. These insights shed light on the relationships between task-specific representations and their adaptability to complex downstream tasks, encouraging further exploration of embedding-level task transfer. Our source code is publicly available.[1]

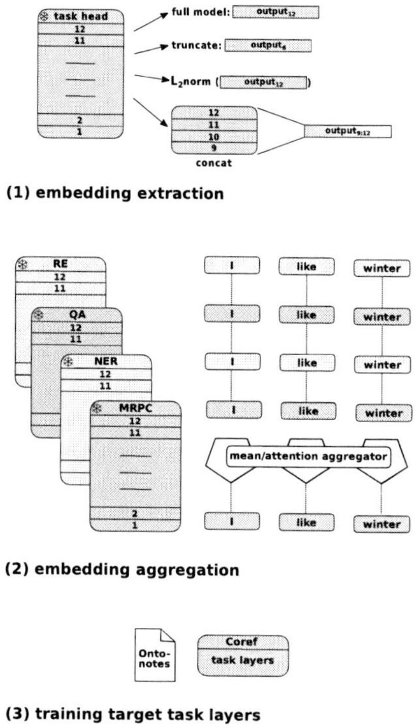

Figure 1: Probing workflow with Coreference Resolution (Coref) as target task and four different source tasks: Relation Extraction (RE), Question Answering (QA), Named Entity Recognition (NER), and Paraphrase Detection (MRPC).

1 Introduction

Language models have exhibited superior performance in most areas of NLP applications, including natural language inference (Williams et al., 2018), question answering (Rajpurkar et al., 2016, 2018), commonsense reasoning (Talmor et al., 2019; Ostermann et al., 2019), and others. Since the establishment of language models with partial superhuman performance, research has aimed to pinpoint which types of knowledge are exactly encoded by such language models. One technique in the field of explainable artificial intelligence for evaluating the presence of such types of knowledge is *probing* (Conneau et al., 2018; Hewitt and Liang, 2019; Tenney et al., 2019a; Belinkov, 2022). Probing involves adding linear classifiers on top of representations extracted from a pre-trained model, which are trained on simple tasks for predicting a

[1]github.com/Cora4NLP/multi-task-knowledge-transfer
* Equal contribution.

Proceedings of the 10th Workshop on Representation Learning for NLP (RepL4NLP-2025), pages 108–119
May 4, 2025 ©2025 Association for Computational Linguistics

feature of choice, such as syntactic structures (Lin et al., 2019), entity types (Tenney et al., 2019b), or specific types of commonsense knowledge (Zhou et al., 2020).

A main intuition behind probing is to evaluate to what degree the representations that are learned from the complex source task can be re-purposed to solve a new, simpler task (Belinkov, 2022). In our work we decide to reverse this paradigm (thus *reverse probing*) and investigate how different source task embeddings, from a model trained on simple tasks, can be adapted to a new, more complex target task. In other words, we try to answer the question: **Can we reuse knowledge from simpler tasks for a more complex task?** Such a *recycling* of knowledge is not only interesting to deepen our understanding of what type of knowledge is encoded in language models, but it also results in more energy-efficient deep learning, by reusing network weights and representations.

We choose **coreference resolution** (Lee et al., 2017) as our target task because solving coreference is - up to date - a challenging NLP problem that even newer large language models struggle with (Bohnet et al., 2023; Martinelli et al., 2024). Coreference resolution involves understanding of context, what counts as a valid mention and which mentions refer to the same entity. Solving coreference may require different types of linguistic knowledge. Our goal is to find out which types of information from which source task models are useful and how this information can be combined and/or adapted to work for the target task.

To isolate the effects of single tasks, we rely on small language models, in our case BERT (Devlin et al., 2019). Such models do not possess sophisticated in-context abilities and require finetuning steps in order to perform well on tasks. Our research questions are as follows:

(1) Which **source tasks** are beneficial for combination into a more complex target task, here coreference resolution?

(2) Which **layers** of source task models contribute most to the target model performance?

(3) What are the effects of **combining embeddings** from different models and layers? How should these embeddings be aggregated? Can we improve word representations by extending the **embedding context** and combining the outputs of several hidden layers?

2 Reverse Probing

The goal of our framework is to evaluate the transferability of knowledge embedded in representations from simpler source tasks to a complex target task. Figure 1 gives an overview.

Let $S = \{s_1, s_2, \ldots, s_k\}$ be a set of source tasks with models pre-trained on simpler NLP tasks, and T be the target task (coreference resolution in this case). M_s is a pre-trained model fine-tuned on source task s. We then define H_s^l to be the output embeddings from layer l of M_s.

For each source task $s_i \in S$, we extract embeddings $\mathbf{H}_s$ from layer l of the corresponding source task model M_s (Figure 1, embedding extraction). We either take the output at a single or multiple consecutive layers. Note that these may be also intermediate layers (model truncation). Optionally, we apply L_2 normalization.

Secondly, we aggregate token embeddings from different source task models by using an aggregation function A to combine embeddings across layers and models. The aggregation is done token-wise, so that every token can be represented as a combination of different model outputs. We define A to be either the mean of all vectors, i.e. as

$$\mathbf{E}_T = \frac{1}{k}\sum_{i=1}^{k}\mathbf{H}_{s_i}$$

Alternative, we use a simple attention mechanism for the combination (Figure 1, embedding aggregation):

$$\mathbf{E}_T = \sum_{i=1}^{k}\alpha_i\mathbf{H}_{s_i}$$

where

$$\alpha_i = \text{softmax}(\mathbf{W}\cdot\mathbf{H}_{s_i})$$

In some experiments we use only a single model. In this case the mean corresponds to the original embedding of the source model and attention simply means self-attention.

Next, the aggregated token embeddings are passed to the target task head that includes several layers with trainable weights (Figure 1, training target task layers which follow the *coref-hoi* implementation by Xu and Choi (2020)).

Figure 1 shows the probing workflow with four different source task models. Each source model is pre-trained separately on a corresponding dataset as described in Section 3. The models are based on *bert-base-cased* contextualized embeddings with different task-specific heads and their weights are frozen. Given that the source models cannot update their weights during probing, our conjecture is that those models that perform better on the coreference task "out-of-the-box" contain some useful information that is relevant for the target task.

3 Tasks

In this section we describe the target task, the source tasks and their respective training data.

3.1 Target Task

As our target model we choose a popular end-to-end coreference resolution model based on the implementation by (Xu and Choi, 2020) and train it on the OntoNotes CoNLL 2012 corpus (Pradhan et al., 2012). We use *bert-base-cased* and the recommended parameters for fine-tuning[2].

3.2 Source Tasks

We focus on the comparison with standard BERT as well as four other task-specific models. As source tasks we take a range of tasks of varying complexity: Paraphrase identification, named entity recognition, relation extraction, and - a (more complex) source task - quesion answering.

The first model is fine-tuned on the Microsoft Research Paraphrase Corpus (MRPC) (Dolan and Brockett, 2005). Since paraphrased sentences describe the same entities and events, such sentence pairs likely contain more coreferent mentions than standard (non-paraphrased) texts. Hence, MRPC embeddings are more tuned towards semantic similarity and could be useful for the coreference task.

Named Entity Recognition (NER) model is trained on the CoNLL 2012 dataset (Pradhan et al., 2012) and can generate one of the 37 labels for each token (e.g., PERSON, PRODUCT, DATE etc.). Named entities are often involved in coreference relations and being able to identify mention spans correctly is crucial for coreference resolution.

Next, we also experiment with the Relation Extraction model (RE) trained on the TACRED dataset (Zhang et al., 2017). It provides annotations for the spans of the subject and object mentions as well as the mention types according to the Stanford NER system and relations (if applicable) between the entities. Similarly to the NER model, RE is important for coreference because one of the tasks that this model performs is mention span detection. However, it also classifies different relations between the mentions and such relations are typically non-referential (e.g. *"per:employee_of"*).

Another source task model used in this project is trained on the SQUAD 2.0 dataset (Rajpurkar et al., 2016) for extractive question answering. This model (QA) can identify answer spans given the question and a paragraph of text. Since answering questions often involves coreference resolution, there is an overlap between these two tasks and word embeddings from one task might be beneficial for another.

For single model experiments we also analyse the performance on the vanilla BERT model [3](Devlin et al., 2019) which was trained with a masked language modeling objective on BookCorpus (Zhu et al., 2015) and English Wikipedia. Note that all the other source models are fine-tuned versions of this model.

Additionally, we experiment with the POS-tagging model[4], the models for semantic tagging[5] and chunking[6] as well as another NER model (NER-dslim)[7] trained on the English version of the CoNLL-2003 Named Entity Recognition dataset (Tjong Kim Sang and De Meulder, 2003). However, we limit the number of experiments for these models and focus mostly on MRPC, NER, RE and QA tasks.

4 Experiments and Results

In this section we describe our experiments with various source models and probe them on the coreference resolution task (§4.2). We also evaluate different embedding aggregation methods (§4.3), measure the effects of using intermediate layer output and normalization (§4.4), vary the embedding context from several hidden layers (§4.5) and compare the performance of multiple vs single models (§4.6).

[2] https://github.com/lxucs/coref-hoi/blob/master/experiments.conf

[3] We use the cased variant from HuggingFace under https://huggingface.co/bert-base-cased.

[4] https://huggingface.co/QCRI/bert-base-cased-pos

[5] https://huggingface.co/QCRI/bert-base-cased-sem

[6] https://huggingface.co/QCRI/bert-base-cased-chunking

[7] https://huggingface.co/dslim/bert-base-NER

4.1 Training Details and Evaluation

The coreference-specific layers are trained with the learning rate 1e-4 and early stopping (maximum number of epochs is set to 100 and patience is set to 5). The learning rate was optimized based on the experiments with the standard frozen BERT model.

For evaluation we use an average F1 score that is a combination of MUC (Vilain et al., 1995), CEAF (Luo, 2005) and B^3 (Bagga and Baldwin, 1998) coreference metrics. We run each experiment with three different seeds and report the average F1 values on the validation set. The target (non-frozen) model trained on the coreference resolution task from scratch achieves 73.75 F1 which is an upper bound for our probing task.

4.2 The Choice of the Source Task Models

Figure 2 shows the comparison between different source task models. Our original set of models that includes MRPC, NER, RE, QA and vanilla BERT has two clear winners: BERT and MRPC (64.01 and 64.32 F1). They are followed by RE (52.43) and QA (47.51) models and, finally, NER achieves the lowest score of 36.03. This comparison is based on a single run with the same seed, the averaged results across three runs with standard deviation can be found in Table 1.

We also have a closer look at the cosine similarity between our source models and the pre-trained coreference model. Figure 3 shows similarity scores averaged across all tokens for 15 random batches. The scores are collected before the embedding aggregation. Hence, they show how close the original source model embeddings are to the "ideal" task embeddings. Unsurprisingly, BERT and MRPC have the most similar embeddings to the coreference target. On the other hand, although both QA and NER embeddings are very different from the target task embeddings, QA achieves much better performance than NER on this task (50.79 vs 35.63 F1, see Table 1). This shows that even though cosine similarity is a good approximation for the task similarity, it is not an ideal predictor for the target task performance and even the source models with very different embeddings (QA) can still achieve the scores comparable to the ones achieved by the models with more similar embeddings (RE).

Additional models that we tested demonstrate rather poor performance on the coreference resolution task (see Figure 2). POS-tagging model struggles to learn anything about coreference and the training does not progress. Another NER model trained on a different version of Ontonotes (NER-dslim) achieves the maximum of 37.83 F1. Chunking and semantic labeling are somewhat more successful and achieve 48.81 and 49.82 F1 each, correspondingly.

4.3 How to Combine Task Embeddings

We employ two different aggregation strategies to combine the embeddings of the source task models: mean and attention-based aggregation. Additionally, we experimented with summing instead of using the mean, but the results were comparable or slightly worse: A combination of frozen MRPC with BERT achieves 62.34 F1 with sum and 63.26 with mean (average values across three runs with different seeds). Hence, in all further experiments we focus on the comparison between the mean and attention-based aggregation.

F1 scores for single models as well as for their 2x, 3x and 4x combinations can be found in Tables 1, 2 and 3. We also summarize the results for single models and for pairs of models graphically in Figure 4 that shows how much models benefit from attention. However, the trend holds even when there is only a single source model. This shows how much improvement we get by simply adding additional projections in the case of attention aggregation. The performance gains are different depending on the model. E.g., if we use pre-trained coreference model as our source task, there is almost no difference between attention and mean aggregation. However, other task-specific models can substantially benefit from selective aggregation. E.g., NER gains almost +19.7% and QA improves by +9%. In general, all models except for the one that has the same source and target tasks (CorefTarget) benefit from attention and improvements are larger for the models that have lower original scores.

For multiple model combinations we also see a similar trend with consistent improvements when attention-based aggregation is used, e.g., +13.23% for NER+MRPC and +9.36% for NER+QA (see Figure 4 and Table 2 for further comparisons). Interestingly, when we combine our source models with the model that was pre-trained on the coreference task (CorefTarget), we have only negligible improvements because the attention aggregator quickly learns which source model is beneficial for the task and starts paying almost all attention

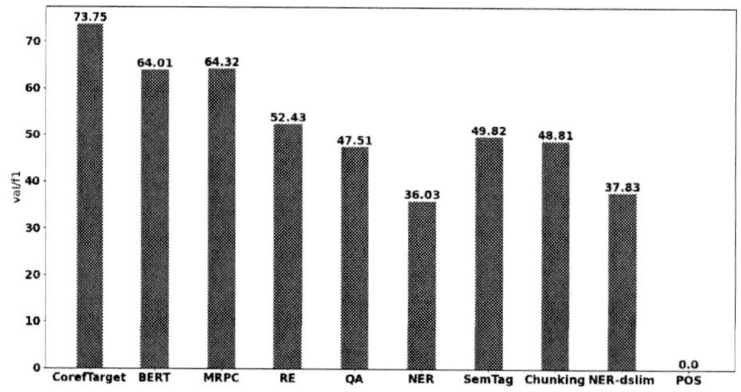

Figure 2: Source task models: CorefTarget, BERT, MRPC, RE, QA, NER, SemTag, Chunking, NER-dslim, POS

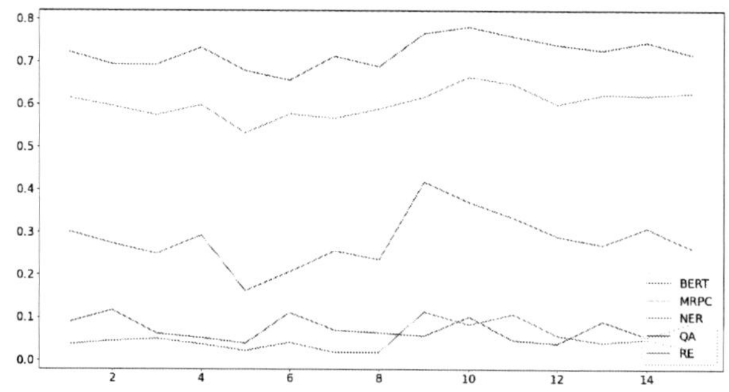

Figure 3: Average cosine similarity between the embeddings of the source tasks and the target coreference task, averaged across all tokens for 15 batches

to the output of this model ignoring all the others. However, if we do not add coreference task to the set of source tasks we observe some interesting patterns that emerge with the combinations of different models. Figure 9 (in the Appendix) shows how attention is distributed across different training epochs for the combination of MRPC, RE and NER. In the beginning, all three models are being paid the same amount of attention (≈33%). However, the aggregator soon starts prioritizing MRPC and NER gets progressively less and less attention. Interestingly, RE model also loses some impact over time but more slowly and remains somewhat important for the aggregator until the end of the training.

4.4 How to Extract Embeddings

We also consider different ways of embedding manipulations since the final layers of BERT-based models might be too specialized on their corresponding tasks, so that their representations are no longer useful for coreference resolution. In fact, after comparing the embeddings from layer 6 to 12 we found that the best performing layer on our probing task was typically not the final one. E.g., it was layer 9 for MRPC and RE, layer 8 for QA and 6 for NER (see Figure 5). Tables 1, 2 and 3 show the detailed comparisons between the original (full) model outputs as well as the normalized and truncated (to the "best" layer) versions for single models and their combinations (see also Figure 6 and 7 for the plot comparison). Truncation seems to be a good strategy for embedding aggregation and consistently yields best results across different settings. Truncation improves NER by up to +26.2%. QA is improved by +14% (Figure 6). Also combinations of models work better with truncation, e.g., RE+QA pair gains +8.17% F1 with mean aggregation and +2.84% with attention aggregation when both models are truncated (Figure 7).

Since combining embeddings from disparate models is a challenging task, especially when the

models	mean			attention			layer concat + attention		
	full	norm	trunc	full	norm	trunc	4	6	12
MRPC$_{(9)}$	61.16$_{\pm 2.84}$	58.61$_{\pm 13.7}$	66.26$_{\pm 0.61}$	67.05$_{\pm 0.70}$	67.49$_{\pm 0.29}$	67.27$_{\pm 0.30}$	**67.94**$_{\pm 1.54}$	67.03$_{\pm 0.99}$	67.28$_{\pm 1.48}$
NER$_{(6)}$	35.63$_{\pm 2.12}$	47.95$_{\pm 3.27}$	61.76$_{\pm 1.53}$	55.30$_{\pm 1.22}$	54.82$_{\pm 1.02}$	64.31$_{\pm 0.22}$	63.80$_{\pm 0.71}$	**66.30**$_{\pm 0.51}$	65.76$_{\pm 0.95}$
RE$_{(9)}$	52.27$_{\pm 2.39}$	48.03$_{\pm 10.8}$	62.40$_{\pm 1.41}$	60.97$_{\pm 0.01}$	41.01$_{\pm 0.14}$	63.73$_{\pm 0.70}$	65.16$_{\pm 1.07}$	**65.79**$_{\pm 0.37}$	65.43$_{\pm 0.93}$
QA$_{(8)}$	50.79$_{\pm 3.01}$	59.56$_{\pm 0.65}$	64.77$_{\pm 0.65}$	59.82$_{\pm 1.51}$	60.98$_{\pm 0.60}$	66.47$_{\pm 0.56}$	**67.70**$_{\pm 0.93}$	66.82$_{\pm 0.11}$	67.63$_{\pm 0.86}$
BERT$_{(10)}$	64.95$_{\pm 0.98}$	66.50$_{\pm 0.09}$	66.40$_{\pm 1.66}$	67.15$_{\pm 0.49}$	43.94$_{\pm 0.70}$	68.19$_{\pm 0.80}$	69.06$_{\pm 0.49}$	**69.07**$_{\pm 1.15}$	68.79$_{\pm 0.99}$
Coref$_{(12)}$	**73.75**$_{\pm 0.29}$	72.33$_{\pm 0.12}$	73.75$_{\pm 0.29}$	73.60$_{\pm 0.31}$	73.11$_{\pm 0.55}$	73.60$_{\pm 0.29}$	73.19$_{\pm 0.65}$	72.70$_{\pm 0.85}$	72.59$_{\pm 0.09}$

Table 1: Results for single models with different settings, mean and attention aggregation. Subscript indicates the best truncation layer for the *trunc* setting.

models	mean			attention		
	full	norm	trunc	full	norm	trunc
RE$_{(9)}$ + MRPC$_{(9)}$	61.76$_{\pm 1.85}$	64.71$_{\pm 0.42}$	64.49$_{\pm 0.76}$	67.56$_{\pm 0.36}$	51.06$_{\pm 13.8}$	**68.78**$_{\pm 0.32}$
NER$_{(6)}$ + MRPC$_{(9)}$	54.71$_{\pm 4.57}$	64.47$_{\pm 0.29}$	65.71$_{\pm 0.22}$	67.94$_{\pm 0.78}$	67.36$_{\pm 0.46}$	**68.67**$_{\pm 0.46}$
RE$_{(9)}$ + NER$_{(6)}$	56.13$_{\pm 1.42}$	60.68$_{\pm 0.48}$	64.38$_{\pm 1.14}$	64.00$_{\pm 0.74}$	62.80$_{\pm 0.36}$	**67.03**$_{\pm 0.31}$
QA$_{(8)}$ + MRPC$_{(9)}$	60.84$_{\pm 1.04}$	65.58$_{\pm 0.48}$	66.46$_{\pm 2.05}$	67.87$_{\pm 0.92}$	59.00$_{\pm 15.0}$	**68.98**$_{\pm 0.44}$
RE$_{(9)}$ + QA$_{(8)}$	57.66$_{\pm 3.61}$	63.55$_{\pm 0.26}$	65.83$_{\pm 0.61}$	65.02$_{\pm 0.39}$	64.49$_{\pm 0.30}$	**67.86**$_{\pm 0.59}$
NER$_{(6)}$ + QA$_{(8)}$	55.66$_{\pm 1.72}$	61.14$_{\pm 0.74}$	65.06$_{\pm 0.68}$	65.02$_{\pm 0.46}$	62.51$_{\pm 0.59}$	**67.65**$_{\pm 0.55}$

Table 2: Results for the pairs of models with different settings, mean and attention aggregation. Subscript indicates the best truncation layer for the *trunc* setting.

source tasks are quite different from each other, we also experiment with applying L_2 norm to the output of each model before aggregating the embeddings. This gives us varied results depending on the model and the aggregation type. E.g., for mean aggregation single NER, QA and BERT benefit from normalization but MRPC and RE result in lower scores. For attention aggregation all models except for MRPC and QA have substantial drop in performance.

It is also interesting to see the effect of normalization on the combinations of different models. For mean aggregation normalization brings substantial improvements, e.g., +9.76 F1 for NE+MRPC and +5.48% for NER+QA and, in general, all 2x models show better performance with normalization (Table 2). However, there is a very different trend for attention-based aggregation. Here we see a large drop in performance for most of the models, e.g., -8.87 F1 for QA+MRPC which indicates that attention can already combine the embeddings from different models quite well and achieves worse results with more uniform normalized embeddings.

4.5 Embedding Context from Multiple Layers

Since we found in our previous experiments that truncation consistently improves the performance for many source models, we decided to explore another setting that involves concatenating the embeddings of the last n hidden layers of the source model before aggregating them with attention. We experiment with the last 4, 6 and 12 layers and compare them to the aggregation that affects only the last layer of each model (see Table 1 for more detail).

Our results show that for single models having more "embedding context" is beneficial. Overall, combinations of the last 4 or 6 layers result in the best F1 scores. However, combining all layers of the model is not necessarily useful and can even hurt the performance. E.g., NER achieves 66.30 F1 with combined 6 layers which is +11 F1 improvement compared to the same model that uses only a single last layer but when we combine all 12 layers of NER the metric decreases from 66.30 to 65.76 F1 (Table 1).

Another interesting observation is that for vanilla BERT combining the outputs of the last 4 or 6 layers does not make any difference, and for other models the difference is more pronounced, although still rather small. NER is the model that gains the most from the increased embedding context, it gains additional +2.5 F1 by combining 6 instead of 4 last layers which is also consistent with our finding for the truncated models and the fact that NER performs better when truncated to 6 layers. The only model that does not show any improvements in the layer concatenation setting is the coreference source model since it is already optimized for the task and performs best as it is, i.e., without truncation, normalization or any other embedding manipulations.

models	mean			attention		
	full	norm	trunc	full	norm	trunc
$RE_{(9)}$ + $NER_{(6)}$ + $QA_{(8)}$	$58.95_{\pm 1.11}$	$63.70_{\pm 0.08}$	$65.04_{\pm 0.71}$	$66.24_{\pm 0.14}$	$64.71_{\pm 0.50}$	$\mathbf{68.98}_{\pm 0.32}$
$MRPC_{(9)}$ + $NER_{(6)}$ + $QA_{(8)}$	$60.35_{\pm 1.42}$	$65.13_{\pm 0.65}$	$65.68_{\pm 0.83}$	$69.21_{\pm 0.17}$	$59.10_{\pm 14.1}$	$\mathbf{69.56}_{\pm 0.35}$
$MRPC_{(9)}$ + $RE_{(9)}$ + $QA_{(8)}$	$61.83_{\pm 0.38}$	$65.22_{\pm 0.20}$	$66.69_{\pm 0.64}$	$68.63_{\pm 0.60}$	$67.17_{\pm 0.21}$	$\mathbf{68.81}_{\pm 0.69}$
$MRPC_{(9)}$ + $RE_{(9)}$ + $NER_{(6)}$	$62.27_{\pm 2.08}$	$65.15_{\pm 0.18}$	$65.96_{\pm 0.52}$	$68.31_{\pm 0.10}$	$66.88_{\pm 0.16}$	$\mathbf{69.30}_{\pm 0.52}$
$MRPC_{(9)}$ + $RE_{(9)}$ + $NER_{(6)}$ + $QA_{(8)}$	$62.19_{\pm 1.49}$	$65.56_{\pm 0.11}$	$65.66_{\pm 0.50}$	$69.03_{\pm 0.45}$	$66.80_{\pm 0.53}$	$\mathbf{69.39}_{\pm 0.74}$

Table 3: Results for multiple models with different settings, mean and attention aggregation. Subscript indicates the best truncation layer for the *trunc* setting.

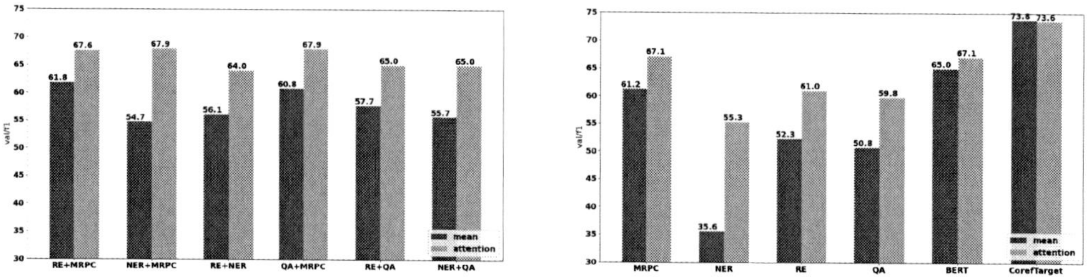

(a) Pairs of models: comparison of two embedding aggregation methods, mean and attention, to combine the source task model outputs

(b) Single models: performance gains by adding attention projections (attention) compared to having no additional parameters (mean)

Figure 4: Mean vs attention aggregation (full setting)

4.6 Combining Multiple Source Models

An interesting research question with respect to the embedding aggregation is how many models are actually needed to achieve good results and whether such models should be more or less similar to each other. E.g., NER and RE both focus on mention span extraction, RE and QA process relations between the entities in the text and MRPC model is more suitable for the semantic similarity tasks.

Firstly, we found that combinations of two models always outperform single models in the attention aggregation setting and, for the mean setting, pairs of models typically also perform better than the individual models except for the combinations with MRPC that tend to have lower scores (see Figure 8 for the comparison with mean and attention). E.g., NER with mean aggregation achieves 35.6 F1, RE achieves 52.3 and the combination of both (RE+NER) has 56.1 F1.

Secondly, we observed that combining three or more models typically works well for the full models. However, for the truncated setting there are only negligible gains when we combine multiple models (e.g., for RE+MRPC with attention we have 68.78 and for RE+MRPC+QA 68.81).

Lastly, model combinations that include MRPC tend to perform better than the rest which likely indicates the importance of semantic similarity for the coreference task. However, the combinations of RE+NER, RE+QA and QA+NER can also be beneficial, especially in the mean aggregation setting.

5 Related Work

Apart from the work on probing that was presented in the introduction, our work is closely related to the idea of *transfer learning* (Torrey and Shavlik, 2010), one of the ubiquitous paradigms in modern NLP. The idea of transfer learning is to train a model on a task A and then transfer the weights to a task B, either with or without further finetuning. This is the basis of most modern language models, which are pretrained and then applied or evaluated on specific downstream tasks (Devlin et al., 2019; Raffel et al., 2020; Jiang et al., 2023; Dubey et al., 2024). The pretraining data of large language models often contains samples from various natural language tasks, which renders most language models as multi-task learners (Yu et al., 2024). Multi-task learning describes a paradigm where a model is simultaneously trained on a range of tasks. While this concept is related to the work presented here, the main difference is that several source tasks are mixed together during (pre-)training usually, which

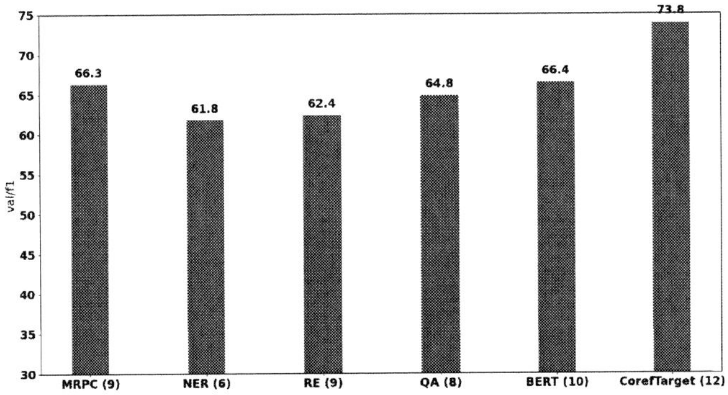

Figure 5: Source task model performance truncated to the best layer (in parentheses) with mean aggregation

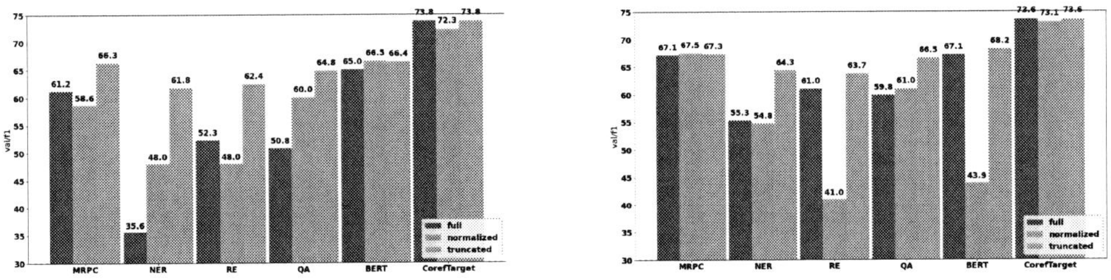

(a) Mean aggregation

(b) Attention aggregation

Figure 6: Single models: full vs normalized vs truncated

is not the case with our work.

In some sense, our work is related to research around task arithmetics (Matena and Raffel, 2022; Chronopoulou et al., 2023; Ilharco et al., 2023; Belanec et al., 2024), which has the goal to explicitly compute task representations in networks, e.g. as differences to a random initalization, and implement transfer learning by means of difference vector arithmetics. In contrast, our work concentrates on hidden representations, rather than the parameters of the network.

6 Conclusion

In this project we "reversed" the classical probing and investigated how different source task embeddings contribute to a target task (coreference resolution). Our experiments with Paraphrase Detection (MRPC), Named Entity Recognition (NER), Relation Extraction (RE) and Extractive Question Answering (QA) as source tasks show there are quite different embedding representations that achieve different scores on the target task ranging from 35.63 F1 (NER) to 61.16 F1 (MRPC) for single models.

Moreover, we found that the best performing embeddings were typically not the outputs of the last hidden layer but rather the representations generated at lower layers. MRPC was found to be the best source model, whereas, surprisingly, NER performed the worst.

We also explored different combinations of source models and found that two or more models typically outperform single ones. We considered mean and attention-based embedding aggregation methods and demonstrated the effectiveness of attention. For single models, we also showed that combining the outputs of several hidden layers instead of only one layer is beneficial. However, combining the outputs of all available layers is not necessarily a good strategy and usually the best scores can be achieved by combining only the outputs of the last 4 hidden layers that possibly contain more high-level, semantic information important for the coreference task.

In the future it would be interesting to experiment with more types of embedding manipula-

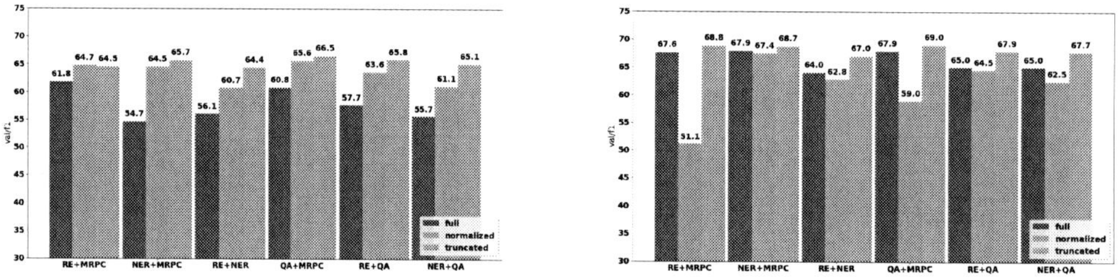

(a) Mean aggregation (b) Attention aggregation

Figure 7: Pairs of models: full vs normalized vs truncated

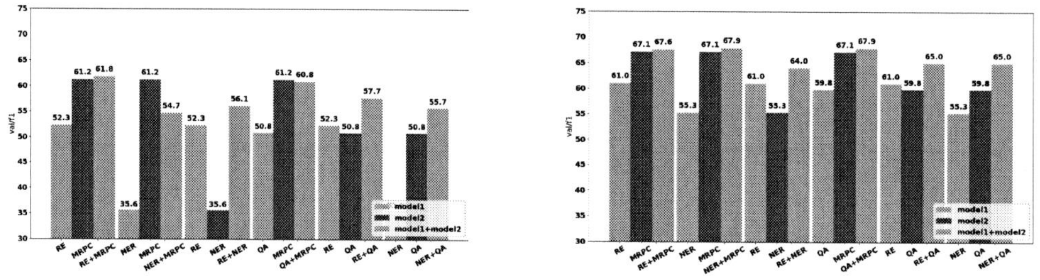

(a) Mean aggregation (b) Attention aggregation

Figure 8: Single and combined (2x) models

tions. Also, a combination of truncation and normalization could possibly bring some gains for single models. Moreover, it would be interesting to check the effects of attention aggregation with hidden layer concatenations for multiple models (e.g., RE+MRPC). Finally, it would be interesting to replicate our experiments on larger (non-BERT) models and tasks (e.g., semantic role labeling, discourse relation classification etc.).

We hope that our experiments can help to clarify the impact of embeddings and their combinations on the target coreference task. We also hope that the reverse probing idea will facilitate further research on finding useful information in the task-specific representations that originate from different fine-tuned models.

Limitations

While this work sheds light on the potential of reverse probing and task embeddings, some limitations arise.

First, we exclusively work with BERT-based models. This gives us a controlled setup, but it also means our findings might not fully translate to larger models or other architectures like GPT, T5, or multilingual models. Future work needs to investigate a broader range of models.

Our choice of source tasks, Paraphrase Detection (MRPC), Named Entity Recognition (NER), Relation Extraction (RE), and Question Answering (QA), is not exhaustive. There are many other NLP tasks, such as sentiment analysis, syntactic parsing, or commonsense reasoning, that might contribute useful embeddings for coreference resolution. Also, some of the tasks are not necessarily simpler than coreference resolution (e.g., QA), which we chose as our target task. Generally, our conclusions are centered around coreference resolution. While this is a challenging and linguistically complex problem, our approach may not directly apply to other NLP tasks, such as machine translation or text summarization.

Lastly, there is the question of computational efficiency. Although we worked with relatively small models, combining embeddings from multiple layers and tasks does introduce extra processing overhead.

Acknowledgments

This work has been supported by the German Ministry of Education and Research (BMBF) as part of the project TRAILS (01IW24005).

References

Amit Bagga and Breck Baldwin. 1998. Entity-based cross-document coreferencing using the vector space model. In *COLING 1998 Volume 1: The 17th International Conference on Computational Linguistics*.

Robert Belanec, Simon Ostermann, Ivan Srba, and Maria Bielikova. 2024. Task prompt vectors: Effective initialization through multi-task soft-prompt transfer. *arXiv preprint arXiv:2408.01119*.

Yonatan Belinkov. 2022. Probing classifiers: Promises, shortcomings, and advances. *Computational Linguistics*, 48(1):207–219.

Bernd Bohnet, Chris Alberti, and Michael Collins. 2023. Coreference resolution through a seq2seq transition-based system. *Transactions of the Association for Computational Linguistics*, 11:212–226.

Alexandra Chronopoulou, Jonas Pfeiffer, Joshua Maynez, Xinyi Wang, Sebastian Ruder, and Priyanka Agrawal. 2023. Language and task arithmetic with parameter-efficient layers for zero-shot summarization. *arXiv preprint arXiv:2311.09344*.

Alexis Conneau, German Kruszewski, Guillaume Lample, Loïc Barrault, and Marco Baroni. 2018. What you can cram into a single $&!#* vector: Probing sentence embeddings for linguistic properties. In *Proceedings of the 56th Annual Meeting of the Association for Computational Linguistics (Volume 1: Long Papers)*, pages 2126–2136, Melbourne, Australia. Association for Computational Linguistics.

Jacob Devlin, Ming-Wei Chang, Kenton Lee, and Kristina Toutanova. 2019. BERT: pre-training of deep bidirectional transformers for language understanding. In *Proceedings of the 2019 Conference of the North American Chapter of the Association for Computational Linguistics: Human Language Technologies, NAACL-HLT 2019, Minneapolis, MN, USA, June 2-7, 2019, Volume 1 (Long and Short Papers)*, pages 4171–4186. Association for Computational Linguistics.

William B. Dolan and Chris Brockett. 2005. Automatically constructing a corpus of sentential paraphrases. In *Proceedings of the Third International Workshop on Paraphrasing (IWP2005)*.

Abhimanyu Dubey, Abhinav Jauhri, Abhinav Pandey, Abhishek Kadian, Ahmad Al-Dahle, Aiesha Letman, Akhil Mathur, Alan Schelten, Amy Yang, Angela Fan, et al. 2024. The llama 3 herd of models. *arXiv preprint arXiv:2407.21783*.

John Hewitt and Percy Liang. 2019. Designing and interpreting probes with control tasks. In *Proceedings of the 2019 Conference on Empirical Methods in Natural Language Processing and the 9th International Joint Conference on Natural Language Processing (EMNLP-IJCNLP)*, pages 2733–2743, Hong Kong, China. Association for Computational Linguistics.

Gabriel Ilharco, Marco Tulio Ribeiro, Mitchell Wortsman, Ludwig Schmidt, Hannaneh Hajishirzi, and Ali Farhadi. 2023. Editing models with task arithmetic. In *The Eleventh International Conference on Learning Representations*.

Albert Q Jiang, Alexandre Sablayrolles, Arthur Mensch, Chris Bamford, Devendra Singh Chaplot, Diego de las Casas, Florian Bressand, Gianna Lengyel, Guillaume Lample, Lucile Saulnier, et al. 2023. Mistral 7b. *arXiv preprint arXiv:2310.06825*.

Kenton Lee, Luheng He, Mike Lewis, and Luke Zettlemoyer. 2017. End-to-end neural coreference resolution. In *Proceedings of the 2017 Conference on Empirical Methods in Natural Language Processing*, pages 188–197, Copenhagen, Denmark. Association for Computational Linguistics.

Yongjie Lin, Yi Chern Tan, and Robert Frank. 2019. Open sesame: Getting inside BERT's linguistic knowledge. In *Proceedings of the 2019 ACL Workshop BlackboxNLP: Analyzing and Interpreting Neural Networks for NLP*, pages 241–253, Florence, Italy. Association for Computational Linguistics.

Xiaoqiang Luo. 2005. On coreference resolution performance metrics. In *Proceedings of Human Language Technology Conference and Conference on Empirical Methods in Natural Language Processing*, pages 25–32, Vancouver, British Columbia, Canada. Association for Computational Linguistics.

Giuliano Martinelli, Edoardo Barba, and Roberto Navigli. 2024. Maverick: Efficient and accurate coreference resolution defying recent trends. In *Proceedings of the 62nd Annual Meeting of the Association for Computational Linguistics (Volume 1: Long Papers)*, pages 13380–13394, Bangkok, Thailand. Association for Computational Linguistics.

Michael S Matena and Colin A Raffel. 2022. Merging models with fisher-weighted averaging. In *Advances in Neural Information Processing Systems*, volume 35, pages 17703–17716. Curran Associates, Inc.

Simon Ostermann, Sheng Zhang, Michael Roth, and Peter Clark. 2019. Commonsense inference in natural language processing (COIN) - shared task report. In *Proceedings of the First Workshop on Commonsense Inference in Natural Language Processing*, pages 66–74, Hong Kong, China. Association for Computational Linguistics.

Sameer Pradhan, Alessandro Moschitti, Nianwen Xue, Olga Uryupina, and Yuchen Zhang. 2012. CoNLL-2012 shared task: Modeling multilingual unrestricted coreference in OntoNotes. In *Joint Conference on EMNLP and CoNLL - Shared Task*, pages 1–40, Jeju Island, Korea. Association for Computational Linguistics.

Colin Raffel, Noam Shazeer, Adam Roberts, Katherine Lee, Sharan Narang, Michael Matena, Yanqi Zhou,

Wei Li, and Peter J Liu. 2020. Exploring the limits of transfer learning with a unified text-to-text transformer. *Journal of machine learning research*, 21(140):1–67.

Pranav Rajpurkar, Robin Jia, and Percy Liang. 2018. Know what you don't know: Unanswerable questions for SQuAD. In *Proceedings of the 56th Annual Meeting of the Association for Computational Linguistics (Volume 2: Short Papers)*, pages 784–789, Melbourne, Australia. Association for Computational Linguistics.

Pranav Rajpurkar, Jian Zhang, Konstantin Lopyrev, and Percy Liang. 2016. SQuAD: 100,000+ questions for machine comprehension of text. In *Proceedings of the 2016 Conference on Empirical Methods in Natural Language Processing*, pages 2383–2392, Austin, Texas. Association for Computational Linguistics.

Alon Talmor, Jonathan Herzig, Nicholas Lourie, and Jonathan Berant. 2019. CommonsenseQA: A question answering challenge targeting commonsense knowledge. In *Proceedings of the 2019 Conference of the North American Chapter of the Association for Computational Linguistics: Human Language Technologies, Volume 1 (Long and Short Papers)*, pages 4149–4158, Minneapolis, Minnesota. Association for Computational Linguistics.

Ian Tenney, Dipanjan Das, and Ellie Pavlick. 2019a. BERT rediscovers the classical NLP pipeline. In *Proceedings of the 57th Annual Meeting of the Association for Computational Linguistics*, pages 4593–4601, Florence, Italy. Association for Computational Linguistics.

Ian Tenney, Patrick Xia, Berlin Chen, Alex Wang, Adam Poliak, R. Thomas McCoy, Najoung Kim, Benjamin Van Durme, Samuel R. Bowman, Dipanjan Das, and Ellie Pavlick. 2019b. What do you learn from context? probing for sentence structure in contextualized word representations. Publisher Copyright: © 7th International Conference on Learning Representations, ICLR 2019. All Rights Reserved.; 7th International Conference on Learning Representations, ICLR 2019 ; Conference date: 06-05-2019 Through 09-05-2019.

Erik F. Tjong Kim Sang and Fien De Meulder. 2003. Introduction to the CoNLL-2003 shared task: Language-independent named entity recognition. In *Proceedings of the Seventh Conference on Natural Language Learning at HLT-NAACL 2003*, pages 142–147.

Lisa Torrey and Jude Shavlik. 2010. Transfer learning. In *Handbook of research on machine learning applications and trends: algorithms, methods, and techniques*, pages 242–264. IGI global.

Marc Vilain, John Burger, John Aberdeen, Dennis Connolly, and Lynette Hirschman. 1995. A model-theoretic coreference scoring scheme. In *Sixth Message Understanding Conference (MUC-6): Proceedings of a Conference Held in Columbia, Maryland, November 6-8, 1995*.

Adina Williams, Nikita Nangia, and Samuel Bowman. 2018. A broad-coverage challenge corpus for sentence understanding through inference. In *Proceedings of the 2018 Conference of the North American Chapter of the Association for Computational Linguistics: Human Language Technologies, Volume 1 (Long Papers)*, pages 1112–1122. Association for Computational Linguistics.

Liyan Xu and Jinho D. Choi. 2020. Revealing the myth of higher-order inference in coreference resolution. In *Proceedings of the 2020 Conference on Empirical Methods in Natural Language Processing (EMNLP)*, pages 8527–8533. Association for Computational Linguistics.

Jun Yu, Yutong Dai, Xiaokang Liu, Jin Huang, Yishan Shen, Ke Zhang, Rong Zhou, Eashan Adhikarla, Wenxuan Ye, Yixin Liu, et al. 2024. Unleashing the power of multi-task learning: A comprehensive survey spanning traditional, deep, and pretrained foundation model eras. *arXiv preprint arXiv:2404.18961*.

Yuhao Zhang, Victor Zhong, Danqi Chen, Gabor Angeli, and Christopher D. Manning. 2017. Position-aware attention and supervised data improve slot filling. In *Proceedings of the 2017 Conference on Empirical Methods in Natural Language Processing*, pages 35–45, Copenhagen, Denmark. Association for Computational Linguistics.

Xuhui Zhou, Yue Zhang, Leyang Cui, and Dandan Huang. 2020. Evaluating commonsense in pretrained language models. In *Proceedings of the AAAI conference on artificial intelligence*, volume 34, pages 9733–9740.

Yukun Zhu, Ryan Kiros, Richard S. Zemel, Ruslan Salakhutdinov, Raquel Urtasun, Antonio Torralba, and Sanja Fidler. 2015. Aligning books and movies: Towards story-like visual explanations by watching movies and reading books. In *2015 IEEE International Conference on Computer Vision, ICCV 2015, Santiago, Chile, December 7-13, 2015*, pages 19–27. IEEE Computer Society.

A Additional Figures

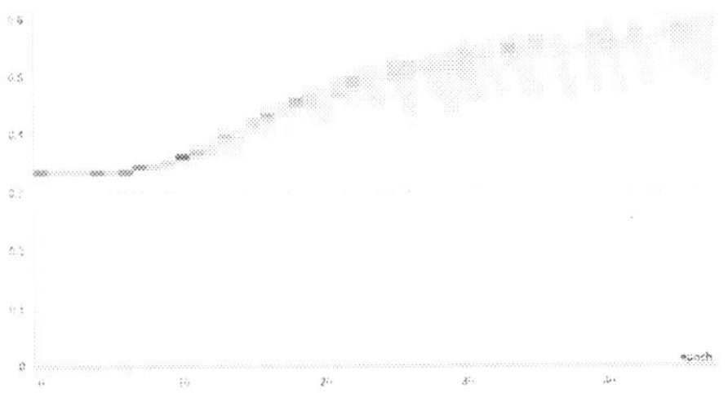

(a) MRPC

(b) RE

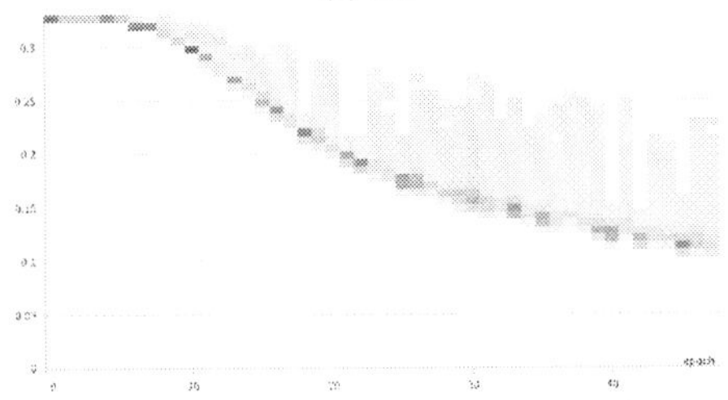

(c) NER

Figure 9: MRPC+RE+NER with attention aggregation (full setting)

Punctuation Restoration Improves Structure Understanding without Supervision

Junghyun Min[1], Minho Lee[2], Woochul Lee, Yeonsoo Lee[3],
[1]Linguistics Department, Georgetown University, Washington, DC, USA
[2]KT Gen AI Lab, Seocho, Seoul, Republic of Korea,
[3]NC AI, Seongnam, Gyeonggi, Republic of Korea
Correspondence: jm3743@georgetown.edu

Abstract

Unsupervised learning objectives like autoregressive and masked language modeling constitute a significant part in producing pre-trained representations that perform various downstream applications from natural language understanding to conversational tasks. However, despite impressive generative capabilities of recent large language models, their abilities to capture syntactic or semantic structure within text lag behind. We hypothesize that the mismatch between linguistic performance and competence in machines is attributable to insufficient learning of linguistic structure knowledge via currently popular pre-training objectives. Working with English, we show that punctuation restoration as a learning objective improves performance on structure-related tasks like named entity recognition, open information extraction, chunking, and part-of-speech tagging. Punctuation restoration results in $\Delta \geq$ 2%p improvement in 16 out of 18 experiments, across 6 out of 7 tasks. Our results show that punctuation restoration is an effective learning objective that can improve structure understanding and yield a more robust structure-aware representations of natural language in base-sized models.

1 Introduction

The modern natural language processing paradigm centers around transformer-based pre-trained language models (PLMs; Peters et al. (2018); Radford et al. (2018); Devlin et al. (2019)). They are optimized on masked language modeling (MLM) and autoregressive language modeling, which provide powerful representations to approach various problems in natural language processing. It is no exaggeration that language models have become effective in tasks like named entity recognition (NER), information extraction, semantic role labeling (SRL) that require understanding of syntactic, semantic, and discourse structure (Wang et al., 2021, 2022). However, the following suggests there is still room for improvement in current language models' abilities to understand such structure in natural language to perform downstream tasks reliably and robustly.

1. **The reversal or factorization curse**. Language models fail to infer "B is A" from "A is B" (Berglund et al., 2024), or their representations are highly dependent on the order (factorization) of the input (Kitouni et al., 2024).

2. **The curse of performance instability**. Model checkpoint initialization and training dataset order strongly affects sensitivity to syntactic structure (Zhou et al., 2020; McCoy et al., 2020; Du and Nguyen, 2023).

3. **Poor out-of-distribution generalization**. Systems report close-to-human performance on one dataset yet perform poorly on other datasets representing the same task, due to their picking up **spurious correlations** rather than learning the task (Gururangan et al., 2018; McCoy et al., 2019; Serrano et al., 2023).

4. **Insufficient or underutilized structure information**. While PLMs do encode some structure, they are poor few-shot structure predictors (Zhao et al., 2023; Bai et al., 2023) and perform better when input is reinforced with linguistic structure information (Strubell et al., 2018; He et al., 2020; Sachan et al., 2021; Wu et al., 2021; Fei et al., 2021; Xie et al., 2023; Huang et al., 2024). This indicates their representations are insufficient or underutilized.

These four phenomena illustrate that current representations as a result of autoregressive (Radford et al., 2018) or masked (Devlin et al., 2019; Liu et al., 2019; Raffel et al., 2019) language modeling are insufficient for structure understanding.

Proceedings of the 10th Workshop on Representation Learning for NLP (RepL4NLP-2025), pages 120–130
May 4, 2025

Efforts to mitigate such shortcomings include data-oriented approaches like syntactic augmentation to improve robustness to spurious correlations (Min et al., 2020; Yaghoobzadeh et al., 2021) and reversing input to mitigate the reversal curse (Golovneva et al., 2024). Architecture oriented efforts include adding explicit graph network layers to encode structure, resulting in improvement in benchmark scores (Zhang et al., 2019; Sachan et al., 2021; Wu et al., 2021) and generalization abilities (He et al., 2020; Sartran et al., 2022).

They are human-in-the-loop methods that require human input or annotation, or a system that requires such annotation. Recent work in distilling linguistic structure knowledge from natural language text to representations without supervision include inside-outside dynamic programming for tree induction (DIORA; Drozdov et al., 2019), dependency-constrained self-attention (Shen et al., 2021; Momen et al., 2023), and augmenting MLM with sentence-level contrastive learning (CLEAR; Wu et al., 2020). With the exception of CLEAR, these methods require additions to the model architecture. Wang et al. (2021) and Wang et al. (2022) propose structure pre-training but use human-annotated data.

In this paper, we investigate whether it is possible for an unsupervised method to mitigate the four shortcomings of the modern language model without implementing additional parser, tree, or graph architecture. In particular, we believe the pre-training stage of current PLMs may be further improved and propose punctuation restoration (PR) as an unsupervised learning objective that improves structure understanding. Punctuation markers, along with capitalization, often serve as boundary markers between different syntactic components of the sentence (Briscoe, 1996; Bayraktar et al., 1998). Punctuation marks also correspond to prosodic features of the sentence (Chafe, 1988), which in turn contain linguistic information (Wilson and Wharton, 2006; Wolf et al., 2023). Thus, the model's ability to predict punctuation from plain text may correlate to its ability to encode syntactic boundaries and thus structure. We hypothesize that additional optimization on punctuation restoration yields representations with increased sensitivity to structure, measured by in-distribution test set score, out-of-distribution generalization performance, and stability across initialization in structure-related natural language processing (NLP) tasks.

Intuitively, punctuation restoration may seem like an easy task. However, predicting punctuation and capitalization given text still remains nontrivial (Păiş and Tufiş, 2022; de Lima et al., 2024; Pang et al., 2024), and is an area of active work especially for post-processing results from automatic speech recognition and trascription systems (Alam et al., 2020; Zhu et al., 2024; You and Li, 2024; Zhong and Sun, 2025). We provide performance on the objective task in Appendix C.1. Although language modeling already includes predicting punctuation and capitalization, explicit optimization on punctuation restoration would allow models to predict them without explicit local context (e.g. beginning of sentence or quotation, following capitalization).

2 Objective and experimental setup

2.1 Objective design

The punctuation restoration objective predicts the original text from its "cleared-formatting" counterpart. In our implementation, we remove the following set of punctuation marks: the comma **,**, the period **.**, the exclamation point **!**, the question mark **?**, the single-quotation mark **'**, and the double-quotation mark **"**, along with capitalization, as shown below. Boldface indicates an addition to or a modification of source text.

- Source: lee faker sang-hyeok (hangul: 이상혁) is a league of legends esports player currently mid laner and part owner at t1
- Target: **L**ee **"F**aker**"** **S**ang-hyeok (**H**angul: 이상혁) is a **L**eague of **L**egends esports player**,** currently mid laner and part owner at **T**1**.**

While it is possible that a different selection yield better results, our selection reflects frequency (Sun and Wang, 2019) as well as syntactic significance (Bayraktar et al., 1998; Brabanter, 2023).

Similarly to popular pre-training objectives like MLM, autoregressive language modeling, and next-sentence prediction, the objective requires no human input. The objective is also architecture-agnostic and can be easily modified as appropriate.

From an internal database of English news articles, accessed between January 2022 and August 2023, we collected a total of 437,031 article excerpts, which are non-overlapping parts separated by a limiting word count of 150. One thousand excerpts each are used as the development and test sets, while the remaining 435,031 excerpts are used for training.

2.2 Experimental setup

Our experiments involve two stages. In the first stage, we take the pre-trained weights of the T5-base[1] model (Raffel et al., 2019), and perform additional pre-training on the punctuation restoration objective to produce PR-T5. Then, in the second stage, we fine-tune PR-T5 on downstream tasks and datasets.

In the first stage, the model f is given the "cleared-formatting" token sequence x comprising of tokens x_t and optimized to predict the original, fully punctuated and capitalized text y comprising of tokens y_t as described in Section 2.1. However, since there is textual overlap between x and y, assuming trivial copy error rate, we can write the model f as a predictor of capitalization and punctuation information $m_t = y_t - x_t$:

$$m_t = f(x, y_{<t}) = \begin{cases} \phi \\ \text{addPunct}(x_t, \theta) \\ \text{addCap}(x_t, \theta) \end{cases}$$

Thus, the effective loss is as follows:

$$\mathcal{L} \approx -\frac{1}{N} \sum_{t=1}^{N} \log P\left(m_t \mid x, y_{<t}\right).$$

In the second stage, we fine-tune PR-T5 and measure the effects of punctuation restoration in downstream tasks. We measure effects across 13 datasets that represent 7 tasks[2] and across 3 settings: generative, discriminative , and multi-task. In the generative setting, fine-tuned PR-T5 makes entity or tag predictions via autoregressive generation. We conduct 16 experiments in the generative setting, with 13 datasets from 7 tasks. In the multitask setting, fine-tuned PR-T5 is trained to make predictions for two tasks at once, namely NER and Open Information Extraction (OpenIE). We conduct 1 experiment in the multitask setting, with 2 datasets from 2 tasks. Generative and multitask predictions are illustrated in Table 4. In the discriminative setting, PR-T5's decoder block is replaced with a classification head, as described in Appendix A.1 and Figure 1. We conduct 1 experiment in the discriminative setting, with 1 dataset from 1 task. We fine-tune the publicly available pre-trained T5 weights on the same downstream tasks and use their performance as comparison baseline for all three settings. We publicly release our architecture, training, and inference code.

[1]See Appendix C.1 for details on model size selection

[2]See Appendix B for task and dataset details

3 Results

We measure the effects of punctuation restoration as an additional pre-training objective on downstream tasks on `t5-base`, with the four behaviors outlined in Section 1 in mind. In this section, we find direct evidence that this method helps mitigate three out of four behaviors we describe in Section 1.

We report our results in Tables 1, 2, 3. Each reported value of precision, recall, and F1 represents an average over the same 5 seed initializations, with the exception of discriminative NER, where we analyze 15 seed initializations.

3.1 Structure information encoding and use

In all 18 experiments across dataset, task, and setting, PR-T5 reports improved performance over T5 baselines. Among them, 16 experiments report improvements $\blacktriangle \geq .02$, and 10 experiments $\blacktriangle \geq .05$ (Tables 1, 2, 3). This is evidence that punctuation restoration makes available a nontrivial amount of structure information that previously may have been unavailable or underutilized, mitigating behavior 4 from Section 1.

3.2 Performance stability and out-of-distribution generalization

An out-of-distribution evaluation measures performance on a dataset that represents the same task but comes from a different source than the training dataset (e.g. evaluating on CaRB (Bhardwaj et al., 2019) after fine-tuning on OIE2016 (Stanovsky and Dagan, 2016)). It is an effective measure of robustness of a representation, as fine-tuned models often learn the dataset, rather than learning the task (Gururangan et al., 2018; McCoy et al., 2019; Serrano et al., 2023). We compare out-of-distribution generalization ability of PR-T5 to that of T5 in 5 experiments across NER, OpenIE, Chunking, and POS tagging, where we observe $\blacktriangle \geq .05$ increase in 4 of them (Table 1). This is evidence that punctuation restoration improves out-of-distribution generalization, mitigating behavior 3 in Section 1.

In addition, we observe that punctuation restoration reduces performance instability. Compared to T5, PR-T5's distribution of NER performance

Task	Training set	Evaluation set	t5-base			+ PR			Δ
			P	R	F1	P	R	F1	F1
NER	Econ-mNER	ID	.69	.65	.67	.90	.89	.89	▲.22
		Econ-sNER	.67	.76	.71	.74	.81	.77	▲.06
	GENIA	ID	.57	.73	.64	.64	.76	.69	▲.05
	CoNLL03	ID	.89	.90	.89	.92	.92	.92	▲.03
	ontonotes	ID	.87	.88	.88	.91	.91	.91	▲.03
OpenIE	EconIE-PRO	ID	.47	.43	.45	.60	.63	.62	▲.17
		CaRB	.22	.16	.19	.62	.42	.50	▲.31
	OIE2016	ID	.16	.19	.18	.19	.19	.19	.01
		CaRB	.10	.15	.12	.26	.27	.27	▲.15
Chunking	CoNLL00	ID	.94	.94	.94	.96	.96	.96	▲.02
		CoNLL03	.41	.41	.41	.41	.42	.42	.01
SRL	CoNLL12	ID	.75	.79	.77	.84	.86	.85	▲.08
SBD	PTB	ID	.97	.72	.81	.98	.98	.98	▲.17
POS	CoNLL00	ID	.96	.96	.96	.98	.98	.98	▲.02
		CoNLL03	.74	.87	.79	.84	.88	.86	▲.07
RE	TACRED	ID			.67			.83	▲.16

Table 1: Our main results where we compare `t5-base` model to `PR-t5-base` (+PR). ID denotes in-distribution evaluation on a dataset from the same source as the training set. See Appendix B for dataset details.

	t5-base (joint)			+ PR			Δ
	P	R	F1	P	R	F1	F1
NER	.86	.84	.85	.87	.86	.87	▲.02
OIE	.57	.60	.58	.60	.62	.61	▲.03

Table 2: Multitask (Econ-mNER, EconIE-PRO) performance.

	t5-base (EO)			+ PR			Δ
	P	R	F1	P	R	F1	F1
min	.67	.91	.78	.74	.90	.82	▲.04
max	.88	.94	.91	.90	.94	.91	.00
avg	.78	.93	.85	.83	.92	.88	▲.03
sdev	.061	.009	.035	.048	.010	.027	▼.008

Table 3: Discriminative Econ-mNER performance.

across initialization seeds is narrower. Minimum-maximum range (▼.04) and standard deviation (▼23%) both decrease with additional pre-training in punctuation restoration, as reported in Table 3. The results support our hypothesis that punctuation restoration increases stability across initialization seed and training dataset order, mitigating behavior 2 discussed in Section 1.

4 Discussion

Results from Section 3 support our hypothesis that complementing MLM with a more structure-related objective improves structure understanding. In particular, we use a punctuation restoration objective, described in Section 2 and evaluate with various structure-related tasks. While it is difficult to investigate the exact mechanism of how additional training on punctuation restoration improves learned representations, we attempt to provide an explanation.

In Section 1, we analyze that current methods for representation learning during the pre-training stage lack sufficient signal, and hypothesize additional training with a structure-sensitive objective should improve structure understanding. Much like how prosody helps disambiguate syntax in human speech processing (Price et al., 1991; Kahn et al., 2005), punctuation can be a useful guide in syntax disambiguation, and eventually toward forming a robust representation of text. Punctuation marks represent prosodic design (Chafe, 1988) which carries linguistic information (Wilson and Wharton, 2006; Wolf et al., 2023). Punctuation marks often also indicate syntactic or semantic boundaries (Briscoe, 1996; Bayraktar et al., 1998). Optimizing a computational system to predict punctuation allows it to predict syntactic and semantic boundaries, even in the absence of punctuation in the original text. Sufficient training in restoring punctuation can imitate effects of explicitly providing a parse, facilitating natural language understanding via a stronger understanding of sentence structure.

Performance improvement from punctuation

restoration is not limited to a specific dataset, task, and setting[3]. and represents an overall increase in representation robustness, as we observe out-of-distribution performance jump in NER, OpenIE, and chunking. Because of the wide range of experiments in which improvement is observed, we interpret this to be a general improvement of structure understanding rather than fortunate task-specific artifacts from the additional training.

Our methods yield a more reliable and robust representation that can be easily implemented and do not interfere with architectural additions. Punctuation restoration can be applied to reinforce structure understanding and improve robustness of learned representations regardless of model choice, or task-specific engineering policy. The effective objective requires no supervision, and one can construct a training corpus with little computational or manual resources.

Limitations

The idea of structure understanding reinforcement via punctuation restoration is still young–many decisions relevant to the learning objective in this paper, including selection of punctuation marks and source of learning corpus warrant additional investigation in future work. Our set of training hyper-parameters also will benefit from additional attention.

Among the 4 behaviors discussed in Section 1, we find direct evidence that punctuation restoration mitigates only three of them. While we predict that unsupervised structure learning via objectives like punctuation restoration can help mitigate the reversal (factorization) curse, this will need explicit verification.

While our experiments show promise in base-sized natural language understanding models for English, its effects in larger models, implications to generative or conversational systems, and generalization to other languages and thus language-agnostic nature also need to be verified.

It is also likely that punctuation restoration is not the only unsupervised learning objective that can be used to improve the representation learning stage of training NLP systems. Other forms of unsupervised structure learning, possibly simpler and more effective methods than punctuation restoration, as well as optimizations on objective combination (e.g. with word prediction methods) should be studied in future work.

Finally, although we believe that additional optimization on punctuation restoration improves the models' encoded linguistic structure, leading to performance jumps between T5 and PR-T5, we do not control for the additional compute or the exposure to novel data in this paper. Future work explicitly controlling for such variables will provide more robust arguments for punctuation restoration as a representation learning objective.

[3] And decoding method, discussed in Appendix B

Responsible research statement

We use OpenAI's GPT-3.5 Turbo (Brown et al., 2020) as a punctuation restoration performance baseline, and as a debugging assistant during the project's technical implementation.

The Econ-mNER dataset was annotated by paid, full-time employees who are trained linguists knowledgeable about their work and the dataset's downstream use. They are compensated similarly to the region's 2021 median income level. Their work has been reviewed by an internal board to not contain any personally identifiable information. Other internal datasets did not require manual annotation.

Acknowledgements

This work was performed during the authors' time at NC AI. We thank Yerang Kim, Tatsuya Aoyama, and Ethan Wilcox for their helpful comments. Any errors remain our own.

References

Tanvirul Alam, Akib Khan, and Firoj Alam. 2020. Punctuation restoration using transformer models for high- and low-resource languages. In *Proceedings of the Sixth Workshop on Noisy User-generated Text (W-NUT 2020)*, pages 132–142.

Xuefeng Bai, Jialong Wu, Yulong Chen, Zhongqing Wang, and Yue Zhang. 2023. Constituency parsing using llms. *arXiv preprint arXiv:2310.19462*.

Murat Bayraktar, Bilge Say, and Varol Akman. 1998. An analysis of english punctuation: The special case of comma. *International Journal of Corpus Linguistics*, 3(1):33–57.

Lukas Berglund, Meg Tong, Maximilian Kaufmann, Mikita Balesni, Asa Cooper Stickland, Tomasz Korbak, and Owain Evans. 2024. The reversal curse: LLMs trained on "a is b" fail to learn "b is a". In *The Twelfth International Conference on Learning Representations*.

Sangnie Bhardwaj, Samarth Aggarwal, and Mausam. 2019. CaRB: A crowdsourced benchmark for open IE. In *Proceedings of the 2019 Conference on Empirical Methods in Natural Language Processing and the 9th International Joint Conference on Natural Language Processing (EMNLP-IJCNLP)*, pages 6262–6267, Hong Kong, China. Association for Computational Linguistics.

Philippe De Brabanter. 2023. Quotation does not need marks of quotation. *Linguistics*, 61(2):285–316.

Ted Briscoe. 1996. The syntax and semantics of punctuation and its use in interpretation. In *Proceedings of the Association for Computational Linguistics Workshop on Punctuation*, pages 1–7. Citeseer.

Tom Brown, Benjamin Mann, Nick Ryder, Melanie Subbiah, Jared D Kaplan, Prafulla Dhariwal, Arvind Neelakantan, Pranav Shyam, Girish Sastry, Amanda Askell, Sandhini Agarwal, Ariel Herbert-Voss, Gretchen Krueger, Tom Henighan, Rewon Child, Aditya Ramesh, Daniel Ziegler, Jeffrey Wu, Clemens Winter, Chris Hesse, Mark Chen, Eric Sigler, Mateusz Litwin, Scott Gray, Benjamin Chess, Jack Clark, Christopher Berner, Sam McCandlish, Alec Radford, Ilya Sutskever, and Dario Amodei. 2020. Language models are few-shot learners. In *Advances in Neural Information Processing Systems*, volume 33, pages 1877–1901. Curran Associates, Inc.

Wallace Chafe. 1988. Punctuation and the prosody of written language. *Written Communication*, 5(4):395–426.

Tiago Barbosa de Lima, Vitor Rolim, André C.A. Nascimento, Péricles Miranda, Valmir Macario, Luiz Rodrigues, Elyda Freitas, Dragan Gašević, and Rafael Ferreira Mello. 2024. Towards explainable automatic punctuation restoration for portuguese using transformers. *Expert Systems with Applications*, 257:125097.

Jacob Devlin, Ming-Wei Chang, Kenton Lee, and Kristina Toutanova. 2019. BERT: Pre-training of deep bidirectional transformers for language understanding. In *Proceedings of the 2019 Conference of the North American Chapter of the Association for Computational Linguistics: Human Language Technologies, Volume 1 (Long and Short Papers)*, pages 4171–4186, Minneapolis, Minnesota. Association for Computational Linguistics.

Andrew Drozdov, Patrick Verga, Mohit Yadav, Mohit Iyyer, and Andrew McCallum. 2019. Unsupervised latent tree induction with deep inside-outside recursive auto-encoders. In *Proceedings of the 2019 Conference of the North American Chapter of the Association for Computational Linguistics: Human Language Technologies, Volume 1 (Long and Short Papers)*, pages 1129–1141, Minneapolis, Minnesota. Association for Computational Linguistics.

Yupei Du and Dong Nguyen. 2023. Measuring the instability of fine-tuning. In *Proceedings of the 61st Annual Meeting of the Association for Computational Linguistics (Volume 1: Long Papers)*, pages 6209–6230, Toronto, Canada. Association for Computational Linguistics.

Hao Fei, Shengqiong Wu, Yafeng Ren, Fei Li, and Donghong Ji. 2021. Better combine them together! integrating syntactic constituency and dependency representations for semantic role labeling. In *Findings of the Association for Computational Linguistics: ACL-IJCNLP 2021*, pages 549–559, Online. Association for Computational Linguistics.

Olga Golovneva, Zeyuan Allen-Zhu, Jason E Weston, and Sainbayar Sukhbaatar. 2024. Reverse training to nurse the reversal curse. In *First Conference on Language Modeling*.

Agustin Gravano, Martin Jansche, and Michiel Bacchiani. 2009. Restoring punctuation and capitalization in transcribed speech. In *2009 IEEE International Conference on Acoustics, Speech and Signal Processing*, pages 4741–4744.

Suchin Gururangan, Swabha Swayamdipta, Omer Levy, Roy Schwartz, Samuel Bowman, and Noah A. Smith. 2018. Annotation artifacts in natural language inference data. In *Proceedings of the 2018 Conference of the North American Chapter of the Association for Computational Linguistics: Human Language Technologies, Volume 2 (Short Papers)*, pages 107–112, New Orleans, Louisiana. Association for Computational Linguistics.

Keqing He, Shuyu Lei, Yushu Yang, Huixing Jiang, and Zhongyuan Wang. 2020. Syntactic graph convolutional network for spoken language understanding. In *Proceedings of the 28th International Conference on Computational Linguistics*, pages 2728–2738.

Xiaosai Huang, Jing Li, Jia Wu, Jun Chang, Donghua Liu, and Kai Zhu. 2024. Flexibly utilizing syntactic knowledge in aspect-based sentiment analysis. *Information Processing & Management*, 61(3):103630.

Jeremy G Kahn, Matthew Lease, Eugene Charniak, Mark Johnson, and Mari Ostendorf. 2005. Effective use of prosody in parsing conversational speech. In *Proceedings of Human Language Technology Conference and Conference on Empirical Methods in Natural Language Processing*, pages 233–240.

J.-D. Kim, T. Ohta, Y. Tateisi, and J. Tsujii. 2003. GENIA corpus—a semantically annotated corpus for bio-textmining. *Bioinformatics*, 19(1):180–182.

Ouail Kitouni, Niklas Nolte, Diane Bouchacourt, Adina Williams, Mike Rabbat, and Mark Ibrahim. 2024. The factorization curse: Which tokens you predict underlie the reversal curse and more. In *Advances in Neural Information Processing Systems*, volume 37, pages 112329–112355. Curran Associates, Inc.

Minho Lee, Junghyun Min, Woochul Lee, and Yeonsoo Lee. 2024. Structured language generation model for robust structure prediction. *arXiv preprint arXiv:2402.08971*.

Frederick Liu, Terry Huang, Shihang Lyu, Siamak Shakeri, Hongkun Yu, and Jing Li. 2022. Enct5: A framework for fine-tuning t5 as non-autoregressive models.

Yinhan Liu, Myle Ott, Naman Goyal, Jingfei Du, Mandar Joshi, Danqi Chen, Omer Levy, Mike Lewis, Luke Zettlemoyer, and Veselin Stoyanov. 2019. Roberta: A robustly optimized bert pretraining approach.

Mitchell P. Marcus, Mary Ann Marcinkiewicz, and Beatrice Santorini. 1993. Building a large annotated corpus of english: The penn treebank. *Comput. Linguist.*, 19(2):313–330.

R. Thomas McCoy, Junghyun Min, and Tal Linzen. 2020. BERTs of a feather do not generalize together: Large variability in generalization across models with similar test set performance. In *Proceedings of the Third BlackboxNLP Workshop on Analyzing and Interpreting Neural Networks for NLP*, pages 217–227, Online. Association for Computational Linguistics.

Tom McCoy, Ellie Pavlick, and Tal Linzen. 2019. Right for the wrong reasons: Diagnosing syntactic heuristics in natural language inference. In *Proceedings of the 57th Annual Meeting of the Association for Computational Linguistics*, pages 3428–3448, Florence, Italy. Association for Computational Linguistics.

Junghyun Min, R. Thomas McCoy, Dipanjan Das, Emily Pitler, and Tal Linzen. 2020. Syntactic data augmentation increases robustness to inference heuristics. In *Proceedings of the 58th Annual Meeting of the Association for Computational Linguistics*, pages 2339–2352, Online. Association for Computational Linguistics.

Omar Momen, David Arps, and Laura Kallmeyer. 2023. Increasing the performance of cognitively inspired data-efficient language models via implicit structure building. In *Proceedings of the BabyLM Challenge at the 27th Conference on Computational Natural Language Learning*, pages 327–338, Singapore. Association for Computational Linguistics.

Vasile Păiş and Dan Tufiş. 2022. Capitalization and punctuation restoration: a survey. *Artificial Intelligence Review*, 55(3):1681–1722.

Yutong Pang, Debjyoti Paul, Kevin Jiang, Xuedong Zhang, and Xin Lei. 2024. Llama based punctuation restoration with forward pass only decoding. *arXiv preprint arXiv:2408.11845*.

Matthew E. Peters, Mark Neumann, Mohit Iyyer, Matt Gardner, Christopher Clark, Kenton Lee, and Luke Zettlemoyer. 2018. Deep contextualized word representations. In *Proceedings of the 2018 Conference of the North American Chapter of the Association for Computational Linguistics: Human Language Technologies, Volume 1 (Long Papers)*, pages 2227–2237, New Orleans, Louisiana. Association for Computational Linguistics.

Sameer Pradhan, Alessandro Moschitti, Nianwen Xue, Olga Uryupina, and Yuchen Zhang. 2012. CoNLL-2012 shared task: Modeling multilingual unrestricted coreference in OntoNotes. In *Joint Conference on EMNLP and CoNLL - Shared Task*, pages 1–40, Jeju Island, Korea. Association for Computational Linguistics.

Patti J Price, Mari Ostendorf, Stefanie Shattuck-Hufnagel, and Cynthia Fong. 1991. The use of prosody in syntactic disambiguation. *the Journal of the Acoustical Society of America*, 90(6):2956–2970.

Alec Radford, Karthik Narasimhan, Tim Salimans, Ilya Sutskever, et al. 2018. Improving language understanding by generative pre-training.

Colin Raffel, Noam Shazeer, Adam Roberts, Katherine Lee, Sharan Narang, Michael Matena, Yanqi Zhou, Wei Li, and Peter J. Liu. 2019. Exploring the limits of transfer learning with a unified text-to-text transformer.

Devendra Sachan, Yuhao Zhang, Peng Qi, and William L Hamilton. 2021. Do syntax trees help pre-trained transformers extract information? In *Proceedings of the 16th Conference of the European Chapter of the Association for Computational Linguistics: Main Volume*, pages 2647–2661.

Laurent Sartran, Samuel Barrett, Adhiguna Kuncoro, Miloš Stanojević, Phil Blunsom, and Chris Dyer. 2022. Transformer grammars: Augmenting transformer language models with syntactic inductive biases at scale. *Transactions of the Association for Computational Linguistics*, 10:1423–1439.

Sofia Serrano, Jesse Dodge, and Noah A. Smith. 2023. Stubborn lexical bias in data and models. In *Findings of the Association for Computational Linguistics: ACL 2023*, pages 8131–8146, Toronto, Canada. Association for Computational Linguistics.

Yikang Shen, Yi Tay, Che Zheng, Dara Bahri, Donald Metzler, and Aaron Courville. 2021. StructFormer: Joint unsupervised induction of dependency and constituency structure from masked language modeling. In *Proceedings of the 59th Annual Meeting of the Association for Computational Linguistics and the 11th International Joint Conference on Natural Language Processing (Volume 1: Long Papers)*, pages 7196–7209, Online. Association for Computational Linguistics.

Gabriel Stanovsky and Ido Dagan. 2016. Creating a large benchmark for open information extraction. In *Proceedings of the 2016 Conference on Empirical Methods in Natural Language Processing*, pages 2300–2305, Austin, Texas. Association for Computational Linguistics.

Emma Strubell, Patrick Verga, Daniel Andor, David Weiss, and Andrew McCallum. 2018. Linguistically-informed self-attention for semantic role labeling. In *Proceedings of the 2018 Conference on Empirical Methods in Natural Language Processing*, pages

5027–5038, Brussels, Belgium. Association for Computational Linguistics.

Kun Sun and Rong Wang. 2019. Frequency distributions of punctuation marks in english: Evidence from large-scale corpora. *English Today*, 35(4):23–35.

Erik F. Tjong Kim Sang and Sabine Buchholz. 2000. Introduction to the CoNLL-2000 shared task chunking. In *Fourth Conference on Computational Natural Language Learning and the Second Learning Language in Logic Workshop*.

Erik F. Tjong Kim Sang and Fien De Meulder. 2003. Introduction to the CoNLL-2003 shared task: Language-independent named entity recognition. In *Proceedings of the Seventh Conference on Natural Language Learning at HLT-NAACL 2003*, pages 142–147.

Chenguang Wang, Xiao Liu, Zui Chen, Haoyun Hong, Jie Tang, and Dawn Song. 2022. DeepStruct: Pretraining of language models for structure prediction. In *Findings of the Association for Computational Linguistics: ACL 2022*, pages 803–823, Dublin, Ireland. Association for Computational Linguistics.

Xinyu Wang, Yong Jiang, Nguyen Bach, Tao Wang, Zhongqiang Huang, Fei Huang, and Kewei Tu. 2021. Automated concatenation of embeddings for structured prediction. In *Proceedings of the 59th Annual Meeting of the Association for Computational Linguistics and the 11th International Joint Conference on Natural Language Processing (Volume 1: Long Papers)*, pages 2643–2660, Online. Association for Computational Linguistics.

Ralph Weischedel, Martha Palmer, Mitchell Marcus, Eduard Hovy, Sameer Pradhan, Lance Ramshaw, Nianwen Xue, Ann Taylor, Jeff Kaufman, Michelle Franchini, Mohammed El-Bachouti, Robert Belvin, and Ann Houston. 2013. Ontonotes.

Deirdre Wilson and Tim Wharton. 2006. Relevance and prosody. *Journal of pragmatics*, 38(10):1559–1579.

Lukas Wolf, Tiago Pimentel, Evelina Fedorenko, Ryan Cotterell, Alex Warstadt, Ethan Wilcox, and Tamar Regev. 2023. Quantifying the redundancy between prosody and text. In *Proceedings of the 2023 Conference on Empirical Methods in Natural Language Processing*, pages 9765–9784, Singapore. Association for Computational Linguistics.

Shengqiong Wu, Hao Fei, Yafeng Ren, Donghong Ji, and Jingye Li. 2021. Learn from syntax: Improving pair-wise aspect and opinion terms extraction with rich syntactic knowledge. In *Proceedings of the Thirtieth International Joint Conference on Artificial Intelligence, IJCAI-21*, pages 3957–3963. International Joint Conferences on Artificial Intelligence Organization. Main Track.

Zhuofeng Wu, Sinong Wang, Jiatao Gu, Madian Khabsa, Fei Sun, and Hao Ma. 2020. Clear: Contrastive learning for sentence representation.

Yifeng Xie, Zhihong Zhu, Xuxin Cheng, Zhiqi Huang, and Dongsheng Chen. 2023. Syntax matters: Towards spoken language understanding via syntax-aware attention. In *Findings of the Association for Computational Linguistics: EMNLP 2023*, pages 11858–11864.

Yadollah Yaghoobzadeh, Soroush Mehri, Remi Tachet des Combes, T. J. Hazen, and Alessandro Sordoni. 2021. Increasing robustness to spurious correlations using forgettable examples. In *Proceedings of the 16th Conference of the European Chapter of the Association for Computational Linguistics: Main Volume*, pages 3319–3332, Online. Association for Computational Linguistics.

Jian You and Xiangfeng Li. 2024. A light-weight and efficient punctuation and word casing prediction model for on-device streaming asr. *arXiv preprint arXiv:2407.13142*.

Yue Zhang, Rui Wang, and Luo Si. 2019. Syntax-enhanced self-attention-based semantic role labeling. In *Proceedings of the 2019 Conference on Empirical Methods in Natural Language Processing and the 9th International Joint Conference on Natural Language Processing (EMNLP-IJCNLP)*, pages 616–626, Hong Kong, China. Association for Computational Linguistics.

Yuhao Zhang, Victor Zhong, Danqi Chen, Gabor Angeli, and Christopher D. Manning. 2017. Position-aware attention and supervised data improve slot filling. In *Proceedings of the 2017 Conference on Empirical Methods in Natural Language Processing (EMNLP 2017)*, pages 35–45.

Haoyu Zhao, Abhishek Panigrahi, Rong Ge, and Sanjeev Arora. 2023. Do transformers parse while predicting the masked word? In *Proceedings of the 2023 Conference on Empirical Methods in Natural Language Processing*, pages 16513–16542, Singapore. Association for Computational Linguistics.

Qishuai Zhong and Aixin Sun. 2025. Punctuation restoration: A case study of bert-based models' task-specific excellence. In *ICASSP 2025 - 2025 IEEE International Conference on Acoustics, Speech and Signal Processing (ICASSP)*, pages 1–5.

Xiang Zhou, Yixin Nie, Hao Tan, and Mohit Bansal. 2020. The curse of performance instability in analysis datasets: Consequences, source, and suggestions. In *Proceedings of the 2020 Conference on Empirical Methods in Natural Language Processing (EMNLP)*, pages 8215–8228, Online. Association for Computational Linguistics.

Xiliang Zhu, Chia-Tien Chang, Shayna Gardiner, David Rossouw, and Jonas Robertson. 2024. Resolving transcription ambiguity in Spanish: A hybrid acoustic-lexical system for punctuation restoration. In *Proceedings of the Third Workshop on Understanding Implicit and Underspecified Language*, pages 33–41, Malta. Association for Computational Linguistics.

A Additional details on experimental setup

We train the model on the punctuation restoration objective for 40 epochs, before fine-tuning with supervised datasets for downstream tasks. The experiments are run on a single V100 GPU with 32GB VRAM, with half precision and gradient accumulation enabled at 16. Our choice of hyper-parameters are as follows: batch size 32, maximum sequence length 256, learning rate 3e-4, maximum grad norm 0.5, and Adam epsilon 1e-8. Number of fine-tuning epochs was 10, with the exception of SRL, which is fine-tuned for 1 epoch only. The additional pre-training lasts about 2 weeks, while the length of each epoch of training varies across datasets between 10 minutes and around 2 hours.

A.1 Discriminative approach

While there exist sophisticated attempts to incorporate the decoder layers in producing a discriminative model from a pre-trained encoder-decoder architecture (Liu et al., 2022), we use a simple architecture where we forgo the decoder block and place a `T5ClassificationHead` on top of the encoder block of the T5 model. That is, we take the hidden state output from model's encoder and use it as input to the classification head. An illustration of the model architecture is shown in Figure 1. After additional pre-training on punctuation restoration objective, the decoder block of the `t5-base` model is removed and a newly initialized classification head is placed on top of the encoder block. The architecture is comparable to those of BERT-like encoder-only models. Even by retaining weights from the encoder blocks only, we observe that additional unsupervised structure learning via punctuation restoration results in downstream task performance improvement.

A.2 Joint multitask generative approach

The joint multitask approach, where we focus on open information extraction using the EconIE-PRO dataset and NER using the Econ-mNER dataset, is similar to the generative approach. The input sequence is identical to the experiments from Section 3, but the output sequence is a concatenation of output sequences from the two datasets, as illustrated in Table 4.

B Additional details on dataset

We use a suite of structure-related NLP tasks to measure model structure understanding. Relevant tasks include named entity recognition (NER), sentence boundary detection (SBD), open information extraction (OpenIE), chunking, semantic role labeling (SRL), part-of-speech tagging, and relation classification. Our selection mostly follows that from Wang et al. (2021) and Lee et al. (2024). We use both public and internal datasets, and check for in- and out-of-distribution generalization. A full list of datasets for each task is shown in Table 5. In the main body of the paper, we discuss effects of punctuation restoration across task, dataset, and setting. Here, we discuss another variable across which punctuation restoration is effective: decoding method.

B.1 Entity generation tasks

NER, OpenIE, SRL, and relation classification are entity generation tasks, where fine-tuned models autoregressively generate entity objects. For example, `(Faker: PER)`, `(Faker, is, a League of Legends esports player)`, `(Faker, employeeAt, T1)` are NER, OpenIE, and relation classification examples, respectively. The order in which entities are generated does not affect evaluation in the case of entity generation tasks.

Source	Faker is a League of Legends esports player, currently mid laner and part owner at T1.
OpenIE	(Faker, is, a League of Legends esports player)
	(Faker, is mid laner and part owner at, T1)
NER	(Faker: PER) (T1: ORG)
Multitask	(Faker: PER)
	(Faker, is, a League of Legends esports player)
	(Faker, is mid laner and part owner at, T1)
	(T1: ORG)

Table 4: Example output from generative NER, OpenIE, and multitask models.

B.2 Tag sequence generation tasks

Chunking and POS tagging are tag sequence generation tasks, where fine-tuned models autoregressively generate tag sequences. `"NP VP ADVP PP NP NP NP"` and `"NP VBZ DT NP IN NP"` are example sequences of chunking and POS tagging, respectively.

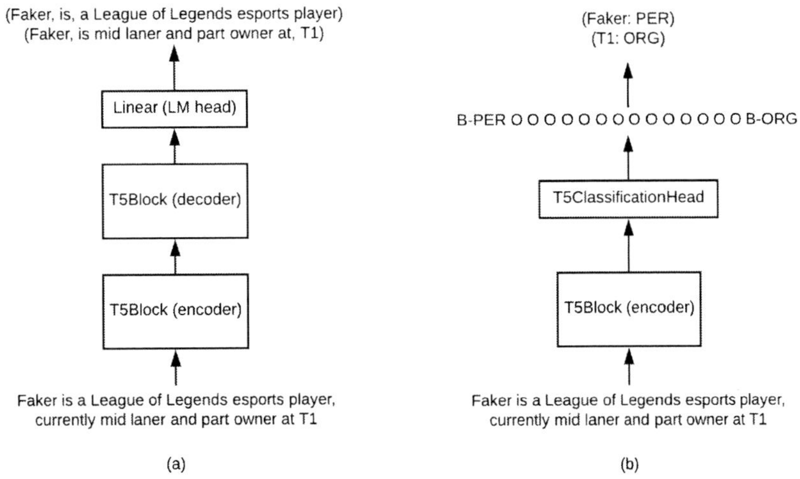

Figure 1: (a) The `t5` architecture for a generative, text-to-text approach to NLP tasks. Here, we illustrate open information extraction. (b) A modification to the `t5` architecture to allow a discriminative approach to NLP tasks. Here, we illustrate named entity recognition.

B.3 Sequence generation tasks

Punctuation restoration and sentence boundary detection are sequence generation tasks. Fine-tuned models auto-regressively generate natural text sequences, with predefined tags to perform the task. For example, a sentence boundary detection model would generate a [<s>] token between sentences, given a passage.

B.4 Token classification tasks

NER in the discriminative setting is a token classification task. Given a sentence of length n, the fine-tuned model outputs an array of length n, each element of which represents whether its corresponding token is part of a named entity. For example, one from a tag set such as `[O, B-PER, I-PER, B-LOC, I-LOC, B-ORG, I-ORG]`, as illustrated in Figure 1.

C Additional details on results

In our results, improvements from punctuation restoration persist across decoding methods–entity generation in NER, OpenIE, SRL, and relation classification; tag sequence generation in chunking and POS tagging; sequence generation in sentence boundary detection; and token classification in discriminative NER.

C.1 Objective results

Punctuation restoration, along with capitalization restoration is no trivial task, especially when the model needs to predict restoration location without local context (Gravano et al., 2009; Alam et al., 2020; Păiş and Tufiş, 2022; de Lima et al., 2024; Zhong and Sun, 2025). Should our hypothesis hold, it is likely that syntactic signals from punctuation restoration transfer more effectively in models with stronger punctuation restoration performances. We experiment with three sizes of the T5 architecture (Raffel et al., 2019). We consider `t5-small`, `t5-base`, and `t5-large`. Table 6 includes their punctuation restoration performance, in addition to ChatGPT's (Brown et al., 2020) zero-shot performance as a reference point, which shows that the objective is nontrivial.

Across the T5 models, there is some correlation between size and punctuation restoration performance. Because the performance gap between `t5-base` and `t5-large` models is small (Δ.00), while gap between `t5-small` and `t5-base` more significant (Δ.05), we use the `t5-base` model for our experiments.

We also note that our selection of the T5 model is due to its ability to perform both generative and discriminative tasks after single pre-training.

Task	Dataset	Source	Task type
Internal datasets			
PR	finPR	Rule-based tagging on finance news	Seq. gen.
NER	Econ-mNER	Manual tagging on finance news and corporate filings	Ent. gen., Tok. cls.
	Econ-sNER	Semi-supervised tagging on finance news	Ent. gen.
OpenIE	EconIE-PRO	Rule-based tagging on finance news, predicate range optimized	Ent. gen.
Public datasets			
NER	GENIA	Kim et al. (2003)	Ent. gen.
	CoNLL 2003	Tjong Kim Sang and De Meulder (2003)	Ent. gen.
	ontonotes	Weischedel et al. (2013)	Ent. gen.
SBD	PTB	Marcus et al. (1993)	Seq. gen.
OpenIE	OIE2016	Stanovsky and Dagan (2016)	Ent. gen.
	CaRB	Bhardwaj et al. (2019)	Ent. gen.
Chunk, POS	CoNLL 2000	Tjong Kim Sang and Buchholz (2000)	Tag gen.
	CoNLL 2003	Tjong Kim Sang and De Meulder (2003)	Tag gen.
SRL	CoNLL 2012	Pradhan et al. (2012)	Ent. gen.
ORE	TACRED	Zhang et al. (2017)	Ent. gen.

Table 5: We use a total of 14 datasets across 8 tasks, including punctuation restoration. Four are internal datasets, while the rest are publicly available.

Model architecture	P	R	F1
ChatGPT 0-shot*	.75	.71	.73
`t5-small`	.91	.86	.88
`t5-base`	.93	.92	.93
`t5-large`	.94	.93	.93

Table 6: Punctuation restoration performance after 50 epochs (small), 40 epochs (base), and 20 epochs (large) of training respectively. *Measured on a small subset of the punctuation restoration evaluation dataset.

C.2 Joint multitask generative setting

Similarly to the generative approach, we observe that additional unsupervised structure learning via punctuation restoration results in downstream task performance improvement (▲.02 NER and ▲.03 OpenIE). While PR-T5 multi-task performance slightly degrades compared to its single-task generative setting (▼.02 NER and .01 OpenIE), multitask-T5 outperforms single task-T5 on EconIE-PRO, an open information extraction dataset (▲.13).

C.3 Discriminative setting

Given the results from the single-task generative approach, the transfer from punctuation restoration to multi-task generative approach may be no big surprise, as there is no drastic difference between the generative nature of the two approaches. However, we report that our improved representations from punctuation restoration non-trivially transfers to the discriminative approach as well, where the decoder block is removed from the model, as illustrated in Figure 1. Although the maximum performance for T5 and PR-T5 are similar at .91 (.00), there is a significant difference in the minimum, at .78 and .82, respectively (▲.04). Punctuation restoration results in not only higher performance, but also more consistent and stable sets across different initializations.

Amuro & Char: Analyzing the Relationship between Pre-Training and Fine-Tuning of Large Language Models

Kaiser Sun **Mark Dredze**
Johns Hopkins University
Baltimore, MD USA
{hsun74,mdredze}@cs.jhu.edu

Abstract

Large language model development relies on the pre-train-then-align paradigm, in which the model is typically pre-trained on a large text corpus and undergoes a tuning stage to align the model with human preference or downstream tasks. We investigate the relationship between pre-training and supervised fine-tuning by considering multiple tasks as well as different pre-trained model checkpoints. Our results on 18 datasets and two models suggest that i) although the model benefits significantly through supervised fine-tuning, it may forget previously known domain knowledge and tasks that are not seen during fine-tuning; ii) the model exhibits high sensitivity to evaluation prompts after supervised fine-tuning, but this sensitivity can be alleviated through further pre-training; iii) continual pre-training improves the model in a latent way that manifests after fi ne-tuning; iv) The model can already solve some tasks after pre-training, while fine-tuning most benefits datasets where the model does not show capability during pre-training. [1]

1 Introduction

The rise of large language models (LLMs) as a general-purpose tool for a diverse range of natural language processing tasks has dramatically transformed the field, introducing new paradigms for data collection and model training (Brown et al., 2020, Biderman et al., 2023, Touvron et al., 2023, Jiang et al., 2023, Chowdhery et al., 2023, Groeneveld et al., 2024, Wang et al., 2024, *inter alia*). Numerous models, training methods, datasets, and evaluation methods continue to be developed on an ongoing basis. Nevertheless, a unified paradigm has emerged for training LLMs:

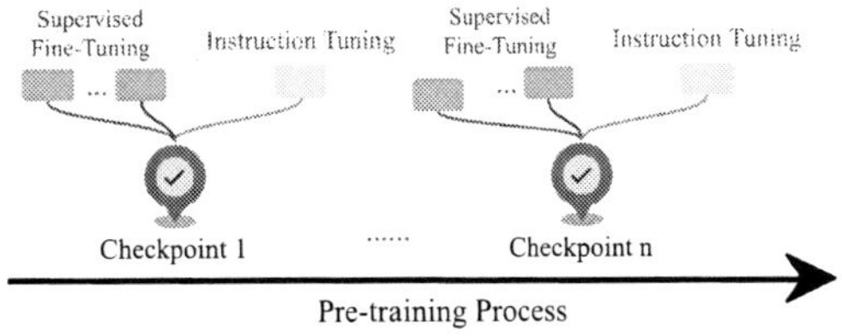

Figure 1: Illustration of the experimental scheme. Intermediate pre-training checkpoints are fine-tuned on different datasets.

pre-train on an enormous corpus of diverse documents, ranging from 250B (Biderman et al., 2023) to 15T (AI@Meta, 2024) tokens, followed by an alignment stage to make the model more useful and performative for various tasks.

Based on this paradigm, work has focused on improving these two stages. Work to improve pre-trained models includes larger training sets (Hoffmann et al., 2022; AI@Meta, 2024; Touvron et al., 2023), different data selection mechanisms (Xia et al., 2024), higher quality data (Zhou et al., 2024), and various model architectures (Su et al., 2024; Touvron et al., 2023). Meanwhile, research on model alignment includes different training objectives (Rafailov et al., 2024; Schulman et al., 2017), new datasets (Narayanan and Aepli, 2024), more efficient training (Hu et al., 2021; Dettmers et al., 2024) and safety tuning (Bianchi et al., 2023). The alignment stage usually involves either supervised fine-tuning for specific tasks or instruction fine-tuning for general-purpose usage. Regardless, fine-tuning (almost always) comes at the end of pre-training and yields remarkable improvements on downstream tasks (Touvron et al., 2023; Groeneveld et al., 2024). Consequently, the benefits of each stage are largely explored independently, with improvements to pretraining being orthogonal to benefits from model alignment.

Rather than exploring these two training regimes independently, we ask: What does the model learn

[1] Code, results, and data to reproduce the experiments are available at github.com/KaiserWhoLearns/AmuroCharPTFTRelationship. All the model checkpoints resulting from this work are available at huggingface.co/KaiserWhoLearns/PTvsSFT_OLMo1b

Proceedings of the 10th Workshop on Representation Learning for NLP (RepL4NLP-2025), pages 131–151
May 4, 2025 ©2025 Association for Computational Linguistics

and forget during pre-training and fine-tuning? Specifically, **how do pretraining and fine-tuning interact to produce the resulting model?** Does more pre-training hinder better fine-tuning results? Answering these questions requires us to examine how models learn during pre-training and how this affects fine-tuning. Therefore, we begin by fine-tuning two language models under a variety of conditions to determine how fine-tuning affects model behavior. We explore both supervised and instruction fine-tuning, testing the models' memorization and forgetting when learning specific tasks and serving as general-purpose language-AI tools. We then explore the affect of pre-training on these behaviors by fine-tuning **multiple pre-training checkpoints** of a large language model (Figure 1), evaluating each checkpoint and its fine-tuned variant on downstream evaluation sets. We track model abilities during pre-training and compare them to improvements achieved after fine-tuning at the corresponding pre-training step.[2]

Our experiments yield the following insights into LLM training: (1) although supervised fine-tuning can improve performance on in-distribution tasks, it can also cause the model to forget domain knowledge or tasks that it was previously capable of solving (§4); (2) fine-tuned models show high sensitivity to evaluation prompts, but this sensitivity can be alleviated by more pre-training (§4); (3) continued pre-training can improve a model in ways that are only revealed after fine-tuning (§6); (4) tasks for which the model already performs well during pre-training benefit much less from fine-tuning than those where the model does not demonstrate capabilities (§5, §6);

Our findings provide insights into model training and can inform methods for both pre-training and fine-tuning. Furthermore, our work shows the value of analyzing the training dynamics, in addition to analyzing the final checkpoint of an LLM, as an aspect of interpretability, and we encourage model developers to release these checkpoints to aid future studies.

2 Background: Model Training

We use "model alignment" as a general term for techniques that align a model with a desired behavior, often accomplished by fine-tuning models after pretraining. The term is also associated with other definitions (Shen et al., 2024).

We begin with a brief survey of the core components of LLM training: pre-training, fine-tuning, and instruction fine-tuning. The first step of training an LLM is pre-training on a massive text corpus (Achiam et al., 2023; Touvron et al., 2023; Groeneveld et al., 2024). Initial work increased model size to hundreds of billions of parameters (Brown et al., 2020; Rae et al., 2021; Chowdhery et al., 2023), along with explorations in model size, training corpus size, and training data characteristics (Radford et al., 2019; Hoffmann et al., 2022; Gururangan et al., 2020). Other work increased the amount of pre-training data (Computer, 2023; Soldaini et al., 2024), with new models now reaching 15 trillion tokens (AI@Meta, 2024).

After the pre-training stage, when a specific task of interest has been identified, supervised fine-tuning can improve a pre-trained model. Task-agnostic tuning became popularized with the advent of T5 models (Raffel et al., 2020), where a pre-trained LLM is tuned using a general text-to-text solution. Instruction fine-tuning is preferred when more general model behaviors are desired. When multiple tasks are given to the model, the model is commonly given a task-specific prefix or an instruction along with the task input, leading to the development of various methods of prefix tuning (Li and Liang, 2021) and instruction tuning (Wei et al., 2021; Mishra et al., 2022; Victor et al., 2022).

Other works explore human preference tuning with or without a reward model (Christiano et al., 2017; Ziegler et al., 2019; Stiennon et al., 2020; Ouyang et al., 2022; Rafailov et al., 2024; Song et al., 2024; Xu et al., 2024). In-context learning utilizes a small amount of supervised data to improve model performance without updating the parameters. In this work, we focus specifically on single-task supervised fine-tuning and multi-task instruction tuning.

3 Experimental Setup

In this section, we describe the models and datasets used. The hyperparameter tuning procedure and setup for each fine-tuning setting can be found in Appendix B.

[2]While we believe that we were the first to explore these issues through intermediate model checkpoints, recently released work has also utilized pre-training checkpoints and are highlighted in Section 8.

[3]https://huggingface.co/datasets/pietrolesci/gpt3_nli

Supervised Fine-Tuning			
Task	**Training**	**ID Test**	**OOD Test**
Summary Generation	XSum	XSum, XLSum	CNN
Question Generation	SocialIQa	SocialIQA	SciQ, TweetQA
Natural Language Inference	MNLI	MNLI1, MNLI2	RTE, GPT3NLI[3]
Paraphrase Detection	Paws	Paws	QQP, STS-B

Instruction Tuning	
Dataset	**Description**
TÜLU-v2	A mixture of instruction datasets.
ARC	Grade-school multiple-choice QA.
OpenbookQA	Open book exam QA.
Hellaswag	Commonsense inference.
BoolQ	Reading comprehension.
SciQ	Science exam multiple choice QA.

Table 1: Dataset information. For Generation tasks, ROUGE-L is used as evaluation metric, and accuracy is used for classification tasks. ID = In-domain, OOD = Out-of-domain.

3.1 Model Choice

We consider two open models of different architectures and scales: Llama3-8B (AI@Meta, 2024) and OLMo-1B (Groeneveld et al., 2024). To minimize potential confounding factors such as multilingual ability and double descent (Belkin et al., 2019; Caballero et al., 2022; Schaeffer et al., 2023), we exclusively select models predominantly pre-trained in English and incorporate significantly more pre-trained tokens than the number of parameters. We do not include models trained in a multi-stage manner to ensure uniformity of the tokens seen by the model during pre-training. Some of our experiments consider intermediate pre-training checkpoints. We select checkpoints uniformly by the number of tokens seen from the pre-training history along with the first and the final checkpoints. Unfortunately, very few large language models release intermediate pre-training checkpoints (summarized in Table 2). Further consideration and reasoning of model selection are included in Appendix A.

3.2 Training Procedure

We fully fine-tune each of the selected model checkpoints using two different procedures to create fine-tuned models: supervised fine-tuning and instruction tuning. The supervised fine-tuning is conducted separately for each model checkpoint and dataset, while the instruction fine-tuning is done once using the instruction dataset. The instruction-tuned model is evaluated on a suite of LLM benchmarks. All experiments are conducted on two Nvidia 80GB A100, with a total cost of approximately 1100 GPU hours. The detailed number of GPU hours consumed for each experiment is included in Appendix E.

Supervised Fine-tuning. We adapt the datasets from Yang et al. (2024) for supervised fine-tuning. For each in-domain dataset, one to two cross-domain evaluation datasets are supplied. OLMo-1B is fully fine-tuned for 3 epochs with a batch size of 8, while Llama3-8B is fine-tuned with a batch size of 16 and 2 training epochs. Both models are trained with learning rates resulting from minimal hyperparameter tuning (Appendix B). Each task is formatted using a default prompt-completion format (Table 5).

Instruction Fine-Tuning. We instruction-tune the model on TÜLU (Ivison et al., 2023), following the decision of Groeneveld et al., 2024. Each model checkpoint is fully fine-tuned for 5 epochs with a batch size of 8 and a learning rate of 2×10^{-6}.

3.3 Evaluation

For each model, we conduct a few-shot evaluation with a shot size of 4, after examining with shot size in $\{0, 2, 4, 6\}$.

Datasets. The datasets are summarized in Table 1 and data licenses are in Table 7. We evaluate the model with an in-domain test set and one or two out-of-domain test sets for each of the supervised fine-tuning tasks. We conduct experiments on the tasks of *summary generation* (Narayan et al., 2018; Hasan et al., 2021; Hermann et al., 2015), *question generation* (Sap et al., 2019; Xiong et al., 2019; Welbl et al., 2017), *natural language inference* (Williams et al., 2018; Wang et al., 2018; Dagan et al., 2006; Bar Haim et al., 2006; Giampiccolo et al., 2007; Bentivogli et al., 2009), and *paraphrase detection* (Zhang et al., 2019; Wang et al., 2018; Agirre et al., 2007). We subsample 6,000 training instances for each set to ensure a fair comparison.

In instruction fine-tuning, we base our downstream evaluation settings on Groeneveld et al. (2024), as OLMo is found to have stable performance on these datasets. The instruction tuned models are evaluated on ARC (both `arc easy` and `arc challenge`) (Clark et al., 2018), OpenbookQA (Mihaylov et al., 2018), Hellaswag (Zellers et al., 2019), BoolQ (Clark et al., 2019),

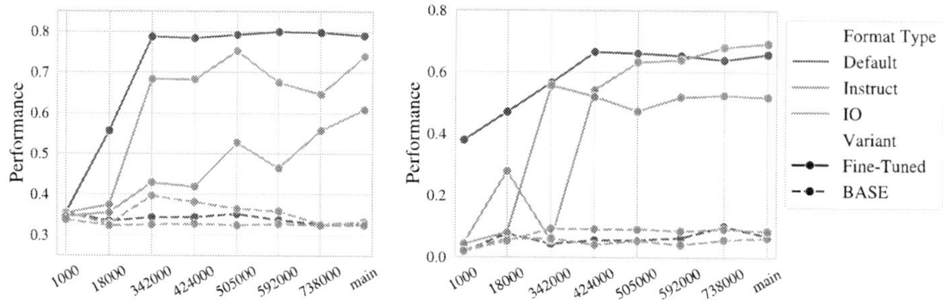

(a) MNLI matched

(b) SocialIQa

Figure 2: Example of model performance with different task formats. The figure of all datasets can be found in Figure 14.

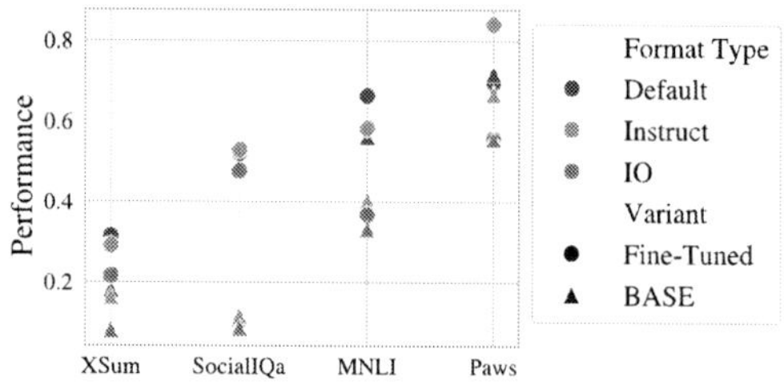

Figure 3: LLAMA3-8B performance with different task format. `Instruct` and `Default` always lead to highest evaluation results.

and SciQ (Welbl et al., 2017).

Metrics. We use accuracy (Pedregosa et al., 2011) for classification tasks and ROUGE-L (Lin, 2004) for generation tasks. The maximum amount of newly generated tokens is set to 5 for classification tasks and 60 for generation tasks. Outputs are generated with greedy decoding. For classification tasks, we experiment with both constrained decoding and logit-based predictions. We find the best performance by selecting the label with the highest logit of its first subtoken (Appendix C).

4 Supervised Fine-Tuning: What does the model learn and forget?

We begin our analysis with the supervised fine-tuning process to understand the downstream results of the training process. Specifically, we explore three dimensions: **task format, task transfer, and domain knowledge**. In each case, we fine-tune both final checkpoints and intermediate pre-training checkpoints to understand the relationship between pre-training and fine-tuning.

4.1 Task Format

LLMs can be extremely sensitive to prompt perturbation in few-shot settings (Sclar et al., 2023; Leidinger et al., 2023; Salinas and Morstatter, 2024; Wahle et al., 2024). We hypothesize that fine-tuning fits the model to a specific task format, resulting in higher performance when the evaluation set matches this format. To test this hypothesis, we vary the task format to either match the training format, use a different format, or rely on instructions.

We carefully construct three different prompt formats for the following settings. 1) `Default` is the same format used for training, where we expect the model to benefit from learning the task format; 2) `IO` format, by contrast, reflects a common way of performing supervised fine-tuning by incorporating only unprocessed input and output; 3) `Instruct` uses a human-readable instruction template to format the input. Table 5 in the Appendix shows an example of each format. The performance of Llama3-8B with different task formats is shown in Figure 3. Checkpoint performance on OLMo before and after fine-tuning is shown in Figure 2.

Across both models, `IO` format leads to the least favorable performance, as the only task-specific information in this format is included in the evaluation shots. Model reports similar performance when evaluated with the `default` and `instruct` format, aligning with the findings in Hewitt et al. (2024) that the models retain their instruction-following ability after fine-tuning without instructions. However, in the early pre-training steps, aligning the task format with fine-tuning data plays a crucial role (Figure 2), suggesting that the instruction-following ability has not yet been developed. In this view, **fine-tuning teaches the model how to format a response for the task, while further pretraining enhances the instruction-following ability**. In other words, the instruction provides a directed prior for the model to behave in a certain way.

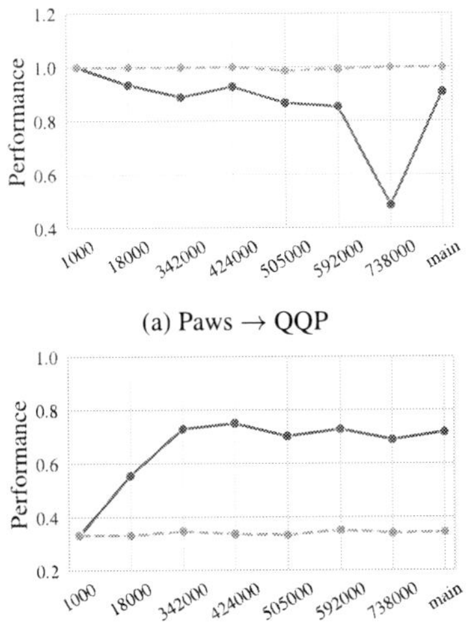

(a) Paws → QQP

(b) MNLI → GPT3NLI

Figure 4: Example of out-of-domain performance for fine-tuned models. The solid blue line represents the fine-tuned checkpoint evaluated on an out-of-domain dataset, and the dashed orange line represents the base checkpoint where the model is not fine-tuned. Figure 4a shows an example of fine-tuning hurting OOD performance, while Figure 4b shows an example of fine-tuning boosting OOD performance as pre-traininng proceeds.

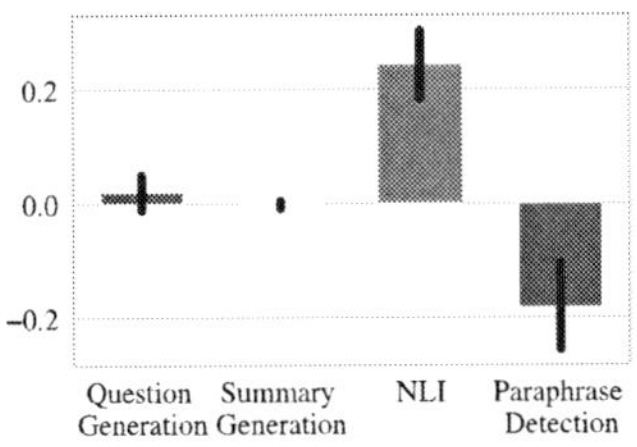

Figure 5: Ratio of out-of-domain performance change for each task, averaged across checkpoints.

4.2 Domain Knowledge

We next explore how the domain-generalization ability is affected by fine-tuning by inspecting whether the model forgets the domain knowledge after fine-tuning on a different domain. An example of OOD model performance is shown in Figure 4, and the mean ratio of change by datasets is presented in Figure 5 and Figure 15.

The models do not benefit equally from the in-domain fine-tuning: Llama shows subtle benefits on question generation tasks, while not benefiting at all on the other tasks (Figure 15). Across OLMo training history (Figure 5), NLI datasets experience a boost when fine-tuning on MNLI, while fine-tuning on Paws is detrimental to other paraphrase detection datasets. This suggests that both forgetting and learning are happening in fine-tuning: the model learns to perform the task with in-domain knowledge, but it may, in turn, forget information more distant from what is learned in fine-tuning. Furthermore, **under the same task, the amount of general-purpose pre-training may not affect the model's reaction to out-of-domain knowledge**. Questions remain, however, about whether domain-specific continual pre-training or continual pretraining on similarly distributed data would bring different conclusions, which requires further study of pre-training dynamics.

4.3 Task Transfer

Model forgetting occurs when model training on new tasks improves those tasks at the expense of previously trained tasks (Luo et al., 2023; Mehta et al., 2023; Li and Lee, 2024). To understand whether the model will forget a previously known task solution when fine-tuned on a different one, we evaluate model forgetfulness by examining whether the model does worse on some tasks after fine-tuning for other tasks. Specifically, we divide our tasks into two types: classification and generation.

We notate the training datasets as D_T and the evaluation datasets as D_E. We represent the performance of a pre-trained model (BASE) on checkpoint i as $\text{Perf}^i_{BASE}(d)$ for an evaluation dataset $d \in D_E$, and the performance of the i-th checkpoint fine-tuned on dataset $t \in D_T$ be $\text{Perf}^i_t(d)$. To normalize the effect caused by uneven performance across different datasets, we compute the mean ratio of change (MRC) in performance for each checkpoint as follows.

$$\text{MRC} = \frac{1}{|D_E \setminus \{t\}|} \sum_{\forall d \in D_E, d \neq t} \frac{\text{Perf}^i_t(d) - \text{Perf}^i_{BASE}(d)}{\text{Perf}^i_{BASE}(d)} \tag{1}$$

Models fine-tuned on classification tasks and evaluated on generation tasks decrease on average 61.4% compared to models that are never fine-tuned. In contrast, models fine-tuned on generation tasks can still perform the same as the BASE model on classification tasks, with a 0.3% MRC, which is not statistically significantly different from a 0% change. Our findings on all pre-training checkpoints align with the findings of Yang et al. (2024) on the final checkpoint of LLAMA-7B and our experiments on the final checkpoint of Llama3-8B (Appendix G).

Regardless of the pre-training stage, **a model maintains classification abilities when trained**

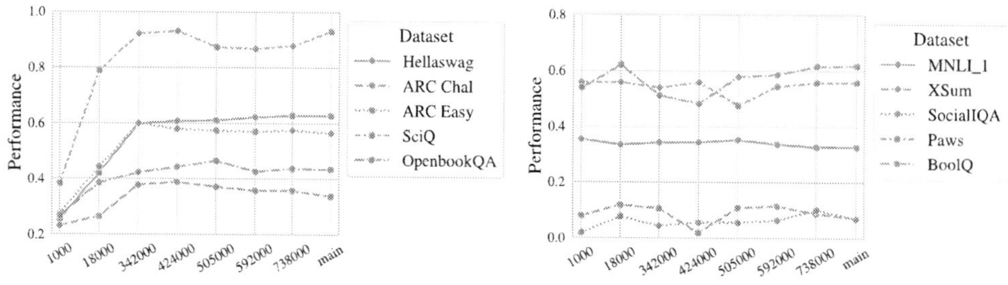

(a) Learned during Pre-training.

(b) Never learned during pre-training.

Figure 6: Few-shot performance on different pre-training steps.

for generation but loses generation abilities when trained for classification. This is not surprising given that classification tasks can be seen as a subset of generation, while the reverse is not true. The model follows a simplicity bias (Shah et al., 2020) and thus is more likely to memorize simple classification tasks than generation tasks with an exponentially larger search space. Additionally, since we evaluate the classification tasks based on the output logits and the base model performs randomly on the classification tasks, it is much easier for the models to maintain the same performance as the BASE models. Regardless of the stage of pre-training, fine-tuning can cause a model to lose abilities when the desired fine-tuning behavior does not support those abilities.

Across these three experimental settings, we find that fine-tuning teaches a model how to perform a task without hurting the model's instruction-following ability, but can sacrifice generalization across domains and tasks.

5 How does the model change across pre-training?

Section 4.1 reveals that the effect brought by fine-tuning could be different depending on the amount of pre-training, but how exactly does pre-training affect downstream fine-tuning results? We begin by considering how additional pre-training changes the **BASE** model. Typically, researchers track the value of the training or held-out loss during training. However, performance improvements on downstream tasks do not always follow the same trend with the loss curves (Groeneveld et al., 2024).

Instead, we evaluate the pre-trained checkpoints with few-shot examples, as models without alignment tend to do poorly in a zero-shot context. Four shots are randomly sampled from the datasets, which are selected based on the highest performance shot amount reported in Yang et al. (2024). The model's performance at each pre-training step is reported in Figure 6.

Broadly speaking, our results suggest that all datasets fall into one of two groups. For the first group of datasets (Figure 6a), although the model shows clear improvement during the early stages of pre-training, performance levels off fairly early on and remains consistent. The dramatic improvements in the early stages of pre-training may result from larger steps in early optimization. We find improvements stop increasing past step 342,000. The second group (Figure 6a) shows tasks that are never learned during pre-training. Performance remains constant throughout the whole pre-training process even when we vary shot sizes. These datasets include MNLI, XSum, and BoolQ. A natural hypothesis for this finding is potential data contamination in the pre-training data. However, the evaluation datasets are selected based on the popularity of the task and the content of pre-training data. All datasets that experience improvement do not exist in the model's pre-training data (Soldaini et al., 2024), while the more likely leaked datasets (MNLI, XSUM) never gain an improvement during the pre-training process.

Overall, these results reveal an interesting dichotomy. **Some tasks can be learned during pre-training, while others cannot**. Next, we explore what exactly the model is learning regarding this second group of datasets during pre-training by exploring the fine-tuned models.

6 Does more pre-training yield better fine-tuning results?

Groeneveld et al. (2024) compares OLMo's performance on several tasks before and after fine-tuning the final checkpoint and finds that fine-tuning enables the model to do well on tasks for which the

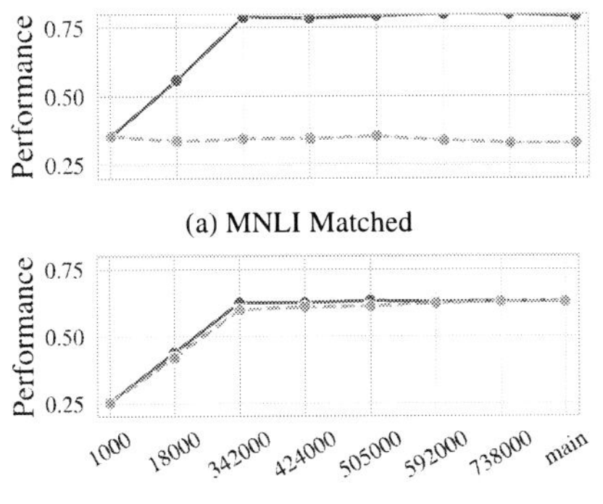

(a) MNLI Matched

(b) Hellaswag

Figure 7: Example of few-shot performance on different pre-training steps of the models that benefited (7a) and did not benefit from fine-tuning (7b). The solid blue line represents the fine-tuned checkpoint, and the dashed orange line represents the base checkpoint. The results of all datasets can be found in Figure 10 and Figure 9.

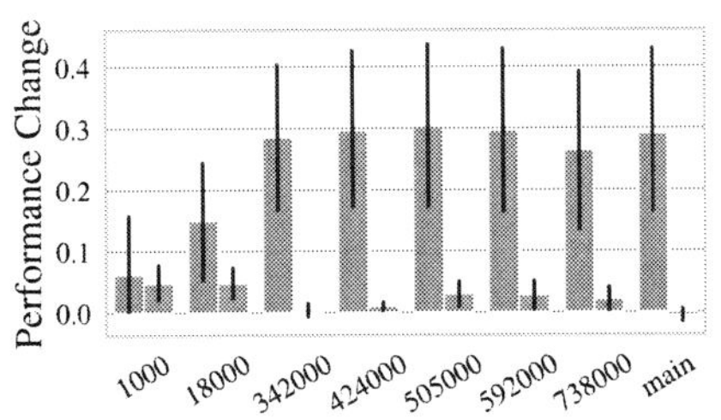

Figure 8: Amount of performance increase brought by fine-tuning between tasks that model can solve in pre-training (mandarin orange) and tasks that the model could not solve until fine-tuning (sage green). The exact number of mean increase is shown in Appendix J.

unaligned model does poorly. We observe (§5) that while some datasets improved during pre-training, there is a group of datasets for which a pre-trained model does poorly. Does the model learn useful information for these tasks but cannot express it without fine-tuning? In this section, we further explore this dataset dichotomy by examining fine-tuned checkpoints for each of the datasets.

Our results appear in Figure 7 and Figure 8. First, we consider those datasets where the pre-trained models do well (Figure 6a). These datasets do not improve with fine-tuning, suggesting that whatever is learned during fine-tuning, which we discuss below, the model already gains the knowledge during pre training. This effect is observed at all checkpoints; fine-tuning simply does not help.

However, a different story is observed for datasets that are not learned during pre-training. For these, fine-tuning yields significant improvements at every model checkpoint, with Figure 8 showing the magnitude of improvement on these datasets compared to no improvement to the datasets already learned during pre-training. Moreover, earlier checkpoints obtain more substantial gains from fine-tuning than later checkpoints. The benefit of fine-tuning continues to increase until a certain threshold in pre-training steps is reached (approximately 424,000). Figure 7 shows representative plots comparing the performance of a pre-trained versus fine-tuned model at different checkpoints for two datasets (full list in Appendix F). For Hellaswag (learned during pre-training), fine-tuning does not benefit the model, even during early checkpoints when the model performs poorly on the task. Nevertheless, for MNLI (not learned during pre-training), fine-tuning dramatically improves the model. Interestingly, later checkpoints achieve better results after fine-tuning, even when the performance of the pre-trained model is unchanged. This suggests that **the model is, in fact, improving during pre-training, but it cannot express that improvement without fine-tuning**.

Our findings suggest that early stopping in pre-training will not be detrimental to downstream fine-tuning performance. When the budget is limited, the benefits of fine-tuning an LLM could exceed the benefits of continued pretraining, which sheds light on the potential of a cost-effective training paradigm with less pre-training. However, directly identifying such stopping criteria without fine-tuning intermediate checkpoints is challenging. We only empirically observed that the point where more pre-training lead to diminishing return on downstream fine-tuning results approximately align with the turning point of few-shot performance in Section 5. Without such a hypothesis, the improvement trend is invisible before fine-tuning the checkpoints. Overall, when resource-intensive pre-trained LLMs are not available, fine-tuning models on checkpoints with less pre-training may be a reasonable practical choice for obtaining a high-quality model.

7 Discussion

Our study fine-tunes model pre-training checkpoints to understand the dynamics of pre-training and fine-tuning on model performance.

Fine-tuning teaches additional task format but leads to forgetting unused abilities. Our results show that fine-tuning guides the model to understand the format and complete a given task. As this information diminishes, the model's overall ability improves. Additionally, more pre-training will lead to a model that reacts better to instruction-style prompts, and the ability to interpret such instruction will not be lost when the model is fine-tuned in a different format. However, fine-tuning comes at the expense of other model abilities, such as the capability of solving tasks or domains that are unrelated or weakly related to the fine-tuning task. This insight can be helpful in our understanding of the multitask abilities of LLMs, where certain tasks can introduce conflicts during multi-task training (Mueller et al., 2022).

Some datasets can be learned without fine-tuning. We discover a dichotomy between datasets. Some are learned during model pre-training, while others show no improvements during pre-training. Furthermore, the datasets learned during pre-training do not benefit from fine-tuning. This observation, combined with our study about what is learned during fine-tuning (§4) suggests that some tasks are presented in a manner that aligns with what the model sees during pre-training, and thus fine-tuning provides no additional information. It may be possible to modify tasks to better align with pre-training and thus make them learnable.

Pre-training can improve models in unseen ways. Some datasets are not learned during pre-training but benefit significantly from fine-tuning (§5). However, these datasets still benefit from additional pre-training, even though those benefits are not revealed without fine-tuning (§6). The model learns important information to solve the task, even though it cannot express that information without fine-tuning. We empirically observe that the point where more pre-training lead to diminishing return on downstream fine-tuning results approximately align with the turning point of few-shot performance in Section 5. Future work may identify ways to verify the turning point and detect these improvements during pre-training, which can better guide pre-training choices to produce models that perform better post-fine-tuning. Perhaps there is a way in which information about these tasks can be included in pre-training, allowing the model to better utilize the massive amount of pre-training data. For example, early stopping during pre-training could lead to better utilization of limited training resources if we know when to stop.

8 Related Work

Recent studies identify *phase transition* of model training (Olsson et al., 2022; Wei et al., 2022), where new capabilities or behaviors suddenly emerge when certain thresholds of model complexity are reached. The aspects of complexity often include model size, amount of training by FLOPs or tokens, and model architecture. Several prior works studied the training dynamics of language models by analyzing the internals of train-from-scratch models (Tirumala et al., 2022; Chen et al., 2023; Tian et al., 2023; Chen et al., 2024; Chang et al., 2024). The results of these works suggest that the behaviors that are often overlooked after training could be valuable signals for model analysis. In addition to train-from-scratch models, Ren and Sutherland (2024) studied the fine-tuning dynamics of language models. This work focuses on *the effect of pre-training dynamics on downstream fine-tuning results* by fine-tuning intermediate pre-training checkpoints on various tasks. Due to the scarcity of publically accessible intermediate pre-training checkpoints, the effect of fine-tuning at different pre-training stages is largely unexplored. Concurrent work (Snell et al., 2024) also fine-tunes intermediate pre-training checkpoints and finds that supervised fine-tuning results can be used as a signal to predict when emergence occurs, while our findings point out a dichotomy of model behavior on different datasets, with the potential for data-efficient and budget-friendly training by understanding the stages of model training.

9 Conclusion

We explore the relationship between fine-tuning and pre-training LLMs through fine-tuning multiple pre-training checkpoints of large language models. Our results on 18 datasets and two models provide insights into LLM training. We identify the aspects that LLM learns and forgets during supervised fine-tuning; By analyzing pre-training history, we find that pre-training improves the model in a latent way that is only observable after fine-tuning. The model may excel at some tasks without fine-tuning. However, the model can rapidly learn datasets that it does not demonstrate capabilities during pre-training with a small amount of supervision. Overall, our study highlights the value of analyzing language model training dynamics. We encourage model developers to release pre-training checkpoints to facilitate research on LLM training.

Limitations

While our insights suggest directions for future work, we note important limitations inherent in our experiments. We discuss the weaknesses and limitations in the following section.

Computing Resource. Due to computational constraints, we can only conduct checkpointing experiments on a 1B model. We supply the final checkpoint of an 8B model to verify the findings that are shared across checkpoints. The amount of GPU hours spent for each experiment in this study is listed in Table 4.

Model Size and Variant. For the analysis with intermediate checkpoints, this study considered a single, relatively small LLM, which may, therefore, conceal the emergent capability brought by larger models (Wei et al., 2022). To combat this, we include the final checkpoint of an 8B model from a different model family. Future work needs to confront these issues on larger models and more datasets.

Availbility of Pre-training Checkpoints. Although Choshen et al. (2024) points out that the behavior of a model can often be predicted with a model with the same architecture but a different family. This study would benefit significantly from including a broader spectrum of models, but the public pre-training checkpoint releases are limited. We list open-source LLMs with intermediate checkpoint release in Appendix A. After a series of preliminary experiments, we select available models' best-performing and robust families.

Analysis Protocol. Wu et al. (2023) show that the evaluation result may be affected by samples that have been memorized by the model during training instead of revealing the reasoning capability. The only analysis protocol used in this work is the downstream performance of a trained model. More investigation should be done into model internals during pre-training dynamics and how they relate to the effects of fine-tuning.

Training Paradigm. Although multiple tuning strategies exist, to create a fair comparison environment where checkpoints receive the same amount of training, models are fine-tuned with a fixed amount of epochs in this work. On different pre-training stages, the model may converge at a different speed. Further study can be done to study the effect of pre-training on different fine-tuning methods or fine-tuning dynamics in different pre-training stages. We only explored the scenario of full-parameter fine-tuning. Whether parameter-efficient fine-tuning or human preference tuning will lead to a different conclusion also remains an open question.

Randomness. In this study, we only assess uncertainty with Bootstrap during evaluation. However, uncertainty may emerge during training, which poses optimizer initialization and data ordering, the study of which requires an extensive amount of computing resources.

Acknowledgments

The authors thank Saleh Soltan, Niyati Bafna, Fan Bai, Miriam Wanner, Xinbo Wu, and Carlos Aguirre for their helpful feedback. This work was supported in part by a grant from the JHU + Amazon Initiative for Interactive AI.

References

Josh Achiam, Steven Adler, Sandhini Agarwal, Lama Ahmad, Ilge Akkaya, Florencia Leoni Aleman, Diogo Almeida, Janko Altenschmidt, Sam Altman, Shyamal Anadkat, et al. 2023. Gpt-4 technical report. *arXiv preprint arXiv:2303.08774*.

Eneko Agirre, Llu'is M'arquez, and Richard Wicentowski, editors. 2007. *Proceedings of the Fourth International Workshop on Semantic Evaluations (SemEval-2007)*. Association for Computational Linguistics, Prague, Czech Republic.

Ai2. 2024. Olmo2 blog.

AI@Meta. 2024. Llama 3 model card.

Roy Bar Haim, Ido Dagan, Bill Dolan, Lisa Ferro, Danilo Giampiccolo, Bernardo Magnini, and Idan Szpektor. 2006. The second PASCAL recognising textual entailment challenge.

Khuyagbaatar Batsuren, Ekaterina Vylomova, Verna Dankers, Tsetsuukhei Delgerbaatar, Omri Uzan, Yuval Pinter, and Gábor Bella. 2024. Evaluating subword tokenization: Alien subword composition and oov generalization challenge. *arXiv preprint arXiv:2404.13292*.

Mikhail Belkin, Daniel Hsu, Siyuan Ma, and Soumik Mandal. 2019. Reconciling modern machine-learning practice and the classical bias–variance trade-off. *Proceedings of the National Academy of Sciences*, 116(32):15849–15854.

Luisa Bentivogli, Ido Dagan, Hoa Trang Dang, Danilo Giampiccolo, and Bernardo Magnini. 2009. The fifth PASCAL recognizing textual entailment challenge.

Federico Bianchi, Mirac Suzgun, Giuseppe Attanasio, Paul Röttger, Dan Jurafsky, Tatsunori Hashimoto, and James Zou. 2023. Safety-tuned llamas: Lessons from improving the safety of large language models that follow instructions. *arXiv preprint arXiv:2309.07875*.

Stella Biderman, Hailey Schoelkopf, Quentin Gregory Anthony, Herbie Bradley, Kyle O'Brien, Eric Hallahan, Mohammad Aflah Khan, Shivanshu Purohit, USVSN Sai Prashanth, Edward Raff, et al. 2023. Pythia: A suite for analyzing large language models across training and scaling. In *International Conference on Machine Learning*, pages 2397–2430. PMLR.

Tom Brown, Benjamin Mann, Nick Ryder, Melanie Subbiah, Jared D Kaplan, Prafulla Dhariwal, Arvind Neelakantan, Pranav Shyam, Girish Sastry, Amanda Askell, et al. 2020. Language models are few-shot learners. *Advances in neural information processing systems*, 33:1877–1901.

Ethan Caballero, Kshitij Gupta, Irina Rish, and David Krueger. 2022. Broken neural scaling laws. *arXiv preprint arXiv:2210.14891*.

Tyler A Chang, Zhuowen Tu, and Benjamin K Bergen. 2024. Characterizing learning curves during language model pre-training: Learning, forgetting, and stability. *Transactions of the Association for Computational Linguistics*, 12:1346–1362.

Angelica Chen, Ravid Schwartz-Ziv, Kyunghyun Cho, Matthew L Leavitt, and Naomi Saphra. 2023. Sudden drops in the loss: Syntax acquisition, phase transitions, and simplicity bias in mlms. *arXiv preprint arXiv:2309.07311*.

Siyu Chen, Heejune Sheen, Tianhao Wang, and Zhuoran Yang. 2024. Training dynamics of multi-head softmax attention for in-context learning: Emergence, convergence, and optimality. *arXiv preprint arXiv:2402.19442*.

Leshem Choshen, Yang Zhang, and Jacob Andreas. 2024. A hitchhiker's guide to scaling law estimation. *arXiv preprint arXiv:2410.11840*.

Aakanksha Chowdhery, Sharan Narang, Jacob Devlin, Maarten Bosma, Gaurav Mishra, Adam Roberts, Paul Barham, Hyung Won Chung, Charles Sutton, Sebastian Gehrmann, et al. 2023. Palm: Scaling language modeling with pathways. *Journal of Machine Learning Research*, 24(240):1–113.

Paul F Christiano, Jan Leike, Tom Brown, Miljan Martic, Shane Legg, and Dario Amodei. 2017. Deep reinforcement learning from human preferences. *Advances in neural information processing systems*, 30.

Christopher Clark, Kenton Lee, Ming-Wei Chang, Tom Kwiatkowski, Michael Collins, and Kristina Toutanova. 2019. BoolQ: Exploring the surprising difficulty of natural yes/no questions. In *Proceedings of the 2019 Conference of the North American Chapter of the Association for Computational Linguistics: Human Language Technologies, Volume 1 (Long and Short Papers)*, pages 2924–2936, Minneapolis, Minnesota. Association for Computational Linguistics.

Peter Clark, Isaac Cowhey, Oren Etzioni, Tushar Khot, Ashish Sabharwal, Carissa Schoenick, and Oyvind Tafjord. 2018. Think you have solved question answering? try arc, the ai2 reasoning challenge. *arXiv preprint arXiv:1803.05457*.

Together Computer. 2023. Redpajama: an open dataset for training large language models.

Ido Dagan, Oren Glickman, and Bernardo Magnini. 2006. The PASCAL recognising textual entailment challenge. In *Machine learning challenges. evaluating predictive uncertainty, visual object classification, and recognising tectual entailment*, pages 177–190. Springer.

Tim Dettmers, Artidoro Pagnoni, Ari Holtzman, and Luke Zettlemoyer. 2024. Qlora: Efficient finetuning of quantized llms. *Advances in Neural Information Processing Systems*, 36.

Xinyang Geng and Hao Liu. 2023. Openllama: An open reproduction of llama.

Danilo Giampiccolo, Bernardo Magnini, Ido Dagan, and Bill Dolan. 2007. The third PASCAL recognizing textual entailment challenge. In *Proceedings of the ACL-PASCAL workshop on textual entailment and paraphrasing*, pages 1–9. Association for Computational Linguistics.

Dirk Groeneveld, Iz Beltagy, Pete Walsh, Akshita Bhagia, Rodney Kinney, Oyvind Tafjord, Ananya Harsh Jha, Hamish Ivison, Ian Magnusson, Yizhong Wang, et al. 2024. Olmo: Accelerating the science of language models. *arXiv preprint arXiv:2402.00838*.

Suchin Gururangan, Ana Marasović, Swabha Swayamdipta, Kyle Lo, Iz Beltagy, Doug Downey, and Noah A. Smith. 2020. Don't stop pretraining: Adapt language models to domains and tasks. In *Proceedings of the 58th Annual Meeting of the Association for Computational Linguistics*, pages 8342–8360, Online. Association for Computational Linguistics.

Tahmid Hasan, Abhik Bhattacharjee, Md. Saiful Islam, Kazi Mubasshir, Yuan-Fang Li, Yong-Bin Kang, M. Sohel Rahman, and Rifat Shahriyar. 2021. XL-sum: Large-scale multilingual abstractive summarization for 44 languages. In *Findings of the Association for Computational Linguistics: ACL-IJCNLP 2021*, pages 4693–4703, Online. Association for Computational Linguistics.

Karl Moritz Hermann, Tomas Kocisky, Edward Grefenstette, Lasse Espeholt, Will Kay, Mustafa Suleyman, and Phil Blunsom. 2015. Teaching machines to read and comprehend. *Advances in neural information processing systems*, 28.

John Hewitt, Nelson F Liu, Percy Liang, and Christopher D Manning. 2024. Instruction following without instruction tuning. *arXiv preprint arXiv:2409.14254*.

Jordan Hoffmann, Sebastian Borgeaud, Arthur Mensch, Elena Buchatskaya, Trevor Cai, Eliza Rutherford, Diego de Las Casas, Lisa Anne Hendricks, Johannes Welbl, Aidan Clark, et al. 2022. Training compute-optimal large language models. *arXiv preprint arXiv:2203.15556*.

Edward J Hu, Yelong Shen, Phillip Wallis, Zeyuan Allen-Zhu, Yuanzhi Li, Shean Wang, Lu Wang, and Weizhu Chen. 2021. Lora: Low-rank adaptation of large language models. *arXiv preprint arXiv:2106.09685*.

Dieuwke Hupkes, Mario Giulianelli, Verna Dankers, Mikel Artetxe, Yanai Elazar, Tiago Pimentel, Christos Christodoulopoulos, Karim Lasri, Naomi Saphra, Arabella Sinclair, et al. 2023. A taxonomy and review of generalization research in nlp. *Nature Machine Intelligence*, 5(10):1161–1174.

Hamish Ivison, Yizhong Wang, Valentina Pyatkin, Nathan Lambert, Matthew Peters, Pradeep Dasigi, Joel Jang, David Wadden, Noah A Smith, Iz Beltagy, et al. 2023. Camels in a changing climate: Enhancing lm adaptation with tulu 2. *arXiv preprint arXiv:2311.10702*.

Albert Q Jiang, Alexandre Sablayrolles, Arthur Mensch, Chris Bamford, Devendra Singh Chaplot, Diego de las Casas, Florian Bressand, Gianna Lengyel, Guillaume Lample, Lucile Saulnier, et al. 2023. Mistral 7b. *arXiv preprint arXiv:2310.06825*.

Teven Le Scao, Angela Fan, Christopher Akiki, Ellie Pavlick, Suzana Ilić, Daniel Hesslow, Roman Castagné, Alexandra Sasha Luccioni, François Yvon, Matthias Gallé, et al. 2023. Bloom: A 176b-parameter open-access multilingual language model.

Alina Leidinger, Robert Van Rooij, and Ekaterina Shutova. 2023. The language of prompting: What linguistic properties make a prompt successful? *arXiv preprint arXiv:2311.01967*.

Chen-An Li and Hung-Yi Lee. 2024. Examining forgetting in continual pre-training of aligned large language models. *arXiv preprint arXiv:2401.03129*.

Xiang Lisa Li and Percy Liang. 2021. Prefix-tuning: Optimizing continuous prompts for generation. In *Proceedings of the 59th Annual Meeting of the Association for Computational Linguistics and the 11th International Joint Conference on Natural Language Processing (Volume 1: Long Papers)*, pages 4582–4597, Online. Association for Computational Linguistics.

Chin-Yew Lin. 2004. ROUGE: A package for automatic evaluation of summaries. In *Text Summarization Branches Out*, pages 74–81, Barcelona, Spain. Association for Computational Linguistics.

LLM360. 2024. K2 blog release.

Yun Luo, Zhen Yang, Fandong Meng, Yafu Li, Jie Zhou, and Yue Zhang. 2023. An empirical study of catastrophic forgetting in large language models during continual fine-tuning. *arXiv preprint arXiv:2308.08747*.

Sanket Vaibhav Mehta, Darshan Patil, Sarath Chandar, and Emma Strubell. 2023. An empirical investigation of the role of pre-training in lifelong learning. *Journal of Machine Learning Research*, 24(214):1–50.

Todor Mihaylov, Peter Clark, Tushar Khot, and Ashish Sabharwal. 2018. Can a suit of armor conduct electricity? a new dataset for open book question answering. In *Proceedings of the 2018 Conference on Empirical Methods in Natural Language Processing*, pages 2381–2391, Brussels, Belgium. Association for Computational Linguistics.

Swaroop Mishra, Daniel Khashabi, Chitta Baral, and Hannaneh Hajishirzi. 2022. Cross-task generalization via natural language crowdsourcing instructions. In *Proceedings of the 60th Annual Meeting of the Association for Computational Linguistics (Volume 1: Long Papers)*, pages 3470–3487, Dublin, Ireland. Association for Computational Linguistics.

David Mueller, Nicholas Andrews, and Mark Dredze. 2022. Do text-to-text multi-task learners suffer from task conflict? In *Findings of the Association for Computational Linguistics: EMNLP 2022*, pages 2843–2858, Abu Dhabi, United Arab Emirates. Association for Computational Linguistics.

Shashi Narayan, Shay B. Cohen, and Mirella Lapata. 2018. Don't give me the details, just the summary! topic-aware convolutional neural networks for extreme summarization. In *Proceedings of the 2018 Conference on Empirical Methods in Natural Language Processing*, pages 1797–1807, Brussels, Belgium. Association for Computational Linguistics.

Manu Narayanan and Noëmi Aepli. 2024. A Tulu resource for machine translation. In *Proceedings of the 2024 Joint International Conference on Computational Linguistics, Language Resources and Evaluation (LREC-COLING 2024)*, pages 1756–1767, Torino, Italia. ELRA and ICCL.

Catherine Olsson, Nelson Elhage, Neel Nanda, Nicholas Joseph, Nova DasSarma, Tom Henighan, Ben Mann, Amanda Askell, Yuntao Bai, Anna Chen, et al. 2022. In-context learning and induction heads. *arXiv preprint arXiv:2209.11895*.

Long Ouyang, Jeffrey Wu, Xu Jiang, Diogo Almeida, Carroll Wainwright, Pamela Mishkin, Chong Zhang, Sandhini Agarwal, Katarina Slama, Alex Ray, et al. 2022. Training language models to follow instructions with human feedback. *Advances in neural information processing systems*, 35:27730–27744.

F. Pedregosa, G. Varoquaux, A. Gramfort, V. Michel, B. Thirion, O. Grisel, M. Blondel, P. Prettenhofer, R. Weiss, V. Dubourg, J. Vanderplas, A. Passos, D. Cournapeau, M. Brucher, M. Perrot, and E. Duchesnay. 2011. Scikit-learn: Machine learning in Python. *Journal of Machine Learning Research*, 12:2825–2830.

Alec Radford, Jeffrey Wu, Rewon Child, David Luan, Dario Amodei, Ilya Sutskever, et al. 2019. Language models are unsupervised multitask learners. *OpenAI blog*, 1(8):9.

Jack W Rae, Sebastian Borgeaud, Trevor Cai, Katie Millican, Jordan Hoffmann, Francis Song, John Aslanides, Sarah Henderson, Roman Ring, Susannah Young, et al. 2021. Scaling language models: Methods, analysis & insights from training gopher. *arXiv preprint arXiv:2112.11446*.

Rafael Rafailov, Archit Sharma, Eric Mitchell, Christopher D Manning, Stefano Ermon, and Chelsea Finn. 2024. Direct preference optimization: Your language model is secretly a reward model. *Advances in Neural Information Processing Systems*, 36.

Colin Raffel, Noam Shazeer, Adam Roberts, Katherine Lee, Sharan Narang, Michael Matena, Yanqi Zhou, Wei Li, and Peter J Liu. 2020. Exploring the limits of transfer learning with a unified text-to-text transformer. *Journal of machine learning research*, 21(140):1–67.

Yi Ren and Danica J Sutherland. 2024. Learning dynamics of llm finetuning. *arXiv preprint arXiv:2407.10490*.

Abel Salinas and Fred Morstatter. 2024. The butterfly effect of altering prompts: How small changes and jailbreaks affect large language model performance. *arXiv preprint arXiv:2401.03729*.

Maarten Sap, Hannah Rashkin, Derek Chen, Ronan Le Bras, and Yejin Choi. 2019. Social IQa: Commonsense reasoning about social interactions. In *Proceedings of the 2019 Conference on Empirical Methods in Natural Language Processing and the 9th International Joint Conference on Natural Language Processing (EMNLP-IJCNLP)*, pages 4463–4473, Hong Kong, China. Association for Computational Linguistics.

Rylan Schaeffer, Mikail Khona, Zachary Robertson, Akhilan Boopathy, Kateryna Pistunova, Jason W Rocks, Ila Rani Fiete, and Oluwasanmi Koyejo. 2023. Double descent demystified: Identifying, interpreting & ablating the sources of a deep learning puzzle. *arXiv preprint arXiv:2303.14151*.

John Schulman, Filip Wolski, Prafulla Dhariwal, Alec Radford, and Oleg Klimov. 2017. Proximal policy optimization algorithms. *arXiv preprint arXiv:1707.06347*.

Melanie Sclar, Yejin Choi, Yulia Tsvetkov, and Alane Suhr. 2023. Quantifying language models' sensitivity to spurious features in prompt design or: How i learned to start worrying about prompt formatting. *arXiv preprint arXiv:2310.11324*.

Harshay Shah, Kaustav Tamuly, Aditi Raghunathan, Prateek Jain, and Praneeth Netrapalli. 2020. The pitfalls of simplicity bias in neural networks. *Advances in Neural Information Processing Systems*, 33:9573–9585.

Hua Shen, Tiffany Knearem, Reshmi Ghosh, Kenan Alkiek, Kundan Krishna, Yachuan Liu, Ziqiao Ma, Savvas Petridis, Yi-Hao Peng, Li Qiwei, Sushrita Rakshit, Chenglei Si, Yutong Xie, Jeffrey P. Bigham, Frank Bentley, Joyce Chai, Zachary Lipton, Qiaozhu Mei, Rada Mihalcea, Michael Terry, Diyi Yang, Meredith Ringel Morris, Paul Resnick, and David Jurgens. 2024. Towards bidirectional human-ai alignment: A systematic review for clarifications, framework, and future directions. *arXiv preprint arXiv:2406.09264*.

Aaditya K Singh and DJ Strouse. 2024. Tokenization counts: the impact of tokenization on arithmetic in frontier llms. *arXiv preprint arXiv:2402.14903*.

Charlie Snell, Eric Wallace, Dan Klein, and Sergey Levine. 2024. Predicting emergent capabilities by finetuning. *arXiv preprint arXiv:2411.16035*.

Luca Soldaini, Rodney Kinney, Akshita Bhagia, Dustin Schwenk, David Atkinson, Russell Authur, Ben Bogin, Khyathi Chandu, Jennifer Dumas, Yanai Elazar, et al. 2024. Dolma: An open corpus of three trillion tokens for language model pretraining research. *arXiv preprint arXiv:2402.00159*.

Feifan Song, Bowen Yu, Minghao Li, Haiyang Yu, Fei Huang, Yongbin Li, and Houfeng Wang. 2024. Preference ranking optimization for human alignment. In *Proceedings of the AAAI Conference on Artificial Intelligence*, volume 38, pages 18990–18998.

Nisan Stiennon, Long Ouyang, Jeffrey Wu, Daniel Ziegler, Ryan Lowe, Chelsea Voss, Alec Radford, Dario Amodei, and Paul F Christiano. 2020. Learning to summarize with human feedback. *Advances in Neural Information Processing Systems*, 33:3008–3021.

Jianlin Su, Murtadha Ahmed, Yu Lu, Shengfeng Pan, Wen Bo, and Yunfeng Liu. 2024. Roformer: Enhanced transformer with rotary position embedding. *Neurocomputing*, 568:127063.

Kaiser Sun, Peng Qi, Yuhao Zhang, Lan Liu, William Wang, and Zhiheng Huang. 2023. Tokenization consistency matters for generative models on extractive NLP tasks. In *Findings of the Association for Computational Linguistics: EMNLP 2023*, pages 13300–13310, Singapore. Association for Computational Linguistics.

Tianhua Tao, Junbo Li, Bowen Tan, Hongyi Wang, William Marshall, Bhargav M Kanakiya, Joel Hestness, Natalia Vassilieva, Zhiqiang Shen, Eric P Xing, et al. 2024. Crystal: Illuminating llm abilities on language and code. *arXiv preprint arXiv:2411.04156*.

Yuandong Tian, Yiping Wang, Beidi Chen, and Simon S Du. 2023. Scan and snap: Understanding training dynamics and token composition in 1-layer transformer. *Advances in Neural Information Processing Systems*, 36:71911–71947.

Kushal Tirumala, Aram Markosyan, Luke Zettlemoyer, and Armen Aghajanyan. 2022. Memorization without overfitting: Analyzing the training dynamics of large language models. *Advances in Neural Information Processing Systems*, 35:38274–38290.

Hugo Touvron, Louis Martin, Kevin Stone, Peter Albert, Amjad Almahairi, Yasmine Babaei, Nikolay Bashlykov, Soumya Batra, Prajjwal Bhargava, Shruti Bhosale, et al. 2023. Llama 2: Open foundation and fine-tuned chat models. *arXiv preprint arXiv:2307.09288*.

Sanh Victor, Webson Albert, Raffel Colin, Bach Stephen, Sutawika Lintang, Alyafeai Zaid, Chaffin Antoine, Stiegler Arnaud, Raja Arun, Dey Manan, et al. 2022. Multitask prompted training enables zero-shot task generalization. In *International Conference on Learning Representations*.

Jan Philip Wahle, Terry Ruas, Yang Xu, and Bela Gipp. 2024. Paraphrase types for generation and detection. In *Proceedings of the 2024 Conference on Empirical Methods in Natural Language Processing*. Association for Computational Linguistics.

Alex Wang, Amanpreet Singh, Julian Michael, Felix Hill, Omer Levy, and Samuel Bowman. 2018. GLUE: A multi-task benchmark and analysis platform for natural language understanding. In *Proceedings of the 2018 EMNLP Workshop BlackboxNLP: Analyzing and Interpreting Neural Networks for NLP*, pages 353–355, Brussels, Belgium. Association for Computational Linguistics.

Zhilin Wang, Yi Dong, Olivier Delalleau, Jiaqi Zeng, Gerald Shen, Daniel Egert, Jimmy J. Zhang, Makesh Narsimhan Sreedhar, and Oleksii Kuchaiev. 2024. Helpsteer2: Open-source dataset for training top-performing reward models. *arXiv preprint arXiv:2406.08673*.

Jason Wei, Maarten Bosma, Vincent Y Zhao, Kelvin Guu, Adams Wei Yu, Brian Lester, Nan Du, Andrew M Dai, and Quoc V Le. 2021. Finetuned language models are zero-shot learners. *arXiv preprint arXiv:2109.01652*.

Jason Wei, Yi Tay, Rishi Bommasani, Colin Raffel, Barret Zoph, Sebastian Borgeaud, Dani Yogatama, Maarten Bosma, Denny Zhou, Donald Metzler, et al. 2022. Emergent abilities of large language models. *arXiv preprint arXiv:2206.07682*.

Johannes Welbl, Nelson F Liu, and Matt Gardner. 2017. Crowdsourcing multiple choice science questions. In *Proceedings of the 3rd Workshop on Noisy User-generated Text*, pages 94–106.

Adina Williams, Nikita Nangia, and Samuel Bowman. 2018. A broad-coverage challenge corpus for sentence understanding through inference. In *Proceedings of the 2018 Conference of the North American Chapter of the Association for Computational Linguistics: Human Language Technologies, Volume 1 (Long Papers)*, pages 1112–1122, New Orleans, Louisiana. Association for Computational Linguistics.

Zhaofeng Wu, Linlu Qiu, Alexis Ross, Ekin Akyürek, Boyuan Chen, Bailin Wang, Najoung Kim, Jacob Andreas, and Yoon Kim. 2023. Reasoning or reciting? exploring the capabilities and limitations of language models through counterfactual tasks. *arXiv preprint arXiv:2307.02477*.

Mengzhou Xia, Sadhika Malladi, Suchin Gururangan, Sanjeev Arora, and Danqi Chen. 2024. Less: Selecting influential data for targeted instruction tuning. *arXiv preprint arXiv:2402.04333*.

Wenhan Xiong, Jiawei Wu, Hong Wang, Vivek Kulkarni, Mo Yu, Shiyu Chang, Xiaoxiao Guo, and William Yang Wang. 2019. TWEETQA: A social media focused question answering dataset. In *Proceedings of the 57th Annual Meeting of the Association for Computational Linguistics*, pages 5020–5031, Florence, Italy. Association for Computational Linguistics.

Haoran Xu, Amr Sharaf, Yunmo Chen, Weiting Tan, Lingfeng Shen, Benjamin Van Durme, Kenton Murray, and Young Jin Kim. 2024. Contrastive preference optimization: Pushing the boundaries of llm performance in machine translation. *arXiv preprint arXiv:2401.08417*.

Aiyuan Yang, Bin Xiao, Bingning Wang, Borong Zhang, Ce Bian, Chao Yin, Chenxu Lv, Da Pan, Dian Wang, Dong Yan, et al. 2023. Baichuan 2: Open large-scale language models. *arXiv preprint arXiv:2309.10305*.

Haoran Yang, Yumeng Zhang, Jiaqi Xu, Hongyuan Lu, Pheng Ann Heng, and Wai Lam. 2024. Unveiling the generalization power of fine-tuned large language models. *arXiv preprint arXiv:2403.09162*.

Rowan Zellers, Ari Holtzman, Yonatan Bisk, Ali Farhadi, and Yejin Choi. 2019. HellaSwag: Can a machine really finish your sentence? In *Proceedings of the 57th Annual Meeting of the Association for Computational Linguistics*, pages 4791–4800, Florence, Italy. Association for Computational Linguistics.

Peiyuan Zhang, Guangtao Zeng, Tianduo Wang, and Wei Lu. 2024. Tinyllama: An open-source small language model. *arXiv preprint arXiv:2401.02385*.

Yuan Zhang, Jason Baldridge, and Luheng He. 2019. PAWS: Paraphrase adversaries from word scrambling.

In *Proceedings of the 2019 Conference of the North American Chapter of the Association for Computational Linguistics: Human Language Technologies, Volume 1 (Long and Short Papers)*, pages 1298–1308, Minneapolis, Minnesota. Association for Computational Linguistics.

Chunting Zhou, Pengfei Liu, Puxin Xu, Srinivasan Iyer, Jiao Sun, Yuning Mao, Xuezhe Ma, Avia Efrat, Ping Yu, Lili Yu, et al. 2024. Lima: Less is more for alignment. *Advances in Neural Information Processing Systems*, 36.

Daniel M Ziegler, Nisan Stiennon, Jeffrey Wu, Tom B Brown, Alec Radford, Dario Amodei, Paul Christiano, and Geoffrey Irving. 2019. Fine-tuning language models from human preferences. *arXiv preprint arXiv:1909.08593*.

A Model and Data Selection

Only a small subset of large language models publicly release their intermediate training checkpoints. We list these models in Table 2 and would like to call for model developers to release intermediate checkpoints in the future to aid the research of training dynamics. To reduce the confounding factor of language and stages of training, we select the models that are dominantly trained in English and followed a single-staged training strategy. Only the models pre-trained with significantly more tokens than the model parameters are considered to avoid the occurrence of double descent (Belkin et al., 2019; Schaeffer et al., 2023) in the middle of pretianing, which could lead to a broken scaling law (Caballero et al., 2022) that complicates the analysis. Additionally, we restrict our selection to models pre-trained on over one trillion tokens, thereby ensuring a sufficiently extended training trajectory is represented. We conduct initial experiments with OLMo and RedPajama-INCITE. We observe that the RedPajama-INCITE shows subtle improvement following instruction-tuning or fine-tuning, and its 7B variant shows lower performance compared to OLMo 1B. Therefore, we select OLMo 1.0 1B as the backbone for analysis.

During this study, several recent initiatives released the intermediate checkpoints. We also list these works in Table 2.

B Hyperparameter Tuning

For both supervised fine-tuning and instruction tuning, we pre-set the effective batch size to 8, and tune the learning rate within $\{2 \times 10^{-5}, 2 \times 10^{-6}, 2 \times 10^{-7}\}$. OLMo-1B is fine-tuned for 3 epochs on the supervised fine-tuning tasks and 5 epochs on Tulu for instruction tuning. Llama3-8B is fine-tuned for 2 epochs with a learning rate of 5×10^{-6}, with learning rate selected from $\{5 \times 10^{-5}, 5 \times 10^{-6}, 5 \times 10^{-7}\}$. In both settings, we adopt an AdamW optimizer with a linear learning rate scheduler. The optimizer is warmed up for the first 3% of the training time.

C Prediction Generation Method

For classification tasks, we examine three different prediction generation methods: Free Generation (`Free`), Constrained Generation (`Constrained`), and Token Probability (`TokenProb`), the results are shown in Table 3. In `Constrained`, we force the output to include at least one label in the acceptable label set. In `TokenProb`, we compare the logits of acceptable labels and select the label with the highest score as the final output. This ablation study is conducted only on the BASE and fine-tuned versions of the final checkpoint of the pre-trained model. We find that, although prediction generation methods have less effect on the evaluation result of a fine-tuned model, BASE variants suffer much more from not knowing the desired output. Therefore, we proceed with all the classification experiments with `TokenProb`.

C.1 Label and Tokenizations

Depending on the tokenizer variant, the label text may be tokenized differently, leading to evaluation unreliability. For example, in paraphrase detection, the model could assign probability on both "`yes`" and " `yes`" (the same label with a prefix space). This behavior is reported and explored in various related work (Sun et al., 2023; Batsuren et al., 2024; Singh and Strouse, 2024). In this study, we leniently regard all individual tokens that contain the whole label or part of the label along with some special characters that do not affect the semantics as an acceptable target label.

D Task Format

We adopt the task format from (Yang et al., 2024), with an additional task format of input-output. How each dataset is formated can be found in Table 5.

E GPU Hours per-Experiment

We show a table of GPU hours spent for each experiment in Table 4. The total number of GPU hours spent on this project is approximately 1067 A100

	Pythia	OpenLLAMA	K2 (LLM360)	Crystal (LLM360)	Baichuan2
Citation	Biderman et al., 2023	Geng and Liu, 2023	LLM360, 2024	Tao et al., 2024	Yang et al., 2023
Size (Param)	70M, 160M, 410M, 1B, 1.4B, 2.8B, 6.9B, 12B	3B, 7B	65B	7B	7B, 13B
Languages	English	English	English	English	English & Chinese
Pre-trained Tokens	300B	1T	1.4T	1300B	2.6T
Note	-	-	Multi-phase pre-training	Multi-phase pre-training	-

	OLMO-2	OLMO	TinyLLaMA	RedPajama-INCITE	Bloom
Citation	Ai2, 2024	Groeneveld et al., 2024	Zhang et al., 2024	Computer, 2023	Le Scao et al., 2023
Size (Param)	4T, 5T	1B, 7B	1B	7B	176B
Languages	English	English	English	English	Multilingual
Pre-trained Tokens	7B, 13B	3T, 2.5T	3T	1.2T	366B
Note	Multi-phase pre-training	-	BOS Token leads to training history inconsistency.	Poor fine-tunablity	-

Table 2: Large language models with public release of intermediate pre-training checkpoints. All models are under Apache 2.0 license.

Dataset	Model	Free	Constrained	TokenProb
MNLI	Fine-tuned	0.786	0.791	0.792
	BASE	0.0	0.0	0.327
RTE	Fine-tuned	0.658	0.662	0.66
	BASE	0.0	0.0	0.241
Paws	Fine-tuned	0.871	0.878	0.878
	BASE	0.0	0.0	0.558
STS-B	Fine-tuned	0.775	0.741	0.744
	BASE	0.0	0.0	0.964

Table 3: Performance of final checkpoint with different prediction generation method.

hours. We lose track of the GPU hours spent on preliminary experiments, so a lower-bound estimation is reported.

F Per-dataset Figures

We show the model performance on each dataset after supervised fine-tuning and instruction tuning correspondingly in Figure 10 and Figure 9. The datasets that already show improvement during pre-training do not benefit from fine-tuning, while performance improves drastically on the datasets that the model has never learned during pre-training.

Out-of-domain Generalization The out-of-domain performance for each dataset with respect to pre-training steps is shown in Figure 11. Overall, the model generalizes well after fine-tuning on NLI tasks, while its performance deteriorates when evaluated on out-of-domain paraphrase detection tasks.

Cross-task Generalization The cross-task performance for each dataset with respect to pre-training steps is shown in Figure 12 and Figure 13.

Task-Format The performance of models on evaluation sets formatted with different prompt formatting methods is shown in Figure 14.

G Llama3-8B Results

To provide more evidence of the findings on a different model architecture and size, we conduct some experiments on the final checkpoint of Llama3-8B.

Task Transfer Similar to our findings with OLMo, Llama3-8B fine-tuned on classification tasks and evaluated on generation tasks decreases on average 61.0% compared to models that are never fine-tuned. In contrast, models fine-tuned on generation tasks perform similarly to the BASE model on classification tasks, with a 10.6% MRC.

Prelinminary Experiments				
Description				**GPU Hours**
Instruction Tuning on LIMA, TULU, and NaturalInstructions				~300
Model Performance Verification, Dataset Selection				120
Instruction Tuning				
Instruction Tuning				360
Evaluation				10
Total				**370**
Fine-Tuning				
	XSum	**SocialIQa**	**MNLI**	**Paws**
Training	12	6	4.6	5.3
Evaluation	8	5.3	3	2
OOD Evaluation	96	32	11	25.6
CrossTask Evauation	5.2	6.5	7.7	8.15
Task Format Evaluation	16	12.8	6	4
Total	137.2 + 62.6 + 32.3 + 45 = 277.1			

Table 4: GPU hours for each experiment. The total amount of GPU hours spent in this project is approximately 1067 A100 hours.

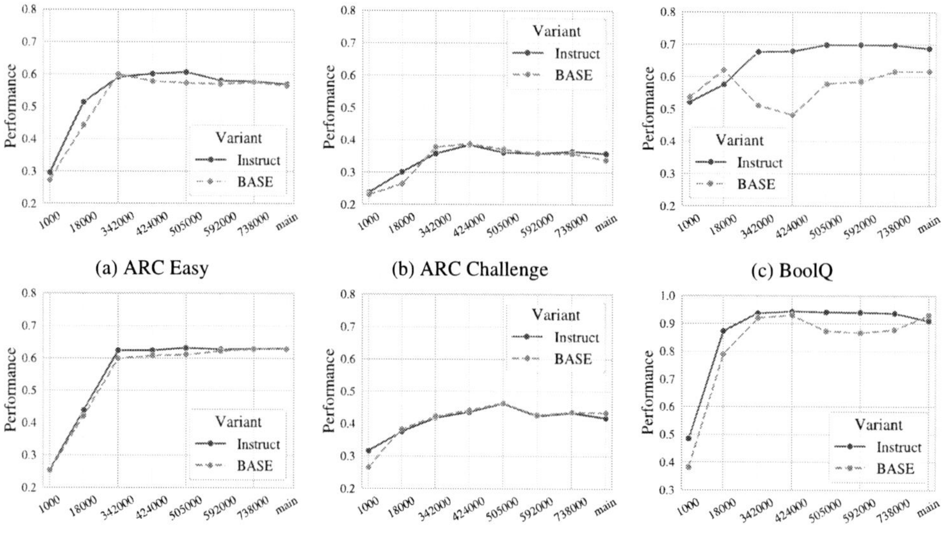

(a) ARC Easy (b) ARC Challenge (c) BoolQ

(d) Hellaswag (e) Openbook QA (f) SciQ

Figure 9: Model performance after instruction tuning on each pre-training step.

Domain Knowledge The ratio of out-of-domain performance change by task is shown in Figure 15. Overall, we observe that Llama and OLMo experience benefits with different tasks after fine-tuning, but both model shows an inconsistent change across tasks.

H License of Artifacts

We include the license of artifacts used in this paper in Table 7

I Full Performance Table

Due to the availability of space and the amount of fine-tuned checkpoints, we omit displaying all exact metric values in the paper. The performance of each fine-tuned variant on each dataset can be found in the csv file under directory `results` in the code base.

J Performance Difference Numbers

The average performance change before and after fine-tuning for each checkpoint is shown in Table 6.

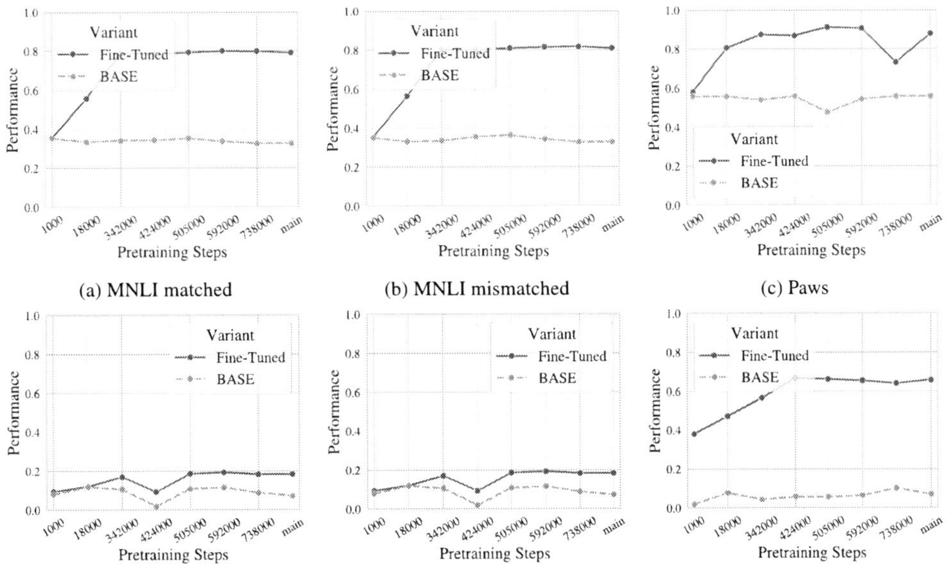

(a) MNLI matched (b) MNLI mismatched (c) Paws

(d) XSum (e) XLSum (f) SocialIQA

Figure 10: Model performance after supervised fine-tuning on each pre-training step.

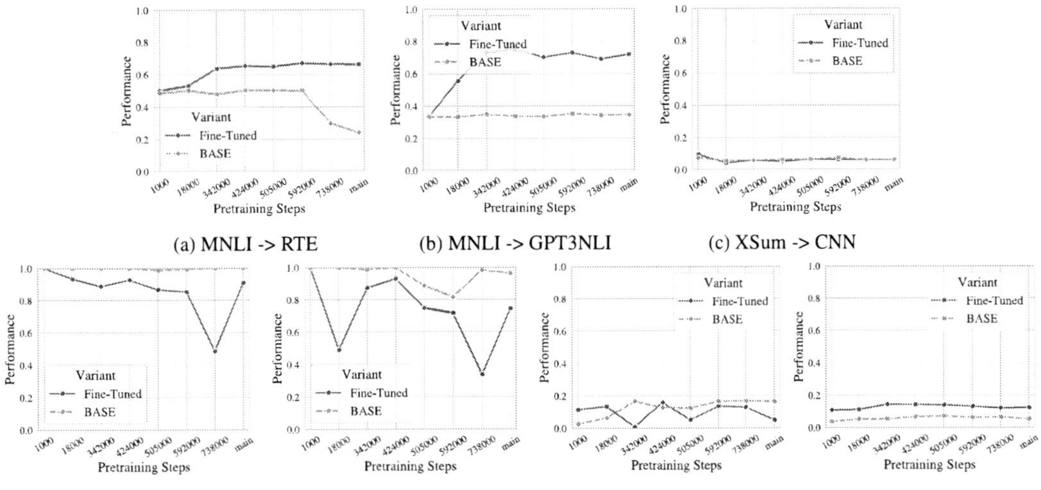

(a) MNLI -> RTE (b) MNLI -> GPT3NLI (c) XSum -> CNN

(d) Paws -> QQP (e) Paws -> STS-B (f) SocialIQA -> SciQ (g) SocialIQA -> TweetQA

Figure 11: Out-of-domain performance after supervised fine-tuning on each pre-training step.

The data in this table is used to create Figure 8.

K Generalization Taxonomy

Following the generalization taxonomy in Hupkes et al. (2023), the evaluation card is included in Table 8.

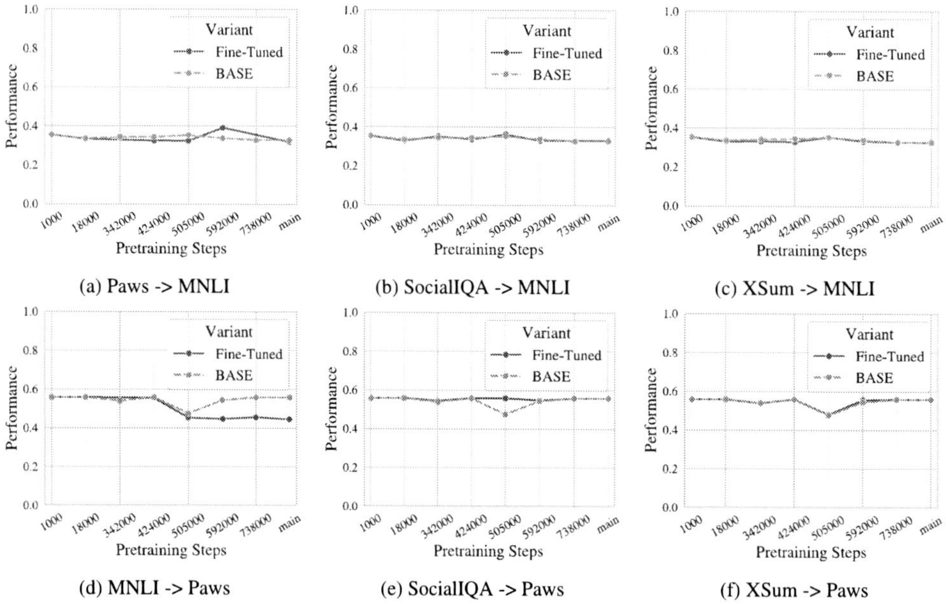

(a) Paws -> MNLI (b) SocialIQA -> MNLI (c) XSum -> MNLI
(d) MNLI -> Paws (e) SocialIQA -> Paws (f) XSum -> Paws

Figure 12: Cross-task performance after supervised fine-tuning on each pre-training step. The model is fine-tuned on a classification task and evaluated on a generation task or a classification task with a different label set.

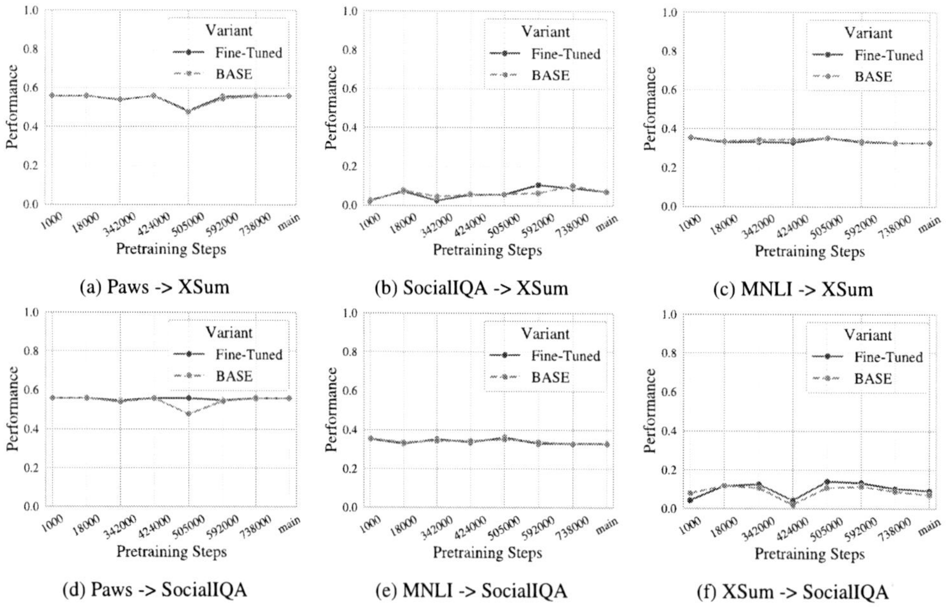

(a) Paws -> XSum (b) SocialIQA -> XSum (c) MNLI -> XSum
(d) Paws -> SocialIQA (e) MNLI -> SocialIQA (f) XSum -> SocialIQA

Figure 13: Cross-task performance after supervised fine-tuning on each pre-training step. The model is fine-tuned on a generation task and evaluated on a classification task.

Task	Default Prompt	Instruction Prompt	IO Prompt	Expected Output
Summary Generation	### Input: {document} ### Summary:	Please read the following text: {document} Provide a summary:	{document}	{summary}
Question Generation	### Input: {context} ### Answer: {answer} ### Question:	Given the context: {context} And the answer: {answer} Generate a suitable question:	{context} {answer}	{question}
Natural Language Inference	### Input_1: {premise} ### Input_2: {hypothesis} ### Inference:	Consider the following texts: Text 1: {premise} Text 2: {hypothesis} The relation is	{premise} {hypothesis}	{label}
Paraphrase Detection	### Input_1: {sentence1} ### Input_2: {sentence2} ### Paraphrase Classification:	Let's compare the two sentences: Sentence_1: {sentence1} Sentence_2: {sentence2} Are they paraphrasing?:	{sentence1} {sentence2}	{label}

Table 5: Formatting of the prompts

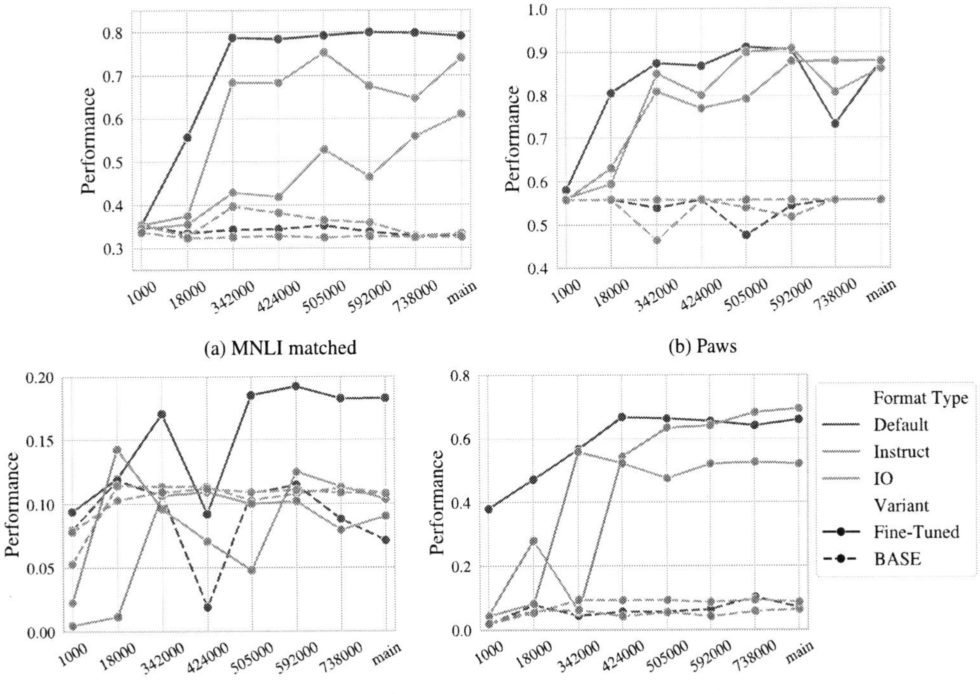

(a) MNLI matched

(b) Paws

(c) XSum

(d) SocialIQa

Figure 14: Model performance with different task formats.

Checkpoint	Learned in Pre-train	Learned in Fine-Tune
1000	0.048	0.062
18000	0.048	0.149
342000	0.004	0.286
424000	0.01	0.297
505000	0.03	0.304
592000	0.027	0.297
738000	0.021	0.264
main	-0.005	0.290

Table 6: Average performance change before and after fine-tuning for each checkpoint (Perf(Fine-tuned) - Perf(BASE)). The group that is never learned during pre-training is picked up by the model during fine-tuning.

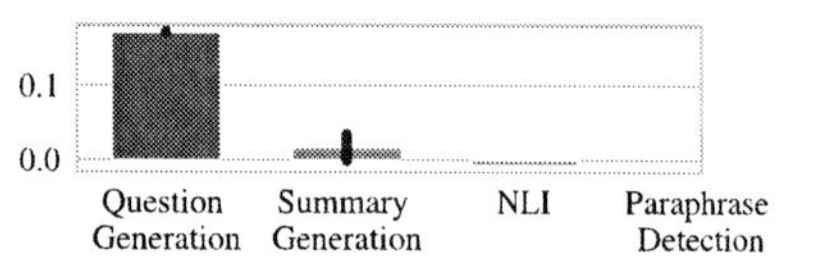

Figure 15: Ratio of out-of-domain performance change for each task on the final checkpoint of LLAMA3-8B.

Name	License	Name	License
OLMo-1b	Apache 2.0	SocialIQa	CC-BY
TULU	ODC-BY	CNN/DailyMail	Apache 2.0
ARC	CC BY-SA	TweetQA	CC BY-SA-4.0
OpenbookQA	Apache 2.0	MNLI	CC-BY-3.0
Hellaswag	MIT	GPT3NLI	MIT
BoolQ	Apache 2.0	RTE	N/A
SciQ	CC-BY-NC-3.0	Paws	Free
XSum	MIT	QQP	Non-Commercial
XLSum	CC-BY-NC-SA 4.0	STS-B	Other

Table 7: License of artifacts used in this paper.

Motivation					
Practical □ △	*Cognitive*	*Intrinsic*	*Fairness*		
Generalisation type					
Compositional	*Structural*	*Cross Task* △	*Cross Language*	*Cross Domain* □	*Robustness*
Shift type					
Covariate □	*Label* △	*Full*	*Assumed*		
Shift source					
Naturally occuring □ △	*Partitioned natural*	*Generated shift*	*Fully generated*		
Shift locus					
Train–test	*Finetune train–test* □ △	*Pretrain–train*	*Pretrain–test*		

Table 8: Generalization experiment summary following taxonomy in Hupkes et al. (2023).

State Space Models are Strong Text Rerankers

Jinghua Yan[◇ 1] **Zhichao Xu**[◇ 12] **Ashim Gupta** [1] **Vivek Srikumar** [1]
[1] Kahlert School of Computing, University of Utah
[2] Scientific Computing and Imaging Institute, University of Utah
{jhyan,brutusxu,ashim,svivek}@cs.utah.edu

Abstract

Transformers dominate NLP and IR; but their inference inefficiencies and challenges in extrapolating to longer contexts have sparked interest in alternative model architectures. Among these, state space models (SSMs) like Mamba offer promising advantages, particularly $O(1)$ time complexity in inference. Despite their potential, SSMs' effectiveness at text reranking — a task requiring fine-grained query-document interaction and long-context understanding — remains underexplored.

This study benchmarks SSM-based architectures (specifically, Mamba-1 and Mamba-2) against transformer-based models across various scales, architectures, and pre-training objectives, focusing on performance and efficiency in text reranking tasks. We find that (1) Mamba architectures achieve competitive text ranking performance, comparable to transformer-based models of similar size; (2) they are less efficient in training and inference compared to transformers with flash attention; and (3) Mamba-2 outperforms Mamba-1 in both performance and efficiency. These results underscore the potential of state space models as a transformer alternative and highlight areas for improvement in future IR applications.[1]

1 Introduction

The transformer architecture (Vaswani et al., 2017) is an established standard within NLP and IR community. Compared to recurrent neural networks (RNNs) transformers better capture long-range dependencies and also admit large scale pre-training. However, for inference with a sequence of length L and D-dimensional hidden states, transformers cost $O(L)$ time and $O(LD)$ space complexity — proving to be less efficient than RNNs.

Recently, there has been a growing interest in developing alternative architectures for modeling sequence data. For example, RWKV (Peng et al., 2023) combines the efficient parallelizable training of transformers with the efficient inference of RNNs. Another notable architecture is the state space model (SSM, Gu and Dao, 2023; Gu et al., 2020, 2021b), which is related to convolutional and recurrent neural networks, and also to signal processing literature.

In essence, state space models compress the context into a smaller state of size N, achieving $O(1)$ time complexity and $O(ND)$ space complexity in inference time. However, the capabilities of SSMs are limited by the amount of information that can be compressed in its hidden state. To mitigate this, Gu and Dao (2023) propose a novel selective state space model named Mamba. Mamba selectively encodes the input to the hidden state to improve model expressiveness, while also addressing the computation problem with a selective scan method and hardware-aware optimization. Gu and Dao (2023) and followup work (Dao and Gu, 2024; Zhu et al., 2024; Wang et al., 2024; Waleffe et al., 2024, *inter alia*) examine the efficacy of Mamba models for various sequence modeling tasks, notably language modeling, and also image and audio tasks. The parameterized SSMs are able to achieve performance close to transformer-based models of similar sizes while also demonstrating efficiency in training and inference.

Despite the growing popularity of state space models, their effectiveness in information retrieval remains underexplored. Modern search systems typically consist of at least two stages: retrieval and reranking. During retrieval, offline indexes first fetch a preliminary list of candidate documents, which is refined by the reranking model. Reranking requires models to understand long context input, and to capture fine-grained query-document interactions. The attention mechanism in the transformer

[◇]Equal Contribution, order decided randomly.
[1]The code for reproducing our experiments is available at https://github.com/zhichaoxu-shufe/RankMambaV2

Proceedings of the 10th Workshop on Representation Learning for NLP (RepL4NLP-2025), pages 152–169

naturally allows for the latter; it allows query tokens to attend to document tokens. In contrast, state space models may fail to model long-range dependencies due to their recurrent nature.

In this paper, we examine the following research questions about Mamba-1 and Mamba-2:

1. **Performance RQ**: How do Mamba models compare to transformers for text reranking?

2. **Efficiency RQ**: How efficient are the Mamba architectures with respect to training throughput and inference speed?

To this end, we conduct a rigorous benchmarking study comparing the two model families, across varying architectures, sizes, pre-training objectives, and attention patterns. Specifically, we train neural reranking models following established training methodologies outlined in prior literature (Gao et al., 2021; Boytsov et al., 2022; Ma et al., 2023). Our experiments allow us to address the two research questions above. We find that:

1. Mamba-based language models can achieve strong text reranking performance, matching transformer-based models of similar scales.

2. Although Mamba architectures have better complexity theoretically, in practice they are less efficient compared to transformer architecture with I/O-aware optimization (e.g., flash attention (Dao, 2024)).

3. Mamba-2 improves upon Mamba-1 in both performance and efficiency.

We discuss the implications of our results and point out future directions of transformer alternative architectures for IR tasks.

2 Background: State Space Models

We will briefly survey state space models and their connection to RNNs and transformers. We use Structured State Space Sequence Models (S4, Gu et al., 2021a) to illustrate the idea behind state space models before describing the Mamba models.

State space models. In its simplest form, an SSM maps a 1-dimensional function or sequence $x(t) \in \mathbb{R}$ to $y(t) \in \mathbb{R}$ via a latent state $h(t) \in \mathbb{R}^N$. Here, t denotes a timestep and N is the state size (different from hidden dimensionality D). It is parameterized by $(\Delta, \boldsymbol{A}, \boldsymbol{B}, \boldsymbol{C})$ and defines a *continuous* sequence-to-sequence transformation as:

$$h'(t) = \boldsymbol{A}h(t) + \boldsymbol{B}x(t) \qquad y(t) = \boldsymbol{C}h(t) \qquad (1)$$

The above transformation can be *discretized* as:

$$h_t = \overline{\boldsymbol{A}}h_{t-1} + \overline{\boldsymbol{B}}x_t \qquad y_t = \boldsymbol{C}h_t \qquad (2)$$

The discretization of $\overline{\boldsymbol{A}}$ and $\overline{\boldsymbol{B}}$ is defined by the *discretization rule*, for example:

$$\overline{\boldsymbol{A}} = \exp(\Delta\boldsymbol{A}) \qquad (3)$$

$$\overline{\boldsymbol{B}} = (\Delta\boldsymbol{A})^{-1}(\exp(\Delta\boldsymbol{A}) - I) \cdot \Delta\boldsymbol{B} \qquad (4)$$

Expanding Eqn. (2) with the whole sequence $x = (x_1, x_2, \ldots, x_n)$ leads to a convolutional form:

$$y = x * \overline{\boldsymbol{K}} \qquad (5)$$

$$\overline{\boldsymbol{K}} = (\boldsymbol{C}\overline{\boldsymbol{B}}, \boldsymbol{C}\overline{\boldsymbol{A}}\overline{\boldsymbol{B}}, \ldots, \boldsymbol{C}\overline{\boldsymbol{A}}^{n-1}\overline{\boldsymbol{B}}) \qquad (6)$$

While Eqn. (2) resembles an RNN, Eqn. (5) looks like a CNN, where $\overline{\boldsymbol{K}}$ is a large convolution kernel over the whole input sequence x. The parameterization of $(\Delta, \boldsymbol{A}, \boldsymbol{B}, \boldsymbol{C})$ is independent of input sequence x and is fixed during all time steps, a property referred to as linear time invariance (LTI). Structured state space models (S4) imposes a structure on the $\boldsymbol{A}$ matrix for efficiency. Existing works (Gu et al., 2021a; Gupta et al., 2022; Smith et al., 2022) employ a diagonal matrix, thus $\boldsymbol{A} \in \mathbb{R}^{N \times N}$, $\boldsymbol{B} \in \mathbb{R}^{N \times 1}$ and $\boldsymbol{C} \in \mathbb{R}^{1 \times N}$ matrices are all represented by N parameters.

The above expressions can be generalized to D-channel features, i.e., $x_t, y_t \in \mathbb{R}^D$. A concrete example might be D-dimensional word embeddings or hidden states. In this case, computation of $\boldsymbol{A}, \boldsymbol{B}, \boldsymbol{C}$ is applied to each channel independently.

Mamba-1 Models. State space models compress potentially unbounded context into a state $h_t \in \mathbb{R}^N$, potentially limiting their effectiveness. Gu and Dao (2023) propose to make the parameters $(\Delta, \boldsymbol{B}, \boldsymbol{C})$ input-dependent. This modification changes the model from time-invariant to time-varying, therefore posing challenges to the model's computational efficiency; the model now cannot be trained in CNN mode. Gu and Dao (2023) address this via a hardware-aware optimization algorithm called *Selective Scan*. We refer the reader to the original paper for details.

Scalar Structured SSM. Mamba-2 (Dao and Gu, 2024) restricts the matrix $\boldsymbol{A}$ to be a scalar times identity matrix; i.e., all the diagonal elements of $\boldsymbol{A}$ are the same value. It also introduces a new hyperparameter P, the SSM head dimension, which is analogous to the transformer head dimension, i.e., $D = P \times \texttt{\#heads}$. Mamba-2 uses different $(\Delta, \boldsymbol{A}, \boldsymbol{B}, \boldsymbol{C})$ for each SSM head, and P is set to 64 or 128, similar to transformers. Further, Dao and Gu (2024) develop efficient implementations for training and inference, enabling much larger state size (from $N = 16$ in Mamba-1 to $N = 64, 256$ or larger in Mamba-2), while simultaneously being faster in training. Subsequent works (Yang et al., 2024; Qin et al., 2024; Dao and Gu, 2024, *inter alia*) also reported Mamba-2's performance and efficiency improvement over Mamba-1.

3 The Text Reranking Problem

Modern IR systems employ a two-stage retrieval-reranking pipeline (Schütze et al., 2008; Zhang et al., 2021; Asai et al., 2024; Xu et al., 2025, *inter alia*). After the initial retrieval by an efficient, scalable first-stage retriever, a reranker refines the ranklist to optimize ranking metrics. Reranking involves ordering texts (passages or documents) by their *relevance* to a query, with passage reranking being a finer-grained form of document reranking. Our focus is to study this second stage and perform a comprehensive analysis of different rerankers for the tasks of both passage reranking and document reranking.

Let q be an input query, and $d \in \mathcal{D}$ be a text, where $\mathcal{D}$ is the set of all texts (passages for passage reranking and documents for document reranking). The reranking model $f_\theta(q, d)$, parameterized by θ, predicts a scalar relevance score. The model f is instantiated as a linear layer on top of a language model. We adopt the common practice of concatenating the query and the document as input to the model (Nogueira et al., 2019; Yates et al., 2021; Boytsov et al., 2022; Ma et al., 2023, *inter alia*).

Training a Reranker. Training the reranking model involves sampling negatives from the document collection. We use the recommended setup from literature (Gao et al., 2021; Ma et al., 2023; Boytsov et al., 2022; Xu, 2024) to sample hard negatives from the retrieval results obtained from the first-stage retriever.

Let us denote the relevant document to query q_i as d_i^+, and sampled negatives as $d_i^- \in \mathcal{D}_i^-$, training pair $(q_i, d_i^+) \in \mathcal{S}$, the reranking model is trained with optimizing the following softmax loss:

$$-\frac{1}{|\mathcal{S}|} \sum_{(q_i,d_i^+)\in\mathcal{S}} \log \frac{\exp f_\theta(q_i,d_i^+)}{\exp f_\theta(q_i,d_i^+)+\sum_{j\in\mathcal{D}_i^-} \exp f_\theta(q_i,d_i^-)} \tag{7}$$

We pack multiple training instances into a mini-batch and jointly optimize the backbone language model and the linear layer.

4 Experiments

In this section, we describe the experimental setup for passage (§ 4.1) and document reranking (§ 4.3). For **Performance RQ**, we report results and analyze the implications in § 4.2 and § 4.4 respectively. Then we address **Efficiency RQ** in § 4.5.

4.1 Passage Reranking

First, let us examine the passage reranking task.

Datasets and Evaluation Metrics. We employ the passage ranking subset of the well-known MS MARCO dataset (Bajaj et al., 2016) which contains a total of 524K training instances. For the passage retriever in the first stage, we use `BGE-large-en-v1.5` (Xiao et al., 2023) due to its strong trade-off between retrieval performance and size of the retriever. (See Table 7 in the appendix for this comparison). The training set for our passage reranker is constructed by uniformly sampling 15 hard negatives from the ranklist of top-1000 passages returned by the BGE retriever. Zhuang et al. (2023); Ma et al. (2023) highlight that increasing the number of negatives along with the global batch size leads to better ranking performance. Training demands significant GPU RAM. We determined these hyperparameters by balancing performance and the available hardware resources.

The in-domain evaluation is conducted using the official passage ranking development set (`Dev`) containing 6,980 queries. We also include TREC DL19/DL20 (Craswell et al., 2020, 2021) evaluation set that contains 43/54 queries with in-depth annotation for passage ranking. We report the official evaluation metrics for passage ranking, i.e., MRR@10 for Dev and NDCG@10 for DL19/DL20. For out-of-domain evaluation, we use 13 publicly available BEIR testsets (Thakur et al., 2021) covering different text domains. Again, we report the official evaluation metric NDCG@10. All evaluations involve first constructing the index with the first-stage retriever, then retrieving pas-

Model	Size	Architecture	Pre-train #Tokens
***Encoder-only Models** (Bi-directional)*			
BERT-base	110M	Transformer	3.3B
RoBERTa-base	120M	Transformer	33B
ELECTRA-base	105M	Transformer	3.3B
BERT-large	330M	Transformer	3.3B
RoBERTa-large	335M	Transformer	33B
ELECTRA-large	320M	Transformer	33B
***Encoder-Decoder Models** (Bi-directional)*			
BART-base	130M	Transformer	33B
BART-large	385M	Transformer	33B
***Decoder-only Models** (Uni-directional)*			
OPT-125M	125M	Transformer	180B
Mamba-1-130M	130M	Mamba-1	300B
Mamba-2-130M	130M	Mamba-2	300B
OPT-350M	350M	Transformer	180B
Mamba-1-370M	370M	Mamba-1	300B
Mamba-2-370M	370M	Mamba-2	300B
Mamba-1-790M	790M	Mamba-1	300B
Mamba-2-780M	780M	Mamba-2	300B
OPT-1.3B	1.3B	Transformer	180B
Mamba-1-1.4B	1.4B	Mamba-1	300B
Mamba-2-1.3B	1.3B	Mamba-2	300B
Llama-3.2-1B	1.3B	Transformer++	15T

Table 1: Details of the Pre-trained language models used in our comparative study. Transformer++ indicates the state-of-the-art transformer architecture. Note the pre-training #tokens is not directly comparable between encoder-only, encoder-decoder and decoder-only models due to different pre-training objectives.

sages with the retriever, followed by refining the ranklist using our trained rerankers.

Language Models Used. We conduct a comparative study between rerankers using state space models and several previously studied language models. Among encoder-only models, we use BERT (Devlin et al., 2019), RoBERTa (Liu et al., 2019), and ELECTRA (Clark et al., 2020) with their `base` as well as `large` variants. For encoder-decoder models, we select both `base` and `large` variants of the BART model (Lewis et al., 2020). Among decoder-only models, we compare with OPT (Zhang et al., 2022), and Llama3 (Dubey et al., 2024) models. The Llama3 model serves as an upper bound for transformer-based models, given that is the state-of-the-art pre-trained model at the 1B scale and high pre-training cost. We compare these with both Mamba-1 and Mamba-2-based rerankers at four different parameter settings. The details of the models used in our comparison study are shown in Table 1.

This extensive selection of pre-trained language models enables the comparison across different architecture types (e.g., encoder-only vs decoder-only), pre-trained model scales (from 110M to 1.4B parameters), as well as different pre-training objectives (e.g., masked language modeling in BERT vs replaced token detection in ELECTRA). It is important to acknowledge that the pre-trained models are trained under different pre-training setups (such as varying datasets and hyperparameter configurations, etc.); comparing them is not entirely fair. Nevertheless, we can gain insights by evaluating different language models using a consistent fine-tuning approach.

Baselines. We include MonoBERT (Nogueira and Cho, 2019), cross-SimLM (Wang et al., 2022), MonoT5 (Nogueira et al., 2020), RankT5 (Zhuang et al., 2023) as well as the state-of-the-art RankLlama model (Ma et al., 2023). Appx. B gives a detailed description of these methods .

Implementation Details. Our code is implemented in PyTorch (Paszke et al., 2019) using the Huggingface library (Wolf, 2019). The weights of the pre-trained language models are obtained from the Huggingface Hub[2]. Wherever applicable, we use Flash Attention 2 (Dao, 2024), gradient accumulation, and activation checkpointing. Note that the models are trained *without* parameter-efficient fine-tuning techniques such as LoRA (Hu et al., 2021) which is different from Ma et al. (2023). We also do not investigate alternative compression techniques for improved parameter efficiency, such as low-rank factorization (Gupta et al., 2024), and leave these avenues for future research.

We do not extensively tune hyperparameters; as discussed by prior works (Boytsov et al., 2022; Ma et al., 2023) fine-tuning of reranking models is less sensitive to hyperparameters. We found the vanilla AdamW optimizer along with learning rate warm-up with linear scheduler to work for all training runs. Refer to Appx. D for an overview of hyperparameters throughout the experiments. Out implementation as well as checkpoints will be made public to facilitate reproducibility.

For the autoregressive models, including Mamba models, we provide input with the following template: `document:` $\{d\}$; `query:` $\{q\}$; `[EOS]`. The linear layer then takes the last layer representation of the `[EOS]` token and outputs the relevance score:

$$f_\theta(q, d) = \text{Linear}\big(\text{model}(\text{input})[-1]\big) \quad (8)$$

For encoder-only and encoder-decoder models, we use a different template: `[CLS]` ; `query:` $\{q\}$;

[2]`https://huggingface.co/models`

document: $\{d\}$. The linear layer in this case uses the representation of the [CLS] token.

4.2 Passage Reranking Results

In-domain Evaluation. We show the in-domain passage reranking results in Table 2. First, note that our trained models are comparable to previously reported results. For example, we report that BERT-base achieves 38.5, 73.3, 73.1 on Dev, DL19, DL20 respectively, compared to MonoBERT (Nogueira and Cho, 2019)'s 37.2, 72.3 and 72.2. This suggests the correctness of our training setup.

Between transformer models of different architectures, we notice that both encoder-only and encoder-decoder models outperform decoder-only models (OPT-125M and 350M in our case), despite OPT being pre-trained with more tokens. We hypothesize the reason is that the bi-directional attention in encoders better capture the interaction between query and document tokens. But decoder-only models are easier to scale.

Between transformer and Mamba architectures, Mamba models are able to achieve strong performance. For example, despite being uni-directional, Mamba-2-370M achieves 38.6, 75.8, and 74.0 on three datasets compared to the best transformer-based model in that parameter range—BERT-large's 39.1, 76.4, and 72.4. The overall best transformer-based model—Llama-3.2-1B outperforms the Mamba models of similar size. However, note that Llama-3.2-1B is pre-trained on 15T tokens compared to Mamba model's 300B tokens. We conclude that Mamba models are competitive in the passage ranking task.

Among Mamba models, despite being trained on the same number of tokens, we notice overall that Mamba-2 achieves better performance than Mamba-1. A similar trend is shown in BEIR and document reranking results. In conclusion, Mamba-2 is a better SSM architecture compared to Mamba-1 for text reranking.

Out-of-domain Evaluation. We report part of BEIR results in § 4.2 and leave full results to Appx. E. Overall, Mamba models are able to achieve competitive performance compared to the transformer-based models of similar sizes. Specifically, Mamba-2-1.3B achieves 53.6 NDCG@10 averaged over 13 datasets compared to OPT-1.3B's 52.7. Compared to baselines, Mamba-based models are only outperformed by the much larger RankLlama — a 7B model based on 7B-sized retrieval model RepLlama. This reinforces our findings from in-domain evaluation, suggesting the efficacy of Mamba models in the passage reranking task.

One surprising observation is the underperformance of the Llama-3.2-1B model. This pre-trained model was not only trained on more tokens (15B) but was also trained on a much more diverse set of web documents. Ideally, a model pre-trained on a more diverse set of documents should perform better on out-of-domain evaluation sets, but we find that to not be the case with Llama-3.2-1B model.

4.3 Document Reranking

Next, we discuss the experimental setup and results for the document reranking task. The setup closely aligns with that used for passage reranking, with specific differences highlighted where applicable.

Datasets and Evaluation Metrics. We use the document ranking subset from the MSMARCO dataset containing 320K training instances. We use Pyserini's implementation of BM25 (Robertson et al., 1995)[3] as the first-stage document retriever and use top-100 documents to uniformly sample 7 hard negatives for each positive query-document pair. We train two model variants — FirstP and LongP — which truncate the input at 512 and 1,536 tokens respectively. Prior works (Boytsov et al., 2022; Ma et al., 2023) note that longer training lengths only yield marginal performance improvements. So we do not experiment with them.

For evaluation, we use the official development set (Dev) containing 5,193 queries and report MRR@100 for comparison. For the TREC DL19/DL20 (Craswell et al., 2020, 2021) evaluation set that includes 43/45 queries, we use the official NDCG@10 as our evaluation metric.

Other Details. Among the baselines, we include MonoT5 (Nogueira et al., 2020), RankT5 (Zhuang et al., 2023) along with RankLlama that is the current state-of-the-art model using 7 Billion parameters. We also report two baseline runs from Boytsov et al. (2022): BERT-base-FirstP and BERT-base-MaxP as a sanity check for our implementation. MaxP method first segments the long document into several shorter passages, then uses the maximum relevance of segmented passages as the relevance of the document. We train document reranking models for each of the pre-trained models highlighted in § 4.1. Note that as encoder-only models

[3]https://github.com/castorini/pyserini

Model	Size	Retriever	Dev MRR@10	DL19 NDCG@10	DL20 NDCG@10
MonoBERT (Nogueira and Cho, 2019)	110 M	BM25	37.2	72.3	72.2
cross-SimLM (Wang et al., 2022)	110 M	bi-SimLM	43.7	74.6	72.7
MonoT5 (Nogueira et al., 2020)	220 M	BM25	38.1	-	-
RankT5 (Zhuang et al., 2023)	335 M	GTR	42.2	-	-
RankLlama (Ma et al., 2023)	7 B	RepLlama	**44.9**†	**75.6**†	**77.4**†
BERT-base [E]	110 M	BGE	38.5	73.3	73.1
RoBERTa-base [E]	120 M	BGE	39.1	**75.4**	72.0
ELECTRA-base [E]	105 M	BGE	**39.8**	73.4	**74.1**
BART-base [ED]	130 M	BGE	37.8	74.7	70.2
OPT-125M [D]	125 M	BGE	35.2	70.6	69.2
Mamba-1-130M [D]	130 M	BGE	37.8	73.7	70.5
Mamba-2-130M [D]	130 M	BGE	37.0	73.8	70.8
BERT-large [E]	330 M	BGE	39.1	**76.4**	72.4
RoBERTa-large [E]	335 M	BGE	37.8	75.1	69.4
ELECTRA-large [E]	320 M	BGE	38.8	74.9	73.2
BART-large [ED]	385 M	BGE	**39.2**	74.6	72.2
OPT-350M [D]	350 M	BGE	36.3	72.1	68.9
Mamba-1-370M [D]	370 M	BGE	38.9	74.7	72.5
Mamba-2-370M [D]	370 M	BGE	38.6	75.8	**74.0**
Mamba-1-790M [D]	790 M	BGE	38.2	76.4	72.9
Mamba-2-780M [D]	780 M	BGE	**39.0**	**76.8**	**73.6**
OPT-1.3B [D]	1.3 B	BGE	38.9	74.2	73.7
Mamba-1-1.4B [D]	1.4 B	BGE	38.9	74.7	72.5
Mamba-2-1.3B [D]	1.3 B	BGE	38.6	75.8	74.0
Llama-3.2-1B [D]	1.3 B	BGE	**40.4**‡	**76.8**‡	**76.2**‡

Table 2: Results for passage reranking in-domain evaluation. We denote BGE-large-en-v1.5 as BGE for simplicity. We mark best results in each section bold; † indicates the overall best result and ‡ indicates the best result among our trained models. For the reranking threshold, RankLlama reranks top-100 results from RepLlama while other models reranks top-1000 results. Superscript E denotes encoder-only model, ED denotes encoder-decoder model and D denotes decoder-only model.

Dataset	BM25 -	MonoT5 220M	RankT5 335M	RankLlama 7B	ELECTRA 335M	BART 385M	Llama-3.2 1.3B	OPT 1.3B	Mamba-1 1.4B	Mamba-2 1.3B
Arguana	39.7	19.4	22.3	**56.0**†	14.6	18.0	32.7	**35.7**‡	33.1	**34.4**
Climate-FEVER	16.5	24.5	20.6	**28.0**†	18.2	20.9	22.6	**26.7**‡	22.6	**26.2**
DBPedia	31.8	41.9	43.5	**48.3**†	43.2	43.5	43.1	**45.8**‡	**45.8**‡	**45.8**‡
FEVER	65.1	80.1	83.5	**83.9**†	76.8	77.5	72.9	**83.0**‡	80.9	**81.9**
FiQA	23.6	41.3	41.6	**46.5**†	38.8	41.4	40.5	**44.3**‡	**43.3**‡	**43.3**‡
HotpotQA	63.3	69.5	71.3	**75.3**†	68.6	71.9	69.2	**74.9**	75.8	**76.3**‡
NFCorpus	32.2	**35.7**	32.6	30.3	33.5	34.9	**37.9**	32.8	38.8	**39.2**†‡
NQ	30.6	56.7	59.6	**66.3**†	49.2	51.0	48.2	**52.6**‡	50.8	**52.1**
Quora	78.9	82.3	82.2	**85.0**†	79.3	73.6	**84.9**‡	84.0	80.9	**83.9**
SCIDOCS	14.9	16.4	**18.2**	17.8	16.5	17.0	17.7	**17.8**	19.0	**19.6**†‡
SciFact	67.9	73.5	**74.9**	73.2	65.9	65.7	71.7	**72.7**	**77.4**†‡	76.8
TREC-COVID	59.5	77.6	75.2	**85.2**†	67.2	70.6	77.0	**81.6**	**83.0**‡	79.9
Touche-2020	44.2	27.7	**45.9**†	40.1	34.3	**34.9**	32.8	33.2	36.7	**37.7**‡
Average	43.7	49.7	51.7	**56.6**†	46.6	47.8	50.1	**52.7**	52.9	**53.6**‡

Table 3: Results for passage reranking out-of-domain evaluation. We show results of the largest encoder-only, encoder decoder model and decoder only models. Full results are referred to Appx. E. We mark best results in each section bold; † indicates the overall best result and ‡ indicates best result among our trained models.

have a fixed context length (ex: BERT with 512), we do not have LongP variants for them.

Model	Size	Dev MRR@100	DL19 NDCG@10	DL20 NDCG@10
BERT-base-FirstP	110 M	39.4	63.1	59.8
BERT-base-MaxP	110 M	39.2	64.8	61.5
MonoT5	3 B	41.1	-	-
RankLlama	7 B	**50.3**†	**67.7**	**67.4**†
FirstP models				
BERT-base [E]	110 M	**41.3**	65.8	61.5
RoBERTa-base [E]	125 M	39.4	65.5	59.3
ELECTRA-base [E]	105 M	39.0	66.3	62.3
BART-base [ED]	130 M	37.5	63.9	59.9
OPT-125M [D]	125 M	38.8	63.8	61.8
Mamba-1-130M [D]	130 M	40.9	66.5	**64.4**
Mamba-2-130M [D]	130 M	38.3	**66.7**	63.9
BERT-large [E]	330 M	40.1	65.9	61.4
RoBERTa-large [E]	355 M	**43.3**‡	66.8	64.2
ELECTRA-large [E]	335 M	40.3	**67.8**	**64.9**
BART-large [ED]	385 M	40.3	64.7	61.6
OPT-350M [D]	350 M	39.0	64.7	63.1
Mamba-1-370M [D]	370 M	42.5	67.8	63.9
Mamba-2-370M [D]	370 M	41.0	67.2	64.7
Mamba1-790M [D]	790 M	**42.0**	67.4	**64.9**
Mamba2-780M [D]	780 M	**42.0**	**68.7**	64.6
OPT-1B [D]	1.3 B	40.8	65.3	61.8
Llama-3.2-1B [D]	1.3 B	40.6	67.6	60.8
Mamba-1-1.3B [D]	1.3 B	OOM	OOM	OOM
Mamba-2-1.3B [D]	1.3 B	**42.1**	**68.3**	**64.6**
LongP models				
OPT-125M [D]	125 M	38.8	63.8	61.8
Mamba-1-130M [D]	130 M	**39.2**	66.0	63.0
Mamba-2-130M [D]	130 M	38.3	**67.3**	**63.6**
OPT-350M [D]	350 M	35.7	64.3	60.5
Mamba-1-370M [D]	370 M	39.3	**67.8**	64.3
Mamba-2-370M [D]	370 M	**41.4**	67.3	**65.1**
Mamba-1-790M [D]	790 M	41.3	68.0	64.9
Mamba-2-780M [D]	780 M	**42.2**	**70.0**†‡	**66.9**‡
OPT-1.3B [D]	1.3 B	**41.8**	68.0	**63.9**
Llama-3.2-1B [D]	1.3 B	40.9	**68.5**	63.5
Mamba-1-1.4B [D]	1.4 B	OOM	OOM	OOM
Mamba-2-1.3B [D]	1.3 B	OOM	OOM	OOM

Table 4: Results for document reranking. We mark the best result in each section bold; † marks the overall best result and ‡ marks best result among our trained models. For the reranking threshold, MonoT5 reranks top-1000 documents from the retriever while others rerank top-100 results. Superscripts E, ED and D are the same as Table 2. OOM denotes Out-Of-Memory Error.

4.4 Document Reranking Results

The task of document reranking necessitates using models that can process lengthy contexts. Although transformer models can accommodate long contexts through adjustments like improved positional embeddings (Su et al., 2024) or specialized training methods (Xiong et al., 2024; Dubey et al., 2024), it remains unclear whether Mamba-based state space models possess this capability. Our experiments in document reranking aim to address this gap. Our document reranking results are shown in Table 4.

We make two important observations. First, in terms of the task performance, Mamba-based rerankers are comparable to their Transformer-based counterparts for every parameter budget. Notably, among the sub-1 billion parameter models, the best model is the 780 million Mamba-2 model trained with 1536 context length. Second, while the Mamba-1 and Mamba-2 variants perform comparably for document reranking, we found that Mamba-2 models in general require less GPU memory. One such instance is the training run with 1.3B parameters for context length of 512 (FirstP settings)—Mamba-1 leads to OOM error but Mamba-2 does not. This echoes prior works' observation that Mamba-2 is more memory efficient during training compared to Mamba-1 (Dao and Gu, 2024; Yang et al., 2024, *inter alia*).

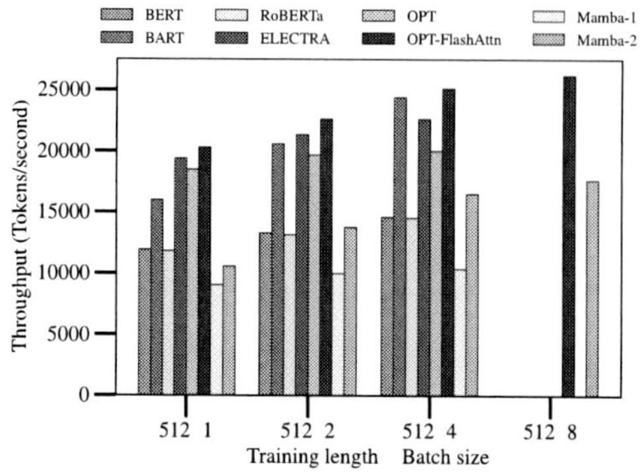

Figure 1: Training throughput comparison between models≈330M. For batch_size=8, all models except OPT-FlashAttn and Mamba-2 run out of memory with a 48 GB VRAM GPU.

4.5 Training Throughput and Inference Speed

To answer the **Efficiency RQ**, we evaluate the training throughput and inference speed of Mamba models and compare them to the transformer-based models. We perform this comparison with document ranking models as it involves a more challenging setting. All the numbers reported here are measured on a server with Intel Xeon Gold 6230 CPU @2.1GHz and a single Nvidia A40 GPU (48 GB VRAM).

We measure training throughput (#tokens/second) with 512 training length and the inference speed (#queries/second) on MS MARCO document ranking dataset with max input length of 512 and 1,536. The results for the training throughput with different training batch sizes are shown in Fig. 1. The average inference speed over the queries from DL19 eval set is

Model	Size	Max. Length	Queries. per Second (↑)
BERT-large	330 M	512	0.65
BART-large	385 M	512	0.65
OPT-350M	350 M	512	**0.69**
Mamba-1-370M	370 M	512	0.53
Mamba-2-370M	370 M	512	0.56
OPT-350M	370 M	1536	**0.45**
Mamba-1-370M	370 M	1536	0.40
Mamba-2-370M	370 M	1536	**0.45**
OPT-1.3B	1.3 B	512	0.29
Llama-3.2-1B	1.3 B	512	**0.33**
Mamba-1-1.4B	1.4 B	512	0.25
Mamba-2-1.3B	1.3 B	512	0.30
OPT-1.3B	1.3 B	1536	0.28
Llama-3.2-1B	1.3 B	1536	**0.31**
Mamba-1-1.4B	1.4 B	1536	0.24
Mamba-2-1.3B	1.3 B	1536	0.29

Table 5: Inference speed of different models. We use half precision and batch size 32 for all models.

shown in Table 5.

First, observe that Mamba-2 has a much higher training throughput than Mamba-1. Additionally, since the Mamba-2 models are more memory efficient during training compared to Mamba-1, we do not notice an Out-Of-Memory (OOM) errors with Mamba-2 — Mamba-1-370M does not train with batch size 8. The throughput of Mamba models is significantly worse than that of the transformer-based models. In other words, the Mamba-based models are much less efficient at training time.

As highlighted in prior research (Waleffe et al., 2024; Gu and Dao, 2023, *inter alia*), the true benefit of the Mamba models is realized with an improved inference speed. We do not observe this to be the case for the document reranking task (see Table 5). The main reason is that for inference, reranking only requires one single forward computation compared to multiple forward computations in autoregressive generation. We further discuss the deficiency of Mamba models in § 4.6.

4.6 Profiling Inference Computation

To better understand the inference performance of Mamba models, we use the PyTorch profiler[4] to analyze the execution time of Mamba models at the operator level, comparing it to Transformer-based models of similar sizes. As in § 4.5, we use the DL19 document ranking evaluation set, an input length of 512, an evaluation batch size of 32, and the same hardware configuration. The results are presented in Fig. 2.

For Transformer-based models like OPT, I/O-related operators (e.g., `aten::copy_`, `aten::to`, `aten::_to_copy`, etc.) account for the majority of the execution time. Flash Attention (Dao, 2024) mitigates this by optimizing the I/O operations involved in attention computation, as seen in the reduced execution time for I/O-related operations in Figs. 2b and 2f. This optimization leads to a noticeable speedup in inference, highlighting the importance of improving I/O efficiency for Transformers.

In contrast, the total execution time of Mamba-1 is dominated by operators such as `aten::is_nonzero`, `aten::item`, and `aten::_local_scalar_dense`. The first operator, `aten::is_nonzero`, checks whether tensors contain any non-zero elements, while `aten::item` and `aten::_local_scalar_dense` are used to extract scalar values from tensors. This suggests that Mamba-1's architecture might suffer from computational inefficiencies due to an over-reliance on these scalar-extraction operations, which could be bottlenecking the performance. We hypothesize that these operations contribute to the model's overall computational deficiency, particularly in comparison to models that utilize more efficient tensor operations. Mamba-2 improves upon this by parameterizing the Mamba-2 block, allowing for more effective utilization of matrix multiplication. This change is reflected in the elimination of the aforementioned scalar-extraction operators, with the new operator `MambaSplitConv1D` now accounting for over half of the total execution time. Mamba-2's shift towards matrix multiplication suggests a more balanced computational load, although it still doesn't fully close the gap in terms of inference speed compared to Transformer models with Flash Attention. This empirical evidence points to the need for further architectural refinement to optimize performance and better leverage compute-optimized hardware.

5 Related Works

Text Ranking with Pre-trained Transformers. Fine-tuning pre-trained transformers has been the standard practice for text ranking tasks (Yates et al., 2021; Karpukhin et al., 2020, *inter alia*). Combining the query and the document as the input, the model predicts a scalar score indicating the

[4] https://pytorch.org/docs/stable/profiler.html

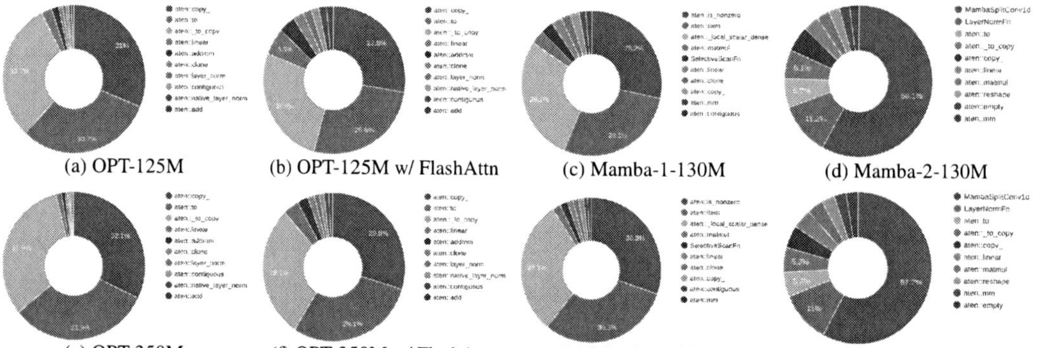

(a) OPT-125M (b) OPT-125M w/ FlashAttn (c) Mamba-1-130M (d) Mamba-2-130M

(e) OPT-350M (f) OPT-350M w/ FlashAttn (g) Mamba-1-370M (h) Mamba-2-370M

Figure 2: Inference profiling results for Mamba models versus OPT models of similar size.

relevance. Prior works have highlighted different aspects of training transformer-based text ranking models. Nogueira and Cho (2019); Nogueira et al. (2020); Dai and Callan (2019) are among the first efforts to showcase the effectiveness of fine-tuning pre-trained transformer-based language models. Gao et al. (2021) studied the retrieval-reranking pipeline and recommended training rerankers by sampling negatives from the results of first-stage retrievers. Li et al. (2023); Hofstätter et al. (2021) studied the effectiveness of chunking and pooling in long document ranking with shorter context transformer models. Boytsov et al. (2022) focused on benchmarking long context pre-trained transformers in long document ranking. Refer to (Yates et al., 2021; Xu et al., 2025) for detailed surveys.

Transformer Alternatives. Different works have explored transformer alternative model architectures for sequence modeling. For example, S4 (Gu et al., 2021b; Smith et al., 2022) demonstrate the effectiveness of structured state space models. Recent works (Peng et al., 2023; Yang et al., 2023, 2024; Qin et al., 2024, *inter alia*) have vastly improved the computational bottleneck of RNN-alike architectures and have shown comparable performance to modern transformer architectures at a moderate scale of comparison. We refer readers to these works for more details.

Within the IR community, works have explored the possibility of using state space models as retriever (Zhang et al., 2024) and reranker (Xu, 2024). This study extends prior works with more comprehensive experiments and points out new directions.

6 Conclusion and Future Work

This study investigates the suitability of Mamba architectures, a novel class of state space models, for text ranking. Our findings demonstrate that Mamba models, particularly Mamba-2, can achieve competitive performance compared to transformer-based models of comparable size, showcasing their potential as viable alternatives for sequence modeling in IR tasks. While Mamba architectures currently exhibit lower training and inference efficiency compared to transformers with flash attention, continuous advancements in model optimization and hardware acceleration have the potential to mitigate these limitations.

We picture two future directions of this work: the task direction and the model direction. From the task perspective, the efficacy of state space models, including Mamba should be further examined in other IR tasks (e.g., text retrieval). From the model perspective, hybrid models (Lieber et al., 2024; Lenz et al., 2024; Glorioso et al., 2024; Nvidia, 2025) have shown promise in certain NLP tasks. We believe the effectiveness of hybrid models should be thoroughly tested. Additionally, optimization for state space models is an interesting challenge that may offer substantial improvements.

Limitations and Potential Risks

This paper studies the efficacy of state space models in text ranking tasks. Our experiments are carried out by fine-tuning pre-trained language models, which differ in the pre-training corpus as well as pre-training FLOPs. Limited by hardware and budget, we are not able to carry out an apples-to-apples comparison with the exact same pre-training setup. We believe this leaves room for future direction.

This paper studies a well established task with publicly available datasets licensed for academic usage (see Appx. A). To the best of our knowledge this paper does not introduce potential risks.

Acknowledgements

This material is based upon work supported in part by NSF under grants 2007398, 2217154, 2318550, 2205418, and 2134223. This research is supported by the National Artificial Intelligence Research Resource (NAIRR) Pilot and the Delta advanced computing and data resource which is supported by the National Science Foundation (award NSF-OAC 2005572). Ashim Gupta is supported by the Bloomberg Data Science Ph.D. Fellowship. Any opinions, findings, and conclusions or recommendations expressed in this material are those of the authors and do not necessarily reflect the views of the sponsers.

References

Akari Asai, Jacqueline He, Rulin Shao, Weijia Shi, Amanpreet Singh, Joseph Chee Chang, Kyle Lo, Luca Soldaini, Sergey Feldman, Mike D'arcy, et al. 2024. Openscholar: Synthesizing scientific literature with retrieval-augmented lms. *arXiv preprint arXiv:2411.14199.*

Payal Bajaj, Daniel Campos, Nick Craswell, Li Deng, Jianfeng Gao, Xiaodong Liu, Rangan Majumder, Andrew McNamara, Bhaskar Mitra, Tri Nguyen, et al. 2016. Ms marco: A human generated machine reading comprehension dataset. *arXiv preprint arXiv:1611.09268.*

Alexander Bondarenko, Maik Fröbe, Meriem Beloucif, Lukas Gienapp, Yamen Ajjour, Alexander Panchenko, Chris Biemann, Benno Stein, Henning Wachsmuth, Martin Potthast, et al. 2020. Overview of touché 2020: argument retrieval. In *Experimental IR Meets Multilinguality, Multimodality, and Interaction: 11th International Conference of the CLEF Association, CLEF 2020, Thessaloniki, Greece, September 22–25, 2020, Proceedings 11*, pages 384–395. Springer.

Vera Boteva, Demian Gholipour, Artem Sokolov, and Stefan Riezler. 2016. A full-text learning to rank dataset for medical information retrieval. In *Advances in Information Retrieval: 38th European Conference on IR Research, ECIR 2016, Padua, Italy, March 20–23, 2016. Proceedings 38*, pages 716–722. Springer.

Leonid Boytsov, Tianyi Lin, Fangwei Gao, Yutian Zhao, Jeffrey Huang, and Eric Nyberg. 2022. Understanding performance of long-document ranking models through comprehensive evaluation and leaderboarding. *arXiv preprint arXiv:2207.01262.*

Kevin Clark, Minh-Thang Luong, Quoc V Le, and Christopher D Manning. 2020. Electra: Pre-training text encoders as discriminators rather than generators. In *International Conference on Learning Representations.*

Arman Cohan, Sergey Feldman, Iz Beltagy, Doug Downey, and Daniel S Weld. 2020. Specter: Document-level representation learning using citation-informed transformers. *arXiv preprint arXiv:2004.07180.*

Nick Craswell, Bhaskar Mitra, Emine Yilmaz, and Daniel Campos. 2021. Overview of the trec 2020 deep learning track. corr abs/2102.07662 (2021). *arXiv preprint arXiv:2102.07662.*

Nick Craswell, Bhaskar Mitra, Emine Yilmaz, Daniel Campos, and Ellen M Voorhees. 2020. Overview of the trec 2019 deep learning track. *arXiv preprint arXiv:2003.07820.*

Zhuyun Dai and Jamie Callan. 2019. Deeper text understanding for ir with contextual neural language modeling. In *Proceedings of the 42nd international ACM SIGIR conference on research and development in information retrieval*, pages 985–988.

Tri Dao. 2024. Flashattention-2: Faster attention with better parallelism and work partitioning. In *The Twelfth International Conference on Learning Representations.*

Tri Dao and Albert Gu. 2024. Transformers are SSMs: Generalized models and efficient algorithms through structured state space duality. In *Proceedings of the 41st International Conference on Machine Learning*, volume 235 of *Proceedings of Machine Learning Research*, pages 10041–10071. PMLR.

Jacob Devlin, Ming-Wei Chang, Kenton Lee, and Kristina Toutanova. 2019. BERT: Pre-training of deep bidirectional transformers for language understanding. In *Proceedings of the 2019 Conference of the North American Chapter of the Association for Computational Linguistics: Human Language Technologies, Volume 1 (Long and Short Papers)*, pages 4171–4186, Minneapolis, Minnesota. Association for Computational Linguistics.

Thomas Diggelmann, Jordan Boyd-Graber, Jannis Bulian, Massimiliano Ciaramita, and Markus Leippold. 2020. Climate-fever: A dataset for verification of real-world climate claims. *arXiv preprint arXiv:2012.00614.*

Abhimanyu Dubey, Abhinav Jauhri, Abhinav Pandey, Abhishek Kadian, Ahmad Al-Dahle, Aiesha Letman, Akhil Mathur, Alan Schelten, Amy Yang, Angela Fan, et al. 2024. The llama 3 herd of models. *arXiv preprint arXiv:2407.21783.*

Luyu Gao and Jamie Callan. 2022. Unsupervised corpus aware language model pre-training for dense passage retrieval. In *Proceedings of the 60th Annual Meeting of the Association for Computational Linguistics (Volume 1: Long Papers)*, pages 2843–2853.

Luyu Gao, Zhuyun Dai, and Jamie Callan. 2021. Rethink training of bert rerankers in multi-stage retrieval pipeline. In *Advances in Information Retrieval: 43rd European Conference on IR Research, ECIR 2021,*

Virtual Event, March 28–April 1, 2021, Proceedings, Part II 43, pages 280–286. Springer.

Paolo Glorioso, Quentin Anthony, Yury Tokpanov, James Whittington, Jonathan Pilault, Adam Ibrahim, and Beren Millidge. 2024. Zamba: A compact 7b ssm hybrid model. *arXiv preprint arXiv:2405.16712*.

Albert Gu and Tri Dao. 2023. Mamba: Linear-time sequence modeling with selective state spaces. *arXiv preprint arXiv:2312.00752*.

Albert Gu, Tri Dao, Stefano Ermon, Atri Rudra, and Christopher Ré. 2020. Hippo: Recurrent memory with optimal polynomial projections. *Advances in neural information processing systems*, 33:1474–1487.

Albert Gu, Karan Goel, and Christopher Re. 2021a. Efficiently modeling long sequences with structured state spaces. In *International Conference on Learning Representations*.

Albert Gu, Isys Johnson, Karan Goel, Khaled Saab, Tri Dao, Atri Rudra, and Christopher Ré. 2021b. Combining recurrent, convolutional, and continuous-time models with linear state space layers. *Advances in neural information processing systems*, 34:572–585.

Ankit Gupta, Albert Gu, and Jonathan Berant. 2022. Diagonal state spaces are as effective as structured state spaces. *Advances in Neural Information Processing Systems*, 35:22982–22994.

Ashim Gupta, Sina Mahdipour Saravani, P Sadayappan, and Vivek Srikumar. 2024. An empirical investigation of matrix factorization methods for pre-trained transformers. *arXiv preprint arXiv:2406.11307*.

Faegheh Hasibi, Fedor Nikolaev, Chenyan Xiong, Krisztian Balog, Svein Erik Bratsberg, Alexander Kotov, and Jamie Callan. 2017. Dbpedia-entity v2: a test collection for entity search. In *Proceedings of the 40th International ACM SIGIR Conference on Research and Development in Information Retrieval*, pages 1265–1268.

Sebastian Hofstätter, Bhaskar Mitra, Hamed Zamani, Nick Craswell, and Allan Hanbury. 2021. Intra-document cascading: learning to select passages for neural document ranking. In *Proceedings of the 44th International ACM SIGIR Conference on Research and Development in Information Retrieval*, pages 1349–1358.

Edward J Hu, Phillip Wallis, Zeyuan Allen-Zhu, Yuanzhi Li, Shean Wang, Lu Wang, Weizhu Chen, et al. 2021. Lora: Low-rank adaptation of large language models. In *International Conference on Learning Representations*.

Vladimir Karpukhin, Barlas Oguz, Sewon Min, Patrick Lewis, Ledell Wu, Sergey Edunov, Danqi Chen, and Wen-tau Yih. 2020. Dense passage retrieval for open-domain question answering. In *Proceedings of the 2020 Conference on Empirical Methods in Natural Language Processing (EMNLP)*, pages 6769–6781, Online. Association for Computational Linguistics.

Tom Kwiatkowski, Jennimaria Palomaki, Olivia Redfield, Michael Collins, Ankur Parikh, Chris Alberti, Danielle Epstein, Illia Polosukhin, Jacob Devlin, Kenton Lee, Kristina Toutanova, Llion Jones, Matthew Kelcey, Ming-Wei Chang, Andrew M. Dai, Jakob Uszkoreit, Quoc Le, and Slav Petrov. 2019. Natural questions: A benchmark for question answering research. *Transactions of the Association for Computational Linguistics*, 7:452–466.

Barak Lenz, Alan Arazi, Amir Bergman, Avshalom Manevich, Barak Peleg, Ben Aviram, Chen Almagor, Clara Fridman, Dan Padnos, et al. 2024. Jamba-1.5: Hybrid transformer-mamba models at scale. *arXiv preprint arXiv:2408.12570*.

Mike Lewis, Yinhan Liu, Naman Goyal, Marjan Ghazvininejad, Abdelrahman Mohamed, Omer Levy, Veselin Stoyanov, and Luke Zettlemoyer. 2020. BART: Denoising sequence-to-sequence pre-training for natural language generation, translation, and comprehension. In *Proceedings of the 58th Annual Meeting of the Association for Computational Linguistics*, pages 7871–7880, Online. Association for Computational Linguistics.

Canjia Li, Andrew Yates, Sean MacAvaney, Ben He, and Yingfei Sun. 2023. Parade: Passage representation aggregation fordocument reranking. *ACM Transactions on Information Systems*, 42(2):1–26.

Opher Lieber, Barak Lenz, Hofit Bata, Gal Cohen, Jhonathan Osin, Itay Dalmedigos, Erez Safahi, Shaked Meirom, Yonatan Belinkov, Shai Shalev-Shwartz, et al. 2024. Jamba: A hybrid transformer-mamba language model. *arXiv preprint arXiv:2403.19887*.

Yinhan Liu, Myle Ott, Naman Goyal, Jingfei Du, Mandar Joshi, Danqi Chen, Omer Levy, Mike Lewis, Luke Zettlemoyer, and Veselin Stoyanov. 2019. Roberta: A robustly optimized bert pretraining approach. *arXiv preprint arXiv:1907.11692*.

Xueguang Ma, Liang Wang, Nan Yang, Furu Wei, and Jimmy Lin. 2023. Fine-tuning llama for multi-stage text retrieval. *arXiv preprint arXiv:2310.08319*.

Macedo Maia, Siegfried Handschuh, André Freitas, Brian Davis, Ross McDermott, Manel Zarrouk, and Alexandra Balahur. 2018. Www'18 open challenge: financial opinion mining and question answering. In *Companion proceedings of the the web conference 2018*, pages 1941–1942.

Arvind Neelakantan, Tao Xu, Raul Puri, Alec Radford, Jesse Michael Han, Jerry Tworek, Qiming Yuan, Nikolas Tezak, Jong Wook Kim, Chris Hallacy, et al. 2022. Text and code embeddings by contrastive pre-training. *arXiv preprint arXiv:2201.10005*.

Jianmo Ni, Gustavo Hernandez Abrego, Noah Constant, Ji Ma, Keith Hall, Daniel Cer, and Yinfei Yang. 2022.

Sentence-t5: Scalable sentence encoders from pre-trained text-to-text models. In *Findings of the Association for Computational Linguistics: ACL 2022*, pages 1864–1874, Dublin, Ireland. Association for Computational Linguistics.

Rodrigo Nogueira and Kyunghyun Cho. 2019. Passage re-ranking with bert. *arXiv preprint arXiv:1901.04085*.

Rodrigo Nogueira, Zhiying Jiang, Ronak Pradeep, and Jimmy Lin. 2020. Document ranking with a pre-trained sequence-to-sequence model. In *Findings of the Association for Computational Linguistics: EMNLP 2020*, pages 708–718.

Rodrigo Nogueira, Wei Yang, Jimmy Lin, and Kyunghyun Cho. 2019. Document expansion by query prediction. *arXiv preprint arXiv:1904.08375*.

Nvidia. 2025. Nemotron-h: A family of accurate, efficient hybrid mamba-transformer models.

Adam Paszke, Sam Gross, Francisco Massa, Adam Lerer, James Bradbury, Gregory Chanan, Trevor Killeen, Zeming Lin, Natalia Gimelshein, Luca Antiga, et al. 2019. Pytorch: An imperative style, high-performance deep learning library. *Advances in neural information processing systems*, 32.

Bo Peng, Eric Alcaide, Quentin Anthony, Alon Albalak, Samuel Arcadinho, Stella Biderman, Huanqi Cao, Xin Cheng, Michael Chung, Leon Derczynski, Xingjian Du, Matteo Grella, Kranthi Gv, Xuzheng He, Haowen Hou, Przemyslaw Kazienko, Jan Kocon, Jiaming Kong, Bartłomiej Koptyra, Hayden Lau, Jiaju Lin, Krishna Sri Ipsit Mantri, Ferdinand Mom, Atsushi Saito, Guangyu Song, Xiangru Tang, Johan Wind, Stanisław Woźniak, Zhenyuan Zhang, Qinghua Zhou, Jian Zhu, and Rui-Jie Zhu. 2023. RWKV: Reinventing RNNs for the transformer era. In *Findings of the Association for Computational Linguistics: EMNLP 2023*, pages 14048–14077, Singapore. Association for Computational Linguistics.

Ronak Pradeep, Rodrigo Nogueira, and Jimmy Lin. 2021. The expando-mono-duo design pattern for text ranking with pretrained sequence-to-sequence models. *arXiv preprint arXiv:2101.05667*.

Zhen Qin, Songlin Yang, Weixuan Sun, Xuyang Shen, Dong Li, Weigao Sun, and Yiran Zhong. 2024. Hgrn2: Gated linear rnns with state expansion. *arXiv preprint arXiv:2404.07904*.

Colin Raffel, Noam Shazeer, Adam Roberts, Katherine Lee, Sharan Narang, Michael Matena, Yanqi Zhou, Wei Li, and Peter J Liu. 2020. Exploring the limits of transfer learning with a unified text-to-text transformer. *Journal of machine learning research*, 21(140):1–67.

Stephen E Robertson, Steve Walker, Susan Jones, Micheline M Hancock-Beaulieu, Mike Gatford, et al. 1995. Okapi at trec-3. *Nist Special Publication Sp*, 109:109.

Hinrich Schütze, Christopher D Manning, and Prabhakar Raghavan. 2008. *Introduction to information retrieval*, volume 39. Cambridge University Press Cambridge.

Jimmy TH Smith, Andrew Warrington, and Scott Linderman. 2022. Simplified state space layers for sequence modeling. In *The Eleventh International Conference on Learning Representations*.

Jianlin Su, Murtadha Ahmed, Yu Lu, Shengfeng Pan, Wen Bo, and Yunfeng Liu. 2024. Roformer: Enhanced transformer with rotary position embedding. *Neurocomputing*, 568:127063.

Nandan Thakur, Nils Reimers, Andreas Rücklé, Abhishek Srivastava, and Iryna Gurevych. 2021. Beir: A heterogeneous benchmark for zero-shot evaluation of information retrieval models.

James Thorne, Andreas Vlachos, Christos Christodoulopoulos, and Arpit Mittal. 2018. Fever: a large-scale dataset for fact extraction and verification. *arXiv preprint arXiv:1803.05355*.

Hugo Touvron, Louis Martin, Kevin Stone, Peter Albert, Amjad Almahairi, Yasmine Babaei, Nikolay Bashlykov, Soumya Batra, Prajjwal Bhargava, Shruti Bhosale, et al. 2023. Llama 2: Open foundation and fine-tuned chat models. *arXiv preprint arXiv:2307.09288*.

Ashish Vaswani, Noam Shazeer, Niki Parmar, Jakob Uszkoreit, Llion Jones, Aidan N Gomez, Łukasz Kaiser, and Illia Polosukhin. 2017. Attention is all you need. *Advances in neural information processing systems*, 30.

Ellen Voorhees, Tasmeer Alam, Steven Bedrick, Dina Demner-Fushman, William R Hersh, Kyle Lo, Kirk Roberts, Ian Soboroff, and Lucy Lu Wang. 2021. Trec-covid: constructing a pandemic information retrieval test collection. In *ACM SIGIR Forum*, volume 54, pages 1–12. ACM New York, NY, USA.

Henning Wachsmuth, Shahbaz Syed, and Benno Stein. 2018. Retrieval of the best counterargument without prior topic knowledge. In *Proceedings of the 56th Annual Meeting of the Association for Computational Linguistics (Volume 1: Long Papers)*, pages 241–251.

David Wadden, Shanchuan Lin, Kyle Lo, Lucy Lu Wang, Madeleine van Zuylen, Arman Cohan, and Hannaneh Hajishirzi. 2020. Fact or fiction: Verifying scientific claims. *arXiv preprint arXiv:2004.14974*.

Roger Waleffe, Wonmin Byeon, Duncan Riach, Brandon Norick, Vijay Korthikanti, Tri Dao, Albert Gu, Ali Hatamizadeh, Sudhakar Singh, Deepak Narayanan, et al. 2024. An empirical study of mamba-based language models. *arXiv preprint arXiv:2406.07887*.

Junxiong Wang, Daniele Paliotta, Avner May, Alexander Rush, and Tri Dao. 2024. The mamba in the llama: Distilling and accelerating hybrid models. *Advances in Neural Information Processing Systems*, 37:62432–62457.

Liang Wang, Nan Yang, Xiaolong Huang, Binxing Jiao, Linjun Yang, Daxin Jiang, Rangan Majumder, and Furu Wei. 2022. Simlm: Pre-training with representation bottleneck for dense passage retrieval. *arXiv preprint arXiv:2207.02578*.

T Wolf. 2019. Huggingface's transformers: State-of-the-art natural language processing. *arXiv preprint arXiv:1910.03771*.

Shitao Xiao, Zheng Liu, Peitian Zhang, and Niklas Muennighof. 2023. C-pack: Packaged resources to advance general chinese embedding. *arXiv preprint arXiv:2309.07597*.

Wenhan Xiong, Jingyu Liu, Igor Molybog, Hejia Zhang, Prajjwal Bhargava, Rui Hou, Louis Martin, Rashi Rungta, Karthik Abinav Sankararaman, Barlas Oguz, et al. 2024. Effective long-context scaling of foundation models. In *Proceedings of the 2024 Conference of the North American Chapter of the Association for Computational Linguistics: Human Language Technologies (Volume 1: Long Papers)*, pages 4643–4663.

Zhichao Xu. 2023. Context-aware decoding reduces hallucination in query-focused summarization. *arXiv preprint arXiv:2312.14335*.

Zhichao Xu. 2024. Rankmamba, benchmarking mamba's document ranking performance in the era of transformers. *arXiv preprint arXiv:2403.18276*.

Zhichao Xu and Daniel Cohen. 2023. A lightweight constrained generation alternative for query-focused summarization. In *Proceedings of the 46th International ACM SIGIR Conference on Research and Development in Information Retrieval*, pages 1745–1749.

Zhichao Xu, Daniel Cohen, Bei Wang, and Vivek Srikumar. 2024a. In-context example ordering guided by label distributions. In *Findings of the Association for Computational Linguistics: NAACL 2024*, pages 2623–2640, Mexico City, Mexico. Association for Computational Linguistics.

Zhichao Xu, Ashim Gupta, Tao Li, Oliver Bentham, and Vivek Srikumar. 2024b. Beyond perplexity: Multi-dimensional safety evaluation of LLM compression. In *Findings of the Association for Computational Linguistics: EMNLP 2024*, pages 15359–15396, Miami, Florida, USA. Association for Computational Linguistics.

Zhichao Xu, Hemank Lamba, Qingyao Ai, Joel Tetreault, and Alex Jaimes. 2023. Counterfactual editing for search result explanation. *arXiv preprint arXiv:2301.10389*.

Zhichao Xu, Hemank Lamba, Qingyao Ai, Joel Tetreault, and Alex Jaimes. 2024c. Cfe2: Counterfactual editing for search result explanation. In *Proceedings of the 2024 ACM SIGIR International Conference on Theory of Information Retrieval*, ICTIR '24, page 145–155, New York, NY, USA. Association for Computing Machinery.

Zhichao Xu, Fengran Mo, Zhiqi Huang, Crystina Zhang, Puxuan Yu, Bei Wang, Jimmy Lin, and Vivek Srikumar. 2025. A survey of model architectures in information retrieval. *arXiv preprint arXiv:2502.14822*.

Songlin Yang, Bailin Wang, Yikang Shen, Rameswar Panda, and Yoon Kim. 2023. Gated linear attention transformers with hardware-efficient training. *arXiv preprint arXiv:2312.06635*.

Songlin Yang, Bailin Wang, Yu Zhang, Yikang Shen, and Yoon Kim. 2024. Parallelizing linear transformers with the delta rule over sequence length. In *The Thirty-eighth Annual Conference on Neural Information Processing Systems*.

Zhilin Yang, Peng Qi, Saizheng Zhang, Yoshua Bengio, William W Cohen, Ruslan Salakhutdinov, and Christopher D Manning. 2018. Hotpotqa: A dataset for diverse, explainable multi-hop question answering. *arXiv preprint arXiv:1809.09600*.

Andrew Yates, Rodrigo Nogueira, and Jimmy Lin. 2021. Pretrained transformers for text ranking: Bert and beyond. In *Proceedings of the 14th ACM International Conference on web search and data mining*, pages 1154–1156.

Hanqi Zhang, Chong Chen, Lang Mei, Qi Liu, and Jiaxin Mao. 2024. Mamba retriever: Utilizing mamba for effective and efficient dense retrieval. In *Proceedings of the 33rd ACM International Conference on Information and Knowledge Management*, pages 4268–4272.

Susan Zhang, Stephen Roller, Naman Goyal, Mikel Artetxe, Moya Chen, Shuohui Chen, Christopher Dewan, Mona Diab, Xian Li, Xi Victoria Lin, et al. 2022. Opt: Open pre-trained transformer language models. *arXiv preprint arXiv:2205.01068*.

Yue Zhang, ChengCheng Hu, Yuqi Liu, Hui Fang, and Jimmy Lin. 2021. Learning to rank in the age of Muppets: Effectiveness–efficiency tradeoffs in multi-stage ranking. In *Proceedings of the Second Workshop on Simple and Efficient Natural Language Processing*, pages 64–73, Virtual. Association for Computational Linguistics.

Lianghui Zhu, Bencheng Liao, Qian Zhang, Xinlong Wang, Wenyu Liu, and Xinggang Wang. 2024. Vision mamba: Efficient visual representation learning with bidirectional state space model. In *Forty-first International Conference on Machine Learning*.

Honglei Zhuang, Zhen Qin, Rolf Jagerman, Kai Hui, Ji Ma, Jing Lu, Jianmo Ni, Xuanhui Wang, and Michael Bendersky. 2023. Rankt5: Fine-tuning t5 for text ranking with ranking losses. In *Proceedings of the 46th International ACM SIGIR Conference on Research and Development in Information Retrieval*, pages 2308–2313.

A Dataset Artifacts and Licenses

Four of the datasets we used in experiments (NF-Corpus (Boteva et al., 2016), FiQA-2018 (Maia et al., 2018), Quora[5], Climate-Fever (Diggelmann et al., 2020)) do not report the dataset license in the paper or a repository. For the rest of the datasets, we list their licenses below:

- MS MARCO (Bajaj et al., 2016): MIT License for non-commercial research purposes.
- ArguAna (Wachsmuth et al., 2018): CC BY 4.0 license.
- DBPedia (Hasibi et al., 2017): CC BY-SA 3.0 license.
- FEVER (Thorne et al., 2018): CC BY-SA 3.0 license.
- HotpotQA (Yang et al., 2018): CC BY-SA 4.0 license.
- NQ (Kwiatkowski et al., 2019): CC BY-SA 3.0 license.
- SCIDOCS (Cohan et al., 2020): GNU General Public License v3.0 license.
- SciFact (Wadden et al., 2020): CC BY-NC 2.0 license.
- TREC-COVID (Voorhees et al., 2021): "Dataset License Agreement".
- Touche-2020 (Bondarenko et al., 2020): CC BY 4.0 license.

B Additional Experiment Details

B.1 Complexity Analysis of State Space Model

We use the complexity analysis from (Dao and Gu, 2024). For details, refer to Section 6 of Dao and Gu (2024). Denote the sequence length as L and state size as N, which means size N per channel. We skip the #channel dimension (D) for ease of comparison. SSD structure used in Mamba-2 is able to achieve better training and inference complexity, as reflected in our experiments (Fig. 1 and Table 5).

[5]https://www.kaggle.com/c/quora-question-pairs

	Attention	SSM	SSD
State size	$O(L)$	$O(N)$	$O(N)$
Training FLOPs	$O(L^2N)$	$O(LN^2)$	$O(LN^2)$
Inference FLOPs	$O(LN)$	$O(N^2)$	$O(N^2)$
(Naive) memory	$O(L^2)$	$O(LN^2)$	$O(LN)$
Matrix multiplication	✓	✗	✓

Table 6: Complexity analysis between state space structure and attention.

B.2 Baselines

B.2.1 Sparse and Dense Retrieval Methods

For both document and passage retrieval, we include the classical BM25 baseline. For passage retrieval, bi-SimLM (Wang et al., 2022) is a competitive baseline that uses specialized pre-training with encoder-only transformer architecture for text retrieval task; GTR (Ni et al., 2022) is based on T5 (Raffel et al., 2020) architecture and is extensively fine-tuned for passage representations; BGE-large-en-v1.5 (Xiao et al., 2023) is based on BERT style encoder architecture and is fine-tuned with millions of synthetic query-passage pairs to achieve strong performance; OpenAI Ada2 (Neelakantan et al., 2022) is a proprietary embedding model developed by OpenAI; RepLlama (Ma et al., 2023) is based on Llama-2 language model (Touvron et al., 2023) and is fine-tuned on the training split of MS MARCO datasets. It achieves state-of-the-art performance on passage retrieval. For document retrieval, a common practice in literature is to segment long documents into several passages to fit into the 512 context length of BERT-style encoder-only transformer models. Each passage is scored individually and the relevance score of the document is an aggregation of individual passage's relevance scores. We include two such retrieval baselines: BM25-Q2D (Nogueira et al., 2019) uses the document expansion technique to enhance BM25's performance. CoCondenser-MaxP is based on CoCondenser technique (Gao and Callan, 2022) and uses max pooling for document relevance.

B.2.2 Reranking Methods

We include results from prior works as a comparison. For long document ranking, a common practice is to segment the long document into shorter passages and score them individually. For example, Dai and Callan (2019) referred to models only computing the relevance between query and the first document segment as FirstP, and methods that use the maximum relevance of passages within the document as the relevance of the document as

MaxP. We refer to document ranking models that based on long context language models as LongP following Boytsov et al. (2022).

For document ranking, we include BERT-base-FirstP and BERT-base-MaxP from Boytsov et al. (2022). We also include another MaxP baseline MonoT5 (Pradeep et al., 2021) and a state-of-the-art LongP model RankLlama (Ma et al., 2023).

For passage ranking, we include results of MonoBERT (Nogueira and Cho, 2019), cross-SimLM (Wang et al., 2022), MonoT5 (Nogueira et al., 2020) and more recent RankT5 (Zhuang et al., 2023) and RankLlama (Ma et al., 2023). An additional note is these ranking models are coupled with different first-stage retrievers and with different training strategies. We refer to RankT5 (Zhuang et al., 2023) for a comprehensive study of loss functions and training strategies involved in training ranking models.

C Retrieval Results

We show the passage retrieval results in Table 7 and document retrieval results in Table 8.

D Hyperparameter Setting

We show the hyperparameters in Table 9 and Table 10.

E Full BEIR Results

We refer the full results on BEIR to Table 11.

Model	Size	Embed. Dim.	Dev		DL19		DL20	
			MRR@10	Recall@1000	NDCG@10	Recall@1000	NDCG@10	Recall@1000
BM25	-	-	18.4	85.3	50.6	75.0	48.0	78.6
bi-SimLM	110M	768	39.1	98.6	69.8	-	69.2	-
GTR-base	110M	768	36.6	98.3	-	-	-	-
GTR-XXL	4.8B	768	38.8	99.0	-	-	-	-
BGE-large-en-v1.5	335M	1024	35.7	97.6	70.8	84.5	70.7	83.0
OpenAI Ada2	?	1536	34.4	98.6	70.4	**86.3**	67.6	**87.1**
RepLlama	7B	4096	**41.2**	**99.4**	**74.3**	-	**72.1**	-

Table 7: Passage retrieval performance of different retrieval models. We mark the best performance bold.

Model	Size	Seg. Y/N	Embed. Dim.	Dev		DL19		DL20	
				MRR@100	Recall@1000	NDCG@10	Recall@100	NDCG@10	Recall@100
BM25	-	N	-	27.7	93.6	52.3	38.5	50.6	58.6
BM25-Q2D	-	Y	-	32.7	95.5	59.7	**39.9**	58.5	**61.8**
CoCondenser-MaxP	110M	Y	768	42.5	93.9	64.8	-	**64.0**	-
RepLlama	7B	N	4096	**45.6**	**98.9**	**65.0**	-	63.2	-

Table 8: Document retrieval performance of different models. We mark the best performance bold.

Model	Size	Architecture	LR	Warmup	#Epochs	Global BZ	AMP	FlashAttn
***Encoder-only Models** (Bi-directional)*								
BERT-base	110M	Transformer	2e-5	10%	2	8	FP16	✗
RoBERTa-base	120M	Transformer	2e-5	10%	2	8	FP16	✗
ELECTRA-base	105M	Transformer	2e-5	10%	2	8	FP16	✗
BERT-large	330M	Transformer	1e-5	10%	2	8	FP16	✗
RoBERTa-large	335M	Transformer	1e-5	10%	2	8	FP16	✗
ELECTRA-large	320M	Transformer	1e-5	10%	2	8	FP16	✗
***Encoder-Decoder Models** (Bi-directional)*								
BART-base	130M	Transformer	2e-5	10%	2	8	FP16	✗
BART-large	385M	Transformer	1e-5	10%	2	8	FP16	✗
***Decoder-only Models** (Uni-directional)*								
OPT-125M	125M	Transformer	2e-5	10%	2	8	BF16	✓
Mamba-1-130M	130M	Mamba-1	2e-5	10%	2	8	BF16	✗
Mamba-2-130M	130M	Mamba-2	2e-5	10%	2	4	BF16	✗
OPT-350M	350M	Transformer	1e-5	10%	2	8	BF16	✓
Mamba-1-370M	370M	Mamba-1	1e-5	10%	2	4	BF16	✗
Mamba-2-370M	370M	Mamba-2	1e-5	10%	2	4	BF16	✗
Mamba-1-790M	790M	Mamba-1	1e-5	10%	1	4	BF16	✗
Mamba-2-780M	780M	Mamba-2	1e-5	10%	1	4	BF16	✗
OPT-1.3B	1.3B	Transformer	1e-5	10%	1	4	BF16	✓
Mamba-1-1.4B	1.4B	Mamba-1	1e-5	10%	1	4	BF16	✗
Mamba-2-1.3B	1.3B	Mamba-2	1e-5	10%	1	4	BF16	✗
Llama-3.2-1B	1.3B	Transformer++	1e-5	10%	1	4	BF16	✓

Table 9: Hyperparameters for passage reranking models. We use 10% of the total training steps for linear learning rate warmup. Global BZ denotes global batch size; AMP denotes automatic mixed precision, FlashAttn denotes whether Flash Attention 2 (Dao, 2024) is used.

Model	Size	Architecture	LR	Warmup	#Epochs	Global BZ	AMP	FlashAttn
Encoder-only Models *(Bi-directional)*								
BERT-base	110M	Transformer	2e-5	10%	2	8	FP16	✗
RoBERTa-base	120M	Transformer	2e-5	10%	2	8	FP16	✗
ELECTRA-base	105M	Transformer	2e-5	10%	2	8	FP16	✗
BERT-large	330M	Transformer	1e-5	10%	2	8	FP16	✗
RoBERTa-large	335M	Transformer	1e-5	10%	2	8	FP16	✗
ELECTRA-large	320M	Transformer	1e-5	10%	2	8	FP16	✗
Encoder-Decoder Models *(Bi-directional)*								
BART-base	130M	Transformer	2e-5	10%	2	8	FP16	✗
BART-large	385M	Transformer	1e-5	10%	2	8	FP16	✗
Decoder-only Models *(Uni-directional)*								
OPT-125M	125M	Transformer	2e-5	10%	2	8	BF16	✓
Mamba-1-130M	130M	Mamba-1	2e-5	10%	2	8	BF16	✗
Mamba-2-130M	130M	Mamba-2	2e-5	10%	2	4	BF16	✗
OPT-350M	350M	Transformer	1e-5	10%	2	8	BF16	✓
Mamba-1-370M	370M	Mamba-1	1e-5	10%	2	4	BF16	✗
Mamba-2-370M	370M	Mamba-2	1e-5	10%	2	4	BF16	✗
Mamba-1-790M	790M	Mamba-1	1e-5	10%	1	4	BF16	✗
Mamba-2-780M	780M	Mamba-2	1e-5	10%	1	4	BF16	✗
OPT-1.3B	1.3B	Transformer	1e-5	10%	1	4	BF16	✓
Mamba-1-1.4B	1.4B	Mamba-1	1e-5	10%	1	4	BF16	✗
Mamba-2-1.3B	1.3B	Mamba-2	1e-5	10%	1	4	BF16	✗
Llama-3.2-1B	1.3B	Transformer++	1e-5	10%	1	4	BF16	✓

Table 10: Hyperparameters for document reranking models. We use 10% of the total training steps for linear learning rate warmup. Global BZ denotes global batch size; AMP denotes automatic mixed precision, FlashAttn denotes whether Flash Attention 2 (Dao, 2024) is used. Note for LongP models, we additionally use gradient accumulation and/or activation checkpoint techniques to maintain a reasonably large global batch size. Mamba-1-1.4B gets OOM in FirstP setting; Mamba-1-1.4B and Mamba-2-1.3B get OOM in LongP setting with batch size 1 despite all optimization techniques at our hands.

Dataset	BM25 -	MonoT5 220M	RankT5 335M	RankLlama 7B	BERT-base 110M	BART-base 130M	RoBERTa-base 120M	ELECTRA-base 105M
Arguana	39.7	19.4	22.3	56.0	15.6	16.1	14.8	18.2
ClimateFever	16.5	24.5	20.6	28.0	16.9	16.6	17.8	20.3
DBPedia	31.8	41.9	43.5	48.3	38.5	42.5	42.1	42.1
FEVER	65.1	80.1	83.5	83.9	73.9	72.9	70.9	78.2
FiQA	23.6	41.3	41.6	46.5	34.6	38.4	36.4	40.1
HotpotQA	63.3	69.5	71.3	75.3	66.0	69.7	70.8	68.9
NFCorpus	32.2	35.7	32.6	30.3	29.3	32.7	26.1	29.9
NQ	30.6	56.7	59.6	66.3	45.2	48.6	49.6	50.1
Quora	78.9	82.3	82.2	85.0	75.8	75.3	74.8	79.3
SCIDOCS	14.9	16.4	18.2	17.8	16.1	15.8	15.4	17.1
SciFact	67.9	73.5	74.9	73.2	65.3	67.7	61.3	66.3
TREC-COVID	59.5	77.6	75.2	85.2	67.8	70.3	70.9	72.3
Touche-2020	44.2	27.7	45.9	40.1	30.7	33.2	30.1	33.3
Average	43.7	49.7	51.7	56.6	44.3	46.1	44.7	47.4

Dataset	OPT-125M 125M	Mamba-1-130M 130M	Mamba-2-130M 130M	BERT-large 330M	BART-large 385M	RoBERTa-large 335M	ELECTRA-large 320M	OPT-350M 350M
Arguana	10.1	32.8	33.8	19.5	18.0	15.4	14.6	21.0
ClimateFever	5.9	21.0	23.1	23.4	20.9	15.1	18.2	8.1
DBPedia	17.6	43.8	43.7	43.1	43.5	42.7	43.2	23.0
FEVER	9.5	76.6	76.3	79.5	77.5	71.9	76.8	19.8
FiQA	11.2	38.9	40.7	38.2	41.4	36.4	38.8	16.1
HotpotQA	31.7	72.2	72.8	70.2	71.9	66.8	68.6	48.1
NFCorpus	10.2	36.3	37.2	35.0	34.9	27.7	33.5	12.9
NQ	22.1	48.3	48.3	51.5	51.0	48.2	49.2	29.0
Quora	34.5	85.1	84.5	76.6	73.6	82.1	79.3	60.2
SCIDOCS	5.2	17.4	17.4	16.8	17.0	15.5	16.5	7.9
SciFact	9.7	72.2	73.0	68.8	65.7	55.4	65.9	28.6
TREC-COVID	51.9	75.9	79.0	68.0	70.6	70.8	67.2	57.3
Touche-2020	10.4	36.4	36.3	48.6	34.9	29.6	34.3	16.1
Average	17.7	50.5	51.2	49.2	47.8	44.4	46.6	26.8

Dataset	Mamba-1-370M 370M	Mamba-2-370M 370M	Mamba-1-790M 790M	Mamba-2-780M 780M	OPT-1.3B 1.3B	Llama-3.2-1B 1.3B	Mamba-1-1.4B 1.4B	Mamba-2-1.3B 1.3B
Arguana	33.3	34.8	34.4	33.7	35.7	32.7	33.1	34.4
ClimateFever	23.3	25.4	24.7	23.9	26.7	22.6	22.6	26.2
DBPedia	45.8	46.0	46.1	46.4	45.8	43.1	45.8	45.8
FEVER	76.5	79.1	81.8	80.4	83.0	72.9	80.9	81.9
FiQA	42.4	41.5	44.8	43.6	44.3	40.5	43.3	43.3
HotpotQA	75.7	75.0	75.6	76.2	74.9	69.2	75.8	76.3
NFCorpus	37.9	39.1	41.0	39.9	32.8	37.9	38.8	39.2
NQ	51.0	51.9	53.4	52.8	52.6	48.2	50.8	52.1
Quora	86.0	83.5	86.0	84.4	84.0	84.9	80.9	83.9
SCIDOCS	18.6	19.1	19.1	19.5	17.8	17.7	19.0	19.6
SciFact	75.2	76.0	77.7	77.1	72.7	71.7	77.4	76.8
TREC-COVID	82.7	81.2	82.7	85.1	81.6	77.0	83.0	79.9
Touche-2020	48.6	36.1	39.6	37.5	33.2	32.8	36.7	37.7
Average	53.6	53.0	54.4	53.9	52.7	50.1	52.9	53.6

Table 11: Full results for passage ranking out-of-domain evaluation.

Large Language Models Are Overparameterized Text Encoders

Thennal D K[1], Tim Fischer[2], Chris Biemann[2],

[1]IIIT Kottayam, [2]University of Hamburg
Correspondence: thennal10@gmail.com

Abstract

Large language models (LLMs) demonstrate strong performance as text embedding models when finetuned with supervised contrastive training. However, their large size balloons inference time and memory requirements. In this paper, we show that by pruning the last $p\%$ layers of an LLM before supervised training for only 1000 steps, we can achieve a proportional reduction in memory and inference time. We evaluate four different state-of-the-art LLMs on text embedding tasks and find that our method can prune up to 30% of layers with negligible impact on performance and up to 80% with only a modest drop. With only three lines of code, our method is easily implemented in any pipeline for transforming LLMs to text encoders. We also propose L^{3}Prune, a novel layer-pruning strategy based on the model's initial loss that provides two optimal pruning configurations: a large variant with negligible performance loss and a small variant for resource-constrained settings. On average, the large variant prunes 21% of the parameters with a -0.3 performance drop, and the small variant only suffers from a -5.1 decrease while pruning 74% of the model. We consider these results strong evidence that LLMs are overparameterized for text embedding tasks, and can be easily pruned.

1 Introduction

In the past few years, the field of natural language processing (NLP) has seen a significant shift towards large-scale language models (LLMs). These models, due to a combination of their large size, extensive pre-training, and instruction-following ability, have achieved state-of-the-art performance on a wide range of NLP tasks, such as language modeling, text generation, and text understanding (Dubey et al., 2024; Brown et al., 2020; Jiang et al., 2023a).

Despite their strong generative capabilities, decoder-only LLMs have seen comparatively little adoption for text embedding tasks until recently (BehnamGhader et al., 2024). Text embedding, which involves mapping a text sequence of varying length to a fixed-dimensional vector representation, is a fundamental task in NLP and is used as a building block for a wide range of downstream tasks, such as semantic textual similarity, information retrieval, text classification, and retrieval-augmented generation (Lewis et al., 2020).

Traditionally, text embedding models have been based on masked language models (MLMs) and bidirectional encoders, such as BERT (Devlin et al., 2019) and T5 (Raffel et al., 2020), typically adapted for text embedding tasks by following a multi-step training pipeline consisting of weakly- and fully-supervised contrastive training (Ni et al., 2022; Li et al., 2023a; Xiao et al., 2024a).

Decoder-only LLMs, however, offer several advantages over their encoder-only counterparts. They are more sample-efficient during pre-training, leverage instruction-following capabilities for task generalization, and benefit from a rich and evolving research ecosystem (Clark et al., 2020; Asai et al., 2023; BehnamGhader et al., 2024). Further, the availability of high-performing public pre-trained LLMs and their continual development make it appealing to explore their use for text embedding tasks. To this end, several studies have experimented with various pipelines, training methods, and architectural modifications, effectively converting LLMs into state-of-the-art text embedding models with small amounts of supervised contrastive training (BehnamGhader et al., 2024; Li and Li, 2024; Ma et al., 2024; Muennighoff, 2022; Springer et al., 2024; Lee et al., 2024).

On the other hand, the increasingly large size of LLMs, with parameters ranging up to 540B (Brown et al., 2020; Chowdhery et al., 2023; Dubey et al., 2024), stands in stark contrast to traditional small bidirectional encoders of sizes almost universally less than 1B parameters (Li et al., 2023a; Xiao et al.,

Proceedings of the 10th Workshop on Representation Learning for NLP (RepL4NLP-2025), pages 170–184

2024a). Even the smallest LLMs in use typically have 3-8B parameters (Abdin et al., 2024). Consequently, inference with LLM-based text encoders is far more demanding in terms of computing and memory requirements.

Therefore, there are a variety of post-training techniques for reducing the cost of LLMs, such as pruning, quantization, and distillation (Zhu et al., 2024). In particular, the recent work of Gromov et al. (2024) showed that LLMs can be pruned to up to half their size with minimal impact on downstream performance (i.e. question answering) by dropping the last half of the model's layers, with the exception of the final layer, and applying a small amount of parameter-efficient finetuning. Layer-dropping as a pruning strategy has particular benefits: it is straightforward to implement, with memory and inference time decreasing linearly with the number of layers dropped, and it can be combined with other efficiency methods such as quantization.

In this work, we build on these findings and apply them in the context of text embedding, resulting in an easy-to-use and efficient approach to transform any pre-trained decoder-only LLM into a much smaller text embedding model. By simply pruning the last $n\%$ layers of a model before supervised contrastive training, we reduce the final model size with a proportional decrease in memory and inference time. We experiment with four different decoder-only LLMs ranging from 3.8B to 8B parameters with a variety of pruning percentages and show that up to 30% of a model's layers may be pruned with almost no impact in performance and may even *increase* it. Even intensive pruning of up to 80% still provides reasonably effective text embedding models, with a drop in performance on the downstream embedding task from 64.9 to 59.8 for our highest-performing model.

Further, we propose **L^{3}Prune**, a simple and novel heuristic that pinpoints particular layers to prune to based on the initial loss without requiring significant testing or experimentation. With no input, our method produces both *a)* a lightly-pruned model, 69-89% of the original size with minimal performance loss of -0.2 on average and even a performance *improvement* in one model, and *b)* a heavily pruned model, 16-36% of their original size with a modest performance drop of -4.4 to -6.9.

Our contributions can be summarized as follows:

- We are the first to apply pruning in a text embedding setting, formulating a simple procedure that can be easily applied to pipelines converting an LLM to a text encoder.
- We demonstrate that LLMs can be pruned by up to 30% with negligible impact on the quality of representations and up to 80% with a modest performance drop.
- We propose and evaluate L^{3}Prune, a novel method that identifies layers to prune by leveraging the model's initial loss, minimizing the need for trial-and-error for effective pruning.

Overall, our work demonstrates that decoder-only LLMs are generally overparameterized for text embedding tasks and that significant reductions in model size can be achieved with minimal impact on performance. We release the full code for L^{3}Prune [1].

2 Related Work

2.1 Encoder-only Text Embedding Models

BERT-based models have largely dominated the field of text representation in the past, relying on supervised training with natural language inference or sentence similarity to produce high-quality sentence embeddings (Conneau et al., 2017; Reimers and Gurevych, 2019). Recent methods have further improved these representations through large-scale contrastive pretraining followed by multi-task fine-tuning (Ni et al., 2022; Wang et al., 2022; Li et al., 2023a; Xiao et al., 2024a). These methods generally require a complex multi-stage training pipeline that demands substantial engineering effort, along with large-scale compute-intensive pretraining (Zhang et al., 2024).

2.2 Decoder-only Text Embedding Models

Various recent works have explored leveraging LLMs and their capabilities to generate high-quality text representations. Generally, a combination of *(a)* a pooling method, *(b)* architectural modifications, and *(c)* supervised or unsupervised fine-tuning are used to effectively convert LLMs to text embedding models.

The majority of prior work considers two straightforward pooling strategies to extract embeddings for a sequence of tokens: mean pooling and last-token pooling (Springer et al., 2024, Jiang et al., 2023b; BehnamGhader et al., 2024; Muennighoff, 2022; Wang et al., 2024b). Mean

[1] https://github.com/thennal10/l3prune

pooling is more effective with bidirectional embedding models (BehnamGhader et al., 2024; Wang et al., 2022) while last-token pooling is generally preferred when working with causal attention (Lee et al., 2024; BehnamGhader et al., 2024). Muennighoff (2022) introduces weighted mean pooling, assigning a higher weight to later tokens to offset the autoregressive nature of decoder-only LLMs, with significant success. Lee et al. (2024) utilizes a trainable latent attention layer as a pooling technique and obtains consistent improvement.

Several studies identify the causal attention mechanism of decoder-only LLMs as an obstacle in obtaining performant representations and suggest modifications to the architecture to compensate. Li and Li (2024) and BehnamGhader et al. (2024) replace the causal attention mechanism with bidirectional attention. Muennighoff et al. (2024) utilizes a hybrid objective with both bidirectional representation learning and causal generation training. Lee et al. (2024) finds that simply removing the causal attention mask works compellingly well.

Finally, both supervised and unsupervised finetuning have been extensively explored to significantly improve the performance of decoder-only LLMs in representational tasks, with supervised training consistently producing the best results (BehnamGhader et al., 2024; Muennighoff, 2022; Jiang et al., 2023b). Several modifications to the training pipeline have been proposed, such as an additional masked token prediction training step (BehnamGhader et al., 2024), or a two-stage instruction-tuning setup (Lee et al., 2024). The zero-shot setting has also been studied with limited success by Springer et al. (2024) and Jiang et al. (2023b).

2.3 LLM Pruning

Pruning as a method of size reduction has a long history in the field of deep learning (Cheng et al., 2024). Classic pruning techniques sparsify networks by removing individual parameters based on various criteria (LeCun et al., 1990; Han et al., 2015). While these models were smaller, these techniques generally lead to irregular sparsification patterns that require specialized hardware or libraries to fully utilize. Structured pruning techniques were developed to remove irrelevant groups of parameters together, such as particular channels or filters in convolutional neural networks (Wen et al., 2016; Li et al., 2022).

Recent work has focused on applying structure pruning methods to transformers. Almost every possible component of the model architecture is studied as candidates for removal, most prominently methods that drop attention heads (Voita et al., 2019; Michel et al., 2019; Kim and Hassan, 2020) and layers (Fan et al., 2020; Zhang et al., 2022; Sajjad et al., 2023; Gromov et al., 2024; Men et al., 2024; Fan et al., 2024). Prior literature on layer pruning generally considers BERT-like models (Fan et al., 2020; Sajjad et al., 2023), with recent studies shifting focus to decoder-only LLMs (Gromov et al., 2024; Men et al., 2024; Fan et al., 2024).

Sajjad et al. (2023) finds that for BERT-like models, dropping the last layers is the best layer pruning strategy. Gromov et al. (2024) extends this research to decoder-only LLMs and presents a layer pruning strategy, pruning a block of layers based on angular distance between layer representations. Their results indicate that the last layer, in particular, is essential for maintaining performance. Informed by this finding, they propose a simpler strategy: dropping the last n layers except the final layer. They conclude that simply dropping the last layers works effectively to prune the model, with a caveat: after dropping the layers, it is required to "heal" the model via finetuning with QLoRA (Dettmers et al., 2023) for 1000 steps.

While these results suggest that the last layer, in particular, is essential when pruning LLMs for text generation, this is not necessarily the case when utilizing the LLM for other tasks. To this end, Fan et al. (2024) finds that for "simpler" tasks such as sentiment analysis, early stopping—stopping the inference after a certain number of layers—is an effective strategy to significantly reduce inference time with minimal impact on performance. The authors suggest that the later layers of LLMs, including the final layer, may not be necessary when using the LLM representations for other tasks.

3 Pruning

We borrow the intuition from Gromov et al. (2024), that the representations in a transformer can be thought of as a slowly changing function of the layer index. Specifically, the representation can be formulated as the following iterative residual equation:

$$x^{(\ell+1)} = x^{(\ell)} + f(x^{(\ell)}, \theta^{(\ell)}), \quad (1)$$

where $x^{(\ell)}, \theta^{(\ell)}$, respectively, are the multi-dimensional input and parameter vectors for layer ℓ, and $f(x, \theta)$ describes the transformation of one multi-head self-attention and MLP layer block.

The authors assert that these representations converge to a slowly changing function:

$$x^{(\ell)} \approx x^{(\ell-1)} + \epsilon \quad (2)$$

with $\epsilon \ll x^{\ell}$ as an approximation. They verify this hypothesis experimentally by calculating the distance between layer representations and using them for a pruning algorithm. Their findings indicate that the earlier layers have a significantly larger impact on the representation compared to the later layers, with a particular caveat: the final layer also modifies the representation significantly. Thus, they propose and verify a simpler pruning strategy, where the last n layers of the model, excluding the final layer, are dropped. This method requires a "healing" step, recovering the downstream performance with a few QLoRA finetuning steps (Dettmers et al., 2023).

Our hypothesis extends theirs and posits that for the text embedding task, the final layer is also not necessary. Our pruning experiments are conducted with the percentage pruned p, between 0% (all layers intact) and 100% (all layers removed). Given a pruning percentage and a total number of layers n, the new number of layers n^* is calculated as

$$n^* = \lfloor n \times (1 - p) \rfloor$$

Given a model and its configuration, this straightforward procedure can be integrated with modern LLM implementations with just three lines of code:

```
n = int(config.num_hidden_layers * (1-p))
model.layers = model.layers[:n]
config.num_hidden_layers = n
```

We then conduct supervised contrastive training, as with prior work on converting LLMs to text encoders. Instead of an explicit healing step, we hypothesize that the aforementioned training acts as such. Thus, no additional or separate training is necessary to execute our method.

4 Experiments

4.1 General Setup

For our experiments, we chose four instruct-tuned decoder-only LLMs across different families ranging from 3.7B to 7.5B: LLaMA-3-8B (`Meta-Llama-3-8B-Instruct`, Dubey et al., 2024), Mistral-7B (`Mistral-7B-Instruct-v0.2`, Jiang et al., 2023a), Qwen2-7B (`Qwen2-7B-Instruct`, Yang et al., 2024), and Phi3-4B (`Phi-3-mini-4k-instruct`, Abdin et al., 2024). These model families were chosen due to their widespread use in open-source communities and LLM literature. As we are conducting pruning and are only concerned with its effects, we pick the smallest model available in each family, and we opt for no modification to the LLM architecture itself. We use weighted mean pooling (Muennighoff, 2022) to generate embeddings from the outputs of the LLM as it is straightforward to implement and outperforms other pooling measures when paired with causal attention (Muennighoff, 2022; BehnamGhader et al., 2024).

We also conduct supervised contrastive finetuning, known to outperform unsupervised finetuning and the zero-shot setting, and considered to be an integral part of effectively utilizing LLMs as embedding models (BehnamGhader et al., 2024; Muennighoff, 2022; Jiang et al., 2023b). We use the replication of the public portion of the E5 dataset (Wang et al., 2024b), curated by Springer et al. (2024), as the training dataset. Consisting of approximately 1.5 million samples, it is a multilingual compilation of various retrieval datasets meant for supervised contrastive training of embedding models. In accordance, we use contrastive loss with hard negatives and in-batch negatives (Springer et al., 2024; BehnamGhader et al., 2024). Further details on the dataset and training are provided in Appendix A.

All experiments were conducted on a single A100 (80GB) GPU, reinforcing the accessible nature of our proposed procedure.

4.2 Zero-shot Loss Evolution Over Layers

As a preliminary test of our hypothesis—that an LLM can form performant text representations even before reaching the final layer—we first calculate how well the output of each layer of the model performs as an embedding. We note that this is equivalent to a zero-shot setting. As we are interested in a comparative measure between layers intra-model, the loss as a metric is sufficient. We take a random sampling of 1280 tuples from the training dataset and calculate the embeddings via weighted mean pooling of the outputs of each layer. Then, the loss is calculated and averaged per layer. We find that the loss values converge fairly quickly,

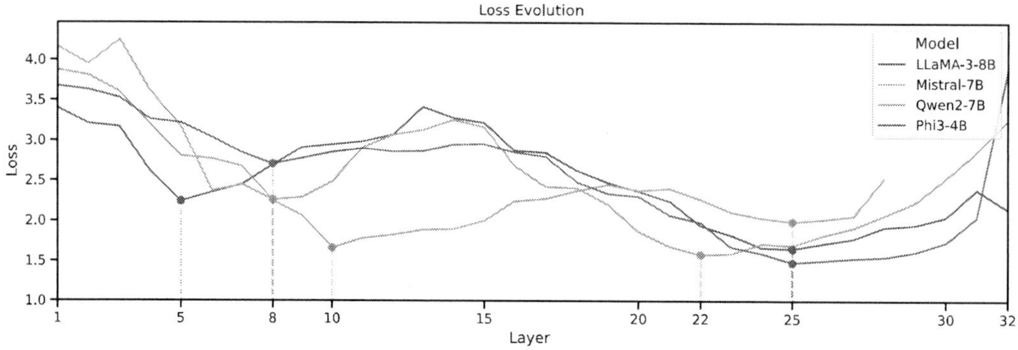

Figure 1: For each layer of an unmodified model, we compute the loss on 1280 randomly sampled examples from the training dataset. The marked points indicate the layer with minimal loss before and after the midpoint.

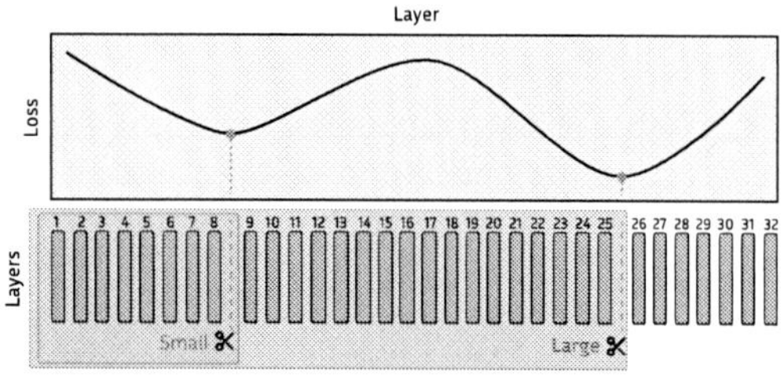

Figure 2: A simplified illustration of L^{3}Prune. The initial loss of the representation of each layer is found, and the two minima before and after 50% of the model correspond to the layers to prune to in the two configurations, `small` and `large`.

so 1280 samples are sufficient for our purposes. The results are aggregated in Figure 1.

The loss for all four models follows a similar curve: an initial drop to around layer 5-10, a subsequent rise around layer 15, and a slower drop up to layer 22-25, where it rises again by the end with layer 28-32. While the specifics of how LLM representations evolve are not well understood, these results suggest that the early layers of the model are generally focused on representation. In contrast, the final layers transform the representation into the specific probability distribution for the next token. Regardless of the underlying dynamics, the drop-rise-drop curve is consistent across model sizes and families in our experiments.

We expect that training will considerably transform the shape of this layerwise evolution. We also have little reason to expect that the final downstream performance of layer-dropped models will be accurately modeled by the effectiveness of these initial representations. However, we posit that these initial loss curves also reveal optimal starting points for pruning. The minima of these curves indicate layers where the text embeddings are best optimized, making them good candidates for pruning without significant performance loss.

Inspired by these findings, we consider the following heuristic for pruning: find the two minima in the layer-loss curve before and after 50% of the layers (the low point of the two drops). We hypothesize that pruning up to these layers provides us with two models: a smaller model with degraded but reasonable performance and a larger model whose performance is close to the original. This procedure would thus produce two text embedding model variants from an LLM, each usable in different circumstances. The two aforementioned models are termed `large` and `small` in the following sections. We term this method **LLM** **L**ayerwise **L**oss **P**runing, or **L^{3}Prune** for short. Figure 2 shows a simple illustration of the process.

4.3 Supervised Training

To verify the general efficacy of our hypothesis—that LLMs can form effective text representations even before reaching their deeper layers—we conduct training on pruned LLMs to convert them into effective text encoders. We keep the training procedure fairly straightforward: supervised contrastive learning for 1000 steps with LoRA modules (Hu et al., 2022). Other hyperparameters are detailed in Appendix A.2. We first test a range of pruning percentages from 10% to 90% at 10% intervals. Figure 3 shows the training loss for all models and pruning percentages. We note that the training loss curves all generally follow the same shape, indicating stability in training even with the modified architecture.

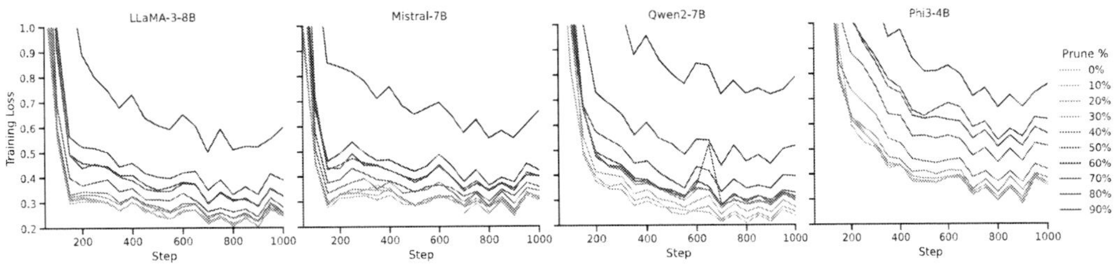

Figure 3: The training loss curves for each model at different pruning percentages.

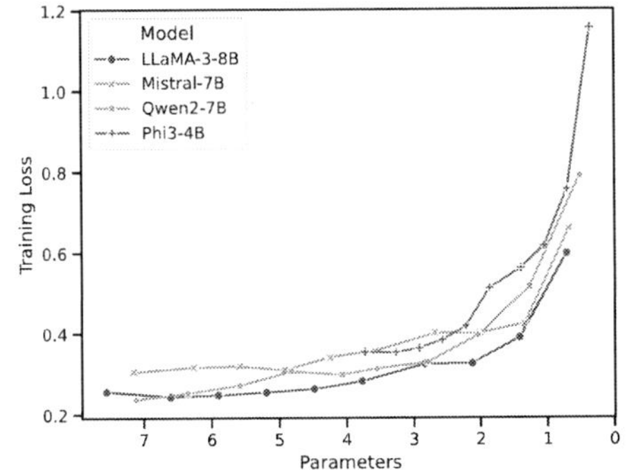

Figure 4: The final loss values at the end of training across different pruning percentages.

Figure 4 shows the final loss in relation to the pruned model parameters, with each marked point representing a model pruned by an additional 10%. The final loss values for each model follow a straightforward trajectory with increasing pruning percentage: minimal increases up to 30-40%, with larger increases as the pruning percentage hits 90%. Notably, we find that the final loss of different models correlates more with the final parameter count after pruning than with the percentage of layers retained. This suggests that the parameter count is a more significant factor in determining the effectiveness of a pruned model than simply the proportion of layers kept.

If we presume that training loss correlates well with downstream accuracy for text embedding, we can make a series of predictions from an analysis of the plots:

- Performance always degrades sharply as the parameter count approaches and goes below 1 billion.
- In contrast, performance degrades little even with 30-50% pruning. LLaMA-3-8B degrades minimally up to 40-50%, Mistral-7B up to 30-40%, and Phi3-4B up to 20-30%. Qwen2-7B degrades more at low pruning percentages, but remains stable between 30-60%.
- Even at high pruning percentages, model performance degrades at a reasonable rate. Models can likely be pruned up to 2 billion parameters while still producing viable embeddings.

4.4 Simple Pruning Evaluation

To validate the predictions made from the training loss, we evaluate the models at various pruning percentages on downstream text embedding tasks. Specifically, to speed up evaluation, we opt for the 15-task subset of the Massive Text Embedding Benchmark (MTEB, Muennighoff et al., 2023) collected and used by BehnamGhader et al. (2024). The subset, which we term MTEB-15 for clarity, covers representative tasks from the full 56 tasks in MTEB, including tasks from each category with almost the same proportion to prevent bias. Further details are provided in Appendix B.1.

In accordance with previous work (BehnamGhader et al., 2024; Springer et al., 2024; Wang et al., 2024b), we evaluate with task-specific instructions. We use the same instructions as Wang et al. (2024b), which can be found in Appendix Table 4. Following BehnamGhader et al. (2024), for symmetric tasks, the same instruction is used for the query and the document. Instruction tokens are excluded from the final pooling.

Figure 5 shows the impact of pruning on MTEB-15 results across a range of pruning percentages. We plot with respect to the number of parameters as opposed to relative pruning percentages because parameter count correlates better with the score. We can see that the training loss and MTEB-15 score also roughly correlate. This confirms that our predictions in Section 4.3, based on the supervised training loss, are fairly accurate.

LLama at 50% pruning (3.77B) is only degraded by -1.89, still providing a strong performance of 63.10. Even at 80% pruning (1.41B), it performs

	LLaMA-3-8B		Mistral-7B		Qwen2-7B		Phi3-4B		BGE	GTE	E5
	Large	**Small**	**Large**	**Small**	**Large**	**Small**	**Large**	**Small**	-	-	-
Layers	25 (-7)	5 (-27)	22 (-10)	8 (-24)	25 (-3)	10 (-18)	25 (-7)	8 (-24)	24	24	24
Params	5.9 (78%)	1.18 (16%)	4.92 (69%)	1.79 (25%)	6.35 (89%)	2.54 (36%)	2.91 (78%)	0.93 (25%)	0.36	0.36	0.36
Score	63.5 (-1.5)	58.1 (-6.9)	63.1 (-0.1)	59.0 (-4.2)	64.5 (+0.3)	60.9 (-3.3)	61.7 (-0.1)	55.5 (-6.3)	61.6	57.1	61.3

Table 1: Comparison of `large` and `small` variants across various models, including number of layers, parameters, and MTEB scores. Changes from the full model are provided in parentheses. The encoder-only models BGE, GTE, and E5 are also provided as a baseline.

at a reasonable 59.69. Mistral's performance decrease is an almost negligible -0.08 up to 30% (4.91B). Qwen's performance *increases* by +0.32 with a pruning of 10%. It drops distinctly at 30% pruning. However, it stabilizes at a reasonable 61.51 up to 60% (2.79B). Phi degrades negligibly up to 20% pruning (2.91B) with -0.03, and -0.53 at 30% (2.56B). Higher pruning percentages degrade it significantly as the model parameter count decreases below the 2 billion mark.

Our results correspond roughly with those of Gromov et al. (2024): sharp transitions in performance around 45%-55% for models in the Llama family, 35% for Mistral, 25% for Phi, and 20% for Qwen. However, instead of a sharp transition to near-random performance, we observe a steady but reasonable decline even at higher pruning percentages. In general, we only observe a significant decline in performance as model size goes below roughly 2 billion parameters. These results also correlate roughly with previous findings by Jiang et al. (2023b), who investigated LLM-based sentence embedding models between 125M to 66B parameters and found diminishing returns at parameter counts over 2B.

We can derive some general insights from these experiments. For one, the resilience of a model to pruning is not entirely consistent across families and sizes. Thus, model-specific experimentation may be required. However, in general, models can be pruned 10-30% with minimal drop in downstream performance. Further, higher pruning percentages up to 80% still yield reasonably effective embedding models.

We note that LLaMa-3-8B at 50% pruning, with 3.77B parameters, outperforms an unpruned Phi3-4B at 3.73B parameters. In conjunction with our other results, we suggest that, given a compute/memory budget, simply dropping layers of a high-performing LLM may be a superior and significantly simpler strategy than training a smaller LM that fits the budget.

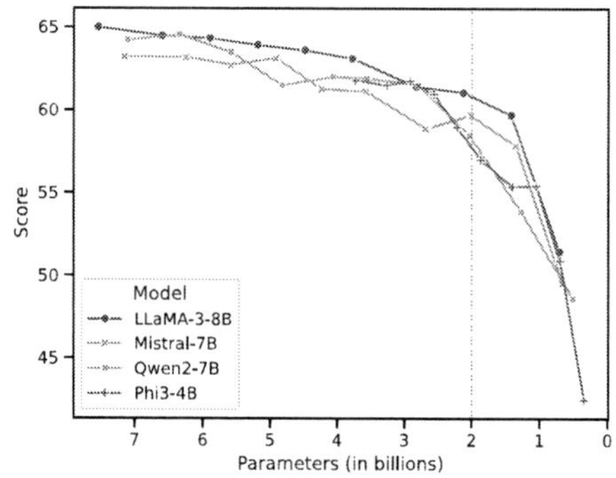

Figure 5: The MTEB (15 task subset) scores with respect to the number of model parameters.

4.5 L^{3}Prune Evaluation

As mentioned in Section 4.2, we hypothesize that the minima in the layer-loss curve before and after the midpoint are particularly effective points for pruning. We prune to those particular layers and conduct the same training and evaluation as described in Sections 4.3 and 4.4. Table 1 aggregates the results across base models for the two resulting prune configurations, termed `small` and `large`, along with three well-known encoder-only models as a baseline (see Section 4.6. It also shows the particular layer numbers and parameter counts.

The results are consistent with our previous findings. The `small` models generally perform worse than the full-sized models, with performance drops ranging between -4.4 and -6.9. However, at 16%-36% of their original size (84%-64% pruning), the models are proportionally compute- and memory-efficient in exchange for the dropped performance. The `large` models, on the other hand, perform almost as well as the unpruned models, with only a slight drop in performance, while pruned to 69%-89% (31%-11% pruning). As we have seen before, Qwen2-7B's performance *increases* slightly with pruning, and both Mistral-7B and Phi3-4B's performance drops are negligible. LLaMA-3-8B's performance drops by -1.4 points but still remains a fairly strong 63.5.

Combined with the results from Section 4.4, we can see that the layers picked by L^{3}Prune are generally optimal. For instance, Mistral-7B, Qwen2-7B, and Phi3-4B show strong performances up to 30%, 10%, and 20% pruning, respectively, and the layers corresponding to those pruning percentages are exactly the layers pinpointed by L^{3}Prune for the `large` variant. As LLaMa-3-8B's performance decrease remains fairly consistent when pruning below 50%, we infer that there is no particularly optimal point for pruning. Similarly, the `small` variants are pruned up to the point before each model's performance drops drastically—roughly 85% for LLAMA-3-8B, 75% for Mistral-7B, 65% for Qwen2-7B, and 75% for Phi3-4B.

Based on these results, we can conclude that the layerwise loss evolution of a model can be used to effectively pick optimal points for pruning. The resulting variants can be used to provide a range of models with different performance and efficiency trade-offs. The `large` models are particularly effective, with a negligible drop (or even an increase) in performance for a significant size reduction. The `small` models can be used for resource-constrained settings with reasonable performance.

We further note that the training of the `small` variants required only 23.6 GB of VRAM at maximum, and the layerwise loss curves can be calculated with less than 17 GB of VRAM. The training is only conducted for 1000 steps and takes less than an hour on average using an A100 GPU. Thus, `small` variant models can be trained on consumer-grade GPUs, making it accessible to open-source and practitioner communities. Further details on training times are given in Appendix A.3.

4.6 Baseline Comparison to Existing Encoder-Only Models

Table 1 also includes the MTEB-15 scores of three high-performing encoder-only embedding models: BGE (`bge-large-en`, Xiao et al., 2024b), GTE (`gte-large`, Li et al., 2023b), and E5 (`e5-large`, Wang et al., 2024a). These models are among the top-performing models with less than 1B parameters on the HuggingFace MTEB Leaderboard, and we evaluated them on our reduced MTEB-15 subset. All the pruned `large` models perform better than the encoder-only models, but the `small` models generally perform on par or worse. As the encoder-only models are significantly smaller, they would indeed be a better choice in a resource-constrained setting. However, we note that these models require long, complex, and computationally intensive multi-stage training pipelines. The E5 model, for instance, requires a contrastive pre-training phase consisting of 20,000 steps with a batch size of 32,768, requiring 64 V100 GPUs and 2 days of training time (Wang et al., 2024a). Li et al., 2023a similarly apply a contrastive pretraining stage for training the GTE model, with 50,000 steps and a batch size of 16,384 on 8 A100 (80GB) GPUs. The BGE model is trained with a three-stage pipeline, with large-scale pre-training using a batch size of 19,200, followed by general-purpose finetuning and task-specific fine-tuning (Xiao et al., 2024b).

In contrast, given an already available LLM, our method can produce a small and reasonably effective pruned embedding model with just an hour of training on a single A100 (80GB) GPU, and will theoretically work with a single V100 (24GB) GPU. Further, our methods scale well with advancements in LLM technology, and the generality of our method allows it to be quickly adapted to any new decoder-only architecture or LLM-to-embedding pipeline.

5 Conclusion

In this work, we presented a simple and effective pruning approach to convert LLMs into lightweight, performant text embedding models. By dropping the last $p\%$ layers of the model, we achieved significant reductions in model size and inference time, with minimal impact on text embedding tasks. Our procedure is straightforward to implement in pipelines converting LLMs to text encoders and requires no additional training, providing smaller models at no cost. Based on the initial model loss, we also proposed L^{3}Prune, a heuristic to pinpoint optimal layers to prune to, providing an efficient strategy for pruning without extensive experimentation. We demonstrated that significant pruning—up to 31%—can be conducted with a negligible performance loss, and substantial pruning—up to 84%—can still produce effective models. Overall, our results show that decoder-only LLMs are overparameterized for text embedding tasks and can be pruned with minimal performance loss.

6 Limitations

Our work only considers the supervised finetuning setting for utilizing LLMs as text encoders, as this is the most common and generally effective. Further, our results may not hold with extensive modifications to the architecture or training process or on models larger than 8 billion parameters. Lastly, even with extensive pruning, our smallest models are still generally larger than traditionally trained encoder-only models. However, as we mention in Section 4.6, these models require a complex and computationally expensive training procedure, in contrast to inexpensive parameter-efficient finetuning required for LLM-based models.

7 Ethical Considerations

Our work provides an effective and efficient method to produce optimized text embedding models from LLMs. As we mentioned in Section 4.5, our method is memory and compute-efficient. It can be conducted on consumer-grade GPUs, making it accessible to a wider audience of practitioners and academics. However, this also enhances potential misuse issues, lowering the bar for malicious actors to train and host embedding models. Regardless, embedding models, in general, have significantly fewer avenues for malicious behavior in comparison to, e.g., generative LLMs.

References

Marah Abdin, Sam Ade Jacobs, Ammar Ahmad Awan, Jyoti Aneja, Ahmed Awadallah, Hany Awadalla, Nguyen Bach, Amit Bahree, Arash Bakhtiari, Jianmin Bao, et al. 2024. Phi-3 technical report: A highly capable language model locally on your phone. *Preprint*, arXiv:2404.14219.

Akari Asai, Timo Schick, Patrick Lewis, Xilun Chen, Gautier Izacard, Sebastian Riedel, Hannaneh Hajishirzi, and Wen-tau Yih. 2023. Task-aware retrieval with instructions. In *Findings of the Association for Computational Linguistics: ACL 2023*, pages 3650–3675, Toronto, Canada. Association for Computational Linguistics.

Payal Bajaj, Daniel Campos, Nick Craswell, Li Deng, Jianfeng Gao, Xiaodong Liu, Rangan Majumder, Andrew McNamara, Bhaskar Mitra, Tri Nguyen, Mir Rosenberg, Xia Song, Alina Stoica, Saurabh Tiwary, and Tong Wang. 2018. MS MARCO: A human generated machine reading comprehension dataset. *Preprint*, arXiv:1611.09268.

Parishad BehnamGhader, Vaibhav Adlakha, Marius Mosbach, Dzmitry Bahdanau, Nicolas Chapados, and Siva Reddy. 2024. LLM2vec: Large language models are secretly powerful text encoders. In *First Conference on Language Modeling*, Pennsylvania, United States.

Samuel R. Bowman, Gabor Angeli, Christopher Potts, and Christopher D. Manning. 2015. A large annotated corpus for learning natural language inference. In *Proceedings of the 2015 Conference on Empirical Methods in Natural Language Processing*, pages 632–642, Lisbon, Portugal. Association for Computational Linguistics.

Tom Brown, Benjamin Mann, Nick Ryder, Melanie Subbiah, Jared D Kaplan, Prafulla Dhariwal, Arvind Neelakantan, Pranav Shyam, Girish Sastry, Amanda Askell, et al. 2020. Language models are few-shot learners. In *Advances in Neural Information Processing Systems*, volume 33, pages 1877–1901. Curran Associates, Inc.

Hongrong Cheng, Miao Zhang, and Javen Qinfeng Shi. 2024. A survey on deep neural network pruning: Taxonomy, comparison, analysis, and recommendations. *IEEE Transactions on Pattern Analysis and Machine Intelligence*, pages 1–20.

Aakanksha Chowdhery, Sharan Narang, Jacob Devlin, Maarten Bosma, Gaurav Mishra, Adam Roberts, Paul Barham, Hyung Won Chung, Charles Sutton, Sebastian Gehrmann, et al. 2023. PaLM: Scaling language modeling with pathways. *Journal of Machine Learning Research*, 24(240):1–113.

Kevin Clark, Minh-Thang Luong, Quoc V. Le, and Christopher D. Manning. 2020. Electra: Pre-training text encoders as discriminators rather than generators. In *International Conference on Learning Representations*, Addis Ababa, Ethiopia.

Alexis Conneau, Douwe Kiela, Holger Schwenk, Loïc Barrault, and Antoine Bordes. 2017. Supervised learning of universal sentence representations from natural language inference data. In *Proceedings of the 2017 Conference on Empirical Methods in Natural Language Processing*, pages 670–680, Copenhagen, Denmark. Association for Computational Linguistics.

Tri Dao. 2024. FlashAttention-2: Faster attention with better parallelism and work partitioning. In *The Twelfth International Conference on Learning Representations*, Vienna, Austria.

Tim Dettmers, Artidoro Pagnoni, Ari Holtzman, and Luke Zettlemoyer. 2023. Qlora: Efficient finetuning of quantized llms. In *Advances in Neural Information Processing Systems*, volume 36, pages 10088–10115, Louisiana, United States. Curran Associates, Inc.

Jacob Devlin, Ming-Wei Chang, Kenton Lee, and Kristina Toutanova. 2019. BERT: Pre-training of deep bidirectional transformers for language understanding. In *Proceedings of the 2019 Conference of the North American Chapter of the Association for*

Computational Linguistics: Human Language Technologies, Volume 1 (Long and Short Papers), pages 4171–4186, Minneapolis, Minnesota. Association for Computational Linguistics.

Abhimanyu Dubey, Abhinav Jauhri, Abhinav Pandey, Abhishek Kadian, Ahmad Al-Dahle, Aiesha Letman, Akhil Mathur, Alan Schelten, Amy Yang, Angela Fan, et al. 2024. The Llama 3 herd of models. *Preprint*, arXiv:2407.21783.

Angela Fan, Edouard Grave, and Armand Joulin. 2020. Reducing transformer depth on demand with structured dropout. In *International Conference on Learning Representations*, Addis Ababa, Ethiopia.

Angela Fan, Yacine Jernite, Ethan Perez, David Grangier, Jason Weston, and Michael Auli. 2019. ELI5: Long form question answering. In *Proceedings of the 57th Annual Meeting of the Association for Computational Linguistics*, pages 3558–3567, Florence, Italy. Association for Computational Linguistics.

Siqi Fan, Xin Jiang, Xiang Li, Xuying Meng, Peng Han, Shuo Shang, Aixin Sun, Yequan Wang, and Zhongyuan Wang. 2024. Not all layers of llms are necessary during inference. *Preprint*, arXiv:2403.02181.

Andrey Gromov, Kushal Tirumala, Hassan Shapourian, Paolo Glorioso, and Daniel A. Roberts. 2024. The unreasonable ineffectiveness of the deeper layers. *Preprint*, arXiv:2403.17887.

Song Han, Jeff Pool, John Tran, and William Dally. 2015. Learning both weights and connections for efficient neural network. In *Advances in Neural Information Processing Systems*, volume 28, Montréal, Canada. Curran Associates, Inc.

Wei He, Kai Liu, Jing Liu, Yajuan Lyu, Shiqi Zhao, Xinyan Xiao, Yuan Liu, Yizhong Wang, Hua Wu, Qiaoqiao She, Xuan Liu, Tian Wu, and Haifeng Wang. 2018. DuReader: a Chinese machine reading comprehension dataset from real-world applications. In *Proceedings of the Workshop on Machine Reading for Question Answering*, pages 37–46, Melbourne, Australia. Association for Computational Linguistics.

Edward J Hu, yelong shen, Phillip Wallis, Zeyuan Allen-Zhu, Yuanzhi Li, Shean Wang, Lu Wang, and Weizhu Chen. 2022. LoRA: Low-rank adaptation of large language models. In *International Conference on Learning Representations*, Online.

Albert Q. Jiang, Alexandre Sablayrolles, Arthur Mensch, Chris Bamford, Devendra Singh Chaplot, Diego de las Casas, Florian Bressand, Gianna Lengyel, Guillaume Lample, Lucile Saulnier, Lélio Renard Lavaud, Marie-Anne Lachaux, Pierre Stock, Teven Le Scao, Thibaut Lavril, Thomas Wang, Timothée Lacroix, and William El Sayed. 2023a. Mistral 7b. *Preprint*, arXiv:2310.06825.

Ting Jiang, Shaohan Huang, Zhongzhi Luan, Deqing Wang, and Fuzhen Zhuang. 2023b. Scaling sentence embeddings with large language models. *Preprint*, arXiv:2307.16645.

Mandar Joshi, Eunsol Choi, Daniel Weld, and Luke Zettlemoyer. 2017. TriviaQA: A large scale distantly supervised challenge dataset for reading comprehension. In *Proceedings of the 55th Annual Meeting of the Association for Computational Linguistics (Volume 1: Long Papers)*, pages 1601–1611, Vancouver, Canada. Association for Computational Linguistics.

Vladimir Karpukhin, Barlas Oguz, Sewon Min, Patrick Lewis, Ledell Wu, Sergey Edunov, Danqi Chen, and Wen-tau Yih. 2020. Dense passage retrieval for open-domain question answering. In *Proceedings of the 2020 Conference on Empirical Methods in Natural Language Processing (EMNLP)*, pages 6769–6781, Online. Association for Computational Linguistics.

Young Jin Kim and Hany Hassan. 2020. FastFormers: Highly efficient transformer models for natural language understanding. In *Proceedings of SustaiNLP: Workshop on Simple and Efficient Natural Language Processing*, pages 149–158, Online. Association for Computational Linguistics.

Yann LeCun, John S Denker, Sara A Solla, Richard E Howard, and Lawrence D Jackel. 1990. Optimal brain damage. In *Advances in neural information processing systems*, pages 598–605.

Chankyu Lee, Rajarshi Roy, Mengyao Xu, Jonathan Raiman, Mohammad Shoeybi, Bryan Catanzaro, and Wei Ping. 2024. NV-Embed: Improved techniques for training LLMs as generalist embedding models. *Preprint*, arXiv:2405.17428.

Patrick Lewis, Ethan Perez, Aleksandra Piktus, Fabio Petroni, Vladimir Karpukhin, Naman Goyal, Heinrich Küttler, Mike Lewis, Wen-tau Yih, Tim Rocktäschel, et al. 2020. Retrieval-augmented generation for knowledge-intensive NLP tasks. *Advances in Neural Information Processing Systems*, 33:9459–9474.

Hao Li, Asim Kadav, Igor Durdanovic, Hanan Samet, and Hans Peter Graf. 2022. Pruning filters for efficient ConvNets. In *International Conference on Learning Representations*, Toulon, France.

Xianming Li and Jing Li. 2024. BeLLM: Backward dependency enhanced large language model for sentence embeddings. In *Proceedings of the 2024 Conference of the North American Chapter of the Association for Computational Linguistics: Human Language Technologies (Volume 1: Long Papers)*, pages 792–804, Mexico City, Mexico. Association for Computational Linguistics.

Zehan Li, Xin Zhang, Yanzhao Zhang, Dingkun Long, Pengjun Xie, and Meishan Zhang. 2023a. Towards general text embeddings with multi-stage contrastive learning. *Preprint*, arXiv:2308.03281.

Zehan Li, Xin Zhang, Yanzhao Zhang, Dingkun Long, Pengjun Xie, and Meishan Zhang. 2023b. Towards

General Text Embeddings with Multi-stage Contrastive Learning. *Preprint*, arXiv:2308.03281.

Xueguang Ma, Liang Wang, Nan Yang, Furu Wei, and Jimmy Lin. 2024. Fine-tuning llama for multi-stage text retrieval. In *Proceedings of the 47th International ACM SIGIR Conference on Research and Development in Information Retrieval*, pages 2421–2425.

Xin Men, Mingyu Xu, Qingyu Zhang, Bingning Wang, Hongyu Lin, Yaojie Lu, Xianpei Han, and Weipeng Chen. 2024. Shortgpt: Layers in large language models are more redundant than you expect. *Preprint*, arXiv:2403.03853.

Paul Michel, Omer Levy, and Graham Neubig. 2019. Are sixteen heads really better than one? In *Advances in Neural Information Processing Systems*, pages 14014–14024.

Niklas Muennighoff. 2022. SGPT: GPT sentence embeddings for semantic search. *Preprint*, arXiv:2202.08904.

Niklas Muennighoff, Hongjin SU, Liang Wang, Nan Yang, Furu Wei, Tao Yu, Amanpreet Singh, and Douwe Kiela. 2024. Generative representational instruction tuning. In *ICLR 2024 Workshop: How Far Are We From AGI*, Vienna, Austria.

Niklas Muennighoff, Nouamane Tazi, Loic Magne, and Nils Reimers. 2023. MTEB: Massive text embedding benchmark. In *Proceedings of the 17th Conference of the European Chapter of the Association for Computational Linguistics*, pages 2014–2037, Dubrovnik, Croatia. Association for Computational Linguistics.

Jianmo Ni, Chen Qu, Jing Lu, Zhuyun Dai, Gustavo Hernandez Abrego, Ji Ma, Vincent Zhao, Yi Luan, Keith Hall, Ming-Wei Chang, and Yinfei Yang. 2022. Large dual encoders are generalizable retrievers. In *Proceedings of the 2022 Conference on Empirical Methods in Natural Language Processing*, pages 9844–9855, Abu Dhabi, United Arab Emirates. Association for Computational Linguistics.

Colin Raffel, Noam Shazeer, Adam Roberts, Katherine Lee, Sharan Narang, Michael Matena, Yanqi Zhou, Wei Li, and Peter J. Liu. 2020. Exploring the limits of transfer learning with a unified text-to-text transformer. *Journal of Machine Learning Research*, 21(140):1–67.

Pranav Rajpurkar, Jian Zhang, Konstantin Lopyrev, and Percy Liang. 2016. SQuAD: 100,000+ questions for machine comprehension of text. In *Proceedings of the 2016 Conference on Empirical Methods in Natural Language Processing*, pages 2383–2392, Austin, Texas. Association for Computational Linguistics.

Nils Reimers and Iryna Gurevych. 2019. Sentence-BERT: Sentence embeddings using Siamese BERT-networks. In *Proceedings of the 2019 Conference on Empirical Methods in Natural Language Processing and the 9th International Joint Conference on Natural Language Processing (EMNLP-IJCNLP)*, pages 3982–3992, Hong Kong, China. Association for Computational Linguistics.

Hassan Sajjad, Fahim Dalvi, Nadir Durrani, and Preslav Nakov. 2023. On the effect of dropping layers of pre-trained transformer models. *Computer Speech & Language*, 77:101429.

Jacob Mitchell Springer, Suhas Kotha, Daniel Fried, Graham Neubig, and Aditi Raghunathan. 2024. Repetition Improves Language Model Embeddings. *Preprint*, arXiv:2402.15449.

James Thorne, Andreas Vlachos, Christos Christodoulopoulos, and Arpit Mittal. 2018. FEVER: a large-scale dataset for fact extraction and VERification. In *Proceedings of the 2018 Conference of the North American Chapter of the Association for Computational Linguistics: Human Language Technologies, Volume 1 (Long Papers)*, pages 809–819, New Orleans, Louisiana. Association for Computational Linguistics.

Elena Voita, David Talbot, Fedor Moiseev, Rico Sennrich, and Ivan Titov. 2019. Analyzing multi-head self-attention: Specialized heads do the heavy lifting, the rest can be pruned. In *Proceedings of the 57th Annual Meeting of the Association for Computational Linguistics*, pages 5797–5808.

Liang Wang, Nan Yang, Xiaolong Huang, Binxing Jiao, Linjun Yang, Daxin Jiang, Rangan Majumder, and Furu Wei. 2022. Text embeddings by weakly-supervised contrastive pre-training. *arXiv preprint*.

Liang Wang, Nan Yang, Xiaolong Huang, Binxing Jiao, Linjun Yang, Daxin Jiang, Rangan Majumder, and Furu Wei. 2024a. Text Embeddings by Weakly-Supervised Contrastive Pre-training. *Preprint*, arXiv:2212.03533.

Liang Wang, Nan Yang, Xiaolong Huang, Linjun Yang, Rangan Majumder, and Furu Wei. 2024b. Improving text embeddings with large language models. In *Proceedings of the 62nd Annual Meeting of the Association for Computational Linguistics (Volume 1: Long Papers)*, pages 11897–11916, Bangkok, Thailand. Association for Computational Linguistics.

Wei Wen, Chunpeng Wu, Yandan Wang, Yiran Chen, and Hai Li. 2016. Learning structured sparsity in deep neural networks. In *Advances in neural information processing systems*, pages 2074–2082, Barcelona, Spain.

Adina Williams, Nikita Nangia, and Samuel Bowman. 2018. A broad-coverage challenge corpus for sentence understanding through inference. In *Proceedings of the 2018 Conference of the North American Chapter of the Association for Computational Linguistics: Human Language Technologies, Volume 1 (Long Papers)*, pages 1112–1122, New Orleans, Louisiana. Association for Computational Linguistics.

Shitao Xiao, Zheng Liu, Peitian Zhang, Niklas Muennighoff, Defu Lian, and Jian-Yun Nie. 2024a. C-pack: Packed resources for general chinese embeddings. In *Proceedings of the 47th International ACM SIGIR Conference on Research and Development in Information Retrieval*, SIGIR '24, page 641–649, New York, NY, USA. Association for Computing Machinery.

Shitao Xiao, Zheng Liu, Peitian Zhang, Niklas Muennighoff, Defu Lian, and Jian-Yun Nie. 2024b. C-Pack: Packed Resources For General Chinese Embeddings. *Preprint*, arXiv:2309.07597.

Xiaohui Xie, Qian Dong, Bingning Wang, Feiyang Lv, Ting Yao, Weinan Gan, Zhijing Wu, Xiangsheng Li, Haitao Li, Yiqun Liu, and Jin Ma. 2023. T2ranking: A large-scale chinese benchmark for passage ranking. In *Proceedings of the 46th International ACM SIGIR Conference on Research and Development in Information Retrieval*, SIGIR '23, page 2681–2690, New York, NY, United States. Association for Computing Machinery.

An Yang, Baosong Yang, Binyuan Hui, Bo Zheng, Bowen Yu, Chang Zhou, Chengpeng Li, Chengyuan Li, Dayiheng Liu, Fei Huang, et al. 2024. Qwen2 technical report. *Preprint*, arXiv:2407.10671.

Zhilin Yang, Peng Qi, Saizheng Zhang, Yoshua Bengio, William Cohen, Ruslan Salakhutdinov, and Christopher D. Manning. 2018. HotpotQA: A dataset for diverse, explainable multi-hop question answering. In *Proceedings of the 2018 Conference on Empirical Methods in Natural Language Processing*, pages 2369–2380, Brussels, Belgium. Association for Computational Linguistics.

Xinyu Zhang, Xueguang Ma, Peng Shi, and Jimmy Lin. 2021. Mr. TyDi: A multi-lingual benchmark for dense retrieval. In *Proceedings of the 1st Workshop on Multilingual Representation Learning*, pages 127–137, Punta Cana, Dominican Republic. Association for Computational Linguistics.

Xinyu Zhang, Nandan Thakur, Odunayo Ogundepo, Ehsan Kamalloo, David Alfonso-Hermelo, Xiaoguang Li, Qun Liu, Mehdi Rezagholizadeh, and Jimmy Lin. 2023. MIRACL: A Multilingual Retrieval Dataset Covering 18 Diverse Languages. *Transactions of the Association for Computational Linguistics*, 11:1114–1131.

Zhehao Zhang, Yan Gao, and Jian-Guang Lou. 2024. e^5: Zero-shot hierarchical table analysis using augmented LLMs via explain, extract, execute, exhibit and extrapolate. In *Proceedings of the 2024 Conference of the North American Chapter of the Association for Computational Linguistics: Human Language Technologies (Volume 1: Long Papers)*, pages 1244–1258, Mexico City, Mexico. Association for Computational Linguistics.

Zhen Zhang, Wei Zhu, Jinfan Zhang, Peng Wang, Rize Jin, and Tae-Sun Chung. 2022. PCEE-BERT: Accelerating BERT inference via patient and confident early exiting. In *Findings of the Association for Computational Linguistics: NAACL 2022*, pages 327–338, Seattle, United States. Association for Computational Linguistics.

Xunyu Zhu, Jian Li, Yong Liu, Can Ma, and Weiping Wang. 2024. A survey on model compression for large language models. *Preprint*, arXiv:2308.07633.

A Training

A.1 Dataset

The dataset we use consists of ELI5 (sample ratio 0.1, Fan et al., 2019), HotpotQA (Yang et al., 2018), FEVER (Thorne et al., 2018), MIRACL (Zhang et al., 2023), MS-MARCO passage ranking (sample ratio 0.5) and document ranking (sample ratio 0.2, Bajaj et al., 2018), NQ (Karpukhin et al., 2020), SNLI (Bowman et al., 2015), MNLI (Williams et al., 2018), SQuAD (Rajpurkar et al., 2016), TriviaQA (Joshi et al., 2017), Quora Duplicate Questions[2] (sample ratio 0.1), Mr- TyDi (Zhang et al., 2021), DuReader (He et al., 2018), and T2Ranking (sample ratio 0.5, Xie et al., 2023). The instructions used for each dataset can be found in Table 5.

A.2 Hyperparameters

All models are trained with LoRA rank $r = 16$ and use brain floating point (`bfloat16`) precision, gradient checkpointing, and FlashAttention-2 (Dao, 2024) to optimize GPU memory consumption. Training is conducted with a batch size of 64 for 1000 steps, gradient accumulation over 1 step, and a maximum sequence length of 512 tokens. The Adam optimizer has a learning rate of 2×10^{-4} and a linear warm-up over the first 300 steps.

A.3 Training Time

	Large	Small
LLaMA-3-8B	2h 48m	35m
Mistral-7B	2h 41m	56m
Qwen2-7B	3h 1m	1h 14m
Phi3-4B	1h 40m	33m

Table 2: Training time for the variants produced by L^{3}Prune.

Table 2 shows the time taken to train the two variants (`large` and `small`) provided by L^{3}Prune for

[2] `https://quoradata.quora.com/First-Quora-Dataset-Release-Question-Pairs`

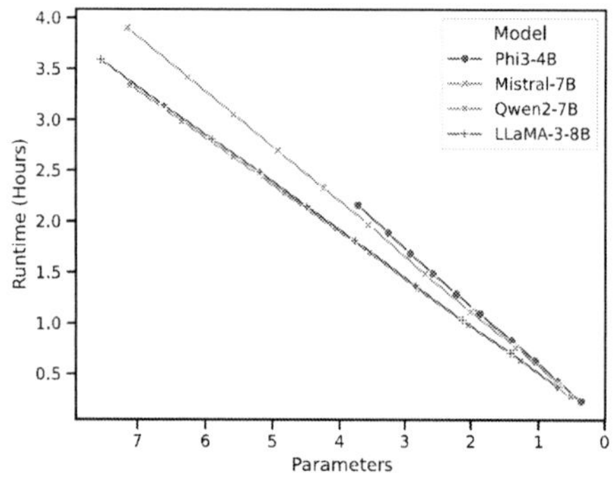

Figure 6: The total training time taken for all models at different pruning percentages.

each model. Figure 6 shows the training time for the models pruned at different pruning percentages, with respect to total parameter count. As we expect, the time taken to train a pruned model is linear to the pruning percentage, and corresponds roughly to the total parameter count. All models were trained on a single NVIDIA A100 GPU. Including evaluation, we estimate that all experiments took a total of 200 GPU hours.

B Massive Text Embeddings Benchmark (MTEB)

B.1 MTEB subset details

MTEB encompasses a diverse array of embedding tasks varying in size, making a full evaluation quite time-consuming—it takes over 160 hours for a full-sized 7B model, such as Qwen2-7B, on an A100 GPU. To expedite our analysis, we use a representative subset of 15 tasks from MTEB, selected and used by BehnamGhader et al. (2024), detailed in Table 3. This subset includes tasks from each category in proportions closely matching those of the full MTEB.

B.2 MTEB instructions

For evaluation on MTEB-15, we use the instructions from Wang et al. (2024b), also used by BehnamGhader et al. (2024). The list of instructions for each task is listed in Table 4.

C Licenses

All four models we used are available for research purposes—LLaMA-3-8B is under its own permissive license, Mistral-7B and Qwen2-7B are under Apache License 2.0, and Phi3-4B is under MIT License. MTEB and the tasks it includes are provided under the Apache License 2.0. We overview the licenses of all datasets used in training below:

Category	Dataset
Retrieval (3)	SciFact ArguAna NFCorpus
Reranking (2)	StackOverflowDupQuestions SciDocsRR
Clustering (3)	BiorxivClusteringS2S MedrxivClusteringS2S TwentyNewsgroupsClustering
Pair Classification (1)	SprintDuplicateQuestions
Classification (3)	Banking77Classification EmotionClassification MassiveIntentClassification
STS (3)	STS17 SICK-R STSBenchmark
SummEval (0)	-
Overall	15 datasets

Table 3: MTEB-15, the subset of MTEB tasks used for our work.

- ELI5: Provided under no specified license, available for research purposes.
- HotpotQA: Provided under CC BY-SA 4.0.
- FEVER: Provided under CC BY-SA 3.0.
- MIRACL: Provided under Apache License 2.0.
- MS-MARCO: Provided under no specific license, available for non-commercial research purposes.
- Natural Questions (NQ): Provided under CC BY 4.0.
- Stanford Natural Language Inference (SNLI): Provided under CC BY-SA 4.0.
- Multi Natural Language Inference (MNLI): Provided under a combination of permissive licenses, elaborated by Williams et al. (2018).
- SQuAD: Provided under CC BY-NC 4.0.
- TriviaQA: Provided under Apache License 2.0.
- Quora Duplicate Questions: Provided under no specified license, available for non-commercial purposes.
- Mr. TyDi: Provided under Apache License 2.0

- DuReader: Provided under Apache License 2.0
- T2Ranking: Provided under Apache License 2.0

Task Name	Instruction
Banking77Classification	Given a online banking query, find the corresponding intents
EmotionClassification	Classify the emotion expressed in the given Twitter message into one of the six emotions: anger, fear, joy, love, sadness, and surprise
MassiveIntentClassification	Given a user utterance as query, find the user intents
BiorxivClusteringS2S	Identify the main category of Biorxiv papers based on the titles
MedrxivClusteringS2S	Identify the main category of Medrxiv papers based on the titles
TwentyNewsgroupsClustering	Identify the topic or theme of the given news articles
SprintDuplicateQuestions	Retrieve duplicate questions from Sprint forum
SciDocsRR	Given a title of a scientific paper, retrieve the titles of other relevant papers
StackOverflowDupQuestions	Retrieve duplicate questions from StackOverflow forum
ArguAna	Given a claim, find documents that refute the claim
NFCorpus	Given a question, retrieve relevant documents that best answer the question
SciFact	Given a scientific claim, retrieve documents that support or refute the claim
STS*	Retrieve semantically similar text.

Table 4: Instructions used for evaluation on the MTEB benchmark. "STS*" refers to all the STS tasks.

Dataset	Instruction(s)
SNLI & MNLI	Given a premise, retrieve a hypothesis that is entailed by the premise Retrieve semantically similar text
DuReader	Given a Chinese search query, retrieve web passages that answer the question
ELI5	Provided a user question, retrieve the highest voted answers on Reddit ELI5 forum
FEVER	Given a claim, retrieve documents that support or refute the claim
HotpotQA	Given a multi-hop question, retrieve documents that can help answer the question
MIRACL	Given a question, retrieve Wikipedia passages that answer the question
MrTyDi	Given a question, retrieve Wikipedia passages that answer the question
MSMARCO Passage	Given a web search query, retrieve relevant passages that answer the query
MSMARCO Document	Given a web search query, retrieve relevant documents that answer the query
NQ	Given a question, retrieve Wikipedia passages that answer the question
QuoraDuplicates	Given a question, retrieve questions that are semantically equivalent to the given question Find questions that have the same meaning as the input question
SQuAD	Retrieve Wikipedia passages that answer the question
T2Ranking	Given a Chinese search query, retrieve web passages that answer the question
TriviaQA	Retrieve Wikipedia passages that answer the question

Table 5: Instructions used for each of the E5 datasets.

Vocabulary-level Memory Efficiency for Language Model Fine-tuning

Miles Williams and **Nikolaos Aletras**
University of Sheffield
{mwilliams15, n.aletras}@sheffield.ac.uk

Abstract

The extensive memory footprint of language model (LM) fine-tuning poses a challenge for both researchers and practitioners. LMs use an embedding matrix to represent extensive vocabularies, forming a substantial proportion of the model parameters. While previous work towards memory-efficient fine-tuning has focused on minimizing the number of trainable parameters, reducing the memory footprint of the embedding matrix has yet to be explored. We first demonstrate that a significant proportion of the vocabulary remains unused during fine-tuning. We then propose a simple yet effective approach that leverages this finding to minimize memory usage. We show that our approach provides substantial reductions in memory usage across a wide range of models and tasks. Notably, our approach does not impact downstream task performance, while allowing more efficient use of computational resources.[1]

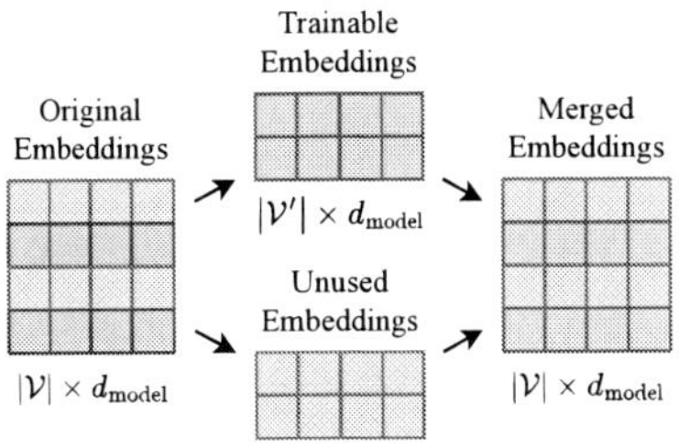

Figure 1: Memory-efficient language model fine-tuning with Partial Embedding Matrix Adaptation (PEMA).

1 Introduction

Language models (LMs) (Chung et al., 2022; Touvron et al., 2023; Warner et al., 2024) form the foundation of contemporary natural language processing (NLP), however they require extensive computational resources to train (Kaplan et al., 2020; Hoffmann et al., 2022). This is contrary to the democratization of NLP, exacerbating economic inequalities and hindering inclusivity (Schwartz et al., 2020; Weidinger et al., 2022). Consequently, there is a growing focus towards developing efficient methods for LM training and fine-tuning (Treviso et al., 2023; Lialin et al., 2023).

The memory footprint of LMs is a major challenge for their application. Storing model parameters requires extensive amounts of memory, constraining the size and architecture of the model (Paleyes et al., 2022). This problem is especially prominent during training as gradients and optimizer states must also be retained (Kingma and Ba, 2017). This can be problematic when using consumer hardware or facing an academic budget (Izsak et al., 2021; Ciosici and Derczynski, 2022).

LMs ordinarily use fixed vocabularies to derive vector representations from text, known as word embeddings. Each element of the vocabulary has a corresponding word embedding, which collectively form an embedding matrix within the LM. The size of the embedding matrix scales with both the vocabulary size and embedding dimension, comprising a substantial proportion of the model parameters (Table 5, Appendix A). This proportion is usually even greater for multilingual LMs, which benefit from larger vocabularies (Conneau et al., 2020; Liang et al., 2023). However, we hypothesize that a significant proportion of LM vocabulary remains unused during fine-tuning on many downstream tasks.

In this paper, we first demonstrate that our hypothesis holds for a variety of downstream tasks, with only a small subset of vocabulary used. We then propose a method to reduce memory usage during fine-tuning by excluding unused embeddings. Finally, we empirically demonstrate the memory savings from our approach across a range of models and tasks. Notably, our approach does not impact downstream task performance and is orthogonal to many existing LM memory efficiency techniques.

[1] https://github.com/mlsw/partial-embedding-matrix-adaptation

Proceedings of the 10th Workshop on Representation Learning for NLP (RepL4NLP-2025), pages 185–196
May 4, 2025 ©2025 Association for Computational Linguistics

2 Related Work

Tokenization. Transformer LMs (Vaswani et al., 2017) typically adopt subword tokenization (Schuster and Nakajima, 2012; Sennrich et al., 2016) to encode text using a finite vocabulary. The use of large subword vocabularies enables improved task performance (Gallé, 2019), inference efficiency (Tay et al., 2022), and multilingual performance (Liang et al., 2023). Conversely, character or byte level tokenization can be used (Clark et al., 2022; Xue et al., 2022), reducing the size of the embedding matrix at the cost of increasing the sequence length.

Reducing embedding parameters. To reduce the size of the embedding matrix, LMs can be trained with embedding factorization (Sun et al., 2020; Lan et al., 2020), albeit with slightly lower task performance. Alternatively, embeddings can be generated from hash functions (Sankar et al., 2021; Xue and Aletras, 2022; Cohn et al., 2023), although this may harm performance due to the many-to-one mapping from tokens to embeddings.

Multilingual vocabulary trimming. The closest work to our own is Abdaoui et al. (2020), which creates smaller multilingual LMs by permanently reducing the number of supported languages. This can harm performance as the removed vocabulary may later be required for a downstream task. Moreover, selecting which vocabulary to remove requires the computationally expensive processing of a large corpus. Ushio et al. (2023) further examine the performance impact of permanently removing LM vocabulary either before or after fine-tuning. However, the same fundamental limitations persist.

Parameter-efficient fine-tuning. PEFT methods, such as adapters (Houlsby et al., 2019), soft prompts (Lester et al., 2021; Li and Liang, 2021), ladder side-tuning (Sung et al., 2022), and low-rank adaptation (Hu et al., 2022), effectively adapt LMs by fine-tuning only a small number of parameters. However, these methods still require all LM parameters to be held in accelerator memory.

Offloading. To minimize accelerator (e.g. GPU) memory usage, LM parameters can be held in separate (e.g. CPU) memory until needed (Pudipeddi et al., 2020; Ren et al., 2021). However, this approach substantially increases inference latency.

Model compression. In Appendix B, we discuss a variety of orthogonal LM compression methods, such as quantization, pruning, and distillation.

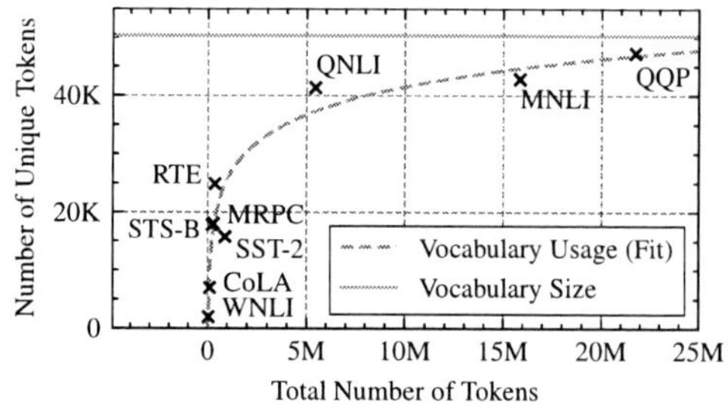

Figure 2: The trend in vocabulary use for the datasets in GLUE when using the vocabulary from GPT-2.

#	Token
49,990	natureconservancy
50,072	;;;;;;;;;;;;
50,160	PsyNetMessage
50,174	rawdownloadcloneembedreportprint
50,243	SolidGoldMagikarp

Table 1: Five examples of tokens from the GPT-2 vocabulary that do not occur within English Wikipedia.

3 Vocabulary Usage Analysis

To empirically assess the level of vocabulary usage during fine-tuning, we first examine the popular GLUE benchmark (Wang et al., 2019). This comprises a series of tasks that are varied in both size and domain (Appendix C). For tokenization, we use the subword vocabulary from GPT-2, which was later adopted by models including RoBERTa (Liu et al., 2019), BART (Lewis et al., 2020), GPT-3 (Brown et al., 2020), and OPT (Zhang et al., 2022).

Figure 2 illustrates the relationship between unique tokens and total tokens in each of the GLUE datasets. Notably, six out of nine datasets fail to use more than half of the vocabulary. Moreover, the smallest dataset, WNLI, uses less than 4%. Interestingly, we observe that the GLUE datasets follow a trend resembling Heaps' Law (Heaps, 1978). This states that as the size of a corpus grows, there are diminishing gains in new vocabulary. However, our use of a finite subword vocabulary means that the trend is asymptotic to the vocabulary size.

Separately, the statistical construction of subword vocabularies can reflect anomalies in their training data, creating tokens that may never be used. To examine the extent of the issue, we identify such tokens by evaluating a processed dump of English Wikipedia, comprising over 20GB of text. Peculiarly, we identify nearly 200 anomalous tokens without a single occurrence (see Table 1).[2]

[2]We refer readers interested in such anomalous tokens to Rumbelow and Watkins (2023) and Land and Bartolo (2024).

4 Partial Embedding Matrix Adaptation

Our empirical analysis (Section 3) suggests that many fine-tuning datasets only use a fraction of LM vocabulary. We leverage this insight to propose Partial Embedding Matrix Adaptation (PEMA), a method that achieves substantial memory savings by selecting only the minimum subset of word embeddings needed for fine-tuning. Notably, this does not impact task performance, as unused word embeddings are not updated during backpropagation.

Preliminaries. Let each token in the vocabulary $\{w_1, \ldots, w_k\}$ be denoted by a unique integer i such that $\mathcal{V} = \{i \in \mathbb{N} \mid i \leq k\}$. The embedding matrix $E \in \mathbb{R}^{|\mathcal{V}| \times d}$ is then used to project each token to a corresponding d-dimensional vector.

Before fine-tuning. Suppose we have fine-tuning dataset $D \in \mathcal{V}^{m \times n}$ where m is the number of examples and n is the length of each example. We compute the partial vocabulary $\mathcal{V}' \subset \mathcal{V}$ consisting of *only* the tokens in D. As the elements of $\mathcal{V}'$ are not necessarily consecutive integers, we define an arbitrary mapping $f \colon \mathcal{V}' \rightarrow \{i \in \mathbb{N} \mid i \leq |\mathcal{V}'|\}$. We then construct the partial embedding matrix $E' \in \mathbb{R}^{|\mathcal{V}'| \times d}$ with entries $E'[:, f(i)] = E[:, i]$ for all $i \in \mathcal{V}'$. That is, E' retains only embedding vectors corresponding to tokens in $\mathcal{V}'$. To adapt D for the partial vocabulary $\mathcal{V}'$, we create an intermediary dataset D' where each entry $D'[i, j] = f(D[i, j])$. Finally, we use D' and E' in place of D and E.

After fine-tuning. Following fine-tuning, our partial embedding matrix E' holds the newly learned embeddings for the partial vocabulary. However, we do not wish to keep only the partial vocabulary, as this would limit future use of the model (i.e. tasks with different vocabulary). Therefore, we merge the newly learned embeddings into the original embedding matrix (stored on-disk). More formally, we update E such that $E[:, f^{-1}(i)] = E'[:, i]$ for all $i \in \mathcal{V}'$. This ensures that the model remains structurally identical, with embeddings for the complete vocabulary.

5 Experimental Setup

Datasets. To offer a fair selection of datasets, we follow existing PEFT literature (Houlsby et al., 2019; Hu et al., 2022; Sung et al., 2022; Zhang et al., 2023) and focus our evaluation on the popular GLUE benchmark. We additionally employ XNLI (Conneau et al., 2018) to assess the performance of our approach with multilingual data. Complete data sources and implementation details are listed in Appendix C and Appendix D, respectively.

Models. Similarly, we select a variety of popular models used in existing work. However, we place an emphasis on having a variety of vocabularies (Table 5, Appendix A). For monolingual models, we use BERT (Devlin et al., 2019), RoBERTa (Liu et al., 2019), and DeBERTaV3 (He et al., 2023). For multilingual models, we use mBERT (Devlin et al., 2019), XLM-RoBERTa (Conneau et al., 2020), and XLM-V (Liang et al., 2023). To evaluate the performance of distilled models, we also use the available distilled counterparts: DistilBERT, DistilRoBERTa, and DistilmBERT (Sanh et al., 2020a). For a fair comparison between models, we consistently select the base size ($d_{\text{model}} = 768$).

Memory efficiency metrics. Following convention in the PEFT literature (Houlsby et al., 2019; Hu et al., 2022; Ben Zaken et al., 2022), we report memory efficiency in terms of model parameters. This is advantageous as it avoids confounding factors such as weight precision, optimizer choice, software implementation, and batch size.

6 Results

Larger vocabularies see more memory savings. Table 2 presents the reduction in parameters for each model across the GLUE benchmark. Following our expectations from Section 3, we generally observe that as vocabulary sizes increase (Table 5, Appendix A), so do the potential memory savings. For example, an average reduction in embedding parameters of 47.3% is achieved for BERT, 52.1% for RoBERTa, and 72.4% for DeBERTaV3.

Memory savings vary between datasets. In line with our expectations from Section 3, the memory savings vary substantially between datasets. For BERT, the embedding matrix can be reduced by 94.3% for the smallest dataset (WNLI), yet only 11.5% for the largest (QQP). We demonstrate that downstream task performance remains consistent across models and datasets in Appendix E.

Distilled models substantially benefit. Considering the distilled models, we observe that they all achieve an identical reduction in embedding parameters to their original counterparts. This is because they use the same vocabulary and embedding size (Sanh et al., 2020a). However, they offer substan-

Model	CoLA	MNLI	MRPC	QNLI	QQP	RTE	SST-2	STS-B	WNLI	Mean
				Reduction in Embedding Parameters (%)						
DistilBERT	80.1	14.8	54.9	13.1	11.5	41.5	57.9	57.2	94.3	47.3
DistilRoBERTa	86.1	14.8	64.0	17.7	5.9	51.6	68.6	64.4	96.0	52.1
DistilmBERT	94.9	76.9	88.2	73.8	72.7	85.0	91.9	88.8	98.4	85.6
BERT	80.1	14.8	54.9	13.1	11.5	41.5	57.9	57.2	94.3	47.3
RoBERTa	86.1	14.8	64.0	17.7	5.9	51.6	68.6	64.4	96.0	52.1
DeBERTaV3	95.0	44.3	85.7	47.1	28.5	79.0	87.5	85.9	98.6	72.4
mBERT	94.9	76.9	88.2	73.8	72.7	85.0	91.9	88.8	98.4	85.6
XLM-RoBERTa	97.8	88.8	94.9	87.6	85.4	93.3	96.3	94.9	99.3	93.1
XLM-V	99.3	93.2	98.0	92.8	90.5	97.1	98.3	98.0	99.8	96.3
				Reduction in Model Parameters (%)						
DistilBERT	28.0	5.2	19.2	4.6	4.0	14.5	20.3	20.0	33.0	16.5
DistilRoBERTa	40.5	7.0	30.1	8.3	2.8	24.3	32.3	30.3	45.1	24.5
DistilmBERT	64.4	52.2	59.9	50.1	49.3	57.7	62.3	60.2	66.8	58.1
BERT	17.1	3.2	11.8	2.8	2.5	8.9	12.4	12.2	20.2	10.1
RoBERTa	26.7	4.6	19.8	5.5	1.8	16.0	21.2	19.9	29.7	16.1
DeBERTaV3	50.7	23.6	45.7	25.1	15.2	42.1	46.7	45.8	52.6	38.6
mBERT	49.0	39.7	45.5	38.1	37.5	43.9	47.4	45.8	50.8	44.2
XLM-RoBERTa	67.5	61.3	65.5	60.5	59.0	64.4	66.5	65.5	68.5	64.3
XLM-V	88.3	82.9	87.2	82.6	80.5	86.4	87.5	87.2	88.8	85.7

Table 2: The reduction in embedding and model parameters (%) for each model across the GLUE benchmark.

Size	CoLA	MNLI	MRPC	QNLI	QQP	RTE	SST-2	STS-B	WNLI	Mean
XSmall	46.7	21.8	42.2	23.2	14.0	38.8	43.1	42.3	48.5	35.6
Small	93.4	43.6	84.3	46.3	28.0	77.7	86.1	84.5	97.0	71.2
Base	93.4	43.6	84.3	46.3	28.0	77.7	86.1	84.5	97.0	71.2
Large	124.6	58.1	112.4	61.8	37.3	103.6	114.8	112.7	129.4	95.0

Table 3: The reduction in model parameters (millions) for each size of DeBERTaV3 across the GLUE benchmark.

tially higher overall savings, as there are fewer parameters allocated to the transformer layers.

Memory savings scale with model size. Table 3 presents the reduction in model parameters for each model from the DeBERTaV3 family. We observe that this reduction continues to increase with model size. On average, the extra small size is reduced by 35.6M parameters, while the large size is reduced by 95.0M parameters. Although the same fixed-size vocabulary is shared across models, the embedding dimension continues to grow (Table 6, Appendix A), offering further memory savings. The exception to this is the small and base sizes, where the only difference is the number of layers.

Multilingual models achieve extreme savings. Unsurprisingly, multilingual models demonstrate extreme memory savings across the monolingual GLUE benchmark. On average, a reduction in model parameters of 44.2% is achieved for mBERT, 64.3% for XLM-RoBERTa, and 85.7% for XLM-V. Table 4 presents the reduction in parameters for the multilingual models when fine-tuning on different subsets of XNLI. Even when fine-tuning on all fifteen languages, these models still demonstrate substantial memory savings from 23.0% to 58.4%.

Model	en	en-de	en-zh	All
	Reduction in Embedding Parameters (%)			
DistilmBERT	77.1	71.7	73.0	44.6
mBERT	77.1	71.7	73.0	44.6
XLM-RoBERTa	89.2	86.0	84.4	56.9
XLM-V	93.6	90.0	90.0	65.7
	Reduction in Model Parameters (%)			
DistilmBERT	52.3	48.6	49.6	30.3
mBERT	39.8	37.0	37.7	23.0
XLM-RoBERTa	61.6	59.4	58.3	39.3
XLM-V	83.2	80.0	80.0	58.4

Table 4: The reduction in parameters across different subsets of XNLI, in addition to all fifteen languages.

7 Conclusion

In this paper, we identified that many fine-tuning datasets do not use the majority of LM vocabulary. We then proposed Partial Embedding Matrix Adaptation (PEMA), a simple yet effective approach to minimize LM memory use during fine-tuning, that is orthogonal to many existing methods. Finally, we empirically demonstrated that our approach offers substantial memory savings across a variety of popular tasks and models, without compromising performance. As future work, we are interested in adapting our approach for the output embedding matrix to offer further memory savings.

Limitations

Processing the fine-tuning dataset to assess vocabulary usage incurs a runtime cost. However, we observe that this cost is negligible. We provide a detailed analysis of this matter in Appendix F.

Ethical Considerations

Our approach improves the memory efficiency of LM fine-tuning, therefore facilitating the use of less powerful hardware. Although we hope that this can reduce the environmental footprint of LM fine-tuning, we acknowledge that it could be used to support the fine-tuning of even larger LMs. We also recognize the dual-use nature of LMs and concede that efforts towards improving efficiency, including our own, can lower the barrier to entry for their misuse (Weidinger et al., 2022).

Acknowledgments

We are sincerely grateful to Nafise Sadat Moosavi, Huiyin Xue, Atsuki Yamaguchi, and the anonymous reviewers for their invaluable feedback. MW is supported by the Centre for Doctoral Training in Speech and Language Technologies (SLT) and their Applications funded by UK Research and Innovation grant EP/S023062/1.

References

Amine Abdaoui, Camille Pradel, and Grégoire Sigel. 2020. Load what you need: Smaller versions of mutililingual BERT. In *Proceedings of SustaiNLP: Workshop on Simple and Efficient Natural Language Processing*, pages 119–123, Online. Association for Computational Linguistics.

Elad Ben Zaken, Yoav Goldberg, and Shauli Ravfogel. 2022. BitFit: Simple parameter-efficient fine-tuning for transformer-based masked language-models. In *Proceedings of the 60th Annual Meeting of the Association for Computational Linguistics (Volume 2: Short Papers)*, pages 1–9, Dublin, Ireland. Association for Computational Linguistics.

Yelysei Bondarenko, Markus Nagel, and Tijmen Blankevoort. 2021. Understanding and overcoming the challenges of efficient transformer quantization. In *Proceedings of the 2021 Conference on Empirical Methods in Natural Language Processing*, pages 7947–7969, Online and Punta Cana, Dominican Republic. Association for Computational Linguistics.

Tom Brown, Benjamin Mann, Nick Ryder, Melanie Subbiah, Jared D Kaplan, Prafulla Dhariwal, Arvind Neelakantan, Pranav Shyam, Girish Sastry, Amanda Askell, Sandhini Agarwal, Ariel Herbert-Voss, Gretchen Krueger, Tom Henighan, Rewon Child, Aditya Ramesh, Daniel Ziegler, Jeffrey Wu, Clemens Winter, and 12 others. 2020. Language models are few-shot learners. In *Advances in Neural Information Processing Systems*, volume 33, pages 1877–1901. Curran Associates, Inc.

Daniel Cer, Mona Diab, Eneko Agirre, Iñigo Lopez-Gazpio, and Lucia Specia. 2017. SemEval-2017 task 1: Semantic textual similarity multilingual and crosslingual focused evaluation. In *Proceedings of the 11th International Workshop on Semantic Evaluation (SemEval-2017)*, pages 1–14, Vancouver, Canada. Association for Computational Linguistics.

Hyung Won Chung, Le Hou, Shayne Longpre, Barret Zoph, Yi Tay, William Fedus, Yunxuan Li, Xuezhi Wang, Mostafa Dehghani, Siddhartha Brahma, Albert Webson, Shixiang Shane Gu, Zhuyun Dai, Mirac Suzgun, Xinyun Chen, Aakanksha Chowdhery, Alex Castro-Ros, Marie Pellat, Kevin Robinson, and 16 others. 2022. Scaling instruction-finetuned language models. *Preprint*, arXiv:2210.11416.

Manuel R. Ciosici and Leon Derczynski. 2022. Training a T5 using lab-sized resources. *Preprint*, arXiv:2208.12097.

Jonathan H. Clark, Dan Garrette, Iulia Turc, and John Wieting. 2022. Canine: Pre-training an efficient tokenization-free encoder for language representation. *Transactions of the Association for Computational Linguistics*, 10:73–91.

Gabrielle Cohn, Rishika Agarwal, Deepanshu Gupta, and Siddharth Patwardhan. 2023. EELBERT: Tiny models through dynamic embeddings. In *Proceedings of the 2023 Conference on Empirical Methods in Natural Language Processing: Industry Track*, pages 451–459, Singapore. Association for Computational Linguistics.

Alexis Conneau, Kartikay Khandelwal, Naman Goyal, Vishrav Chaudhary, Guillaume Wenzek, Francisco Guzmán, Edouard Grave, Myle Ott, Luke Zettlemoyer, and Veselin Stoyanov. 2020. Unsupervised cross-lingual representation learning at scale. In *Proceedings of the 58th Annual Meeting of the Association for Computational Linguistics*, pages 8440–8451, Online. Association for Computational Linguistics.

Alexis Conneau, Ruty Rinott, Guillaume Lample, Adina Williams, Samuel Bowman, Holger Schwenk, and Veselin Stoyanov. 2018. XNLI: Evaluating cross-lingual sentence representations. In *Proceedings of the 2018 Conference on Empirical Methods in Natural Language Processing*, pages 2475–2485, Brussels, Belgium. Association for Computational Linguistics.

Ido Dagan, Oren Glickman, and Bernardo Magnini. 2006. The pascal recognising textual entailment challenge. In *Machine Learning Challenges. Evaluating Predictive Uncertainty, Visual Object Classification, and Recognising Tectual Entailment*, pages 177–190, Berlin, Heidelberg. Springer Berlin Heidelberg.

Tim Dettmers, Mike Lewis, Younes Belkada, and Luke Zettlemoyer. 2022. GPT3.int8(): 8-bit matrix multiplication for transformers at scale. In *Advances in Neural Information Processing Systems*.

Jacob Devlin, Ming-Wei Chang, Kenton Lee, and Kristina Toutanova. 2019. BERT: Pre-training of deep bidirectional transformers for language understanding. In *Proceedings of the 2019 Conference of the North American Chapter of the Association for Computational Linguistics: Human Language Technologies, Volume 1 (Long and Short Papers)*, pages 4171–4186, Minneapolis, Minnesota. Association for Computational Linguistics.

William B. Dolan and Chris Brockett. 2005. Automatically constructing a corpus of sentential paraphrases. In *Proceedings of the Third International Workshop on Paraphrasing (IWP2005)*.

Elias Frantar and Dan Alistarh. 2023. SparseGPT: Massive language models can be accurately pruned in one-shot. In *Proceedings of the 40th International Conference on Machine Learning*, volume 202 of *Proceedings of Machine Learning Research*, pages 10323–10337. PMLR.

Elias Frantar, Saleh Ashkboos, Torsten Hoefler, and Dan Alistarh. 2023. OPTQ: Accurate quantization for generative pre-trained transformers. In *The Eleventh International Conference on Learning Representations*.

Matthias Gallé. 2019. Investigating the effectiveness of BPE: The power of shorter sequences. In *Proceedings of the 2019 Conference on Empirical Methods in Natural Language Processing and the 9th International Joint Conference on Natural Language Processing (EMNLP-IJCNLP)*, pages 1375–1381, Hong Kong, China. Association for Computational Linguistics.

Pengcheng He, Jianfeng Gao, and Weizhu Chen. 2023. DeBERTaV3: Improving DeBERTa using ELECTRA-style pre-training with gradient-disentangled embedding sharing. In *The Eleventh International Conference on Learning Representations*.

Harold Stanley Heaps. 1978. *Information Retrieval: Computational and Theoretical Aspects*. Library and information science series. Academic Press.

Geoffrey Hinton, Oriol Vinyals, and Jeffrey Dean. 2015. Distilling the knowledge in a neural network. In *NIPS Deep Learning and Representation Learning Workshop*.

Jordan Hoffmann, Sebastian Borgeaud, Arthur Mensch, Elena Buchatskaya, Trevor Cai, Eliza Rutherford, Diego de Las Casas, Lisa Anne Hendricks, Johannes Welbl, Aidan Clark, Thomas Hennigan, Eric Noland, Katherine Millican, George van den Driessche, Bogdan Damoc, Aurelia Guy, Simon Osindero, Karén Simonyan, Erich Elsen, and 3 others. 2022. An empirical analysis of compute-optimal large language model training. In *Advances in Neural Information Processing Systems*, volume 35, pages 30016–30030. Curran Associates, Inc.

Neil Houlsby, Andrei Giurgiu, Stanislaw Jastrzebski, Bruna Morrone, Quentin De Laroussilhe, Andrea Gesmundo, Mona Attariyan, and Sylvain Gelly. 2019. Parameter-efficient transfer learning for NLP. In *Proceedings of the 36th International Conference on Machine Learning*, volume 97 of *Proceedings of Machine Learning Research*, pages 2790–2799. PMLR.

Edward J Hu, yelong shen, Phillip Wallis, Zeyuan Allen-Zhu, Yuanzhi Li, Shean Wang, Lu Wang, and Weizhu Chen. 2022. LoRA: Low-rank adaptation of large language models. In *International Conference on Learning Representations*.

Shankar Iyer, Nikhil Dandekar, Kornél Csernai, and 1 others. 2017. First Quora dataset release: Question pairs.

Peter Izsak, Moshe Berchansky, and Omer Levy. 2021. How to train BERT with an academic budget. In *Proceedings of the 2021 Conference on Empirical Methods in Natural Language Processing*, pages 10644–10652, Online and Punta Cana, Dominican Republic. Association for Computational Linguistics.

Jared Kaplan, Sam McCandlish, Tom Henighan, Tom B. Brown, Benjamin Chess, Rewon Child, Scott Gray, Alec Radford, Jeffrey Wu, and Dario Amodei. 2020. Scaling laws for neural language models. *Preprint*, arXiv:2001.08361.

Diederik P. Kingma and Jimmy Ba. 2017. Adam: A method for stochastic optimization. *Preprint*, arXiv:1412.6980.

Eldar Kurtic, Daniel Campos, Tuan Nguyen, Elias Frantar, Mark Kurtz, Benjamin Fineran, Michael Goin, and Dan Alistarh. 2022. The optimal BERT surgeon: Scalable and accurate second-order pruning for large language models. In *Proceedings of the 2022 Conference on Empirical Methods in Natural Language Processing*, pages 4163–4181, Abu Dhabi, United Arab Emirates. Association for Computational Linguistics.

Eldar Kurtic, Torsten Hoefler, and Dan Alistarh. 2024. How to prune your language model: Recovering accuracy on the "sparsity may cry" benchmark. In *Conference on Parsimony and Learning*, volume 234 of *Proceedings of Machine Learning Research*, pages 542–553. PMLR.

Zhenzhong Lan, Mingda Chen, Sebastian Goodman, Kevin Gimpel, Piyush Sharma, and Radu Soricut. 2020. ALBERT: A lite bert for self-supervised learning of language representations. In *International Conference on Learning Representations*.

Sander Land and Max Bartolo. 2024. Fishing for magikarp: Automatically detecting under-trained tokens in large language models. In *Proceedings of the 2024 Conference on Empirical Methods in Natural Language Processing*, pages 11631–11646, Miami, Florida, USA. Association for Computational Linguistics.

Yann LeCun, John Denker, and Sara Solla. 1989. Optimal brain damage. In *Advances in Neural Information Processing Systems*, volume 2. Morgan-Kaufmann.

Brian Lester, Rami Al-Rfou, and Noah Constant. 2021. The power of scale for parameter-efficient prompt tuning. In *Proceedings of the 2021 Conference on Empirical Methods in Natural Language Processing*, pages 3045–3059, Online and Punta Cana, Dominican Republic. Association for Computational Linguistics.

Hector J. Levesque, Ernest Davis, and Leora Morgenstern. 2012. The Winograd schema challenge. In *Proceedings of the Thirteenth International Conference on Principles of Knowledge Representation and Reasoning*, KR'12, pages 552–561. AAAI Press.

Mike Lewis, Yinhan Liu, Naman Goyal, Marjan Ghazvininejad, Abdelrahman Mohamed, Omer Levy, Veselin Stoyanov, and Luke Zettlemoyer. 2020. BART: Denoising sequence-to-sequence pre-training for natural language generation, translation, and comprehension. In *Proceedings of the 58th Annual Meeting of the Association for Computational Linguistics*, pages 7871–7880, Online. Association for Computational Linguistics.

Quentin Lhoest, Albert Villanova del Moral, Yacine Jernite, Abhishek Thakur, Patrick von Platen, Suraj Patil, Julien Chaumond, Mariama Drame, Julien Plu, Lewis Tunstall, Joe Davison, Mario Šaško, Gunjan Chhablani, Bhavitvya Malik, Simon Brandeis, Teven Le Scao, Victor Sanh, Canwen Xu, Nicolas Patry, and 13 others. 2021. Datasets: A community library for natural language processing. In *Proceedings of the 2021 Conference on Empirical Methods in Natural Language Processing: System Demonstrations*, pages 175–184, Online and Punta Cana, Dominican Republic. Association for Computational Linguistics.

Xiang Lisa Li and Percy Liang. 2021. Prefix-tuning: Optimizing continuous prompts for generation. In *Proceedings of the 59th Annual Meeting of the Association for Computational Linguistics and the 11th International Joint Conference on Natural Language Processing (Volume 1: Long Papers)*, pages 4582–4597, Online. Association for Computational Linguistics.

Vladislav Lialin, Vijeta Deshpande, and Anna Rumshisky. 2023. Scaling down to scale up: A guide to parameter-efficient fine-tuning. *Preprint*, arXiv:2303.15647.

Davis Liang, Hila Gonen, Yuning Mao, Rui Hou, Naman Goyal, Marjan Ghazvininejad, Luke Zettlemoyer, and Madian Khabsa. 2023. XLM-V: Overcoming the vocabulary bottleneck in multilingual masked language models. In *Proceedings of the 2023 Conference on Empirical Methods in Natural Language Processing*, pages 13142–13152, Singapore. Association for Computational Linguistics.

Yinhan Liu, Myle Ott, Naman Goyal, Jingfei Du, Mandar Joshi, Danqi Chen, Omer Levy, Mike Lewis, Luke Zettlemoyer, and Veselin Stoyanov. 2019. RoBERTa: A robustly optimized BERT pretraining approach. *Preprint*, arXiv:1907.11692.

Andrei Paleyes, Raoul-Gabriel Urma, and Neil D. Lawrence. 2022. Challenges in deploying machine learning: A survey of case studies. *ACM Comput. Surv.*, 55(6).

Adam Paszke, Sam Gross, Francisco Massa, Adam Lerer, James Bradbury, Gregory Chanan, Trevor Killeen, Zeming Lin, Natalia Gimelshein, Luca Antiga, Alban Desmaison, Andreas Kopf, Edward Yang, Zachary DeVito, Martin Raison, Alykhan Tejani, Sasank Chilamkurthy, Benoit Steiner, Lu Fang, and 2 others. 2019. PyTorch: An imperative style, high-performance deep learning library. In *Advances in Neural Information Processing Systems*, volume 32. Curran Associates, Inc.

Bharadwaj Pudipeddi, Maral Mesmakhosroshahi, Jinwen Xi, and Sujeeth Bharadwaj. 2020. Training large neural networks with constant memory using a new execution algorithm. *Preprint*, arXiv:2002.05645.

Pranav Rajpurkar, Jian Zhang, Konstantin Lopyrev, and Percy Liang. 2016. SQuAD: 100,000+ questions for machine comprehension of text. In *Proceedings of the 2016 Conference on Empirical Methods in Natural Language Processing*, pages 2383–2392, Austin, Texas. Association for Computational Linguistics.

Jie Ren, Samyam Rajbhandari, Reza Yazdani Aminabadi, Olatunji Ruwase, Shuangyan Yang, Minjia Zhang, Dong Li, and Yuxiong He. 2021. ZeRO-Offload: Democratizing billion-scale model training. In *2021 USENIX Annual Technical Conference (USENIX ATC 21)*, pages 551–564. USENIX Association.

Jessica Rumbelow and Matthew Watkins. 2023. SolidGoldMagikarp (plus, prompt generation).

Victor Sanh, Lysandre Debut, Julien Chaumond, and Thomas Wolf. 2020a. DistilBERT, a distilled version of BERT: smaller, faster, cheaper and lighter. *Preprint*, arXiv:1910.01108.

Victor Sanh, Thomas Wolf, and Alexander Rush. 2020b. Movement pruning: Adaptive sparsity by fine-tuning. In *Advances in Neural Information Processing Systems*, volume 33, pages 20378–20389. Curran Associates, Inc.

Chinnadhurai Sankar, Sujith Ravi, and Zornitsa Kozareva. 2021. ProFormer: Towards on-device LSH projection based transformers. In *Proceedings of the 16th Conference of the European Chapter of the Association for Computational Linguistics: Main Volume*, pages 2823–2828, Online. Association for Computational Linguistics.

Mike Schuster and Kaisuke Nakajima. 2012. Japanese and Korean voice search. In *2012 IEEE International Conference on Acoustics, Speech and Signal Processing (ICASSP)*, pages 5149–5152.

Roy Schwartz, Jesse Dodge, Noah A. Smith, and Oren Etzioni. 2020. Green AI. *Commun. ACM*, 63(12):54–63.

Rico Sennrich, Barry Haddow, and Alexandra Birch. 2016. Neural machine translation of rare words with subword units. In *Proceedings of the 54th Annual Meeting of the Association for Computational Linguistics (Volume 1: Long Papers)*, pages 1715–1725, Berlin, Germany. Association for Computational Linguistics.

Sheng Shen, Zhen Dong, Jiayu Ye, Linjian Ma, Zhewei Yao, Amir Gholami, Michael W. Mahoney, and Kurt Keutzer. 2020. Q-BERT: Hessian based ultra low precision quantization of bert. *Proceedings of the AAAI Conference on Artificial Intelligence*, 34(05):8815–8821.

Pranaydeep Singh and Els Lefever. 2022. When the student becomes the master: Learning better and smaller monolingual models from mBERT. In *Proceedings of the 29th International Conference on Computational Linguistics*, pages 4434–4441, Gyeongju, Republic of Korea. International Committee on Computational Linguistics.

Richard Socher, Alex Perelygin, Jean Wu, Jason Chuang, Christopher D. Manning, Andrew Ng, and Christopher Potts. 2013. Recursive deep models for semantic compositionality over a sentiment treebank. In *Proceedings of the 2013 Conference on Empirical Methods in Natural Language Processing*, pages 1631–1642, Seattle, Washington, USA. Association for Computational Linguistics.

Zhiqing Sun, Hongkun Yu, Xiaodan Song, Renjie Liu, Yiming Yang, and Denny Zhou. 2020. MobileBERT: a compact task-agnostic BERT for resource-limited devices. In *Proceedings of the 58th Annual Meeting of the Association for Computational Linguistics*, pages 2158–2170, Online. Association for Computational Linguistics.

Yi-Lin Sung, Jaemin Cho, and Mohit Bansal. 2022. LST: Ladder side-tuning for parameter and memory efficient transfer learning. In *Advances in Neural Information Processing Systems*, volume 35, pages 12991–13005. Curran Associates, Inc.

Yi Tay, Mostafa Dehghani, Dara Bahri, and Donald Metzler. 2022. Efficient transformers: A survey. *ACM Comput. Surv.*, 55(6).

Hugo Touvron, Thibaut Lavril, Gautier Izacard, Xavier Martinet, Marie-Anne Lachaux, Timothée Lacroix, Baptiste Rozière, Naman Goyal, Eric Hambro, Faisal Azhar, Aurelien Rodriguez, Armand Joulin, Edouard Grave, and Guillaume Lample. 2023. LLaMA: Open and efficient foundation language models. *Preprint*, arXiv:2302.13971.

Marcos Treviso, Ji-Ung Lee, Tianchu Ji, Betty van Aken, Qingqing Cao, Manuel R. Ciosici, Michael Hassid, Kenneth Heafield, Sara Hooker, Colin Raffel, Pedro H. Martins, André F. T. Martins, Jessica Zosa Forde, Peter Milder, Edwin Simpson, Noam Slonim, Jesse Dodge, Emma Strubell, Niranjan Balasubramanian, and 3 others. 2023. Efficient methods for natural language processing: A survey. *Transactions of the Association for Computational Linguistics*, 11:826–860.

Asahi Ushio, Yi Zhou, and Jose Camacho-Collados. 2023. Efficient multilingual language model compression through vocabulary trimming. In *Findings of the Association for Computational Linguistics: EMNLP 2023*, pages 14725–14739, Singapore. Association for Computational Linguistics.

Ashish Vaswani, Noam Shazeer, Niki Parmar, Jakob Uszkoreit, Llion Jones, Aidan N Gomez, Ł ukasz Kaiser, and Illia Polosukhin. 2017. Attention is all you need. In *Advances in Neural Information Processing Systems*, volume 30. Curran Associates, Inc.

Alex Wang, Amanpreet Singh, Julian Michael, Felix Hill, Omer Levy, and Samuel R. Bowman. 2019. GLUE: A multi-task benchmark and analysis platform for natural language understanding. In *International Conference on Learning Representations*.

Benjamin Warner, Antoine Chaffin, Benjamin Clavié, Orion Weller, Oskar Hallström, Said Taghadouini, Alexis Gallagher, Raja Biswas, Faisal Ladhak, Tom Aarsen, Nathan Cooper, Griffin Adams, Jeremy Howard, and Iacopo Poli. 2024. Smarter, better, faster, longer: A modern bidirectional encoder for fast, memory efficient, and long context finetuning and inference. *Preprint*, arXiv:2412.13663.

Alex Warstadt, Amanpreet Singh, and Samuel R. Bowman. 2019. Neural network acceptability judgments. *Transactions of the Association for Computational Linguistics*, 7:625–641.

Laura Weidinger, Jonathan Uesato, Maribeth Rauh, Conor Griffin, Po-Sen Huang, John Mellor, Amelia Glaese, Myra Cheng, Borja Balle, Atoosa Kasirzadeh, Courtney Biles, Sasha Brown, Zac Kenton, Will Hawkins, Tom Stepleton, Abeba Birhane, Lisa Anne Hendricks, Laura Rimell, William Isaac, and 4 others. 2022. Taxonomy of risks posed by language models. In *Proceedings of the 2022 ACM Conference on Fairness, Accountability, and Transparency*, FAccT '22, page 214–229, New York, NY, USA. Association for Computing Machinery.

Adina Williams, Nikita Nangia, and Samuel Bowman. 2018. A broad-coverage challenge corpus for sentence understanding through inference. In *Proceedings of the 2018 Conference of the North American Chapter of the Association for Computational Linguistics: Human Language Technologies, Volume 1 (Long Papers)*, pages 1112–1122, New Orleans, Louisiana. Association for Computational Linguistics.

Thomas Wolf, Lysandre Debut, Victor Sanh, Julien Chaumond, Clement Delangue, Anthony Moi, Pierric Cistac, Tim Rault, Remi Louf, Morgan Funtowicz, Joe Davison, Sam Shleifer, Patrick von Platen, Clara Ma, Yacine Jernite, Julien Plu, Canwen Xu, Teven Le Scao, Sylvain Gugger, and 3 others. 2020. Transformers: State-of-the-art natural language processing. In *Proceedings of the 2020 Conference on Empirical Methods in Natural Language Processing: System Demonstrations*, pages 38–45, Online. Association for Computational Linguistics.

Huiyin Xue and Nikolaos Aletras. 2022. HashFormers: Towards vocabulary-independent pre-trained transformers. In *Proceedings of the 2022 Conference on Empirical Methods in Natural Language Processing*, pages 7862–7874, Abu Dhabi, United Arab Emirates. Association for Computational Linguistics.

Linting Xue, Aditya Barua, Noah Constant, Rami Al-Rfou, Sharan Narang, Mihir Kale, Adam Roberts, and Colin Raffel. 2022. ByT5: Towards a token-free future with pre-trained byte-to-byte models. *Transactions of the Association for Computational Linguistics*, 10:291–306.

Zhewei Yao, Reza Yazdani Aminabadi, Minjia Zhang, Xiaoxia Wu, Conglong Li, and Yuxiong He. 2022. ZeroQuant: Efficient and affordable post-training quantization for large-scale transformers. In *Advances in Neural Information Processing Systems*, volume 35, pages 27168–27183. Curran Associates, Inc.

Ofir Zafrir, Guy Boudoukh, Peter Izsak, and Moshe Wasserblat. 2019. Q8BERT: Quantized 8bit bert. In *2019 Fifth Workshop on Energy Efficient Machine Learning and Cognitive Computing - NeurIPS Edition (EMC2-NIPS)*, pages 36–39.

Qingru Zhang, Minshuo Chen, Alexander Bukharin, Pengcheng He, Yu Cheng, Weizhu Chen, and Tuo Zhao. 2023. Adaptive budget allocation for parameter-efficient fine-tuning. In *The Eleventh International Conference on Learning Representations*.

Susan Zhang, Stephen Roller, Naman Goyal, Mikel Artetxe, Moya Chen, Shuohui Chen, Christopher Dewan, Mona Diab, Xian Li, Xi Victoria Lin, Todor Mihaylov, Myle Ott, Sam Shleifer, Kurt Shuster, Daniel Simig, Punit Singh Koura, Anjali Sridhar, Tianlu Wang, and Luke Zettlemoyer. 2022. OPT: Open pre-trained transformer language models. *Preprint*, arXiv:2205.01068.

Sanqiang Zhao, Raghav Gupta, Yang Song, and Denny Zhou. 2021. Extremely small BERT models from mixed-vocabulary training. In *Proceedings of the 16th Conference of the European Chapter of the Association for Computational Linguistics: Main Volume*, pages 2753–2759, Online. Association for Computational Linguistics.

Yi Zhou, Jose Camacho-Collados, and Danushka Bollegala. 2023. A predictive factor analysis of social biases and task-performance in pretrained masked language models. In *Proceedings of the 2023 Conference on Empirical Methods in Natural Language Processing*, pages 11082–11100, Singapore. Association for Computational Linguistics.

A Language Model Vocabulary Sizes

Table 5 presents the vocabulary sizes ($|\mathcal{V}|$) for the models used in our experiments, as identified by the Hugging Face Hub. We also report the number of embedding parameters (N_{emb}), the number of model parameters (N), and the overall proportion of embedding parameters (N_{emb}/N). These metrics are also presented in Table 6 for each size of DeBERTa, in addition to model hyperparameters.

Model	$\lvert\mathcal{V}\rvert$	N_{emb}	N	N_{emb}/N
DistilBERT	28,996	22.3M	65.8M	33.9%
DistilRoBERTa	50,265	38.6M	82.1M	47.0%
DistilmBERT	119,547	91.8M	135.3M	67.8%
BERT	28,996	22.3M	108.3M	20.6%
RoBERTa	50,265	38.6M	124.6M	31.0%
DeBERTaV3	128,100	98.4M	184.4M	53.3%
mBERT	119,547	91.8M	177.9M	51.6%
XLM-RoBERTa	250,002	192.0M	278.0M	69.1%
XLM-V	901,629	692.5M	778.5M	88.9%

Table 5: The vocabulary size and allocation of parameters for each of the models used in our experiments. In all cases, we select the base model size ($d_{\text{model}} = 768$).

Size	l	h	d_{model}	N_{emb}	N	N_{emb}/N
XSmall	12	6	384	49.2M	70.8M	69.4%
Small	6	12	768	98.4M	141.9M	69.3%
Base	12	12	768	98.4M	184.4M	53.3%
Large	24	16	1024	131.2M	435.1M	30.2%

Table 6: The DeBERTaV3 (He et al., 2023) family of models. Columns l, h, and d_{model} show the number of hidden layers, number of attention heads, and hidden embedding size, respectively.

B Language Model Compression

Supplementary to our discussion of related work (Section 2), we additionally discuss the relation to variety of popular LM compression approaches. We emphasize that these methods are orthogonal to our proposed approach.

Knowledge distillation. Knowledge distillation (Hinton et al., 2015) aims to achieve comparable performance by training a smaller model using the predictions from a larger model. This approach has been successfully applied to LMs (Sanh et al., 2020a; Sun et al., 2020). It can also be used to train models with a smaller vocabulary than the original (Zhao et al., 2021; Singh and Lefever, 2022).

Pruning. Neural network pruning (LeCun et al., 1989) seeks to remove redundant weights while preserving performance. Existing approaches focus on pruning the linear and attention weights in LMs (Sanh et al., 2020b; Kurtic et al., 2022; Frantar and Alistarh, 2023). However, pruning the embedding matrix is widely avoided, as it can substantially harm performance (Kurtic et al., 2024).

Quantization. The aim of quantization is to represent neural network weights using lower precision, therefore reducing computational costs. Recent LM quantization efforts generally focus on quantizing the linear layers (Dettmers et al., 2022; Yao et al., 2022; Frantar et al., 2023). The embedding matrix can also be quantized (Zafrir et al., 2019; Bondarenko et al., 2021), although Shen et al. (2020) find that it is more sensitive to quantization.

C Datasets

In all cases, we use the publicly available version of each dataset available from Hugging Face (Lhoest et al., 2021). The GLUE benchmark comprises a diverse range of tasks, including linguistic acceptability (CoLA, Warstadt et al. 2019), sentiment analysis (SST-2, Socher et al. 2013), paraphrasing/sentence similarity (MRPC, Dolan and Brockett 2005; STS-B, Cer et al. 2017; QQP, Iyer et al. 2017), and natural language inference (RTE, Dagan et al. 2006; WNLI, Levesque et al. 2012; QNLI, Rajpurkar et al. 2016; MNLI, Williams et al. 2018). The number of examples per split in each dataset are listed in Table 7. The XNLI dataset (Conneau et al., 2018) extends MNLI to 15 languages: Arabic, Bulgarian, Chinese, English, French, German, Greek, Hindi, Russian, Spanish, Swahili, Thai, Turkish, Vietnamese, and Urdu.

D Implementation & Hardware

We implement our experiments using PyTorch (Paszke et al., 2019), Hugging Face Transformers (Wolf et al., 2020) and Hugging Face Datasets (Lhoest et al., 2021). Since downstream task performance is not relevant to this study, we do not perform hyperparameter tuning. Instead, we broadly follow the hyperparameters from Devlin et al. (2019), listed in Table 8.

We fine-tune all models using a single NVIDIA Tesla V100 (SXM2 32GB) GPU and Intel Xeon Gold 6138 CPU. For consistency, each model type is evaluated on the same physical hardware.

E Fine-tuning on GLUE

Table 10 presents the task performance for each model across the GLUE benchmark. We observe that the performance is largely identical, although there are occasional fluctuations where PEMA performs fractionally better or worse than the baseline. Finally, we note that XLM-RoBERTa and XLM-V both demonstrate very low performance on CoLA, although this issue has also been observed in other studies, e.g. Zhou et al. (2023).

F Runtime Impact

Table 9 presents the mean duration and standard deviation of applying PEMA to RoBERTa and the subsequent fine-tuning process. It also shows the proportion of time spent applying PEMA relative to fine-tuning. We observe that for five of the nine datasets in GLUE, applying PEMA takes less than half a second. For eight out of nine datasets, applying PEMA takes less than 1% of the fine-tuning duration. We note that the time taken to apply PEMA correlates with the size of the fine-tuning dataset (Figure 2). Overall, we note that the time taken to apply PEMA is generally fractional compared to the fine-tuning duration, even though we made no effort to optimize our implementation. As guidance for future optimization efforts, we note that the dataset processing operations in PEMA are trivially parallelizable.

Dataset	Train	Validation	Test	Total
CoLA	8,551	1,043	1,063	10,657
MNLI	392,702	19,647	19,643	431,992
MRPC	3,668	408	1,725	5,801
QNLI	104,743	5,463	5,463	115,669
QQP	363,846	40,430	390,965	795,241
RTE	2,490	277	3,000	5,767
SST-2	67,349	872	1,821	70,042
STS-B	5,749	1,500	1,379	8,628
WNLI	635	71	146	852

Table 7: The number of examples per split in each of the GLUE datasets.

Hyperparameter	GLUE	XNLI
Adam ϵ	1e-8	
Adam β_1	0.9	
Adam β_2	0.999	
Batch Size	32	
Dropout (Attention)	0.1	
Dropout (Hidden)	0.1	
Learning Rate (Peak)	2e-5, 7.5e-6 (XLM)	
Learning Rate Schedule	Linear	
Sequence Length	128	
Training Epochs	3	2

Table 8: The hyperparameters used for each set of experiments.

Dataset	PEMA	Fine-tuning	%
CoLA	$0.4_{0.0}$	$172.7_{0.9}$	0.2
MNLI	$8.8_{0.2}$	$7817.8_{16.6}$	0.1
MRPC	$0.3_{0.0}$	$78.7_{0.7}$	0.4
QNLI	$2.4_{0.0}$	$2092.8_{2.0}$	0.1
QQP	$13.3_{0.5}$	$7235.5_{4.9}$	0.2
RTE	$0.4_{0.0}$	$55.4_{0.6}$	0.7
SST-2	$1.2_{0.0}$	$1329.2_{0.3}$	0.1
STS-B	$0.4_{0.0}$	$118.7_{0.5}$	0.3
WNLI	$0.3_{0.0}$	$18.3_{0.8}$	1.4

Table 9: The mean duration (seconds) and standard deviation over five runs of applying PEMA to RoBERTa and fine-tuning on the GLUE datasets.

Model	PEMA	CoLA	MNLI	MRPC	QNLI	QQP	RTE	SST-2	STS-B	WNLI	Mean
DistilBERT	✗	49.3	82.2	84.2	88.5	86.7	59.6	90.5	86.5	49.3	$75.2_{1.5}$
	✓	49.3	82.2	84.2	88.6	86.7	59.6	90.5	86.5	49.3	$75.2_{1.5}$
DistilRoBERTa	✗	56.4	84.2	85.0	90.9	87.2	65.7	92.3	87.2	53.0	$78.0_{0.9}$
	✓	56.4	84.2	85.0	90.9	87.2	65.7	92.3	87.2	53.0	$78.0_{0.9}$
DistilmBERT	✗	29.7	78.3	81.8	86.7	85.8	60.9	89.1	84.4	48.2	$71.6_{0.3}$
	✓	29.6	78.3	81.8	86.7	85.8	60.9	89.2	84.4	48.2	$71.6_{0.4}$
BERT	✗	56.4	84.3	84.3	91.1	87.9	64.4	92.6	88.1	37.7	$76.3_{0.7}$
	✓	56.7	84.3	84.3	91.3	87.8	64.4	92.5	88.1	37.7	$76.3_{0.8}$
RoBERTa	✗	57.6	87.8	88.4	92.8	88.4	71.1	94.2	89.9	52.1	$80.3_{1.2}$
	✓	57.6	87.8	88.4	92.7	88.4	71.1	94.2	89.9	52.1	$80.3_{1.2}$
DeBERTaV3	✗	67.4	90.2	88.5	93.9	89.9	79.8	95.6	90.9	53.0	$83.2_{0.8}$
	✓	67.4	90.2	88.3	93.9	89.9	79.8	95.5	90.9	53.0	$83.2_{0.8}$
mBERT	✗	35.3	82.3	85.8	91.1	87.1	69.0	91.0	88.0	53.0	$75.8_{2.0}$
	✓	35.4	82.2	85.8	91.1	87.2	69.0	90.8	88.0	53.0	$75.8_{2.0}$
XLM-RoBERTa	✗	22.6	83.9	76.9	89.5	86.9	57.3	92.2	84.2	52.1	$71.7_{2.0}$
	✓	22.4	84.0	76.8	89.5	86.8	57.3	92.0	84.2	52.1	$71.7_{2.0}$
XLM-V	✗	0.0	84.5	68.8	89.6	86.7	54.1	91.8	80.8	55.2	$68.0_{0.6}$
	✓	0.0	84.5	68.8	89.6	86.7	54.1	91.6	80.8	55.2	$67.9_{0.6}$

Table 10: Results on the validation set for each task from GLUE. We present the mean performance over five different seeds, accompanied by the overall mean and standard deviation. We report Matthews correlation for CoLA, F1 for QQP, Spearman correlation for STS-B, and accuracy for the remaining tasks.

Author Index

Association for Computational Linguistics
209 N. Eighth Street
Stroudsburg, Pennsylvania 18360

ISBN 979-8-3313-1928-1

9 798331 319281

CURRAN ASSOCIATES INC.
proceedings.com